OXFORD DATA PROTECTION AND PRIVACY LAW

Series Editors

CHRISTOPHER KUNER
Professor of Law, VUB Brussel

GRAHAM GREENLEAF
Professor of Law and Information Systems, University of New South Wales

Vulnerability and Data Protection Law

OXFORD DATA PROTECTION AND PRIVACY LAW

Series Editors

Christopher Kuner, Professor of Law, VUB Brussel
Graham Greenleaf, Professor of Law and Information Systems, University of New South Wales

The aim of this series is to publish important and original books on legal issues of data protection and privacy. This includes many different areas of law, including comparative law, EU law, human rights law, international law, privacy on the Internet, and others.

Prospective authors are welcome to submit proposals for the series, as outlined on the series website: global.oup.com/academic/content/series/o/oxford-data-protection-and-privacy-law-odppl/

Vulnerability and Data Protection Law

GIANCLAUDIO MALGIERI
Leiden University

OXFORD
UNIVERSITY PRESS

OXFORD
UNIVERSITY PRESS

Great Clarendon Street, Oxford, OX2 6DP,
United Kingdom

Oxford University Press is a department of the University of Oxford.
It furthers the University's objective of excellence in research, scholarship,
and education by publishing worldwide. Oxford is a registered trade mark of
Oxford University Press in the UK and in certain other countries

First Edition published in 2023

Published in the United States of America by Oxford University Press
198 Madison Avenue, New York, NY 10016, United States of America

British Library Cataloguing in Publication Data

Data available

Library of Congress Control Number: 2023932449

ISBN 978–0–19–287033–9

DOI: 10.1093/oso/9780192870339.001.0001

Printed and bound in the UK by
TJ Books Limited

To my families,
enshrining my vulnerable part

Foreword

Looking into the vulnerabilities of the digital with legal magic

I was reading Rebecca Solnit's *Hope in the Dark* (Nation Books 2004, 2016, 3rd edn) when Gianclaudio Malgieri asked me to write the Foreword to his book.

Hope in the Dark is the kind of book that mentors its readers. It helps activists of all sorts resist despair, and explains to those seeking change and digging into the grounds of truisms and commonplaces that change often happens quietly and is often overlooked after it occurs.

A generous and long-term perspective on change and human action should temper impatient verdicts about events, changes, political decisions, and (why not?) laws. The GDPR (the General Data Protection Regulation 2016/679, replacing the 1995 European Union Data Protection Directive (Directive 95/46/EC)) is a law that begs for being treated generously and for a postponement of each final judgment on it.

The GDPR aims to protect and give consumers more control of their data and it applies to controllers and processors of EU citizens' data, including those companies that process data but are based outside the EU. The GDPR came into force in the EU on 25 May 2018. Four years later, it is still too soon to tell whether this law has succeeded in its ambition to empower the citizens and alter the data collection and processing ecosystem of the digital economy erected in the second decade of the twenty-first century.

'Revolutions are often considered to be spontaneous, but less visible long-term organising and groundwork ... often laid the foundation. Changes in ideas and values also result from work done by writers, scholars, public intellectuals, social activists, and participants in social media" (p. xiii), Rebecca Solnit writes in her Foreword to *Hope in the Dark*. These observations help us understand revolutions and set our expectations about them. If they exist, they often announce themselves quietly, happen quietly, and install themselves in our minds equally quietly.

The Brussels data protection field, which generously allows me to be an observer, has had half a decade to discuss the replacement of the 1995 Directive by the new GDPR. Five years of fascinating conferences and panels at the annual Computer Privacy and Data Protection (CPDP) Conferences held in the heart of Brussels, and at other events. The buzz surrounding the current AI Proposal comes somewhere near that energetic storm around data protection and digital regulation in Brussels, but its ambitions are more limited, and the principles used to regulate AI are familiar to everyone who works with the GDPR.

From environmental law we know that healthy laws do not necessarily mean a healthy environment. So how is our data protected? How well are we performing in terms of privacy and the protection of human rights? Malgieri's approach in *Vulnerability and Data Protection Law* is not only to show problems but to offer *critical optimism* towards viable solutions. The essence of critical optimism, he argues, is making the most of the existing laws but never giving up on making substantial improvements to them for the future.

Malgieri has won me over with his critical optimism, although it is a demanding approach and not necessarily a successful one. Gloom is often the easier way to impress, 'for the bearer of bad news is less likely to get shot than to acquire a certain authority that those bringing better, or more complicated news won't' (Solnit, p. 21). In law, gloom is seldom successful. We train our legal students to make the most of existing laws, and we value those that excel in this. There are backdrops to this approach. Clarity—seeing the problems—is already hard enough since it demands to be rooted in this world, but imagination—seeing what might lie beyond and pushing the perceived immutable forwards—is a rare gift. Malgieri found an entry to change in vulnerability theory.

This theory, developed by Martha Albertson Fineman, amongst others, in *The Vulnerable Subject: Anchoring Equality in the Human Condition* (2008) and later work, replaces the starting point for regulation of the legal subject as an autonomous and rational adult with that of the embodied individual who experiences vulnerability in all stages of life in all sorts of settings. Fineman used the starting point (followed by others) to criticize non-discrimination law with its classical liberal and formal insistence on the same treatment for similarly situated individuals and its fixed list of 'particular vulnerable groups' (disabled, children, the elderly, etc). For Fineman, non-discrimination thus rooted will always fail to achieve a more just society or more substantive equality. These objectives could be more ably reached if we understood the human condition as one of universal and constant human vulnerability: *we can all be vulnerable* (not to be confused with *we are all victims or vulnerable*): 'harm, injury, and misfortune' can come to us 'whether accidental, intentional, or otherwise'. Our position in social, economic, and institutional relationships and institutions explains how (hard) vulnerability can hit us, but the bottom line should be more awareness and some much needed destabilization of our belief in US or possessive individualism.

Ed Cohen applies the vulnerability lens to the recent pandemic and observes that a much more diverse range of people now recognize other people's vulnerability in and as their own:

> They are beginning to have a sense that your vulnerability is my vulnerability—which is empirically true, right? That's what the SARS-CoV-2 virus teaches us. And, moreover, that there are all kinds of economic, political, sexual, and racial determinants of such vulnerabilities. So, I do think more people—or at least I'm

> optimistically hoping that more people—have begun to recognize these entangled vulnerabilities as being significant problems in the face of which they might agree that certain kinds of structural transformations are necessary. ('The biopolitics of pandemics: interview with Ed Cohen' (2022) 36(3) *Cultural Studies* 396–409)

Closer to the topic of the book is Shoshana Zuboff's insistence on novel, epistemic inequalities (*The Age of Surveillance Capitalism: The Fight for a Human Future at the New Frontier of Power* (Profile Books 2018)). In her fifth chapter, Zuboff depicts all users of digital services as 'cornered' by tech firms and their hunger for data. A range of administrative, technical, and material capabilities 'rob' or 'dispossess' us of our data and use data 'to make us dance' to the music that big tech composes. Legal and popular resistance to specific cornering practices and manipulations (*incursion*) is broken by subsequent strategies (*habituation*, *adaptation*, and *redirection*) that create a *world of no escape*, in which we find us 'cornered' by converging, overlapping, and relentlessly expanding operations of data dispossession, where knowledge and rights are systematically transferred from the many to the few.

Malgieri has grasped these critiques and is, in my understanding, pioneering in legal studies by introducing the vulnerability lens in data protection law, where universal and constant human vulnerability is partly recognized, but also partly ignored. His chapters on the 'average' data subject (Chapter 2), the 'vulnerable' human (Chapter 3), and vulnerable data subjects (Chapter 4) will enjoy a long-standing reputation in legal literature. The question of vulnerability is rich and substantive and is successfully used by this talented author to rewrite the traditional handbook analysis of the GDPR principles (Chapter 5) and the GDPR rights and duties (Chapter 6). Moral philosophers would be amazed by the ambition of some of those principles (fairness in particular), and it takes a skilled author like Malgieri to give substance to them without running the risk of distancing himself too far from traditional legal interpretation methods. Chapter 7 on data protection impact assessment might look more technical and the future will have to judge whether it is successful in dealing with vulnerability. These assessments, organized by Article 35 GDPR, might indeed offer a possible solution to how to treat vulnerability, since they force data controllers (including tech providers) to analyse possible consequences of personal data processing operations in order to mitigate adverse impacts before they occur. The legal provisions on these assessments are broad enough. They warrant an analysis beyond privacy that covers all risks to the rights and freedoms of natural persons. They also oblige, where appropriate, data controllers to seek the views of data subjects, which could contribute to the empowerment of (less represented) citizens and should bring clarity about vulnerabilities. Future, more empirical research is needed to verify that the promise the GDPR offers is realized. As I said, I am in favour of generous, long-term perspectives on change. Law needs a richer account of the cornered human whose data is out in the world and who must be offered options to give consent that are not currently available to her. This is a deeply urgent problem, written about here by one of the most talented lawyers of this era, an author that makes the most of existing laws without erring, and who displays imagination (legal magic) on every page.

Paul De Hert
Vrije Universiteit Brussels (LSTS)
University of Tilburg (TILT)

Preface

This book is the result of five incredible years of research and personal growth that I experienced when living and working in Brussels, Lille, and Pisa (and many other inspiring venues around the world, where my research grew). When I started to reflect on the concept of vulnerable people in the field of data protection, at the end of 2016, I could not imagine how important this topic would become in the following years of dramatic uncertainties, with humanitarian and pandemic crises inducing new vulnerabilities every day.

Human vulnerability is the hallmark of human beings in the twenty-first century. In the digital environment, this is becoming increasingly evident. We are used to considering vulnerability according to a group-based approach: ethnic minorities, children, the elderly, LGBTIQ+ people, people with disabilities, etc. However, this static approach is not only theoretically disputable but also technologically inaccurate: the digital media have reshaped groups and individuals by inducing new vulnerabilities and creating different contextually vulnerable sub-groups of users, consumers, citizens, and data subjects.

However, this book was conceived not only to highlight problems but to suggest viable solutions. The EU General Data Protection Regulation (GDPR) is not just the legal instrument used to address many issues in the existing digital world, it also and primarily comprises a forward-looking set of tools that, though largely underexplored, might be essential to rebalance power asymmetries and mitigate induced vulnerabilities in the age of artificial intelligence. Ultimately, the anticipated impact of this book is to begin promoting the concept of data subjects' *layered* vulnerability as a *heuristic tool* to reinterpret the whole system of rights, duties, and safeguards in the GDPR, and to reconceptualize the risk-based approach of the GDPR on an individual-centred basis.

After an introductory chapter (Chapter 1), the book develops into three parts: definitions, protections, criticisms. Defining the 'average' data subject (Chapter 2) is essential to investigating the notion of 'vulnerable' humans (Chapter 3) and, in particular, vulnerable data subjects (Chapter 4). With a clearer view of who is the vulnerable party in the data protection framework, it is then possible to examine how the GDPR principles (Chapter 5), data protection rights and duties (Chapter 6), and the data protection impact assessment model (Chapter 7) can be interpreted and implemented to protect vulnerable data subjects. This structure has limitations which is why it is also necessary to reflect on some policy recommendations for the future (Chapter 8). This is the essence of critical optimism: making the most of existing laws but never giving up on substantial improvements to them for the future.

This ambitious project has had one author but a whole team of invisible co-authors. This Preface is my only opportunity to make that team more visible. First, three mentors guided me in the troubled waters of my doctoral research (especially in lockdown days): Paul De Hert, Frederik Zuiderveen Borgesius, and Giovanni Comandé offered me, respectively, vision, methods, and passion. Together with them, the whole doctoral Jury Committee gave me precious support and suggestions: Gloria González Fuster, Serge Gutwirth, Orla Lynskey, and Joris Van Hoboken.

This book is also the product of many preliminary works. My (additional) co-authors were essential partners and I am highly indebted to Jędrzej Niklas, Margot Kaminski, Frank Pasquale, Bart Custers, Paul Quinn, Václav Janeček, and Antonio Davola.

My previous working team (the EDHEC Business School's Augmented Law Institute) and my current one (eLaw Research Center at Leiden University) gave me the final energy to complete this publication. I also received fundamental support from the Brussels Privacy Hub (which I have the honour to co-direct with Professor Christopher Kuner). I would like also to thank the anonymous reviewer at Oxford University Press for their invaluable help.

I had several families that supported me in this journey. My academic families are the LSTS group of Vrije Universiteit Brussel (co-directed by Mireille Hildebrandt, who was an invaluable guide in these years, and Gloria González Fuster), and the Lider-Lab group at the Sant'Anna School of Advanced Studies of Pisa (led by Giovanni Comandé).

And then my daily families: in Pisa, Francesco who supported me in the last precious years; Luca, who has always been there; Carlotta (precious help in the final steps of this book), Maria Adelaide, Maria Ida, Jasmine, Giuseppe, and all my friends; in Telese, my mother and her partner, my sister and her daughter and husband, and my father.

This book is the sum of the love and stimuli I have undeservedly received for years.

Gianclaudio Malgieri
Leiden,
October 2022

Contents

Table of Cases

COURT OF JUSTICE OF THE EUROPEAN UNION

EUROPEAN COURT OF HUMAN RIGHTS

Table of Legislation

Abbreviations

AI	artificial intelligence
AIA	Artificial Intelligence Act
CFR	Charter of Fundamental Rights
CJEU	Court of Justice of the European Union
CNLI	*Commission nationale de l'informatique et des libertés*
CoE	Council of Europe
CPDP	Computer Privacy and Data Protection
CTR	Clinical Trials Regulation EU 536/2014
DCFR	Draft Common Frame of Reference for European Contract Law
DPAs	Data Protection Authorities
DPbD	data protection by design
DPD	Data Protection Directive
DPIA	Data Protection Impact Assessment
DPO	Data Processing Officer
ECHR	European Convention on Human Rights
ECtHR	European Court of Human Rights
EDPB	European Data Protection Board
EDPS	European Data Protection Supervisor
ENISA	European Network and Information Security Agency
EUDPR	European Data Protection Regulation
GDPR	General Data Protection Regulation
ICO	Information Commissioner Officer
IPA	Instrument for Pre-accession Assistance
LED	Law Enforcement Directive
LGBT	Lesbian, Gay, Bisexual, and Transgender
LGBTQI+	Lesbian, Gay, Bisexual, and Transgender, Queer and Questioning, and Intersex
LGBTQIA+	Lesbian, Gay, Bisexual, and Transgender, Queer and Questioning, Intersex, and Asexual
NGOs	non-governmental organizations
NIST	National Institute of Standard and Technology
PNR	Passenger Name Record
SEO	search engine optimization
TEU	Treaty of the European Union
TFEU	Treaty on the Functioning of the EU
UPCD	Unfair Commercial Practice Directive 2005/29/EC
WP29	Article 29 Data Protection Working Party on the Protection of Individuals with regard to the Processing of Personal Data

1

The reasons for research on data subjects

1. The notion(s) of the data subject(s) in a digital changing world

The new potentialities of machine learning, automated decision-making, hyper-personalization of behavioural advertising, and predictive analytics increase the power imbalance between individuals and entities processing data in the digital environment. The effects of such an unfair imbalance are evident from several perspectives: discrimination,[1] manipulation,[2] commodification of identities,[3] intrusions in personal intimacy, and stigmatization[4] are just some of the manifestations of this. Imbalance is intrinsic in nearly every mass commercial relationship since the Industrial Revolution, but what triggers the attention of the EU legislator is the variable level of (un)fairness of such an imbalance; in other words the ability of the data processing environment to affect the autonomy, dignity, and integrity of the individuals, who are thus increasingly *vulnerable*.

The increasing awareness of bounded rationality[5] and cognitive biases is challenging traditional notions of the 'average' consumer, citizen, user, and data subject in the digital ecosphere. Personal circumstances are increasingly becoming important to define different groups of individuals in need of protection from the unfair imbalance described above. The need for higher protection is evident in many EU legal fields, in particular (but not only) in the data protection framework.

[1] S Barocas and AD Selbst, 'Big Data's Disparate Impact' (2016) 104 California Law Review 671; AD Selbst, 'Disparate Impact in Big Data Policing' (2018) 52 Georgia Law Review 109; S Wachter, 'Affinity Profiling and Discrimination by Association in Online Behavioural Advertising' (2021) 35 Berkeley Technology Law Journal 369.

[2] R Calo, 'Digital Market Manipulation' (2014) 82 George Washington Law Review 995; TZ Zarsky, 'Privacy and Manipulation in the Digital Age' (2019) 20 Theoretical Inquiries in Law <http://www7.tau.ac.il/ojs/index.php/til/article/view/1612> accessed 23 January 2019; D Susser and others, 'Online Manipulation: Hidden Influences in a Digital World' (2019) 4 Georgetown Law Technology Review 1; M Sax, *Between Empowerment and Manipulation: The Ethics and Regulation of For-profit Health Apps* (Kluwer Law International 2021).

[3] N Purtova, 'Illusion of Personal Data as No One's Property' (2015) 7 Law Innovation and Technology 83.

[4] On stigmatization see P Quinn, *Stigma, State Expressions and the Law: Implications of Freedom of Speech* (1st edn, Routledge 2019).

[5] The term 'bounded rationality' generally refers to the idea that human rationality is limited (or 'bounded') by cognitive limitations of the mind and other variables (the time available to make decisions, the tractability of the decision). See, largely, D Kahneman, 'A Perspective on Judgment and Choice: Mapping Bounded Rationality' (2003) 58 The American Psychologist 697.

Vulnerability and Data Protection Law. Gianclaudio Malgieri, Oxford University Press. © Gianclaudio Malgieri 2023.
DOI: 10.1093/oso/9780192870339.003.0001

However, while in EU data protection law there are clear definitions and classification of, for example, 'data controllers' and 'data processors' (according to size, responsibility, data protection risks, territoriality, etc),[6] there is no precise classification of *data subjects*.

In many other EU legal fields, there are more explicit definitions of the different individuals involved and possible sub-categories of these individuals. This is the case in, for example, EU private law, consumer law,[7] car insurance regulation,[8] regulation of scientific research,[9] etc. In these fields there are, for example, descriptions of *average* subjects and separate descriptions of *vulnerable* individuals (classified either generally or based on the specific groups to which they belong). Still, in the data protection framework these definitions, distinctions, and categorizations might be even more critical but they are absent.

Privacy and data protection law seek to counterbalance the unfair imbalance between the processing party and the data subject[10] and, thus, to mitigate the vulnerability of the individual to exploitation.[11] However, increased awareness in the social sciences about the personal conditions of individuals (in terms of understanding, awareness, exposure to manipulation and discrimination, resilience to attacks, etc)[12] forces us to consider the different layers of data subjects' vulnerability. In the EU's General Data Protection Regulation (GDPR) (and in the Data Protection Directive (DPD) that preceded it), it is clear that some rules are conceived as applicable to 'average' (rational, aware, and circumspect) data subjects. However, an increasing number of provisions seem to refer to a broad notion of the data subject, which also includes vulnerable subjects.

The *sui generis* protection of children's personal data is meaningful but we should investigate analogous (adult) cases where vulnerability exists. Understanding different sources of vulnerability is necessary to implement more effective protection of the fundamental rights and freedoms of data subjects. As several authors have argued, the EU fundamental rights protection framework (including the

[6] See, in particular, B Van Alsenoy, *Data Protection Law in the EU: Roles, Responsibilities and Liability* (Intersentia Uitgevers NV 2019).

[7] Directive 2005/29/EC of the European Parliament and of the Council of 11 May 2005 concerning unfair business-to-consumer commercial practices in the internal market and amending Council Directive 84/450/EEC, Directives 97/7/EC, 98/27/EC and 2002/65/EC of the European Parliament and of the Council and Regulation (EC) No 2006/2004 of the European Parliament and of the Council ('Unfair Commercial Practices Directive') (Text with EEA relevance) 2005 [32005L0029].

[8] Third Council Directive 90/232/EEC of 14 May 1990 on the approximation of the laws of the Member States relating to insurance against civil liability in respect of the use of motor vehicles.

[9] See eg Regulation (EU) No 536/2014 of the European Parliament and of the Council of 16 April 2014 on clinical trials on medicinal products for human use, and repealing Directive 2001/20/EC Text with EEA relevance 2014 (OJ L).

[10] See O Lynskey, *The Foundations of EU Data Protection Law* (Oxford University Press 2015) 213.

[11] R Calo, 'Privacy, Vulnerability, and Affordance' (2017) 66 DePaul Law Review 591–604.

[12] See eg MG Haselton and others, 'The Evolution of Cognitive Bias' in DM Buss (ed), *The Handbook of Evolutionary Psychology* (John Wiley & Sons, Inc 2015).

fundamental right to data protection) is based on the principle of dignity.[13] The principle of dignity imposes a consideration of human vulnerability[14] so that when protecting fundamental rights, the legislator and the commentator need to implement greater protections for more vulnerable subjects.

Traditionally, the legal notion of vulnerability has been linked to historically sensitive categories of individuals such as patients, children, elderly people, asylum seekers, mentally ill people, etc. Considering the implications of the revolution in the use of computer algorithms, and the asymmetry of power between consumers (data subjects) and companies (data controllers), the traditional categorizations of 'vulnerable' individuals may appear inadequate. This categorization should perhaps increasingly include the general category of consumers, at least when they act in the algorithmic environment where data on them are collected and exploited, and when their vulnerabilities are exploited. Indeed, the sunset of economic theories on rational consumers[15] and the emergence of behavioural law and economics[16] highlight how every consumer is vulnerable under certain circumstances. Moreover, today such vulnerabilities are more easily detectable and exploitable by data mining and machine learning technologies.[17]

The traditional legal tools used to protect individuals in the information society (such as the distinction between different categories of personal data and the data subject 'control' rights, including consent and transparency)[18] have often proved ineffective. Several scandals have shown the dimension of the problem. The case of Cambridge Analytica,[19] where individual's political opinions were unduly influenced through unlawful data processing, has highlighted the manipulative powers of social media platforms and behavioural advertising.[20] Similarly, Facebook has

[13] R Andorno, 'Is Vulnerability the Foundation of Human Rights?' in A Masferrer and E García-Sánchez (eds), *Human Dignity of the Vulnerable in the Age of Rights: Interdisciplinary Perspectives* (Springer International Publishing 2016).

[14] BS Turner, *Vulnerability and Human Rights* (Pennsylvania State University Press 2006) 6.

[15] A Rouvroy, 'The End(s) of Critique: Data-behaviourism vs. Due-process' in M Hildebrandt and E De Vries (eds), *Privacy, Due Process and the Computational Turn. Philosophers of Law Meet Philosophers of Technology* (Routledge 2012). See also D Clifford, 'Citizen-Consumers in a Personalised Galaxy: Emotion Influenced Decision-Making, a True Path to the Dark Side?' [2017] SSRN Electronic Journal <https://www.ssrn.com/abstract=3037425> accessed 16 December 2018.

[16] A Acquisti, 'Nudging Privacy: The Behavioral Economics of Personal Information' (2009) 7 IEEE Security & Privacy Magazine 82.

[17] Calo, 'Digital Market Manipulation' (n 2) 995.

[18] See eg JE Cohen, 'Turning Privacy Inside Out' (2019) 20 Theoretical Inquiries in Law <http://www7.tau.ac.il/ojs/index.php/til/article/view/1607> accessed 23 January 2019.

[19] C Cadwalladr and E Graham-Harrison, 'Revealed: 50 Million Facebook Profiles Harvested for Cambridge Analytica in Major Data Breach' *Guardian* (17 March 2018) <https://www.theguardian.com/news/2018/mar/17/cambridge-analytica-facebook-influence-us-election> accessed 17 December 2018.

[20] Y-A de Montjoye and others, 'Cambridge Analytica Is Only the Beginning and You Might Have Your Friends to Blame for It' (*Computational Privacy Group*) <https://cpg.doc.ic.ac.uk> accessed 2 June 2019.

proved the ease with which users' emotions can be controlled through newsfeeds.[21] At the same time, ProPublica has revealed how algorithms can be racially biased and how significant the impact of these biases can be on individuals' lives.[22] In sum, automated decision-making systems can generate manipulation[23] and discrimination through unaccountable, hidden, and incontestable data processing systems.[24] This makes every data subject vulnerable, at least in some circumstances and situations. The lack of a clear definition of the data subject and of a precise analysis of what data subjects' vulnerability can be constitutes a severe obstacle to thorough and attentive protection of the individual in different situations.

2. Research question

This book asks what the notion of the data subject in the GDPR is, considering different levels of data subjects' vulnerabilities, and how we can improve the protection of vulnerable data subjects.

To analyse such a research question adequately, we need to examine its main components separately: (i) the *definition* of the data subject and different categories of data subjects; and (ii) the *protection* of particularly vulnerable data subjects. These two components are composed of many more elements.

As for the question regarding the definition, we first need to wonder what the notion of the data subject in the EU data protection framework is, and, in particular, if there is an implicit or explicit average data subject. Building on this, I then try to examine whether the GDPR directly or indirectly defines vulnerable data subjects. To do that, it is first necessary to understand what individual 'vulnerability' means in general theoretical terms, and then more specifically what it means in EU primary and secondary law, including other legal fields than data protection, especially consumer protection. Considering the GDPR, I then analyse whether and how data protection principles, data protection rights, and accountability duties consider and protect the special conditions of data subjects, particularly vulnerable ones.

As for the protection issue, the first sub-question concerns interpreting the GDPR provisions to mitigate data subjects' vulnerability. However, in order to

[21] R Booth, 'Facebook Reveals News Feed Experiment to Control Emotions' *Guardian* (29 June 2014) <https://www.theguardian.com/technology/2014/jun/29/facebook-users-emotions-news-feeds> accessed 2 June 2019.

[22] J Angwin and others, 'Machine Bias—There's Software Used across the Country to Predict Future Criminals. And It's Biased against Blacks' (23 May 2016) ProPublica <https://www.propublica.org/article/machine-bias-risk-assessments-in-criminal-sentencing> accessed 2 June 2019.

[23] SC Matz and others, 'Psychological Targeting as an Effective Approach to Digital Mass Persuasion' [2017] 114 Proceedings of the National Academy of Sciences of the United States of America 12714.

[24] DK Citron and F Pasquale, 'The Scored Society: Due Process for Automated Predictions' (2014) 89 Washington Law Review 1; F Pasquale, *The Black Box Society: The Secret Algorithms That Control Money and Information* (Harvard University Press 2015).

suggest improved interpretations of the data protection law based on an understanding of what constitutes vulnerability, it is necessary first to address an adequate vulnerability assessment method, following the GDPR risk analysis indications (namely, the Data Protection Impact Assessment (DPIA)). The final step is to look at the limits of that interpretation of the GDPR which may be sensitive to the issue of vulnerability, such as the risk of paternalism, hermeneutic limitations, and the limited effectiveness of the suggested measures. Consequently, it is necessary to look at possible ways of overcoming these limitations, both under *de lege lata* and *de lege ferenda* perspectives.

3. Three related research objectives

The goals of this book are threefold:

1. Investigating the notion of the data subject and understanding whether and how special circumstances of the individual influence the definition of the data subject and the protection of their rights. This goal responds to the lack of precise analysis of the concept of the data subject in the data protection framework literature. This gap appears even greater when compared to other fields (eg consumer law) where there is a robust and solid analysis of personal differences and different types of individuals classified within that field of law (eg average consumers, vulnerable consumers), or when compared to other actors within data processing (eg the data controller), whom the law defines more precisely and who are discussed more fully in the literature.[25]
2. Reconceptualizing the notion of vulnerability in the data protection framework, proposing thus a contextual, relational, and layered notion that can effectively respond to the challenges of the algorithmic environment and protect the fundamental rights of individuals. This objective is grounded on the lack of clarity about data subjects' vulnerability in the GDPR, considering in particular that there is only one explicit vulnerable category (children) listed, but the whole data protection framework is based on an implicit (broader, layered, and contextual) notion of vulnerability, as revealed by the risk-based approach,[26] by the references to the imbalance of power between data subjects and those entities which collate, process, and use their data, and vulnerable data subjects in the GDPR preamble[27]

[25] See R Mahieu and others, 'Responsibility for Data Protection in a Networked World: On the Question of the Controller, "Effective and Complete Protection" and Its Application to Data Access Rights in Europe' (2019) 10 Journal of Intellectual Property, Information Technology and Electronic Commerce Law 39; Van Alsenoy (n 6).

[26] See arts 24, 25, 32, 35 of the GDPR.

[27] See Recitals 43 and 72 of the GDPR.

and by the frequent references to vulnerable data subjects in the EDPB Opinions.[28]

3. Promoting a vulnerability-aware interpretation of the GDPR. This objective is based on the necessity to adapt the GDPR principles, rights, and duties to the specific challenges of the algorithmic environment, considering, in particular, the higher risk of vulnerabilities exploitation in the digital market. I am aware that this goal can have limits and criticisms; that is why it is also necessary to address possible alternative methods of protection of the data subject and potential reforms to the GDPR.

The three objectives are related: each evolves from the previous one and is the basis for the following one. In particular, to understand what data subject vulnerability is in the GDPR (goal 2) it is necessary first to analyse the notion of the data subject and the relevance of personal situations in the application of the law (goal 1). However, the reason to improve the identification of those who are vulnerable data subjects is not merely speculative but practical: promoting specific protections for these data subjects (through vulnerability-tailored interpretations of the existing law and potential reforms of the data protection law) (goal 3).

In light of the above, this book promotes the concept of the data subjects' layered vulnerability as a *heuristic tool* which may be used to reinterpret the whole system of rights, duties, and safeguards in the GDPR, and primarily to reconceptualize the risk-based approach the GDPR takes on an individual-centred basis.[29] This goal has been explicitly declared by the Article 29 Working Party,[30] which affirmed that the 'origin, nature, particularity and severity of the risks' the collection and use of data pose should be appreciated '*from the perspective of the data subjects*'.[31] Indeed, this approach has been defined as 'subjective, individual-centred'.[32]

On this last matter, it is essential to clarify that this book does not adopt an individualistic perspective of vulnerability and does not underestimate the importance

[28] See Article 29 Data Protection Working Party on the Protection of Individuals with regard to the Processing of Personal Data (WP29), Guidelines on Transparency, WP260rev.01, 10; WP29, Opinion on legitimate interest, WP217, 40–41; WP29, Opinion on purpose limitation, WP203, 25 and 32; WP29 Guidelines on DPIA, WP248, 9; WP29, Guidelines on Profiling, WP251rev.01, 22. See indirectly also EDPB, Opinion 3/2019, 23 January 2019, 6.

[29] A similar goal is declared in G Malgieri and J Niklas, 'The Vulnerable Data Subject' (2020) 37 Computer Law & Security Review 105415.

[30] The Article 29 Working Party after the entry into force of the GDPR was renamed the 'European Data Protection Board' (EDPB). This book refers to the Article 29 Working Party (WP29) for all guidelines and opinions by that entity prior to the entry into force of the GDPR. All opinions and guidelines after the entry into force of the GDPR will refer to the new name, 'European Data Protection Board'.

[31] WP29, Guidelines on Data Protection Impact Assessment (DPIA) and determining whether processing is 'likely to result in a high risk' for the purposes of Regulation 2016/679, 4 April 2017, 21. Emphasis added. See also, on this point, K Demetzou, 'Risk to the "Rights and Freedoms"—A Legal Interpretation of the Scope of Risk Under the GDPR' in R Leenes and others (eds), *Data Protection and Privacy* (Bloomsbury 2020).

[32] M Macenaite, 'The "Riskification" of European Data Protection Law through a Two-Fold Shift' (2017) 8 European Journal of Risk Regulation 506, 536.

of group-based protection. Addressing vulnerability on a contextual, relational, and case-by-case basis does not mean that I reject any form of group-based vulnerability. As Chapter 3 clarifies, this book does not address *traditionally* vulnerable *groups* (children, elderly, workers, people with disabilities, LGBTQIA+, etc) as such, since it aims to overcome an *ex-ante* labelled approach to vulnerability: that approach might even lead to increased existing stigmatization for those individuals (so-called pathogenic vulnerability).[33] However, considering (context-dependant) vulnerable groups is still important: in many cases, different individuals might suffer from similar vulnerability risks, experience similar personal limitations leading to similar unfair effects (eg children of the same age exposed to certain kinds of behavioural advertising might all be considered as belonging to the same 'vulnerability' group and demand protection on a collective level). An exhaustive taxonomy of these 'new' groups is not possible here since an *ex-ante* exercise would be incomplete. Still, I consider that in these groups, similar individuals experience homogenous risks to fundamental rights and freedoms. Layered vulnerability is inherently *intersectional*: the intersection of different conditions (including individuals being members of different disadvantaged groups) qualifies the level of vulnerability of a data subject.

4. Approach and scope

This book contains normative and descriptive research. In particular, the analysis of the definition of the data subject and of vulnerability is descriptive, but the study of a vulnerability-based development of data protection law is normative. In other words, this book considers both what the law is and what the law should be. Nevertheless, the two elements (descriptive and normative) are not and could not be totally separate. Indeed, the normative element is not purely a proposal to change the existing law but also an operational consideration of how to interpret the existing law. This proposed interpretation is just one of the possible interpretations that the broad concepts and the open clauses in the GDPR allow, but, in my view, it is the most respectful of the essence of the fundamental right to data protection and the most effective way to deal with the current level of risk to these rights in the digital ecosphere.

Indeed, the GDPR is based on a collaborative governance framework grounded on the accountability principle:[34] the law posits some goals (fairness, lawfulness, transparency, etc) and is open to different possible actions of the data controller to

[33] See W Rogers and others, 'Why Bioethics Needs a Concept of Vulnerability' (2015) 5(2) International Journal of Feminist Approaches to Bioethics 25 <https://www.utpjournals.press/doi/abs/10.3138/ijfab.5.2.11> accessed 11 April 2020.

[34] ME Kaminski, 'Binary Governance: Lessons from the GDPR's Approach to Algorithmic Accountability' (2019) 92 Southern California Law Review 110.

reach those objectives.[35] In addition, the whole system of accountability is based on the level of risk for fundamental rights and freedoms of data subjects involved in data processing: the higher the risk, the higher the safeguards required to protect individuals.[36] Accordingly, implementing and complying with data protection rules is not a binary variable (yes or no) but a layered and gradual notion.[37] Therefore, the central part of this book is neither purely descriptive nor purely normative. It suggests implementing a broad interpretation of existing principles and rules that are in line with the goal of the GDPR: respecting the fundamental rights of the data subjects, particularly (but not only) the right to data protection.

While the first part of this book (Chapters 2–6) focuses primarily on the existing provisions in the GDPR (*de lege lata*), the final part focuses mostly on possible alternatives *de lege ferenda* (Chapters 7 and 8).

A doctrinal legal research methodology is applied throughout with reference to the relevant legislative frameworks. The legal instruments have been selected based on their substantive and material scope and the interdisciplinary insights have been gathered via a literature review of key insights into the role of human vulnerability, the relationship between human weakness and human rationality, under different (neither fully alternative nor fully complimentary) perspectives: fundamental rights, law and economics analyses of consumers' behaviour, and research ethics. Some parts of this book build on some of the conclusions of the author's earlier work.[38]

EU law constitutes the reference legal framework and references to extra-EU law are made when relevant to offer comparisons with EU law. The choice to take an EU-wide perspective for this book, as opposed to studying national laws, was imposed by the high level of harmonization reached in the EU about personal data protection through the GDPR. National differences about the way to define and deal with data subjects' vulnerability might be either isolated cases or in contradiction with the GDPR. It does not mean that this book does not consider national

[35] However, the data controller in some cases has less room for manoeuvre in complying with the GDPR rules (eg when designating a data protection officer or when guaranteeing the exercise of data protection rights), while in some other cases they have more choice (eg when implementing security measures under arts 32 of data protection by design and by default rules under art 25).

[36] Macenaite (n 32); Ca Quelle, '"The 'Risk Revolution" in EU Data Protection Law: We Can't Have Our Cake and Eat It, Too' in R Leenes and others (eds),, *Data Protection and Privacy: The Age of Intelligent Machines* (Hart Publishing 2017); R Gellert, 'We Have Always Managed Risks in Data Protection Law: Understanding the Similarities and Differences between the Rights-Based and the Risk-Based Approaches to Data Protection' (2016) 2 European Data Protection Law Review 481.

[37] K Demetzou, 'GDPR and the Concept of Risk' in E Kosta and others (eds), *Privacy and Identity Management. Fairness, Accountability, and Transparency in the Age of Big Data: 13th IFIP WG 9.2, 9.6/11.7, 11.6/SIG 9.2.2 International Summer School, Vienna, Austria, August 20–24, 2018, Revised Selected Papers* (Springer International Publishing 2019) <https://doi.org/10.1007/978-3-030-16744-8_10> accessed 19 September 2019.

[38] See, in particular, Malgieri and Niklas (n 29); G Malgieri, 'The Concept of Fairness in the GDPR: A Linguistic and Contextual Interpretation' *Proceedings of the 2020 Conference on Fairness, Accountability, and Transparency* (Association for Computing Machinery 2020) <https://doi.org/10.1145/3351095.3372868> accessed 29 January 2020.

legislation. The GDPR allows EU Member States to specify several provisions in national laws. In many cases, this book considers national laws as relevant examples or case studies for specific possible implementations of the GDPR.

The EU (rather than the national) focus also influences the selection of sources. For instance, this book gives a relatively large amount of attention to the opinions of the Article 29 Working Party, now the European Data Protection Board (EDPB), an EU entity in which national Data Protection Authorities (DPAs) cooperate. Though the EDPB's opinions are not legally binding, Article 70 of the GDPR states that the EDPB is required to issue opinions, guidelines, and recommendations to ensure the consistent application of the GDPR. Accordingly, the interpretational activity of the EDPB is not only influential for commentators but also for the activity of the EU Member States' DPAs. In particular, for our purposes, the role of the EDPB is meaningful: the notion of the vulnerable subject is present in many opinions and guidelines, constituting a solid basis for this research.[39]

The scope of this book is limited to the EU law on *data protection*. Other EU legal fields that might also be very relevant for the consideration of individual vulnerability—such as consumer law, research regulation, contract law—are used only as a comparative reference but they are not the object of specific analyses. However, this book focuses mainly on the comparison and the overlaps between data protection law and consumer law, discussed in Chapters 2 and 3. Although I am aware that this perspective might appear limited (since it does not investigate deeply the overlap between, for example, labour law and data protection law or administrative law and data protection law), consumer protection has been taken as a reference because the theorization of the notions of average and vulnerable individuals is highly developed in EU consumer law at each level (legislation, case law, scholarly debate). In addition, many scholars have suggested that consumer law should be taken as a reference when analysing the notion of average and vulnerable data subjects in the data protection field.[40] Another instance of secondary legislation is taken as a reference too: medical research and, in particular, clinical trials. This choice is because the Clinical Trials Regulation EU 536/2014 (hereinafter CTR) proposes a precise and advanced classification of vulnerable subjects, which seems compatible with the layered vulnerability theory that this book adopts.[41] In addition, as shown in Chapter 8, the protection of vulnerable individuals in CTR

[39] See WP29, Guidelines on Transparency, WP260rev.01, 10; WP29, Opinion on legitimate interest, WP217, 40–41; WP29, Opinion on purpose limitation, WP203, 25 and 32; WP29 Guidelines on DPIA, WP248, 9; WP29, Guidelines on Profiling, WP251rev.01, 22. See indirectly also EDPB, Opinion 3/2019, 23 January 2019, 6.

[40] See eg G González Fuster, 'How Uninformed Is the Average Data Subject? A Quest for Benchmarks in EU Personal Data Protection' (2014) 19 Revista de Internet, Derecho y Política 92; See also N Helberger and others, 'The Perfect Match? A Closer Look at the Relationship between EU Consumer Law and Data Protection Law' (2017) 54 Common Market Law Review 1427.

[41] É Gennet and others, 'Does the New EU Regulation on Clinical Trials Adequately Protect Vulnerable Research Participants?' (2015) 119 Health Policy (Amsterdam, Netherlands) 925.

can be viewed as an interesting possible development *de lege ferenda* for the data protection framework, proposing an approach to vulnerability of the individual which seems a sensible alternative to the approach taken in EU consumer law. Chapter 3 also mentions other EU legal fields that address the definition of vulnerable individuals in different sectors and contexts. Still, in those other pieces of legislation, the mention of the vulnerable subject is merely eventual, incidental, and without the systemic efforts at definition that we can find in consumer law and in clinical trials legislation.

As regards the data protection framework, my focus is on the GDPR, not on specific *lex speciales* or sectoral data protection legislation, like the law enforcement directive,[42] the Passenger Name Record (PNR) Directive,[43] the Regulation of data protection for the EU bodies,[44] the ePrivacy directive,[45] etc, even though these pieces of legislation are also considered for comparison when necessary. The Council of Europe's sources, and, in particular, the Modernized Convention 108 on the protection of personal data,[46] are also taken into account as elements of comparison with the GDPR.

The choice of the GDPR as the main object of investigation is based on two main reasons: (i) since the research question investigates the general notion of the data subject, it is appropriate to consider the *lex generalis* on data protection rather than any *lex specialis* where the definitions might depend on the specific sector or context at issue; (ii) the GDPR is the most harmonized and detailed legal source in the EU data protection framework, and considering such a robust and systemic legal text helps the interpreter to gain a more comprehensive picture, for example, about the rationales for protection, the balancing of different interests, the different safeguards, etc.

This book will not address the specific traditional cases of vulnerability usually considered under EU law (children, elderly, mentally disabled people, asylum seekers, employees, patients, foreigners, pregnant women, etc). This choice is not

[42] Directive (EU) 2016/680 of the European Parliament and of the Council of 27 April 2016 on the protection of natural persons with regard to the processing of personal data by competent authorities for the purposes of the prevention, investigation, detection or prosecution of criminal offences or the execution of criminal penalties, and on the free movement of such data, and repealing Council Framework Decision 2008/977/JHA 2016 [32016L0680].

[43] Directive (EU) 2016/681 of the European Parliament and of the Council of 27 April 2016 on the use of passenger name record (PNR) data for the prevention, detection, investigation and prosecution of terrorist offences and serious crime 2016 [32016L0681].

[44] Regulation (EU) 2018/1725 of the European Parliament and of the Council of 23 October 2018 on the protection of natural persons with regard to the processing of personal data by the Union institutions, bodies, offices and agencies and on the free movement of such data, and repealing Regulation (EC) No 45/2001 and Decision No 1247/2002/EC (text with EEA relevance.) 2018 (OJ L).

[45] Directive 2002/58/EC of the European Parliament and of the Council of 12 July 2002 concerning the processing of personal data and the protection of privacy in the electronic communications sector (Directive on privacy and electronic communications) 2002 [32002L0058].

[46] Council of Europe, Modernised Convention for the Protection of Individuals with Regard to the Processing of Personal Data, CM/Inf(2018)15-final, 18 May 2018, 128th Session of the Committee of Ministers (Elsinore, Denmark, 17–18 May 2018).

based on the lack of literature or empirical data but on a theoretical reason: this book prefers not to consider vulnerability as merely based on traditional labels. Considering the new potentialities of the digital market as described in Section 1 above, the new awareness about cognitive biases of any individual[47] and the new philosophical sensitivity about the general condition of vulnerability,[48] this book looks for a broader definition of vulnerability that goes beyond any traditional label. That is why the taxonomy that I propose (Chapter 4) is not about specific social groups but specific *layers* of vulnerability, considering power distribution (modal or causal), vulnerability manifestation (*during the data processing* or at the *outcome* of the data processing), and effects (lack of self-determination in the data processing or risks of discrimination and manipulation as a consequence of the data processing). Moreover, a group-by-group analysis of vulnerable data subjects would have implied overlaps, inconsistencies, or unnecessary repetitions.

As a last disclaimer, this book will not cover anti-discrimination law in detail, even while recognizing its relevance for the protection of vulnerable and marginalized people. As Chapter 3 shows, anti-discrimination law (legislation, case law, and the scholarly debate) is undoubtedly a field that can enrich the discussion about individual vulnerability. A layered notion of vulnerability might help mitigate eventual pitfalls of anti-discrimination law, particularly the adverse effect experienced by individuals who do not belong to groups that are victims of traditional discrimination (protected explicitly by law). However, the vulnerability framework can only *complement and not substitute* anti-discrimination law, which is still an essential safeguard for the rights and freedoms of individuals.

5. Societal and scientific relevance and the state of the art

This book might be relevant both from a scientific and a societal perspective. In the socio-legal discussion, the notion of vulnerability has even been considered one of the rationales for protecting fundamental rights.[49] Other scholars have argued that the founding principle of fundamental rights in Europe is dignity.[50] The concept of dignity is, however, related to the protection of vulnerable individuals: protecting human dignity means primarily protecting the weakest individuals.[51] In other words, if we want to protect the essence of fundamental rights, we need to

[47] See eg European Commission, 'Consumer Vulnerability across Key Markets in the European Union' (2016) <https://ec.europa.eu/info/sites/info/files/consumers-approved-report_en.pdf> accessed 20 February 2023.
[48] See eg J Butler, *Precarious Life: The Powers of Mourning and Violence* (Verso 2006); C Mackenzie and others (eds), *Vulnerability: New Essays in Ethics and Feminist Philosophy* (1st edn, Oxford University Press 2013).
[49] Turner (n 14) 6.
[50] Andorno (n 13).
[51] ibid 264.

look for tailored protections for vulnerable individuals. In the field of privacy and data protection, the dignity principle has a relevant role too.[52]

Some scholars have suggested that information privacy protection is based on the motivation to mitigate the individual's vulnerability.[53] The assumption that there is a clear power imbalance between data controllers and data subjects is evident not just in the text of the GDPR[54] but in many foundational principles of the data protection framework in Europe.[55]

In similar fields, the analysis of individual vulnerability constitutes an important area of research. This is the case of consumer protection law: essential studies have been conducted not only in the economics and behavioural domain[56] but also in the legal domain.[57] Analogously, in the research regulation field, many scholars addressed the issue of research subjects' vulnerability.[58] The academic attention on

[52] See G González Fuster, *The Emergence of Personal Data Protection as a Fundamental Right of the EU* (Springer International Publishing 2014) 23. See also eg art 1 of the Italian Data Protection Code 2003, affirming that the rationale of data protection law is, among others, protecting individual dignity. See also the German Federal Constitutional Court (Mikrozensus-Urteil, 16 July 1969 [1 BVerfGE 27, Rn. 20] affirming that the protection of personal data is grounded on the principle of dignity, See eg P De Hert and S Gutwirth, 'Privacy, Data Protection and Law Enforcement. Opacity of the Individual and Transparency of Power' in E Claes and others (ed), *Privacy and the Criminal Law* (Intersentia 2006) 81; JQ Whitman, 'The Two Western Cultures of Privacy: Dignity Versus Liberty' (2004) 113 The Yale Law Journal 72; L Floridi, 'On Human Dignity as a Foundation for the Right to Privacy' (2016) 29 Philosophy & Technology 307 See more details in Chapter 3.

[53] Calo, 'Privacy, Vulnerability, and Affordance' (n 11). On the role of data protection in redressing the balance of power see Lynskey (n 10) 213–15.

[54] See Recital 43, GDPR.

[55] See D Clifford and J Ausloos, 'Data Protection and the Role of Fairness' (2018) 37 Yearbook of European Law 130; I Graef and others, 'Fairness and Enforcement: Bridging Competition, Data Protection, and Consumer Law' (2018) 8 International Data Privacy Law 200; See also Malgieri, 'The Concept of Fairness in the GDPR' (n 38).

[56] See eg R Burden, *Vulnerable Consumer Groups: Quantification and Analysis* (Office of Fair Trading 1998); SM Baker and others, 'Building Understanding of the Domain of Consumer Vulnerability' (2005) 25(2) Journal of Macromarketing 128; S Commuri and A Ekici, 'An Enlargement of the Notion of Consumer Vulnerability' [2008] 28(2) Journal of Macromarketing <https://journals.sagepub.com/doi/10.1177/0276146705280622> accessed 23 February 2020; P Lunn and S Lyons, 'Behavioural Economics and "Vulnerable Consumers": A Summary of Evidence' [2010] Communications Consumer Panel <https://www.esri.ie/system/files?file=media/file-uploads/2015-07/BKMNEXT180.pdf> accessed 5 February 2023; European Commission (n 47); P Cartwright, 'Understanding and Protecting Vulnerable Financial Consumers' (2015) 38 Journal of Consumer Policy 119; J Stearn, 'Tackling Consumer Vulnerability an Action Plan for Empowerment' (2012) <https://www.bl.uk/collection-items/tackling-consumer-vulnerability-an-action-plan-for-empowerment> accessed 23 February 2020.

[57] FW Morgan and others, 'A Framework for Examining the Legal Status of Vulnerable Consumers' (1995) 14 Journal of Public Policy & Marketing 267; T Wilhelmsson, 'The Informed Consumer v the Vulnerable Consumer in European Unfair Commercial Practices Law—A Comment' in G Howells and others (eds), *The Yearbook of Consumer Law 2007* (Routledge 2007); L Waddington, 'Reflections on the Protection of "Vulnerable" Consumers Under EU Law' Maastricht Faculty of Law Working Paper No. 2013-2 (2014) <https://papers.ssrn.com/abstract=2532904> accessed 1 March 2020; J Mulder, 'Comparing Vulnerability? How Can EU Comparative Law Methods Shed Light on the Concept of the Vulnerable Consumer' (2019) 6 Journal of International and Comparative Law 209.

[58] Gennet and others (n 41); Rogers and others (n 33); F Luna, 'Elucidating the Concept of Vulnerability: Layers Not Labels' (2009) 2 International Journal of Feminist Approaches to Bioethics 121; D Schroeder and E Gefenas, 'Vulnerability: Too Vague and Too Broad?' (2009) 18 Cambridge Quarterly of Healthcare Ethics 113; F Luna, 'Identifying and Evaluating Layers of Vulnerability—A Way Forward' (2019) 19 Developing World Bioethics 86.

this topic was due not only to the explicit mentioning of human vulnerability in different sectoral laws[59] but also to the scientific evidence about limited rationality and limited freedom of (even average) individuals.[60]

In the field of data protection law too, several scholars, like Gloria Gonzàlez Fuster and Peter Blume, have called for a systematic study on the status and conditions of the data subject to analyse, in particular, whether an 'average' data subject exists[61] and how data subjects' vulnerability might be defined and protected.[62] This might be important to improve understanding of the benchmark for analysing many data protection principles (eg fairness and transparency) and for more effective protection of data subjects and a better (and more individual-centred) understanding of the risk-based approach.

Indeed, as already argued in Section 1, the status and characteristics of other actors in the data protection framework are well defined in the GDPR,[63] and better analysed and classified in the legal literature.[64] Such analysis is missing for what concerns data subjects; this book aims not to cover that gap wholly but to open a meaningful research path that can be developed further in the future.

This book might have many societal implications. Understanding how to analyse the characteristics of the data subject might help gain higher protection for all individuals whose personal data are processed, particularly in more critical and sensitive circumstances (behavioural marketing, health data tracking, surveillance in public areas, etc). A more attentive and individual-centred application of the risk-based approach could produce several benefits for different groups of data subjects. In addition, a vulnerability-tailored application of many data protection principles could be beneficial both for the data subject and the data controller. The latter might profit from more clarity about how to implement transparency and fairness principles, for example, and how to undertake a test which looks at the balance between the different interests at issue.[65]

Moreover, using the DPIA as a tool to analyse human vulnerability in the data environment (mostly—but not only—in the digital market) could be a way to profit from an existing GDPR tool that is often accused of being too vague and

[59] See eg art 5 of the Unfair Commercial Practice Directive. See also arts 10 and 30–33 of the Clinical Trial Regulation.

[60] See eg O Thomas, 'Two Decades of Cognitive Bias Research in Entrepreneurship: What Do We Know and Where Do We Go from Here?' (2018) 68 Management Review Quarterly 107; Matz and others (n 23).

[61] González Fuster, 'How Uninformed Is the Average Data Subject?' (n 40).

[62] P Blume, 'The Data Subject' (2015) 1 European Data Protection Law Review 258; N Helberger and others, 'The Perfect Match? A Closer Look at the Relationship between Eu Consumer Law and Data Protection Law' (2017) 54 Common Market Law Review 1427.

[63] The definition and the role of the data controller is well defined at arts 4(7)–(8), 24–29 of the GDPR.

[64] See, in particular, Van Alsenoy (n 6).

[65] This balancing test is relevant not only for processing data on the basis of legitimate interests under art 6(1)(f) but also for the exercise of the right to object at art 21 and for the analysis of necessity and proportionality as requested at art 35(7).

general[66] and a pragmatic way to address different risks and needs of vulnerable data subjects. In sum, promoting data subjects' vulnerability as a heuristic tool of the whole data protection framework might prove beneficial not only for stakeholders who need to apply and implement the law but also for the addressee of the protections contained in the law (the data subjects).

The ultimate societal relevance of this book might be to identify, prevent, or at least mitigate individual vulnerabilities in the digital ecosphere. The general notions of traditionally vulnerable groups (children, elderly, mentally disabled people, etc) have proved ineffective to address many challenges of the algorithmic age. Adopting an extensive, dynamic, and layered notion of vulnerability could help reduce many harms to fundamental rights and freedoms (discrimination, impairment of freedom of thought and freedom of speech, attacks on physical and psychological integrity of the vulnerable individual, etc.).

6. Outline

This book is composed of nine chapters. Each chapter (excluding the first and the last) replies to one of the research sub-questions posed in Section 2.

In particular, Chapter 2 addresses the notion of the data subject in the GDPR. The chapter starts with a descriptive analysis of the wording of the GDPR (and of the related legal texts) about the definition of the data subject, the living natural person to whom the processed data are related. The chapter proceeds with an analysis on whether the general notion of data subjects in the GDPR implicitly refers to an 'average' data subject counterposed to the idea of a 'vulnerable' data subject. Accordingly, Chapter 2 compares the data protection framework with consumer protection law, where the definition of 'average' and 'vulnerable' consumers is well-rooted in the robust case law of the Court of Justice of the European Union (CJEU) and in EU legislation.[67]

Subsequently, Chapter 3 analyses the concept of data subjects' vulnerability in detail. To respond to the question about whether the GDPR contains an (implicit or explicit) notion of vulnerable data subjects, the chapter analyses first the theoretical concept of human vulnerability starting from other fields (political philosophy, research ethics, and law and economics) and trying to adapt the different theoretical insights to the needs and peculiarities of the data protection field.

After this comparative analysis, Chapter 3 examines EU law: how primary and secondary law address the issue of vulnerability. Although in the European

[66] See eg the discussion in K Demetzou, 'Data Protection Impact Assessment: A Tool for Accountability and the Unclarified Concept of "High Risk" in the General Data Protection Regulation' (2019) 35 Computer Law & Security Review 105342.

[67] See, in particular, the Unfair Commercial Practice Directive.

Convention on Human Rights, in the European Union Charter of Fundamental Rights, and the EU treaties there is no explicit mentioning of subjects' vulnerability, the case law of the European Court of Human Rights (ECtHR) offers interesting insights. In addition, the secondary EU law has paid growing attention to vulnerable individuals; in particular, two fields are analysed in more detail: consumer protection law and scientific research regulation. Building on the theoretical and legal discussion, the chapter proposes focusing on a comprehensive and extensive understanding of vulnerability, based on a layered approach. This investigation allows a strong evaluative analysis of the GDPR, where a layered (though implicit) notion of the vulnerable data subject already exists. Under this layered perspective, Chapter 4 analyses the two main categories of vulnerability considering power asymmetries, their manifestations (during data processing and to the outcome of data processing), their effects (cognitive impairment and adverse effects to fundamental rights), and their driving factors (data subject's characteristics, data controller's power, and vulnerability drivers).

Chapters 5 and 6 analyse in more detail the GDPR provisions to understand the role of personal conditions of the data subjects (particularly the state of vulnerability) to interpret and implement the existing rules. Chapter 5 analyses data protection principles, focusing on four: fairness, lawfulness, transparency, and purpose limitation. In particular, the concept of fairness proves to be meaningful to address subjects' vulnerability: Chapter 5 analyses four possible nuances of fairness (also through a linguistic analysis) and how fairness could mitigate the individual vulnerability. As for the lawfulness principle, the personal condition of the data subject (and their eventual state of vulnerability) is pivotal in selecting the lawful basis for processing personal data. That is why the chapter analyses the role of consent, the role of the legitimate interest provision, and also the *sui generis* protection for special categories of sensitive data as a possible way to mitigate the individual vulnerability. As for transparency and purpose limitation, the chapter analyses how the GDPR suggests valourizing personal characteristics when implementing those principles.

Chapter 6 proceeds with an analysis of the GDPR wording considering the data subjects' rights and accountability duties. The rights considered more relevant for this study are the following: the right to receive information (Articles 13 and 14), the right to access (Article 15), the right to erasure (Article 17), the right to object to the processing (Article 21), and the right not to be subject to automated decision-making (Article 22). On the other hand, the accountability duties where the special circumstances of the data subjects (and in particular, data subjects' vulnerability) play a more significant role are mainly the following ones: data controllers' duties grounded on a risk-based approach (see eg Articles 24 and 32), data protection by default and by design (Article 25), and the DPIA (Article 35).

The descriptive analysis of the GDPR in Chapters 5 and 6 is the basis for more evaluative research presented in Chapter 7. This chapter proposes a vulnerability-centred interpretation of the data protection provisions. Indeed, considering the strong link between vulnerability layers assessment and data protection risk assessment, the DPIA model is used as a basis for evaluating and mitigating vulnerability. In particular, Chapter 7 starts by analysing what harm to 'fundamental rights and freedoms' could mean under the vulnerability perspective. The chapter proceeds by analysing the severity and likelihood of such harms. In assessing severity, different degrees of effects of data processing on data subjects are explored through a textual analysis of the GDPR provisions (mere effects, substantial effects, significant effects, legal or similarly significant effects, damages). Chapter 7 offers recommendations about vulnerability mitigation measures.

Chapter 8 analyses the possible criticisms to a vulnerability-based interpretation and implementation of the GDPR: the risk of paternalism, the lack of legal certainty and foreseeability, the problem of analogical interpretation, and the inconvenience or ineffectiveness of specific vulnerability-aware interpretations of the GDPR provisions. Chapter 8 offers a reply to each of these criticisms *de lege lata*, but also proposes—in its last sections—some possible alternatives *de lege ferenda* (namely a category-based recognition of vulnerable groups in the GDPR, following the CTR model, or a general definition following the Unfair Commercial Practice Directive Model).

Chapter 9 concludes, summarizing the notion of the data subject in the GDPR, distinguishing an average data subject from a vulnerable one, and synthesizing the ways to define and mitigate such data subjects' vulnerability.

2

The notion of the data subject: an average individual?

1. Introduction

This chapter answers the following question: what is the notion of the data subject in the GDPR? This question can have two different kinds of answers: one more descriptive and the other more evaluative. As regards the description of an 'average' data subject, it is necessary to analyse the wording of the GDPR to understand the characteristics and properties of the data subject. However, on a more speculative ground, this chapter analyses whether the general structure of rights, safeguards, and duties in the data protection field assumes a 'standard' data subject, in other words, whether an average data subject actually exists. To answer this, the chapter compares data protection law with consumer law, a field in which the definitions of average and vulnerable individuals are well-established. The CJEU and the EU legislator have developed an 'average consumer test' as a counterpart to a vulnerable consumer standard. Accordingly, the author wonders whether the notion of an 'average' data subject in the GDPR is comparable to the notion of average consumers in EU consumer law.

Section 2 addresses the definition of the data subject in the EU data protection framework, taking a *literal interpretation*. It takes into account not only the wording of the GDPR but also its current interpretation by the Court of Justice of the European Union (CJEU) and the European Data Protection Board (EDBP). In particular, to reply to the research question about the notion of the data subject, I analyse all the requirements of this notion in the GDPR: a living person (Section 3), a natural person (Section 4), an identified or identifiable person (Section 5), and a person to whom the data are related (Section 6).

Section 7 proposes a summary of the normative definition of the data subject in the data protection framework, highlighting how the wording of the GDPR and the scholarly discussion do not pay enough attention to the personal conditions of the data subjects. Section 8 introduces a comparative and contextual interpretation of the definition and role of the data subject to explore the notion of the average data subject. In particular, Section 8 compares consumer law to data protection law with regard to the status of individuals. Section 9 analyses the concept of the average consumer in EU legislation and the CJEU *acquis*. Section 10 considers

Vulnerability and Data Protection Law. Gianclaudio Malgieri, Oxford University Press. © Gianclaudio Malgieri 2023.
DOI: 10.1093/oso/9780192870339.003.0002

some critical remarks that have been levelled at such a definition and further developments of that concept into what has become the current benchmark.

Based on the consumer protection framework analysis, Section 11 seeks to understand whether an average data subject exists in the GDPR (and previously in the Data Protection Directive (DPD)) and how similar this average subject is to the average consumer in EU law. The preliminary answer is that the notion of the data subject is universal and dynamic. However, analysing the structure of the data protection framework and comparing it to consumer protection discussions about average and vulnerable consumers, we can affirm that an implicit notion of average data subject exists and is based on the concept of a rational and well-informed individual, but, as Section 12 reveals, many parts of the GDPR suggest that this standard notion can coexist with the notion of vulnerable subjects (that I will explore in further chapters).

2. The notion of the data subject in the EU data protection framework in general

The first question addressed by this section relates to the current definition of the data subject in the EU data protection framework: how did the CJEU and the EDPB (formerly, WP29 (Article 29 Data Protection Working Party on the Protection of Individuals with regard to the Processing of Personal Data)) interpret that definition?

The GDPR indirectly defines the data subject when defining what 'personal data' means in Article 4(1): 'personal data' means any information relating to an identified or identifiable natural person ('data subject'). More explicitly, the data subject is the identified or identifiable natural person to whom the personal data are related. Starting from this definition, we can infer at least three details: they are a *natural person* and not a legal person; some data must be *related* to them; they must be *identified or identifiable*. The definition in the Data Protection Directive was similar.[1]

As for the definition of natural persons, the WP29 has clarified that under the application of the Data Protection Directive, a natural person means a living human being.[2] Data subjectivity cannot be restricted to citizens or nationals or residents of a particular country; in other words, the right to the protection of personal data is a universal one that is not restricted to nationals or residents in a certain country. Indeed, as Recital 4 of the GDPR clarifies,[3] 'the processing of personal data should be designed to serve mankind' and that it 'must, whatever

[1] See art 2, point (a) of the Data Protection Directive.
[2] WP29, Opinion 4/2007 on the concept of personal data, Adopted on 20 June 2007, WP136, 21.
[3] And previously Recital 22 of the Data Protection Directive.

the nationality or residence of natural persons, respect … fundamental rights and freedoms' of individuals (Recital 2). In order to refine its definition of a 'natural person', the WP29 refers to Article 6 of the Universal Declaration of Human Rights, according to which '[e]veryone has the right to recognition everywhere as a person before the law'. The first conclusion from these considerations is that the notion of the data subject is in principle general, comprehensive, unique, and universal.[4] The Council of Europe's Convention 108 for the Protection of Personal Data of 1981[5] shares this universalistic understanding of the data subject, that everyone is equally potentially vulnerable.

As the WP29 adds, the concept of 'natural person' is related to a human being's legal personality, generally understood as the capacity to be the subject of legal relations, usually starting with the individual's birth and ending with their death.[6] However, Member States' legislation, especially in private law, can delimit the boundaries of legal personality more precisely.[7]

3. The first requirement of the GDPR definition: the 'living' person

The notion of the 'living' individual triggers a relevant question: can unborn children and deceased persons be considered data subjects? The WP29 replies that, in principle, neither unborn children nor deceased persons are under the scope of the definition of data subjects. However, they affirm that the Directive (and now the GDPR) leaves the Member States the possibility to regulate data protection rights for unborn or deceased subjects.[8]

The issue of post-mortem privacy and data protection has triggered a vivid scholarly debate.[9] Several commentators have argued that although in principle the concept of privacy should apply in the case of deceased individuals, the specific

[4] See WP29, Opinion 4/2007, 21: 'The right to the protection of personal data is, in that sense, a universal one that is not restricted to nationals or residents in a certain country.'

[5] Council of Europe, Convention for the Protection of Individuals with regard to Automatic Processing of Personal Data, no 108, Strasbourg, 28 January 1981. See art 1: 'The purpose of this Convention is to secure in the territory of each Party for every individual, *whatever his nationality or residence*' (emphasis added).

[6] WP29, WP136, 22.

[7] ibid.

[8] ibid.

[9] E Harbinja, 'Post-mortem Privacy 2.0: Theory, Law, and Technology' (2017) 31(1) International Review of Law, Computers & Technology 26–42; L Edwards and E Harbinja, 'Protecting Post-Mortem Privacy: Reconsidering the Privacy Interests of the Deceased in a Digital World' (2013) 32(1) Cardozo Arts & Entertainment Law Journal 101–47; JC Buitelaar, 'Post-Mortem Privacy and Informational Self-Determination' (2017) 19(2) Ethics and Information Technology 129–42; G Malgieri, 'R.I.P.: Rest in Privacy or Rest in (Quasi-)Property? Personal Data Protection of Deceased Data Subjects between Theoretical Scenarios and National Solutions' in R Leenes and others (eds), *Data Protection and Privacy: The Internet of Bodies* (Hart Publishing, 2018) 143–67.

extension of data protection rules after the death of data subjects depends on national legislation.[10] The GDPR has made this even more explicit. Recital 27 affirms: 'This Regulation does not apply to the personal data of deceased persons. The Member States may provide for rules regarding the processing of personal data of deceased persons.' In their national data protection laws, several EU Member States afford some form of data protection rights for deceased data subjects. This is the case, for example, in France,[11] Spain,[12] and Italy.[13]

The other aspect to be considered when talking about the 'living natural person' is the status of unborn children. The WP29 affirms that national civil law may have different rules about the legal status of the unborn, but that this is beyond the scope of EU data protection law. Accordingly, we should consider the general approach of the various national legal systems, 'together with the idea that the purpose of data protection rules is to protect the individual'.[14]

The WP29 also underlines that the situation of unborn children is not just limited in time to the period of pregnancy but may last considerably longer, as in the case of frozen embryos. In that case, we should look at particular provisions on reproduction techniques, dealing with the use of medical or genetic information about embryos.[15] More recently, the European Data Protection Supervisor has also mentioned unborn children as potential subjects.[16] In the Opinion on Data

[10] Harbinja (n 9).

[11] Loi no 78-17 du 6 janvier 1978 relative à l'informatique, aux fichiers et aux libertés (Modifié par LOI no 2016-1321 du 7 octobre 2016, art 63), art 40-1. The French law provides that although data protection rights terminate when the data subjects dies, they can formulate some register of will for post-mortem data processing (determining how and whether personal data related to their can be processed), in which they can also mandate the exercise of these rights to a specific representative. The data subject can modify or withdraw these directives (which are kept in a national registry) at any moment. Malgieri (n 9) 150.

[12] Ley Orgánica 3/2018, art 3. According to the Spanish law, the heirs, the persons related to the deceased person or previously mandated by the deceased person, can exercise the right to access, rectify, and erase the personal data of the deceased data subject, unless the data subject has prohibited it through an official declaration during their life. Interestingly, for minors or incapacitated persons also the legal representative can exercise any right after the death of the data subject. PG Santiago, 'La Llamada "Personalidad Pretérita": Datos Personales de Las Personas Fallecidas y Protección Post Mortem de Los Derechos al Honor, Intimidad y Propia Imagen' (2016) 5(1) 201–38 <http://roderic.uv.es/handle/10550/56708> accessed 21 January 2020.

[13] Codice in materia di Protezione dei Dati Personali, d.lgs. 196/2003 as amended by d.lgs. 101/2018, art 2-terdecies. The Italian law provides that any person can exercise the rights at arts 15–22 GDPR on behalf of the deceased data subject for personal interests, family reasons or because they were nominated representative by the deceased person. See what was defined the 'Kantian' model in Malgieri (n 9). See also more in general on this Kantian approach to post-mortem privacy Buitelaar (n 9) The exercise of these rights can be limited by a specific declaration that the deceased data subject has made during their life. Such declaration can be withdrawn or modified at any moment before the death. See Codice in materia di Protezione dei Dati Personali, art 2-terdecies.

[14] WP29, WP136, 23.

[15] ibid.

[16] EDPS, A Preliminary Opinion on Data Protection and Scientific Research, 13.

Protection and Research, the EDPS mentions foetuses in the list of *vulnerable research subjects.*[17]

In conclusion, it does not seem possible to affirm clearly whether unborn or deceased people are 'data subjects' or not. However, what seems clear is that their subjectivity in the data protection legislation depends on national rules and specific situations and is, thus, contextual.

4. The second requirement of the GDPR definition: the natural person (and not legal persons)

The reference to natural persons also means that legal persons cannot be considered data subjects. Actually, the European data protection framework has not always excluded legal persons from the scope of data subjects. The Council of Europe's Convention 108 of 1981 protected 'every individual',[18] without mentioning legal or physical persons. In addition, Article 3(2) point (b) specified that any state might give notice 'that it will also apply this Convention to information relating to groups of persons, associations, foundations, companies, corporations and any other bodies consisting directly or indirectly of individuals, whether or not such bodies possess legal personality'. In other words, the Convention—depending on the legislation of a Council of Europe (CoE) Member State—was potentially applicable to legal persons. Still, even collective subjects without legal personality could have been considered data subjects.[19] The Modernized Convention 108 of 2018 has kept the broad notion of the data subject ('every individual').[20] Still, the new Article 3 has no more references to the potential for the Member States to expand the protection to legal persons.

The Data Protection Directive did not exclude legal persons from the definition of data subjects. Recital 24 of the Directive clarified that 'the legislation concerning the protection of legal persons with regard to the processing data which concerns

[17] ibid. That mention, however, is within the sections about history of ethical standards in research and cannot be exploited beyond that limited context. On the vulnerable nature of foetuses see also R Andorno, 'Is Vulnerability the Foundation of Human Rights?' in A Masferrer and E García-Sánchez (eds), *Human Dignity of the Vulnerable in the Age of Rights: Interdisciplinary Perspectives* (Springer International Publishing 2016) <https://doi.org/10.1007/978-3-319-32693-1_11> accessed 6 April 2020.

[18] Convention 108, art 1: The purpose of this Convention is to secure in the territory of each Party for every individual, whatever his nationality or residence, respect for his rights and fundamental freedoms, and in particular his right to privacy, with regard to automatic processing of personal data relating to him ('data protection'). See also art 2: '"personal data" means any information relating to an identified or identifiable *individual* ("data subject")' (emphasis added).

[19] See also the Explanatory Report of Convention 108, 3: 'In all countries the legislation covers data relating to natural persons, but in some it also covers data concerning legal persons.'

[20] See CoE's Modernized Convention 108, art 1.

them is not affected by this Directive'. However, there was no specific legislation of data protection for legal persons at the EU level. Accordingly, Member States were free to regulate the protection of the personal data of legal persons. This was also confirmed by the CJEU, which affirmed that nothing prevents Member States from extending the scope of the national legislation implementing the Directive's provisions to areas not included within the Directive's scope, provided that no other provision of Community Law (now EU Law) precludes it.[21] Only some Member States extended the notion of data subjects to legal persons: Italy, Austria, and Luxembourg.[22]

However, the repealing of the DPD has diminished the *room for manoeuvre* of Member States in extending the scope of definitions and protection in the EU data protection framework since the GDPR is a regulation requiring higher harmonization. The preamble of the GDPR is more assertive about the issue of data subjectivity of legal persons than the DPD. Recital 14 affirms: 'This Regulation does not cover the processing of personal data which concerns legal persons and in particular undertakings established as legal persons, including the name and the form of the legal person and the contact details of the legal person.'

While the GDPR guarantees that Member States may provide rules regarding the processing of personal data of deceased persons (Recital 27), there is no reference to Member States' derogations as to what concerns the protection of legal persons' personal data. Consequently, considering that Member States have no margin of appreciation beyond what is explicitly stated in an EU regulation, we can conclude that the notion of the data subject cannot include legal persons, not even at the national level.

Moreover, while the title of the Data Protection Directive mentioned only individuals ('Directive . . . on the protection of *individuals* with regard to the processing of personal data'),[23] the title of the GDPR mentions explicitly only natural persons ('Regulation . . . on the protection of *natural persons* with regard to the processing of personal data').[24]

[21] CJEU Case C-101/2001 *Lindqvist* [6 November 2003] ECLI:EU:C:2003:596, §98.

[22] WP29 Opinion, WP136, 24.

[23] Emphasis added.

[24] Emphasis added. Interestingly, some provisions of the e-privacy Directive 2002/58/EC apply also to legal persons. art 1(2) thereof provides that '[t]he provisions of this Directive particularise and complement Directive 95/46/EC for the purposes mentioned in paragraph 1. Moreover, they provide for protection of the legitimate interests of subscribers who are *legal persons*' (emphasis added). Accordingly, arts 12 and 13 extend the application of some provisions concerning directories of subscribers and unsolicited communication also to legal persons. However, I remind readers that the e-privacy directive has not entirely the same scope and legal basis of the GDPR, since its rationale is confidentiality of electronic communication and not mere protection of personal data. In other words, we cannot use the extension of rights at art 1(2) to infer an extension of the definition of data subject in the EU data protection framework.

5. The third requirement of the data subject definition: identified or identifiable

Concerning the meaning of 'identified or identifiable, directly or indirectly', Article 4 clarifies the list of identifiers: 'a name, an identification number, location data, an online identifier or to one or more factors specific to the physical, physiological, genetic, mental, economic, cultural or social identity of that natural person'.

The WP29 has generally adopted a broad notion of 'identified or identifiable'. 'Identified' refers to a person who is known or distinguished in a group, and 'identifiable' is a person who is not identified yet, but identification is possible.[25] One is directly identified or identifiable most commonly by reference to a name, in combination with additional information if the name is not unique; one is 'indirectly identifiable' by the so-called unique combinations of not unique identifiers that allow the individual to be singled out.[26]

In addition, also Recital 26 explains what identifiable means: 'To determine whether a natural person is identifiable, account should be taken of all the means reasonably likely to be used, such as singling out, either by the controller or by another person to identify the natural person directly or indirectly'. The notion of 'reasonably likely to be used' is the key to that definition, but it is not an easy concept. That is why Recital 26 further explains: 'To ascertain whether means are reasonably likely to be used to identify the natural person, account should be taken of all objective factors, such as the costs of and the amount of time required for identification, taking into consideration the available technology at the time of the processing and technological developments.'

The CJEU has accepted this broad notion of identifiability (and reasonable likelihood to identify) in the *Breyer* case,[27] where the Court affirms that it is not necessary 'that all the information enabling the identification ... must be in the hands of one person'.[28] More recently, the *Nowak* judgment has reaffirmed these concepts.[29] The Court, in *Breyer*, also states that identifiability is not 'reasonably likely' if it is 'prohibited by law or practically impossible' due to 'a disproportionate effort in terms of time, cost and man-power, so that the risk of identification appears in reality to be insignificant'.[30] In other terms, the Court introduces the factor

[25] WP29, WP 136, 4–5. N Purtova, 'The Law of Everything. Broad Concept of Personal Data and Future of EU Data Protection Law' (2018) 10 Law, Innovation and Technology 40–81.

[26] WP136, 4–5. Purtova (n 25) 7; FJZ Borgesius, 'Singling out People without Knowing Their Names—Behavioural Targeting, Pseudonymous Data, and the New Data Protection Regulation' (2016) 32(2) Computer Law & Security Review 256–71.

[27] Case C-582/14 *Patrick Breyer v Bundesrepublik Deutschland* [2016] ECLI:EU:C:2016:779.

[28] ibid §43.

[29] CJEU, Case C-434/16 *Peter Nowak v Data Protection Commissioner* [2017] §31; see also Opinion of Advocate General Kokott delivered on 20 July 2017. *Peter Nowak v Data Protection Commissioner*. Case C-434/16 §23.

[30] *Patrick Breyer v Bundesrepublik Deutschland* (n 27) §46.

of legality among the means of identification. The Court has recently confirmed these considerations.[31]

However, this topic is still very controversial: scholars have highlighted the contradictions between the risk-based definition of 'identifiability' in Recital 26 of the GDPR and the authoritative guidelines of WP29,[32] whose wording (referring to 'irreversible' anonymization and 'reasonably impossible' re-identification) seems to refer to a 'zero-risk' approach.[33]

In general terms, taking into account the existing guidelines,[34] the CJEU rulings and the scholarly discussion on the point, the resulting standard of the reasonable likelihood of identification is quite broad and context-dependent,[35] the consequence of this broad definition is that the status of data as 'personal' is dynamic, that is, the same dataset may not be identifiable (referring to an identifiable data subject) at the start of processing from the perspective of a given controller, but might be (or start to be) identifiable from the perspective of another data controller or once the circumstances change.[36]

This is particularly true if also we take into account Article 11, according to which if the purposes for which a controller processes personal data do not (or no longer) require the identification of a data subject by the controller, that controller shall not be obliged to take steps to identify the data subject for the sole purpose of complying with the GDPR. In addition, in these cases, if 'the controller is able to demonstrate that it is not in a position to identify the data subject, the controller shall inform the data subject accordingly' and 'Articles 15 to 20 shall not apply except where the data subject, for the purpose of exercising his or her rights under those articles, provides additional information enabling his or her identification'. This provision seems to add more complexity not only to the difference between anonymous and personal data (including pseudonymized data) but also to the definition of the data subject itself. Indeed, if we agree that under Article 4(1) a person that is not (or no longer) identifiable cannot be called 'data subject',

[31] ECJ Case C-597/19 *Mircom International Content Management & Consulting (MICM) Limited v Telenet BVBA* [2021] §103.

[32] WP29, 'Opinion 05/2014 on Anonymisation Techniques, WP216' (2014).

[33] S Stalla-Bourdillon and A Knight, 'Anonymous Data v. Personal Data—A False Debate: An EU Perspective on Anonymization, Pseudonymization and Personal Data' (2017) 34 Wisconsin International Law Journal 284, 288; M Finck and F Pallas, 'They Who Must Not Be Identified—Distinguishing Personal from Non-Personal Data under the GDPR' (2020) 10 International Data Privacy Law 11, 15.

[34] In addition to WP29 (n 32), see also Information Commissioner's Officer, 'Anonymisation: Managing Data Protection Risk Code of Practice' (2012) 108 <https://ico.org.uk/media/for-organisations/documents/1061/anonymisation-code.pdf> accessed 20 February 2023; CNIL, 'Comment prévenir les risques et organiser la sécurité de vos données?' (2019) <https://www.cnil.fr/fr/comment-prevenir-les-risques-et-organiser-la-securite-de-vos-donnees> accessed 5 May 2022.

[35] Purtova (n 25) 7.

[36] ibid 7; B-J Koops, 'The Trouble with European Data Protection Law' (2014) 4(4) International Data Privacy Law 250.

we might wonder why Article 11, at both paragraphs (1) and (2), keeps referring to these persons as 'data subjects'. Article 11 suggests that non-identifiable data subjects (specifically the individuals to whom anonymous data might be referring if they provide additional information that enables their identification) might exercise data protection rights. Apart from this grey zone of subjects—who might be seen as occupying an intermediate zone between data subjects and non-data subjects—Article 11 reveals that the correct application of purpose limitation and data storage limitation principles influence the identifiability of the subject: when the purpose ends, identifiability should end; where the purpose does not require identifiability at all, such identifiability should not be made possible.

The logical consequence of such reflections is also that the nature of the 'data subject' is *dynamic*, as personal data are dynamic, changing over time.. The relational, risk-based, and context-dependent definition of the data subject, as largely discussed in the legal literature,[37] is something that Chapter 3 explores in depth, especially regarding what concerns the notion of the vulnerable data subjects.

6. The fourth requirement of the data subject definition: to whom data are related

The understanding of what (information) 'relating' (to an identified or identifiable natural person) means is very broad too. The WP29 has interpreted 'relating' as referring to three possible cases: the relation might be based on the *content* (the information is *about* a natural person),[38] on the *purpose* (the data 'are used or are likely to be used with the purpose to evaluate, treat in a certain way or influence the status or behaviour of an individual'),[39] or on the *impact* (the information regardless of its content or any purpose of processing may relate to a person in result when its use is likely to affect a particular person's rights and interests).[40]

The CJEU, initially in *YS and others*,[41] interpreted 'related' as only content-based (information *about* a natural person).[42] More recently, in the *Nowak* case,[43] the Court adopted an approach similar to the WP29, accepting that the relation may be by reason of *content*, *purpose*, or *effect*.[44]

[37] See eg Stalla-Bourdillon and Knight (n 33); M Mourby and others, 'Are "Pseudonymised" Data Always Personal Data? Implications of the GDPR for Administrative Data Research in the UK' (2018) 34 Computer Law & Security Review 222; Finck and Pallas (n 33).

[38] WP136, 10.

[39] ibid 10. Emphasis added.

[40] ibid 11. Emphasis added.

[41] Joined Cases C-141/12 and C-372/12 *YS and M. and S. v Minister of Immigration*, Integration and Asylum [2016] ECLI:EU:C:2014:2081.

[42] ibid §46.

[43] Case C-434/16 *Peter Nowak v Data Protection Commissioner* [2017] ECLI:EU:C:2017:994.

[44] ibid §35.

In sum, the understanding of 'related' in the EU definition of personal data—and therefore in the definition of the data subject—is broad and dynamic as well: if the data processing is about an identified or identifiable person or even if it is just potentially having the purpose of dealing with a given identifiable person or having an impact on such a person, the information processed is personal data, and that person is a data subject.[45]

As I observe in Chapter 6, the relationship between the data subject and the data controller is relevant for our purposes because it helps to qualify the level of vulnerability of a data subject. As we will see in the following chapters, the notion of the vulnerable (or non-vulnerable) data subject is relational: the encounter between the personal characteristics of a given data subject and the power position of a given data controller characterizes the level of the data subject's vulnerability. In particular, assuming an impact-based understanding of the term 'related', we observe that the eventually adverse 'effects' of data processing on an individual are essential to define the data subject and their condition.

7. Preliminary conclusions: universalism versus particularism

The previous sections answered a central research sub-question of this book: what is the definition of the data subject in the GDPR?

We observed that this definition is *broad* and *dynamic*. Still, at the same time, it is limited to natural living persons (with the possibility for the Member States to extend it to deceased persons, but not to legal persons). I also observed that the definition of the data subject is comprehensive, singular, and universal. In particular, nationality or citizenship cannot be criteria to delimit the notion of the data subject.

However, one can still wonder whether this definition is singular and universal only in nominal terms or even in substantial terms. In other words, even assuming that there is just one data subject in legal terms, we might wonder whether the personal conditions of that subject are relevant in data protection law (particularly as to what regards safeguards, rights, duties, etc). As for personal conditions, I am referring to their particular characteristics in a broad sense: legal status (legal capacity, familiar status, etc), mental conditions (including age, maturity, psychological health status), level of awareness and understanding of data protection risks and rights, the likelihood of being at risk in their fundamental rights, resilience, or reaction to such risks.

[45] Finck and Pallas (n 33) 13.

In addition, if the conditions of the data subject are relevant, how does the data protection framework consider these conditions (eg considering factors of vulnerability, sensitive categories of subjects, etc)? In particular, if there is no relevance to the status of the data subjects (ie if their personal conditions have no influence in the application of data protection rights and duties), does the EU data protection framework assume an 'average' data subject as a benchmark?

At first sight, the only special category of data subjects in the GDPR is children. Their particular condition is mentioned at Recital 38, and they are subject to a specific provision in case of consent in relation to information society services (Article 8) and to several other safeguards within the text of the GDPR.[46] However, the *sui generis* protection for children seems only an exception to the monolithic notion of data subjects and, considered alone, it does not help reply to the research questions just posed.

8. The average data subject as the average consumer?

I acknowledge that the GDPR (and before it, the DPD) makes no explicit reference to the personal conditions or to particular categories of data subjects.[47] However, some scholars have wondered about the idea of the data subject(s) and whether the structure of the EU data protection framework seems to suggest an 'average data subject' and how average this data subject is (in terms of mental capabilities, awareness, and understanding of rights and risks, maturity, exposure to risks, etc).[48]

The discussion about average and non-average individuals is meaningful in a legal area close to data protection law: consumer law. Indeed, in EU consumer protection law, there is relevant case law and scholarly reflection about the notion of the average consumer.[49] At the same time, consumer protection legislation in the EU also often distinguishes between average and vulnerable consumers.[50]

[46] See also arts 6(1)(f), 12(1), 40(2)(g), and 57(1)(b). See also Recitals 58, 65, 71, 75. See Information Commissioner Officer (ICO), 'Children and the GDPR' (ICO 2020) <https://ico.org.uk/for-organisations/guide-to-data-protection/guide-to-the-general-data-protection-regulation-gdpr/children-and-the-gdpr/> accessed 28 March 2020.

[47] As argued in Chapter 6, the only reference to 'categories of data subject' is just incidental at arts 28 and 30, but there is no clear indication about which categories to consider and why.

[48] P Blume, 'The Data Subject' (2015) 1 European Data Protection Law Review 258; G González Fuster, 'How Uninformed Is the Average Data Subject? A Quest for Benchmarks in EU Personal Data Protection' (2014) 19 Revista de Internet, Derecho y Política 92; G González Fuster and S Gutwirth, 'The Legal Significance of Individual Choices about Privacy and Personal Data Protection 1' in J P Burgess and others (eds), *Surveillance, Privacy and Security* (Routledge 2017) 184; see also the interplay between data 'subjecthood' and feminism. See in particular JT Theilen and others, 'Feminist Data Protection: An Introduction' (2021) 10 Internet Policy Review <https://policyreview.info/articles/analysis/feminist-data-protection-introduction> accessed 5 May 2022; about the traditional neo-liberal approach to the notion of data subjects see also the critical approach in APL Kadiri, 'Data and Afrofuturism: An Emancipated Subject?' (2021) 10 Internet Policy Review <https://policyreview.info/articles/analysis/data-and-afrofuturism-emancipated-subject> accessed 5 May 2022.

[49] See Chapter 9.

[50] See Chapter 8.

As noted, consumer law and data protection law cannot be considered as two separate monoliths.[51] Although grounded on different EU legal bases and different principles, the goals of protection of the two fields are similar, and the two legal frameworks should be seen as complementary.[52] Also, all consumers are potentially data subjects, at least in the digital market, where most data subjects are also consumers.[53]

González Fuster suggests comparing the notion of standard (and vulnerable) data subjects to the well-rooted concept of the average consumer in the EU consumer law.[54] Similarly, Helberger, Zuiderveen Borgesius, and Reyna have called for an integrated approach to data protection and consumer law. In particular, they wonder what consumer law could add to the existing level of protection under data protection law and they find some specific areas in which such a complementary approach might be fruitful: one of these areas is 'consumer vulnerability'.[55]

Before looking at the concept of vulnerability (Chapter 3), we need to understand what 'average' (data subject and consumer) means. Accordingly, the following sections analyse how consumer law has conceptualized the notion of the 'average' consumer by replying to the call of a complementary approach to data protection and consumer protection. Consequently, I compare such a notion with the data protection scenario, looking for compatibility or incompatibility between the definition of 'average' consumer and the definition of 'average' data subject.

Building on these reflections, Chapter 3 analyses the concept of vulnerability in general, with particular attention to—*inter alia*—consumer law to discover whether the comparison between the data protection framework and the consumer protection framework can be helpful to understand the different nuances of the notion of the data subject.

[51] W Kerber, 'Digital Markets, Data, and Privacy: Competition Law, Consumer Law and Data Protection' (2016) 11 Journal of Intellectual Property Law & Practice 856.

[52] N Helberger and others, 'The Perfect Match? A Closer Look at the Relationship between EU Consumer Law and Data Protection Law' (2017) 54 Common Market Law Review 1427. See also EDPS, 'Privacy and competitiveness in the age of big data: The interplay between data protection, competition law and consumer protection in the Digital Economy' <secure.edps.europa.eu/EDPSWEB/webdav/shared/Documents/Consultation/Opinions/2014/14-03-26 _competitition_law_big_data_EN.pdf> accessed 1 May 2022.

[53] González Fuster, 'How Uninformed Is the Average Data Subject?' (n 48) 99.

[54] ibid.

[55] Helberger and others (n 52) 1456–58; A similar call for an integrative approach between Data Protection Law and Consumer and Competition Law can be found in I Graef and others. 'Fairness and Enforcement: Bridging Competition, Data Protection, and Consumer Law' (2018) 8 International Data Privacy Law 200.

9. The average consumer in EU law: the Unfair Commercial Practices Directive

I first consider the notion of the 'average' consumer to understand whether it could serve as a benchmark for the notion of the 'average' data subject.

The notion of 'average' consumer has a solid tradition in EU consumer protection law. Although the Unfair Commercial Practice Directive 2005/29/EC (UCPD) offered the first legislative definition of the average consumer as a benchmark to determine whether a commercial practice is unfair, such a notion was proposed several years earlier. The CJEU first formulated who an average consumer is. After a long process of elaboration on the notion of model consumers starting from the *Cassis de Dijon* case in 1979,[56] in the *Gut Springenheide* case[57] the Court defined the average consumer as 'reasonably well informed and reasonably observant and circumspect'.

As commentators have argued, this concept is the final step towards the judicial portrayal of the consumer as 'sensible, attentive, and cautious, as well as able to analyse, critically and discerningly, the messages behind advertising and commercial practices in general'.[58] As the Advocate General in *Estée Lauder* affirmed: 'the presumption is that consumers will inform themselves about the quality and price of products and will make intelligent choices'.[59] In other words, the consumer, duly informed and thereby protected, is able to participate fairly and effectively in the market.[60]

However, the Court in *Lauder* mitigated this average consumer test, making it more flexible to different contexts in the various Member States. The so-called *Lauder test* referred to an interpretational rule: when interpreting the average consumer test, 'several considerations must be borne in mind. In particular, it must be determined whether social, cultural or linguistic factors may justify the [use of a

[56] See CJEU Case C-120/78 *Rewe-Zentral AG v Bundesmonopolverwaltung fuer Branntwein* [1979] ECR 649, judgment of the ECJ of 20 February 1979. See R Incardona and C Poncibò, 'The Average Consumer, the Unfair Commercial Practices Directive, and the Cognitive Revolution' (2007) 30 Journal of Consumer Policy 21, 29.

[57] CJEU Case C-210/96 *Gut Springenheide GmbH and Others v Oberkreisdirektor des Kreises Steinfurt Ä Amt für Lebensmittelüberwachung* [16 July 1998]. See also a preliminary attempt to define the average group of consumers, on a quantitative analysis, in the *Nissan* case, Case C-373/90, *Nissan* [16 January 1992] §§15–16: 'to ascertain in the circumstances of the particular case and bearing in mind the consumers to which the advertising is addressed, whether the [advertisement] could be misleading in so far as [it] would have deterred *a significant number of consumers* from making a purchase, had they known it' (emphasis added).

[58] MA Dauses, 'Consumer Information in the Case Law of the European Court of Justice: A German View' (1998) 100 British Food Journal 244–53.

[59] Case C-220/98 *Estée Lauder Cosmetics GmbH & Co. OHG v Lancaster Group GmbH*[2000] ECR I-117, Opinion of Advocate General Fennelly delivered on 16 September 1999.

[60] G Howells and S Weatherill, *Consumer Protection Law* (Ashgate Publishing Group 2005).

specific commercial term] meaning something different to the German consumer as opposed to consumers in other Member States.'[61]

In the Unfair Commercial Practices Directive, the EU regulator introduced both the average consumer test and the *Lauder* formula.[62] Recital 18 states:

> In line with the principle of proportionality, and to permit the effective application of the protections contained in it, this Directive takes as a benchmark the average consumer, who is reasonably well-informed and reasonably observant and circumspect, taking into account social, cultural and linguistic factors, as interpreted by the Court of Justice.

10. Criticisms and developments: the relatively average consumer

Despite all these indications, the notion has been considered vague: courts and commentators have largely focused on interpreting the notion of 'average'.[63] In particular, it has been noted that the figure of the average consumer is nebulous[64] given the lack of definition of the average consumer in the body of the Directive (it appears in Recital 18 alone)[65] and the problematic reference to cultural and social aspects, susceptible to meaningful differences between each individual.[66]

[61] Case C-220/98 *Estée Lauder Cosmetics v Lancaster Group* (n 59) [29]. This case adapts the Graffione case in trademark law (Case C-313/94 *Fratelli Graffione SNC v Ditta Fransa* [1996] ECR 1-6039 at [22]). In particular, scholars observed that differences amongst consumers on cultural grounds can be determined by: 'power distance', 'degree of acceptance', 'individualistic vs collectivistic' structure, significance of 'masculinity/femininity', 'uncertainty avoidance' thinking, 'long vs short-term' orientation, and 'indulgence-restraint' attitude. On the contrary, social factors pertain to concepts such as taste and decency, comprising values such as human dignity and personality, freedom, equality, honour, public health and order, public decency, and childhood. For an evaluation of the characteristics of these elements, see T Wilhelmsson, 'Harmonizing Unfair Commercial Practices Law: The Cultural and Social Dimensions' (2007) 44 Osgoode Hall Law Journal 461, 489.

[62] Even if in the initial proposal this provision was introduced in an article, due to the opposition of Member States (that were not prepared to demand so much to their consumers) the Common Position of the Council left it out from the articles and put the definition in the preamble. See Proposal for a Directive of the European Parliament and of the Council concerning unfair business-to-consumer commercial practices in the Internal Market and amending directives 84/450/EEC, 97/7/EC, and 98/27/EC, COM/2003/0356 final, art 2[b] in comparison with the Statement of the Council's reasons, 1163/2/04 REV 2 ADD 1, 11. See also, on this point, T Wilhelmsson, 'The Informed Consumer v the Vulnerable Consumer in European Unfair Commercial Practices Law—A Comment' in G Howells and others (eds), *The Yearbook of Consumer Law 2007* (Routledge 2007).

[63] ibid; A Beater, *Verbraucherschutz Und Schutzzweckdenken Im Wettbewerbsrecht* (Mohr Siebeck 2000) 95; A Davola, 'The Death of Traditional Consumer Law at the Crossroads of Law, Economics and Cognitive Sciences: A Tentative Reaction' (Doctoral thesis, Sant'Anna School of Advanced Studies of Pisa 2019) 63.

[64] Davola (n 63) 63; Wilhelmsson (n 62).

[65] See eg Wilhelmsson (n 62) affirming that the lack of an average consumer test in the body of the Directive might be used to 'downplay' the normative role of the Average Consumer test and to make it thus more flexible.

[66] LR Carleo, 'Consumatore, consumatore medio, investitore e cliente: frazionamento e sintesi nella disciplina delle pratiche commerciali scorrette' (2010) 3 Europea e Diritto Privato 685, 690; G De

In addition, the meaning of 'observant' and 'circumspect' is problematic. Some scholars have tried to define these two concepts as consumers' *awareness* of their interests and their *critical attitude* in searching, evaluating, and selecting information in a way that is neither superficial nor inattentive.[67] Nonetheless, such broad notions give the courts a relevant margin of appreciation to adapt the average consumer test to practical cases.

The concept of the average consumer is nebulous also because both the Court, building on the *Lauder* case, and the legislator[68] have largely referred to a notion of 'relatively average consumer'.[69] According to that notion, the interpreter must consider the characteristics of the group of consumers to which a commercial practice is directed. In other words, if there is a specifically targeted group of people—for example, sophisticated consumers—this group should be considered as average.[70] In that case, the courts must evaluate whether a given company's marketing/commercial strategy can mislead the 'average member' of that community and adapt the parameters defining that 'average consumer' to the characteristics of the considered group.[71] This fragmentation of the notion of average consumer leads to an eclectic understanding of what constitutes the average consumer defined on a case-by-case basis.[72] As Recital 18 of the Unfair Commercial Practices Directive suggests when referring to the 'interpretation of the Court of Justice', robust case law could help us to understand who the average consumer is in every situation. The Court could, thus, mitigate the fragmentation of the concept of the average consumer.[73]

Cristofaro, 'Art. 20 Codice Del Consumo' in G De Cristofaro and A Zaccaria (eds), *Commentario breve al diritto dei consumatori (Codice del consumo e legislazione complementare)* (Cedam 2014) 161; GG Howells and others, *Rethinking EU Consumer Law* (Routledge 2018); Davola (n 63) 57.

[67] VM Meli, 'Pratiche Commerciali Scorrette' (2012) Diritto on line, Treccani <https://www.treccani.it/enciclopedia/pratiche-commerciali-scorrette_(Diritto-on-line)/> accessed 5 February 2023; Davola (n 63) 58.

[68] See, *mutatis mutandis*, the reference to vulnerable consumers and the relative notion of them at Recital 19: 'Where certain characteristics such as age, physical or mental infirmity or credulity make consumers particularly susceptible to a commercial practice or to the underlying product and the economic behaviour only of such consumers is likely to be distorted by the practice in a way that the trader can reasonably foresee, it is appropriate to ensure that they are adequately protected by assessing the practice from the perspective of the average member of that group.' On this topic, see largely Chapter 3.

[69] E Guerinoni, *Pratiche commerciali scorrette. Fattispecie e rimedi* (Giuffrè 2010) 111.

[70] Incardona and Poncibò (n 56) 27; C Poncibò, '"Il Consumatore Medio"' (2007) 12(2) Contratto e impresa Europa 734; C Alvisi, 'Il Consumatore Ragionevole e Le Pratiche Commerciali Sleali' (2008) 24(3) Contratto e impresa 700; CE Mayr, 'Il Parametro Del Consumatore' [2008] AIDA, issue 2008, 274, 274.

[71] Wilhelmsson (n 62) 211; H-W Micklitz, 'Unfair Commercial Practices and Misleading Advertising' in N Reich and others (eds), *European Consumer Law* (Intersentia 2014) 88.

[72] S Weatherill, 'Who is the Average Consumer' in S Weatherill and U Bernitz (eds), *The Regulation of Unfair Commercial Practices under EC Directive 2005/29: New Rules and New Techniques* (1st edn, Hart Publishing Ltd 2007) 119; V Mak, 'Standards of Protection: In Search of the "Average Consumer" of EU Law in the Proposal for a Consumer Rights Directive' (2011) 19 European Review of Private Law 25; C Van Dam, 'De Gemiddelde Euroconsument—Een Pluriform Fenomeen' (2009) 3 Tijdschrift voor Europees en economisch recht 11.

[73] Micklitz (n 72) 87.

From *Lauder*, the Court tried to develop this contextual notion through objective criteria (leaving a minor role to the subjective criteria of cultural, social, and linguistic factors): if it is proven that the commercial practice is targeting a specific category of consumers, then the particular *literacy* and *education* of that category of consumer should be the benchmark to determine what behaviours are expected, *ex ante*, from the professional (a company). This means that, in some cases, the commercial counterparty should implement a higher standard of transparency or clarity. In contrast, in different cases, the consumers are expected to exercise a higher degree of caution in their commercial choices, depending on the specific characteristics of their category.[74]

However, even when considering the context, commentators have affirmed that the average consumer should never be identified as a 'weak party': they must be able to select and face commercial offers properly.[75] In other words, the EU consumer protection framework expects consumers to act sensibly, be informed about interchangeable products offered in the market, and make conscious choices.[76]

Recital 18 clarifies that the average consumer test 'is not a statistical test'. In other terms, quantitative parameters about the average population (eg studies on the behaviour of specific consumers) should not be taken into account:[77] national authorities and courts should be able to determine whether a practice is liable to mislead the average consumer exercising their own judgment by taking into account the 'general presumed consumers' expectations'[78] qualified in juridical and qualitative terms.

[74] J Minor, 'Consumer Protection in the EU: Searching for the Real Consumer' (2012) 13 European Business Organization Law Review 163.

[75] C Camardi, 'La protezione dei consumatori tra diritto civile e regolazione del mercato. A proposito dei recenti interventi sul Codice del consumo' (2013) 5 Jus Civile 305; J Trzaskowski, 'Behavioural Economics, Neuroscience, and the Unfair Commercial Practises Directive' (2011) 34 Journal of Consumer Policy 377, 380; H Rösler, 'Protection of the Weaker Party in European Contract Law—Standardised and Individual Inferiority in Multi-Level Private Law Schutz Des Schwächeren Im Europäischen Vertragsrecht Typisierte und Individ' (2009) 73 Rabels Zeitschrift für ausländisches und internationales Privatrecht (RabelsZ) 889, 729.

[76] E Tzoulia, 'Imprints of Behavioural Research in EU Consumer Protection Legislation: The "Average Consumer Test" in the Unfair Commercial Practices Directive' (2017) 6 Tijdschrift voor Consumentenrecht en handelspraktijken (TvC) 257, 258.

[77] Case C-210/96 *Gut Springenheide and Tusky v Oberkreisdirektor Steinfurt* [1998] ECR I-4657, paras 31, 32, 36, and 37. See also Case C-220/98 *Estée Lauder Cosmetics GmbH & Co. ORG, v Lancaster Group* (n 59), Opinion of Advocate General Fennelly, para 28.

[78] Commission Staff Working Document, *Guidance on the Implementation/Application of Directive 2005/29/EC on Unfair Commercial Practices Accompanying the Document Communication from The Commission to the European Parliament, the Council, the European Economic and Social Committee and the Committee of the Regions. A comprehensive approach to stimulating cross-border e-Commerce for Europe's citizens and businesses*, SWD/2016/0163 final <https://eur-lex.europa.eu/legal-content/EN/TXT/?uri=CELEX%3A52016SC0163> accessed 20 February 2023.

'Average consumers' in other parts of EU consumer law

Other subfields of EU consumer law also employ the notion of the average consumer. In particular, in food law, Regulation (EU) 1169/2011 often refers to the average consumer,[79] but it does not define the phrase. In that Regulation, the benchmark seems to be based on a less informed and circumspect buyer (the food information is required to be 'simple and easily understood'),[80] but this is probably because of the particular subfield at issue.[81]

Looking at the regulation of consumer contracts, the Unfair Terms Directive[82] does not explicitly refer to average consumers. On the contrary, the consumer is generally considered to be a potential victim of abuse of power (Recital 9) and imbalance in rights and obligations arising from a contract (Article 2). Although the Court, in *Océano*, does not refer to average or vulnerable consumers in the field of consumer contracts, there is at least one case in which the judges accepted the ignorance of '*the* consumer' (ie of the standard consumer) for what concerns their legal rights.[83] However, this case referred to access to courts[84] and not to the average attitude of consumers in being well informed, observant, and circumspect. In addition, in contract law, the concept of vulnerability is partly absorbed by the traditional legal notions of contractual incapacitated persons at the level of national legislation.[85] Also, commentators consider the consumer as an inherently vulnerable market player for whom contract law must be adapted and rebalanced.[86] This is not in contradiction to different layers of vulnerability (eg the relatively average and the *stricto sensu* vulnerable consumer).

After this overview, I propose a summary of the notion of the average consumer so that in what follows, it is possible to compare the average consumer to the notion of the (average) data subject. The EU consumer protection framework (considering legislation, court decisions, and opinions of commentators) generally considers the consumer a vulnerable market player due to the imbalance of

[79] See Recitals 41 and 43, art 45, point (d) of Directive.

[80] See Recital 41.

[81] Recital 41 explicitly affirms: 'given the current level of knowledge on the subject of nutrition'.

[82] Council Directive 93/13/EEC of 5 April 1993 on unfair terms in consumer contracts.

[83] Joined Cases C-240/98–244/98 *Océano Grupo Editorial SA v Rocìo Murciano Quintero* [2000] ECR I-4941, §26: 'While it is the case that, in a number of Member States, procedural rules enable individuals to defend themselves in such proceedings, there is a real risk that the consumer, particularly because of ignorance of the law, will not challenge the term pleaded against him on the grounds that it is unfair' (emphasis added). See also Wilhelmsson (n 62).

[84] V Zeno-Zencovich and MC Paglietti, 'Le droit processuel des consommateurs' (2014) 91 Revue de droit international et de droit comparé 321, 338.

[85] For an international approach to legal capacity see E Varney, 'Redefining Contractual Capacity? The UN Convention on the Rights of Persons with Disabilities and the Incapacity Defence in English Contract Law' (2017) 37 Legal Studies 493.

[86] J Stuyck and others, 'Confidence through Fairness? The New Directive on Unfair Business-to-Consumer Commercial Practices in the Internal Market' (2006) 43 Common Market Law Review 107, 109; G Howells and others, *European Fair Trading Law: The Unfair Commercial Practices Directive* (1st edn, Routledge 2006).

power (based in particular on information asymmetry) between themself and the commercial counterparty (seller, provider). However, among consumers, EU consumer protection law distinguishes the notion of average consumers from vulnerable consumers (that I will consider more deeply in the next chapter). The first is—on a qualitative and not statistical basis—reasonably well informed, observant, circumspect, also taking into account the context (through a case-by-case analysis, considering the characteristics of the consumer, of the seller, the specific market conditions, and so on) and, in particular, social, cultural, and linguistic factors.

Critical remarks on the notion of 'average' consumer

Some authors argued that this notion of consumer reflects a neo-liberal approach to market regulation[87] and it is inadequate to deal with the challenges emphasized by recent research in behavioural law and economics:[88] the exploitation of consumer cognitive biases (made even more accessible and more powerful in the age of Big Data and predictive analytics) may render 'vulnerable' *every* average consumer.[89] However, unfortunately, at the moment there are no legislative proposals questioning the formula about average consumers.[90]

Several theoreticians criticize the normative definition of the 'average' person since they see it as a tool to strengthen dominant categories (white, male, heterosexual, wealthy individuals) and stigmatize minorities or vulnerable groups.[91] Although this discussion is beyond the scope of this research, we can observe that in the consumer protection framework, the notion of the average consumer may not be likely to stigmatize vulnerable consumers or to empower only dominant categories: the consideration of social, cultural, and linguistic differences even within the notion of 'average' individual[92] makes the concept of the average subject more comprehensive and inclusive.

[87] See eg Davola (n 63) passim.

[88] Incardona and Poncibò (n 56) 32–33; see, in general, RH Thaler, 'The Psychology of Choice and the Assumptions of Economics' in AE Roth (ed), *Laboratory Experimentation in Economics: Six Points of View* (Cambridge University Press 2005); RH Thaler and CR Sunstein, 'Libertarian Paternalism' (2003) 93 American Economic Review 175.

[89] MG Haselton and others, 'The Evolution of Cognitive Bias' in DM Buss (ed), *The Handbook of Evolutionary Psychology* (John Wiley & Sons, Inc 2015); O Thomas, 'Two Decades of Cognitive Bias Research in Entrepreneurship: What Do We Know and Where Do We Go from Here?' (2018) 68 Management Review Quarterly 107.

[90] The proposed European Commission reforms of consumer law do not address the notion of average and vulnerable consumers. See eg Proposal for a Directive of the European Parliament and of the Council on representative actions for the protection of the collective interests of consumers, and repealing Directive 2009/22/EC.

[91] See, in general, M Moran, *Are Objective Standards Worth Saving? Exploring the Feminist Debate* (Oxford University Press 2003); see also N Naffine, *Law and the Sexes: Explorations in Feminist Jurisprudence* (Allen & Unwin 1990).

[92] Incardona and Poncibò (n 56) 27; BB Duivenvoorde, *The Consumer Benchmarks in the Unfair Commercial Practices Directive* (Springer International Publishing 2015) 71 <https://www.springer.com/gp/book/9783319139234> accessed 8 March 2020.

However, on a critical note, the notion of the average consumer is unrealistic: rather than actual behaviour, the rational, observant, and circumspect individual definition describes desired behaviours.[93] Similarly, the protection of vulnerable consumers does not seem adequate: its paradigm is similar to the average consumer benchmark. Duivenvoorde argues that even in the context of the protection of vulnerable groups, the ideas underlying the average consumer benchmark (ie that consumers are expected to take care of themselves and try their best to make a rational decision) should be borne in mind. According to them, vulnerable groups are, therefore, only protected if they are unable to make an informed choice. This means that in particular, consumers who are credulous without a specific reason that would make them unable to make an informed decision are not protected.[94] As I will analyse in Chapter 3, consumer law does not provide specific protections: vulnerable consumers are relevant only if one particular commercial practice can foreseeably distort their commercial behaviour and, in that case, the 'unfairness' benchmark should be tailored to the average member of the vulnerable group at issue.[95]

In sum, there is a well-established notion of the average consumer in EU consumer law: a reasonably well-informed, observant, circumspect consumer. Although this definition seems flexible, because the enforcement bodies and the judges should also take into account the contextual social, cultural, and linguistic factors, it is still unrealistic and inadequate to represent the actual average consumer and to protect them adequately, in particular considering new research findings in terms of cognitive biases and bounded rationality.

11. Is there an average data subject in the GDPR?

This section addresses the question of whether the structure of safeguards, rights, and duties in EU data protection law assumes an average data subject as an implicit standard and if such an average data subject reflects the above-analysed definition of the average consumer, in particular in terms of awareness, understanding, and attitude of the consumer to be informed, observant, and circumspect.

As explained above in Section 7, there is no explicit distinction in the GDPR between different categories of data subjects, apart from children. At first sight, the structure of the data protection framework (both in the DPD and in the GDPR) seems to rely on a well-informed and rational data subject.[96] Indeed, the safeguards

[93] Duivenvoorde (n 92) 66–68.

[94] ibid 70. See also K Fezer, *Lauterkeitsrecht: UWG (Kommentar zum Gesetz gegen den unlauteren Wettbewerb)* (Beck 2010), 860–61, 878–81.

[95] See art 5(3) of the Unfair Commercial Practice Directive.

[96] A Reyna, 'The Psychology of Privacy—What Can Behavioural Economics Contribute to Competition in Digital Markets?' (2018) 8 International Data Privacy Law 240, 243 affirming: 'A well-informed rational consumer would always be aware of the risks associated with sharing his or her personal data with firms because this rational consumer always reads the privacy notices and is aware of his or her rights under the General Data Protection Regulation.'

for rebalancing the structural power imbalance of data subjects have been generally based on transparency, information duties, emphasis on consent as a legal basis, and data protection rights, which are typically based on the expectation that the data subject may exercise them autonomously.

This structure seems to date back to the first international legal tools on personal data protection.[97] For example, the Explanatory Memorandum of the Council of Europe Convention 108 on data protection (1981) refers to this idea of an autonomous and rational data subject, whose subjecthood is 'defined' by their rights of control (controlling information about themself).[98] We can observe a similar approach also in the first national legislations about data protection. An example is the French *Loi Informatique et Libertés* (1978), which mentioned in its very first articles as one of the main goals of data protection law the objective to enable transparency and contestation rights to be vested in data subjects.[99] In parallel, even the most important national case law which laid the foundation for the right to data protection in Europe seems to be based on this assumption about data subjects that they are autonomous and rational actors with regard to the processing of their personal data. In particular, the German Constitutional Court's judgment which introduced the 'right to informational self-determination' in Germany in 1983[100] based this new right on the 'individual's *power* to determine for himself or herself the disclosure and use of his or her personal data'.[101] In other terms, the Court acknowledges a data subject who is capable of deciding 'about actions to be taken or refrained from, including the possibility of actually behaving in accordance with this decision'. In sum, the right to informational self-determination, strictly connected to the right to data protection,[102] is based on transparency and control of data regarding autonomous individuals.[103]

[97] On the link between autonomy and the development of data protection law in Europe see E Kosta, *Consent in European Data Protection Law* (Martinus Nijhoff Publishers 2013) 135–38.

[98] Council of Europe, 'Explanatory Report to the Convention for the Protection of Individuals with Regard to Automatic Processing of Personal Data' (1981) <https://rm.coe.int/16800ca434> accessed 20 February 2023. See in particular §29: 'The notion of "data subject" expresses the idea that a person has a subjective right with regard to information about himself, even where this is gathered by others.'

[99] See Loi No 78-17 du 6 Janvier 1978 relative à l'informatique, aux fichiers et aux libertés, art 3: Toute personne a le droit de connaître et de contester les informations et les raisonnements utilisés dans les traitements automatisés dont les résultats lui sont opposés.

[100] *Bundesverfassungsgericht—Urteil des Ersten Senats vom 15 Dezember 1983—1 BvR 209/83, Rn 1-215*, §§145–147.

[101] ibid §147: 'Das Grundrecht gewährleistet insoweit die Befugnis des Einzelnen, grundsätzlich selbst über die Preisgabe und Verwendung seiner persönlichen Daten zu bestimmen' (translated by the author), emphasis added.

[102] See G González Fuster, *The Emergence of Personal Data Protection as a Fundamental Right of the EU* (Springer International Publishing 2014) 177. On the link between the 'right to informational self-determination' and the latest developments of the EU data protection law, see F Thouvenin, 'Informational Self-Determination: A Convincing Rationale for Data Protection Law?' (2021) 12 Journal of Intellectual Property, Information Technology and Electronic Commerce Law 246.

[103] *Bundesverfassungsgericht—Urteil des Ersten Senats vom 15. Dezember 1983—1 BvR 209/83, Rn. 1-215*, (n 100) §145: 'Sie können darüber hinaus—vor allem beim Aufbau integrierter Informationssysteme—mit anderen Datensammlungen zu einem teilweise oder weitgehend

Moreover, looking back at the initial proposal of the Commission for the Data Protection Directive, we can find several references to a rational and well-informed average data subject. In particular, the right to information is seen as a tool to 'enable the data subject *to weigh the risks and advantages of the intended processing* of data relating to him and to exercise his rights under Article 14 of the Directive (rectification, erasure, blocking)'; accordingly 'the controller of the file has to provide the data subject with such information as is relevant to the data subject's decision'.[104] In other words, the legislator was relying on the rational decision-making capabilities of the data subject, who is able to assess risks and advantages of data processing and take informed decisions about that. They seem similar to the reasonably informed, observant, and circumspect consumer that can 'make intelligent choices'[105] described in the consumer law *acquis*.

In the original Commission's proposal of the DPD, even the notions of lawfulness and fairness were related to the rational decision-making capabilities of the data subject, able to decide whether or not to disclose their personal data.[106] Similarly, the regulation of automated profiling was seen as a means 'designed to protect the interest of the data subject in participating in the making of decisions which are of importance to him'.[107]

As Schermer and colleagues affirmed, the emphasis on information duties in the data protection discourse presupposes a rational, informed data subject who makes conscious decisions.[108] The emphasis on consent, as the outcome of the data subject's rational and informed decision-making process, reflects the same approach. Consistently, the Explanatory Memorandum for the Proposed Data Protection Directive affirmed that the lawfulness of data processing 'may

vollständigen Persönlichkeitsbild zusammengefügt werden, ohne daß der Betroffene dessen Richtigkeit und Verwendung zureichend kontrollieren kann' ('Furthermore, they can—especially when integrated information systems are set up—be combined with other data collections to form a partially or largely complete picture of the personality, without the person concerned being able to adequately control its accuracy and use.' Translated by the author).

[104] Commission of the European Communities, Communication on the protection of Individuals in relation to the processing of personal data in the Community and Information security; Proposal for a Council Directive concerning the protection of individuals in relation to the processing of personal data Draft, COM(90) 314 final, SYN 287 and 288, Brussels, 13 September 1990 <https://eur-lex.europa.eu/legal-content/EN/TXT/PDF/?uri=CELEX:51990DC0314&from=EN> accessed 20 February 2023, 26.

[105] *Estée Lauder Cosmetics GmbH & Co. OHG v Lancaster Group GmbH*, Opinion of Advocate General Fennelly (n 59).

[106] Commission of the European Communities, COM(90) 314 final, 27: 'The fair and lawful collection of personal data presuppose, that the data subject makes his decision whether or not to disclose data relating to him.'

[107] ibid 29.

[108] BW Schermer and others, 'The Crisis of Consent: How Stronger Legal Protection May Lead to Weaker Consent in Data Protection' (2014) 16 Ethics and Information Technology 171, 171.

stem from the consent of the data subject' or 'from a provision Community law, or from a national legal instrument'.[109] Similarly, the European Union Charter of Fundamental Rights at Article 8 mentions only 'consent' among the legal grounds for processing personal data.[110]

Consent has not always been a milestone in the European data protection framework.[111] The first international data protection convention, Convention 108 of the Council of Europe, did not mention consent as a legal basis: the only constraint for processing personal data was the respect of the principles of fairness, lawfulness, purpose limitation, data minimization (the collection and processing of adequate, relevant, and not excessive data, and no more), accuracy, and storage limitation (preserved in a form which permits identification of the data subjects for no longer than is required).[112] But there was no indication of which legal bases were considered lawful for processing data. However, recently, the modernized version of Convention 108 has introduced the concept of consent and has given this concept a central role in the whole system. The new Article 5, even before mentioning the list of data processing principles to be respected (lawfulness, fairness, transparency, purpose limitation, data minimization, accuracy, and storage limitation),[113] mentions consent as the first legal basis for processing personal data: 'each Party shall provide that data processing can be carried out on the basis of the *free, specific, informed and unambiguous consent* of the data subject or of some other legitimate basis laid down by law'.[114]

In legal-philosophical terms, consent has been defined as based on the capacity for moral judgments. The person must have sufficient information about the context and consequences of the consent transaction.[115] It has been argued that this emphasis on free and informed consent in the data protection law is based on a theoretical understanding of consent as an 'autonomous authorization model',[116] as theorized by Faden and Beauchamp in 1986.[117] Such a model is generally based on the assumption of our right as rational human beings to choose our course of action freely, and it is reflected in our ability to consent.[118] An overemphasis on this autonomous authorization model of consent has led the EU data protection framework to focus on a conception of data subject capable of making a free, conscious, and rational decision to consent on the basis of the available information.[119]

109 Commission of the European Communities, COM(90) 314 final, 23.

110 See art 8 of the EU Charter of Fundamental Rights: 'Such data must be processed fairly for specified purposes and *on the basis of the consent of the person concerned or some other legitimate basis* laid down by law. . . .' Emphasis added.

111 See eg Kosta (n 97) 12.

112 Convention 108, art 5.

113 See Modernized Convention 108, art 5(3).

114 ibid art 5(2). Emphasis added.

115 Schermer and others (n 108) 172.

116 ibid 174, 176.

117 RR Faden and others, *A History and Theory of Informed Consent* (Oxford University Press 1986).

118 Schermer and others (n 108) 174.

119 ibid 176.

According to Schermer and colleagues, the shift from the DPD to the GDPR has not decreased but instead has increased this reliance on an average and rational data subject, inspired by the rational consumer in the EU consumer law. In particular, considering the new emphasis on the characteristics of valid *consent* (Article 7),[120] the introduction of *transparency* as an explicit data protection principle (Article 5(1), point (a)) and the consequent development of information duties (see Articles 12–14), it seems that the GDPR is 'based on the idea that all data subjects are rational actors that will read all privacy statements and carefully weigh and balance the consequences of consent'.[121]

In addition, the GDPR introduced new data protection rights (namely, the right to limitation, portability, and erasure, or the right 'to be forgotten') with the declared purpose to 'further strengthen the control' of the data subjects 'over his or her own data'.[122] In other words, the average data subject is not only capable of understanding the information received about the data processing and giving consent to it but also of exercising a broad and complex range of individual rights. This appears clear also from other provisions in the GDPR. For example, Article 80 about the new concept of the 'representation of data subjects' does not provide that the representative of the data subjects may exercise on their behalf the data protection rights (access, rectification, objection, erasure, portability, limitation). The representative's role is limited to judicial actions (Articles 77–79) and the right to receive compensation. In other words, the GDPR does not state that data protection rights (at Articles 15–22) are 'mandatable' or exercisable by other persons apart from the data subject.[123] This may suggest that the 'average' data subject is reasonably rational and informed enough to exercise all data protection rights, without any institutional incentive to mandate their exercise to expert entities that could represent them.

[120] About the paradoxical effect of the new emphasis of consent in the GDPR see J van Hoboken, 'The Privacy Disconnect' in RF Jørgensen (ed), *Human Rights in the Age of Platforms* (MIT Press 2019) 266, 268.

[121] Schermer and others (n 108) 179.

[122] See Recitals 7 and 69 of the GDPR.

[123] See S Delacroix and ND Lawrence, 'Bottom-up Data Trusts: Disturbing the "One Size Fits All" Approach to Data Governance' (2019) 9(4) International Data Privacy Law 236–52, affirming that data protection rights cannot be mandated to third persons. In general terms, the possibility to mandate data protection rights is not excluded in the GDPR. In purely private law terms, individual rights can be mandated or delegated to other subjects (eg legal representatives). However, several scholars have excluded the applicability of private law rules in the data protection sphere considering the 'fundamental rights character' of data protection rights, see O Lynskey, *The Foundations of EU Data Protection Law* (Oxford University Press 2015) 40. The CJEU, Case C-498/16 *Maximilian Schrems v Facebook Ireland Limited* [25 January 2018] §49, affirmed that 'assigning' rights under EU consumer law was not possible in the specific case at stake for jurisdictional reasons, but the Court did not discuss whether mandating consumer or data protection rights is forbidden or allowed. We can generally conclude that, considering the fundamental rights nature of the right to personal data protection, what is prohibited is waiving rights, while mandating rights is still possible according to national private law conditions and limitations.

After this brief and preliminary overview, it seems that, according to several commentators, the EU data protection framework may be interpreted as accepting an implicit understanding of an average data subject, who—similarly to the average consumer—reads the information policy and makes free rational and conscious decisions to give consent to the data processing and to exercise all data protection rights. The new emphasis on consent and individual rights (that cannot be mandated to formal representatives) in the GDPR seems in line with this analysis.

12. The hybrid approach of the GDPR to average subjects and the room for contextual vulnerability

As has been noted, the average data subject in practice is very different from the normative notion of an informed and rational 'average' data subject: individuals not only might be unaware of their rights and risks in the field of data processing but are also sometimes willing to give consent easily to any request[124] and are often not interested in reading privacy policies.[125] Recent statistical research has confirmed this worrying trend.[126]

We have already observed that the normative notion of the data subject (though implicit) is different from the statistical one that emerged from the empirical studies.[127] Accordingly, we might affirm that—similarly to the average consumer test—the average data subject standard is not based on quantitative analyses or statistical tests.[128] In other words, the interpreters should consider the 'general

[124] Schermer and others (n 108) 176–79; I Pollach, 'What's Wrong with Online Privacy Policies?' (2007) 50 Communications of the ACM 103; A Acquisti, 'Nudging Privacy: The Behavioral Economics of Personal Information' (2009) 7 IEEE Security & Privacy Magazine 82; R Böhme and S Köpsell, 'Trained to Accept? A Field Experiment on Consent Dialogs' *Proceedings of the SIGCHI Conference on Human Factors in Computing Systems* (Association for Computing Machinery 2010) <https://doi.org/10.1145/1753326.1753689> accessed 20 January 2020; I Adjerid and others, 'Sleights of Privacy: Framing, Disclosures, and the Limits of Transparency', *Proceedings of the Ninth Symposium on Usable Privacy and Security* (Association for Computing Machinery 2013) <https://doi.org/10.1145/2501604.2501613> accessed 20 January 2020; DJ Solove, 'Privacy Self-Management and the Consent Dilemma' (2013) 126 Harvard Law Review 1880; Koops (n 36) 252; FJZ Borgesius, 'Behavioural Sciences and the Regulation of Privacy on the Internet' in A Alemanno and A-L Sibony (eds), *Nudge and the Law: A European Perspective* (Hart Publishing 2015) 192–200.

[125] González Fuster, 'How Uninformed Is the Average Data Subject?' (n 48).

[126] European Commission (Directorate General for Justice and Consumers), *Special Eurobarometer 487a—The General Data Protection Regulation: Report* (Publications Office 2019) <https://data.europa.eu/doi/10.2838/579882> accessed 7 May 2022 According to this statistical research conducted by the European Commission on the EU population in 2019, only 31 per cent of the survey respondents had heard about all six rights in the GDPR (p 24). In addition, 62 per cent of the respondents did not feel in full control of their data (p 39) and only 22 per cent of them affirmed that they were 'always informed' about the conditions of data collection (p 42). In particular, only 13 per cent of the respondents affirmed reading privacy policy fully (p 47). The reasons why most of the respondents affirmed not to read privacy policies were their excessive length (66 per cent of the respondent) and their difficulty (31 per cent) (p 51).

[127] Pollach (n 124); Böhme and Köpsell (n 124).

[128] See Recital 18 of UCPD.

presumed [data subjects'] expectations',[129] rather than any statistical study on the average population.

In addition, as already argued, the GDPR takes into particular account only children (see Chapter 3) and does not identify any other category of cognitively impaired individuals. This lack of reference to other vulnerable data subjects may suggest that all adults are considered well informed and rational enough to deal with data protection choices.

Many scholars have criticized this EU data protection framework interpretation based on the notice-and-consent model.[130] Indeed, it has been argued that consent, though important, is neither the only nor the primary lawful basis for data processing. In particular, there is a growing academic interest on alternative legal bases, like legitimate interest.[131] Moreover, as the WP29 has often affirmed, even in the case of data processing based on consent, all data processing principles (including, eg, fairness and limitation and lawfulness of purposes) apply anyway: consent can never be a basis for limiting or waiving data protection principles (Article 5).[132] Zuiderveen Borgesius highlights that the prevalence of mandatory rules on consent (and on default rules) in data protection should not be considered unduly paternalistic:[133] these mandatory rules should be regarded as not only to strengthen individual autonomy (undue paternalism[134] or libertarian paternalism[135]) but also to protect broader interests (collective interests).[136] In other words, and for our

[129] Commission Staff Working Document, *Guidance on the Implementation/Application of Directive 2005/29/EC on Unfair Commercial Practices. A comprehensive approach to stimulating cross-border e-Commerce for Europe's citizens and businesses*, SWD/2016/0163 final.

[130] JE Cohen, 'Turning Privacy Inside Out' (2019) 20 Theoretical Inquiries in Law <http://www7.tau.ac.il/ojs/index.php/til/article/view/1607> accessed 23 January 2019.

[131] EML Moerel and others, *Homo Digitalis* (Wolters Kluwer 2016); Schermer and others (n 108); About the potentialities of legitimate interests as a legal basis in the GDPR see also I Kamara and P De Hert, 'Understanding the Balancing Act behind the Legitimate Interest of the Controller Ground: A Pragmatic Approach' in E Selinger and others (eds), *The Cambridge Handbook of Consumer Privacy* (1st edn, Cambridge University Press 2018) <https://www.cambridge.org/core/product/identifier/9781316831960%23CN-bp-19/type/book_part> accessed 28 March 2020.

[132] See also WP29, Guidelines on consent under Regulation 2016/679, adopted on 28 November 2017, as last revised and adopted on 10 April 2018, WP259 rev.01, 3–4: 'obtaining consent also does not negate or in any way diminish the controller's obligations to observe the principles of processing enshrined in the GDPR, especially art 5 of the GDPR with regard to fairness, necessity and proportionality, as well as data quality. Even if the processing of personal data is based on consent of the data subject, this would not legitimize collection of data which is not necessary in relation to a specified purpose of processing and be fundamentally unfair'. See also WP29, Opinion 15/2011 on the definition of Consent, WP187, 7.

[133] FJZ Borgesius, *Improving Privacy Protection in the Area of Behavioural Targeting* (Kluwer Law International 2015) 179, 264.

[134] ibid 268.

[135] Thaler and Sunstein (n 88).

[136] Z Borgesius, *Improving Privacy Protection in the Area of Behavioural Targeting* (n 134) 178; A Rouvroy and Y Poullet, '"The Right to Informational Self-Determination and the Value of Self-Development: Reassessing the Importance of Privacy for Democracy"' in S Gutwirth and others (eds), *Reinventing Data Protection?* (Springer 2009); P De Hert and S Gutwirth, 'Privacy, Data Protection and Law Enforcement. Opacity of the Individual and Transparency of Power' in E Claes and others (ed), *Privacy and the Criminal Law* (Intersentia 2006).

purposes, the balancing between consent and mandatory rules suggests that the standard data subject is not purely informed and rational following the concept of the average consumer.

In addition, many references to technical and organizational measures to safeguard the interests of data subjects (including the risk-based approach and data protection by default and by design) suggest a less consent-based approach to data protection.[137] De Hert and Gutwirth have noticed that the data protection paradigm is not based only on transparency but also on opacity.[138] In other words, informing data subjects (about the characteristics of the data processing) and relying on their capability to understand such information and the significance and envisaged implications of being involved in specific data processing activities is not the only strategy to protect data subjects. The other strategy is based on mandatory rules: prohibitions (eg prohibition to process some specific categories of data, as in case of special categories of data cited in Article 9, or to process data in particular ways, as in the case of automated decision-making systems cited in Article 22) and binding principles (fairness, necessity, proportionality, purpose limitation, including lawfulness of purposes). The first strategy relies on empowering an already 'average' data subject, a rational decision-maker. The second strategy counterbalances such an approach that individuals must be protected beyond their capacity to give consent,[139] for example, through fairness, proportionality, necessity, and a list of prohibited data processing activities, considering that every individual might be potentially vulnerable (due to inherent power imbalance and higher risks of adverse effects in the online world, as I will analyse in the following chapters).[140]

Moreover, recently the CJEU has accepted a more flexible notion of the reasonably informed and circumspect data subject. In the *Planet49* case, a case concerning the validity of consent in case of cookies under Articles 2(f) and 5(3) of the e-Privacy Directive in combination with Article 6(1)(a) of the GDPR, the Court argued: 'it is not inconceivable that a user would not have read the information

[137] G Fortuna-Zanfir, 'Forgetting about Consent. Why the Focus Should Be on "Suitable Safeguards" in Data Protection Law' in S Gutwirth and others (eds), *Reloading Data Protection* (Springer 2014); S van der Hof and E Lievens, 'The Importance of Privacy by Design and Data Protection Impact Assessments in Strengthening Protection of Children's Personal Data under the GDPR' (2018) 23 Communications Law 33.

[138] De Hert and Gutwirth (n 136) 78.

[139] See van Hoboken (n 120) 267.

[140] Many scholars have highlighted the dualism of control rights and default protection in the EU data protection framework. See, among others, N Purtova, 'Default Entitlements in Personal Data in the Proposed Regulation: Informational Self-Determination Off the Table ... and Back on Again?' (2014) 30 Computer Law & Security Review 6; A Cavoukian and others, 'The Unintended Consequences of Privacy Paternalism' (Information and Privacy Commissioner, Ontario, Canada 2014) <https://collections.ola.org/mon/28003/326077.pdf> accessed 20 February 2023; C Quelle, 'Not Just User Control in the General Data Protection Regulation. On the Problems with Choice and Paternalism, and on the Point of Data Protection' in A Lehmann and others (eds), *Privacy and Identity Management. Facing up to Next Steps, 11th IFIP International Summer School* (Springer International Publishing 2017); De Hert and Gutwirth (n 136).

accompanying the preselected checkbox, or even would not have noticed that checkbox, before continuing with his or her activity on the website visited'.[141] In other terms, the Court has finally accepted that an average data subject, though reasonably rational and informed, may also disregard important information about the processing of their data. Although this ruling is limited to the specific case of cookies and although the wording of the Court is very prudent ('it is not inconceivable'), it seems that the Court is perhaps accepting a more flexible understanding of the standard data subject, a data subject who can also sometimes ignore reading data processing information.

In other words, even though we consider the notion of the average data subject as similar to the notion of the average consumer—an aware, observant and circumspect individual that can rationally understand and control risks and rights of data processing—there are substantial differences to highlight. In particular, there is more flexibility of the benchmark of informed and circumspect persons. Also, as we will see in the following chapters, there is room for considering the vulnerability of data subjects in the GDPR. The EU data protection framework seems to adopt a hybrid approach, according to which data subjects are rational and informed by default. Still, in specific contexts and situations, every individual is potentially vulnerable. As we will observe in the following chapters, the EU legal framework seems flexible enough to take into account such contextual vulnerability of data subjects, both through *ex-ante* mechanisms (prohibitions and mandatory principles) and through case-by-case solutions (the risk-based approach, the safeguards that every controller needs to implement, the impact assessment, etc).

I agree with González Fuster, who argues that having a clearer understanding of the average data subject might be helpful to recognize the cases of unlawful or unfair data processing in practice:[142] the average data subject would be a benchmark used to predict potential adverse effects of some practices on data subjects. It is also true that a fixed notion of the average data subject might prove inconsistent with the dynamic and contextual notion of the data subject as suggested in the GDPR and analysed above.[143] Also, the idea of a standard data subject as either circumspect and observant[144] or uniformed and unaware by default[145] could be not only unrealistic but also ineffective to protect different data subjects with the necessary adaptive flexibility.

Blume[146] doubts the suitability of uniform rules (eg on a standard 'data subject' definition) in protecting different individuals. He suggests three options to solve

[141] CJEU Case C-673/17 *Bundesverband der Verbraucherzentralen und Verbraucherverbände—Verbraucherzentrale Bundesverband e. V. v Planet49 GmbH*, Grand Chamber [1 October 2019] §55.

[142] González Fuster, 'How Uninformed Is the Average Data Subject?' (n 48) 104.

[143] See the general idea of privacy as a moving target in M Hildebrandt, *Law for Computer Scientists and Other Folk* (Oxford University Press 2020) 134.

[144] Schermer and others (n 108) 174.

[145] González Fuster, 'How Uninformed Is the Average Data Subject?' (n 48).

[146] Blume (n 48) 264.

this uniformity issue: (i) taking account the particular characteristics of the person when applying the rules in practice, (ii) creating rules concerning different types of data subjects, or (iii) having a general rule that states differences must be taken into account when applying specific data protection rules.[147] As we will see, the GDPR adopts a hybrid approach that combines all the three different options, but this is true only under a broad interpretation of the GDPR wording.

In sum, despite the similarities between the average consumer and what I defined here as a potential 'average data subject', a broader understanding of the GDPR imposes to look at the particularities of the data subjects and to understand in which conditions we could consider a data subject as 'vulnerable'.

13. Concluding remarks

This chapter addressed the issue of the notion of the data subject in the GDPR under two different perspectives: a *literal* interpretation and a *contextual and comparative* interpretation.

Under the literal interpretation perspective, we have observed the characteristics of the data subject as a living identified or identifiable natural person to whom data are related. Such concept is:

- *well-circumscribed*, because it excludes legal persons and unborn or deceased persons (but Member States may provide for post-mortem data protection);
- *universal*, that is, there are no limitations to this notion related to nationality or citizenship; and
- *dynamic*, since identifiability and 'relation'—according to the GDPR preamble and the CJEU and the EDPB—are two relative and dynamic concepts.[148]

However, the literal interpretation of the data subject definition does not clarify whether just one data subject is considered (an 'average' or 'standard' data subject) or if the particular situation of different data subjects must be considered. That is why this chapter also addresses a contextual and a comparative interpretation.

Considering the distinction in EU consumer law between average and vulnerable consumers, I first analysed the notion of the average consumer to understand if it can be compared to a standard or average data subject. It seems that the rational and informed understanding possessed by average consumers resembles the GDPR notion of the data subject.[149] Considering the first explanatory report of data protection law at the European level and the general emphasis on information

[147] ibid.
[148] See WP29, WP136.
[149] Schermer and others (n 108).

policies, consent, and the complex web of data protection rights (without an explicit provision about the possibility to mandate or delegate these rights) in the GDPR, it seems that the average data subject may also correspond to a rational, circumspect, informed person. However, the CJEU recently accepted a more flexible understanding in specific contexts.[150]

However, the new awareness about cognitive biases of even 'average' subjects[151] and the empirical studies on data subjects' expectations and behaviour[152] have revealed that such a positive view of an average data subject is unrealistic and even counterproductive.[153] That is why the following two chapters analyse the notion of the vulnerable data subject. I will start from the theoretical discussion about the notion of vulnerable individuals, and then I will look in particular at the consumer protection discussion on that notion. Building on these reflections, it will be easier to look at the concept of the vulnerable person in the European framework in general and in the data protection framework in particular: the GDPR has several (often implicit) references to vulnerable data subjects that deserve specific attention. That analysis will help us to understand the notion of the average data subject and, in addition, contribute to analysing whether a flexible definition of vulnerability can be adopted to respond to new inputs of behavioural law and economics.

[150] CJEU Case C-673/17 *Planet49* [2019] §55.
[151] Thaler (n 88).
[152] Pollach (n 124); Schermer and others (n 108); Acquisti (n 124).
[153] Blume (n 48); González Fuster, 'How Uninformed Is the Average Data Subject?' (n 48).

3

Who is the vulnerable individual?

1. From the average to the vulnerable data subject

As analysed in the previous chapter, the general notion of data subjects is dynamic, limited, and universal. In addition, even though it is not explicit in the wording of the GDPR, we can assume—through a systematic interpretation of data protection duties and rights—that a notion of the average data subject exists and seems to refer to a reasonably rational, circumspect, informed person. However, considering that human rationality is often a disputed concept in scholarly debate[1] and taking into account the risks of exploitation of individual weaknesses in the digital sphere, I focus on the notion of non-average individuals, considering in particular data subjects who are more vulnerable to harms to their fundamental rights and freedoms. Accordingly, the question this chapter poses is: what is a 'vulnerable' person? In other words, what does the term 'vulnerable person' mean?

In the next chapter, the consequent question will ask: does the GDPR contain an (implicit or explicit) notion of the vulnerable data subject?

To answer this question we need first to understand the notion of the vulnerable individual in general. Section 2 summarizes theories of human vulnerability from different sectors, especially political philosophy and bioethics. A key concept in the theoretical conceptualization of vulnerability is power imbalance and Section 3 analyses how power imbalance can induce vulnerability in different contexts and under different variables.

The discussion about vulnerability emerged in various fields including political philosophy, gender studies, law, ethics, and sociology, etc. Scholars from those very different fields often engage with each other and they have adapted an understanding of vulnerability developed in other areas; for example, transferring and adapting the idea of vulnerability developed in political theory to the field of bioethics). Throughout the chapter, I refer to the legal literature on vulnerability. However, most of the legal reflections in this field are based on a dialogue with the work of theoreticians of other fields. Presenting those different theoretical

[1] D Clifford, 'Citizen-Consumers in a Personalised Galaxy: Emotion Influenced Decision-Making, a True Path to the Dark Side?' in L Edwards and others, *Future Law: Emerging Technology, Regulation and Ethics* (Edinburgh University Press 2020); A Rouvroy, 'The End(s) of Critique: Data Behaviourism versus Due Process' in K de Vries and M Hildebrandt (eds), *Privacy, Due Process and the Computational Turn* (Routledge 2013).

Vulnerability and Data Protection Law. Gianclaudio Malgieri, Oxford University Press. © Gianclaudio Malgieri 2023.
DOI: 10.1093/oso/9780192870339.003.0003

approaches helps situate the origins of this notion and understand how it changes the perception of institutions, rules, and the individual's place in society.

This chapter argues that the layered vulnerability theory (deriving from Luna)[2] is one of the most suitable approaches to address those issues and the best response to several criticisms. Such a theory seems to align very well with an intersectional approach to vulnerable people (Section 4). Building on those theoretical definitions of the vulnerable individual, I look at how EU law has employed the notion of vulnerable persons in different sectors. Section 5 analyses how the notion of vulnerability might be conceived as it relates to the concept of dignity in human rights discourse. Section 6 analyses the European Court of Human Rights (ECtHR) case law that has tried to conceptualize the notion of individual vulnerability. Section 7 looks at how secondary legislation in the EU has referred to vulnerable individuals in different fields. I give special attention to two sectors that seem particularly relevant compared to data protection law: research regulation (Section 8) and consumer protection (Section 9). In addition, the consumer protection framework is helpful for this research because several legal and economics scholars who have contributed to that area have identified and classified consumer vulnerability.

2. Theorizing individual vulnerability: the layered theory

For many scholars, vulnerability becomes a term to describe, for example, social marginalization, economic insecurity, precarious employment conditions, or violence caused by wars. For example, Martha Fineman and Judith Butler state that the concept has great potential to redefine some of the existing thinking about injustice, dependency, or privilege.[3] Scholars have portrayed vulnerability as a 'heuristic device' that permits analysing 'hidden assumptions and biases folded into legal practices'.[4] Vulnerability is a major category in bioethics and research ethics.[5] While the field engaged in understanding the nature of vulnerability and exploring its associations and consequences for political practice, ethics, research and law is wide, the term is still deemed vague, complex and ambiguous.[6]

[2] F Luna, 'Elucidating the Concept of Vulnerability: Layers Not Labels' (2009) 2 International Journal of Feminist Approaches to Bioethics 121; F Luna, 'Identifying and Evaluating Layers of Vulnerability—A Way Forward' (2019) 19 Developing World Bioethics 86.

[3] MA Fineman, 'The Vulnerable Subject: Anchoring Equality in the Human Condition' (2008) 20 Yale Journal of Law and Feminism 23; MA Fineman, 'Vulnerability and Social Justice' [2019] SSRN Electronic Journal <https://www.ssrn.com/abstract=3352825> accessed 4 August 2019; J Butler, *Precarious Life: The Powers of Mourning and Violence* (Verso 2004).

[4] Fineman, 'The Vulnerable Subject: Anchoring Equality in the Human Condition' (n 3) 9.

[5] W Rogers and others, 'Why Bioethics Needs a Concept of Vulnerability' (2012) 5 International Journal of Feminist Approaches to Bioethics 11, 12–13.

[6] L Peroni and A Timmer, 'Vulnerable Groups: The Promise of an Emerging Concept in European Human Rights Convention Law' (2013) 11 International Journal of Constitutional Law 1056, 1058; Fineman, 'The Vulnerable Subject: Anchoring Equality in the Human Condition' (n 3) 9.

Some early definitions and conceptualizations of vulnerability stressed its links to fragilities, harms, and the fact of being wounded, as its etymology suggests ('*vulnus*' in Latin means wound).[7] The term served almost as a synonym of dependency, helplessness, pain, violence, weakness. As Goodin affirmed, 'to be vulnerable is to be susceptible to harm to one's interests'.[8] Many other scholars and institutions followed this view of conceptualizing vulnerability around exposure to harm and the likelihood of being harmed in the context of an individual's autonomy, dignity, or integrity.[9]

However, vulnerability is a condition situated in opposition to the actual harm or injustice rather than indicating its potentiality.[10] The well-established views also stress that vulnerability is a condition that should be avoided, something negative, and a risk that should be mitigated.[11] This approach was subject to some criticisms, mostly from feminist scholars, who explored the positive sides of vulnerability, showing it as a precondition of empathy, social connectedness, and intimacy.[12] Therefore, vulnerability is not just a limitation but also something that allows us to act and feel. For example, Erinn Gilson formulates vulnerability as 'openness to being affected and affecting'.[13]

Nonetheless, many problematic dichotomies and uncertainties affect the application of the concept of vulnerability in the institutional environment. One of these dichotomies is between the *particular* and *universal* character of vulnerability.

In more traditional approaches, vulnerability is a distinctive character of *particular* weaker individuals and groups based on specific situations or socio-economic contexts.[14] Typical examples of such groups are racial minorities, asylum seekers, and people with disabilities. It is a predominant way of using the concept of vulnerability in more practical circumstances like research, social policy, or policing.[15] However, several authors criticized this way of understanding vulnerability since it might bring stigmatizing effects and harmful regulation for minorities.[16]

[7] C Mackenzie and others, 'Introduction: What Is Vulnerability, and Why Does It Matter for Moral Theory?', in C Mackenzie and others (eds), *Vulnerability* (Oxford University Press 2013) 4–5.

[8] RE Goodin, *Protecting the Vulnerable: A Reanalysis of Our Social Responsibilities* (University of Chicago Press 1985); See, similarly, also the vulnerability definition in D Schroeder and E Gefenas, 'Vulnerability: Too Vague and Too Broad?' (2009) 18 Cambridge Quarterly of Healthcare Ethics 113.

[9] Mackenzie and others (n 7) 6–11.

[10] EC Gilson, *The Ethics of Vulnerability: A Feminist Analysis of Social Life and Practice* (2016) 7–8.

[11] G Malgieri and J Niklas, 'The Vulnerable Data Subject' (2020) 37 Computer Law & Security Review.

[12] A Cole, 'All of Us Are Vulnerable, But Some Are More Vulnerable than Others: The Political Ambiguity of Vulnerability Studies, an Ambivalent Critique' (2016) 17 Critical Horizons 260, 264.

[13] Gilson (n 10) 76.

[14] MA Fineman, 'Beyond Identities: The Limits of an Antidiscrimination Approach to Equality' (2012) 92 Boston University Law Review 59, 1750.

[15] For example, RM Hewer, 'A Gossamer Consensus: Discourses of Vulnerability in the Westminster Prostitution Policy Subsystem' (2019) 28 Social & Legal Studies 227–49; NL Asquith, and others (eds), *Policing Encounters with Vulnerability* (Springer International Publishing: Palgrave Macmillan 2017).

[16] Cole (n 12) 262.

For these reasons, some critical scholars reformulate the understanding of vulnerability as a *universal* human condition, which can change in different situations, periods, and spaces. They portray this concept as a general feature of human existence, a characteristic of every human being.[17] However, some critics take the view that emphasizing the universal nature of vulnerability may ignore the structural injustice and exploitation that particular groups experience.[18] On the other hand, apologists of a universalized notion of vulnerability show this can be a way to run from failures of existing diversity and equality policies and anti-discrimination laws.[19]

Commentators in the field of research ethics also stress that there are two ways of conceptualizing and addressing the consequences of vulnerability.[20] The first approach focuses on harms and ways to eliminate them.[21] The second approach focuses on individuals' ability to overcome their vulnerable position and empower them with various decision-making and procedural safeguards. In other terms, in the first approach, the emphasis is put on harms (physical or psychological), while in the second, the focus is on consent or participation in decision-making in the research process.

Those two problems discussed at the theoretical level (the tension between the universalistic (everyone is equally vulnerable) versus the particularistic (some individuals are more vulnerable than others) character of vulnerability, and questions about how vulnerability manifests itself and related mitigation strategies) also have far-reaching consequences for the practical use of the concept of vulnerability. However, some scholars have tried to reconcile these different views and overcome dichotomies between them. One of them is Luna, who attempted to reply to various criticisms through a new conception of vulnerability as comprising *layers*.[22] According to Luna, layers of vulnerability are not fixed attributes of specific individuals or groups but are features constructed by an individual's status, time, and location. In this sense, the concept of layering provides an opening to

[17] Fineman, 'The Vulnerable Subject: Anchoring Equality in the Human Condition' (n 3) 23; Butler, *Precarious Life* (n 3) 26–28; M Nussbaum, *Frontiers of Justice: Disability, Nationality, Species Membership* (Harvard University Press 2006) 221.

[18] FR Cooper, 'Always Already Suspect: Revising Vulnerability Theory' (2014) 93 North Carolina Law Review 43; Cole, 'All of Us Are Vulnerable, But Some Are More Vulnerable than Others' (n 12) 260–77.

[19] Fineman, 'The Vulnerable Subject: Anchoring Equality in the Human Condition' (n 3) 18, 23 Another area of disputes about vulnerability concerns the organizational, legal, and political responses to vulnerability. Fineman calls for responsive institutions that recognize human vulnerability. She criticizes existing systems of rights and laws that depend on the formal equality and embrace an individualistic, self-sufficient, and rationalist liberal subject. In a similar tone, for Goodin, vulnerability implies a justification for welfare state institutions that could help in addressing the lack of essential goods and services, Goodin (n 8) 145.

[20] D Schroeder and E Gefenas, 'Vulnerability: Too Vague and Too Broad?' (2009) 18(2) Cambridge Quarterly of Healthcare Ethics 18.

[21] É Gennet and others, 'Does the New EU Regulation on Clinical Trials Adequately Protect Vulnerable Research Participants?' (2015) 119(7) Health Policy 925–31.

[22] Luna, 'Elucidating the Concept of Vulnerability' (n 2); Luna, 'Identifying and Evaluating Layers of Vulnerability—A Way Forward' (n 2).

a more intersectional approach and stresses its cumulative and transitory potential.[23] As Luna indicates, it is true that vulnerability is a universal condition of human beings. Still, it is also true that such a condition of weakness and marginalization may vary from one individual to another; it may have different degrees of severity and many different factors.

We could summarize this universal versus particular theory: all individuals are vulnerable (and as such, there should be no labels placed on some groups as being 'vulnerable'), but some individuals have more layers of vulnerability based on particular contexts and relational balances.[24] The intensity of legal protection of vulnerable individuals should be proportional to the quantity and quality of layers of vulnerability.[25] The identification and assessment of layers of vulnerability should be based on several criteria, including an analysis of the origins of vulnerability (an analysis of the stimulus conditions including if some layers have the potential to cause 'cascade vulnerability', ie layers that have a cascade effect on other sources of vulnerability) and of its impact (ie probability and intensity of harms).[26] Lastly, Luna's theory on layered vulnerability suggests that each vulnerability layer has its own mitigation measures. The obligations originated by evaluation of these layers should be to avoid exacerbating layers, eradicate those layers, and minimize layers of vulnerability using different strategies (protections, safeguards, empowerment).[27]

In sum, the discussion about human vulnerability can lead to different paradoxes and dichotomies, particularly considering the vagueness and changing nature of this concept. This chapter relies on this theory of vulnerability comprising different layers in order to understand vulnerability in the data protection field.

3. Vulnerability and power imbalance: structural imbalance

The layered theory reveals how the concept of vulnerability is not a monolith but is instead a contextual notion which depends on the relationship between a person and their counterpart. Accordingly, a relevant context to analyse is the relationship between consumers and suppliers (see Section 8). Indeed, law and economics discussion in that field is advanced, and we can adapt the reflections developed in that area to the relationship between the data subject and the data controller. The identifying criterion of the consumer–supplier relationship is power asymmetry.[28]

[23] Luna, 'Elucidating the Concept of Vulnerability' (n 2).
[24] ibid.
[25] ibid 86–95.
[26] ibid 92 and 93.
[27] ibid 93.
[28] M Mourali and A Nagpal, 'The Powerful Select, the Powerless Reject: Power's Influence in Decision Strategies' (2013) 66 Journal of Business Research 874.

Accordingly, before addressing the discussion about consumer protection derived from law and economics, we analyse layered vulnerability from the perspective of power imbalance.

Hildebrandt noted that power is a 'framing power' in the digital realm, able to 'reconfigure *choice architectures* in line with whoever pays for them'.[29] Abusive and architectures of unfair choice are precisely the tools that, for example, digital companies can use to force customers to accept undesirable data processing conditions[30] in exchange for access to a particular digital platform in which they are 'locked-in'.

In broader terms, power has been defined as the 'capacity of A to motivate B to think or do something that B would otherwise not have thought or done'.[31] This is in line with EU consumer law definitions,[32] and it is, thus, not limited to brute force but also includes (undue) influences.[33]

In their study on the role of power in consumer decision-making, Mourali and Nagpal note that 'power is commonly defined as a person's relative capacity to control valuable resources or administer punishments'.[34] In broad terms, consumer vulnerability could therefore be seen as a lack of power to control marketplace interactions.[35] This power imbalance comes mostly from information asymmetry. In the digital realm, this information asymmetry is even more substantial: companies not only possess more information about a transaction than the individual consumer but also greater powers to predict new information and to prescribe further actions.[36]

However, power can have different dimensions and classifications. Rephrasing Weber, we can preliminarily identify power as the probability that one actor within a social relationship will be in a position to carry out her own will despite resistance from the other, regardless of the basis on which this probability rests.[37] Power positions have been traditionally considered on a *causal* basis: a power imbalance can *cause* harm to the powerless individual (the individual that we can call

[29] M Hildebrandt, 'The Issue of Bias: The Framing Powers of ML' in M Pelillo (ed), *Machine Learning and Society: Impact, Trust, Transparency* (MIT Press 2021).

[30] M Sax, *Between Empowerment and Manipulation: The Ethics and Regulation of For-profit Health Apps* (Kluwer Law International 2021) 97.

[31] R Forst, 'Noumenal Power' (2015) 23 Journal of Political Philosophy 111.

[32] See art 5 of the Unfair Consumer Practice Directive.

[33] C Véliz, *Privacy is Power: Why and How You Should Take Back Control of Your Data* (Bantam Press 2020).

[34] Mourali and Nagpal (n 28) 874.

[35] European Commission, 'Consumer Vulnerability across Key Markets in the European Union' (2016) 43 <https://ec.europa.eu/info/sites/info/files/consumers-approved-report_en.pdf> accessed 20 February 2023.

[36] D Citron and F Pasquale, 'The Scored Society: Due Process for Automated Predictions' (2014) 89 Washington Law Review 1>; FJ Zuiderveen Borgesius, *Improving Privacy Protection in the Area of Behavioural Targeting* (Kluwer Law International 2015) 203–05.

[37] M Weber, *Economy and Society: An Outline of Interpretive Sociology* (University of California Press 1978) 53; ME Warren, 'Max Weber's Nietzschean Conception of Power' (1992) 5 History of the Human Sciences 19, 19.

vulnerable).[38] In other terms, the power imbalance is defined on the basis of the actual adverse effects that it produces to the person in a disadvantaged position, regardless of any *ex-ante* considerations. More recently, power relationships have been defined on a *modal* basis. What matters is not just the impact but the context in which the powerful and the powerless are, and their role, the conditions in which power is exercised, and the possible lack of alternatives.[39] A causal or modal approach to power can be classified either as *relational* or *structural*.[40]

The power imbalance is inherent in many social relationships (eg between the consumer and the supplier, the citizen and the state, the employee and the employer, the student and the teacher, etc). Still, it can lead to vulnerability when it produces higher risks of harm to fundamental rights and freedoms. This higher risk of harm may depend on the one-to-one relationship between the powerful and the powerless, or it might be generated by the circumstances and contexts of the powerless individual in a bigger structural context, including societal and market structures (eg lack of available alternatives open to the individual consumer, such as in a monopoly, etc).[41]

In rational choice theory, consumers and citizens are modelled as 'actors' who must choose from a 'set of choices', or a choice set, of possible actions to achieve desired outcomes. This choice set is influenced by 'incentive structure'. An actor's 'incentive structure' encompasses (her beliefs about) the costs of different actions in the choice set and the estimated likelihood that some actions will lead to desired outcomes.[42]

In the digital platform scenario, even if there is no brute force forcing us to give consent to data processing, the 'architecture' can nudge us to act in the way that

[38] M Renner, 'Machtbegriffe Zwischen Privatrecht und Gesellschaftstheorie' in F Möslein (ed), *Private Macht* (Mohr Siebeck 2016) 513; M Rölli, 'Vorüberlegungen Zu Einer Philosophie Der Privaten Macht—Im Ausgang von Einigen Allgemeinen Bemerkungen Zum Philosophischen Stand der Machttheorie' in F Möslein (ed), *Private Macht* (Mohr Siebeck) 88.

[39] N Luhmann, *Macht* (4th edn, UTB/UVK 2012) 20; Renner (n 38) 516.

[40] H Richter, 'The Power Paradigm in Private Law' in M Bakhoum and others (eds), *Personal Data in Competition, Consumer Protection and Intellectual Property Law: Towards a Holistic Approach?* (Springer Berlin Heidelberg 2018) 533–34. In the first case (the relational perspective), it is the relationship between two individuals that qualifies power imbalance. Under this perspective, power is generated mainly on a one-to-one basis. Causal-relational power is thus based on the specific causes and effects (impact) of power imbalance between two specific subjects (the powerful and the vulnerable), Rölli (n 38) 88. While modal-relational power is based on the circumstances and context of the relationship between two individuals, Luhmann (n 39) 20. Under the structural perspective, it is the social structure that induces the power imbalances: what matters is not merely the relationship between the powerful and the powerless but how the general structure (of the market, of the institutions, of current business models, etc) generate power asymmetry. The causal-structural approach to power is based on the analysis of causes and effects between two subjects considering the general structure of society, market, public administration, etc. See Renner (n 38) 513. On the other hand, the modal-structural approach focuses on the circumstances and context of the powerless individual in a bigger structural context. According to Foucault, power is inherent in institutions or social conventions, but it might be hidden behind the daily norms of society M Foucault and others, *Microfisica del potere. Interventi politici* (Einaudi 1977) 130.

[41] Foucault and others (n 40) 130.

[42] KM Dowding, *Power* (Open University Press 1996).

our powerful counterparts prefer, thus reducing our resistance to giving away our personal data.

Moreover, Véliz noted that power—like energy—can transform itself from one kind to another (economic power can become political power, for instance).[43] In our example, market power (the relative dominance of a particular company or platform in the market and the consequent locking in of customers to that company or platform) can become knowledge power (customers will consent to give—with little or no resistance—more personal data to data controllers). Such knowledge power could create an increasingly personalized environment (choice architecture) where the user is increasingly easily nudged to accept new requests for personal data and so on, in a self-reinforcing loop that creates vicious circles.[44]

4. Layered vulnerability and intersectionality

The layered theory of vulnerability seems to align with theories of intersectionality which, as conceived and developed in the last three decades,[45] aims to analyse and address discrimination and inequalities from a composite perspective, where more than one vulnerability factor is considered simultaneously.[46] In particular, intersectionality was conceived to analyse the conditions of Black women, victims of discrimination because of their double condition as women and Black persons:[47] the main idea is that where different sources of domination converge, 'intervention strategies based solely on the experiences of women who do not share the same class or race backgrounds will be of limited help to women who because of race *and* class face different obstacles'.[48]

Intersectionality is, thus, traditionally based on three vulnerability factors: race, gender, and class. However, more sources of inequality have been

[43] Véliz (n 33).

[44] JE Cohen, *Between Truth and Power: The Legal Constructions of Informational Capitalism* (Oxford University Press 2019) 180; M Hildebrandt, 'The Dawn of a Critical Transparency Right for the Profiling Era' in J Bus (ed), *Digital Enlightenment Yearbook* (IOS Press 2012) 47; see in general S Zuboff, *The Age of Surveillance Capitalism: The Fight for a Human Future at the New Frontier of Power* (1st edn, Public Affairs 2017).

[45] See the seminal work on intersectionality: K Crenshaw, 'Mapping the Margins: Intersectionality, Identity Politics, and Violence against Women of Color' (1991) 43 Stanford Law Review 1241.

[46] See, in general, *ex multis*, MT Berger and K Guidroz, *Intersectional Approach: Transforming the Academy through Race, Class, and Gender* (ReadHowYouWant 2012); S Atrey, *Intersectional Discrimination* (Oxford University Press 2019); J Kantola and K Nousiainen, 'Institutionalizing Intersectionality in Europe' (2009) 11 International Feminist Journal of Politics 459; KW Crenshaw, 'From Private Violence to Mass Incarceration: Thinking Intersectionally about Women, Race, and Social Control' (2012) 59 UCLA Law Review 1418.

[47] Crenshaw, 'Mapping the Margins' (n 45) 1243–45.

[48] ibid 1246.

analysed over the years, including language, sexual orientation, disability, age, ethnicity, sexual orientation, religion, and disability.[49] The main legal goal of intersectionality has been anti-discrimination through a structural analysis of 'intersections' of vulnerabilities.[50] However, intersectional discourse has not been limited to discrimination but has included broader legal and philosophical reflections on the condition of vulnerable people, such as autonomy and identity.[51]

Vulnerability studies have recently considered the importance of intersectionality in their analysis.[52]

The layered approach to human vulnerability[53] described in the previous section seems to be especially in line with an intersectional approach. Vulnerable people are not vulnerable 'because of their age' or 'because of their mental condition', etc, but because of the *intersection* of different micro- or macro-sources of vulnerabilities, that we can call *layers*. In other words, what determines the vulnerable condition of individuals is not one factor (eg their membership in a protected category) but *the intersection of different layers*.

Layers can be of different relevance and importance, temporary or permanent, physiological or pathological. The intersection of these layers (eg age, sexual orientation, sexual identity, cognitive issues, occupation, socioeconomic condition, literacy, addictions, etc) in a given structural and relational context qualifies a data subject's vulnerability level. It is also important to clarify that vulnerability theories (and in particular the layered vulnerability theory)[54] do not focus solely on discrimination: they address the broader perspective of any adverse effect on individuals (eg manipulation, limitations to the freedom of speech, information, movement, etc) caused by a structural, institutional, or relational power imbalance.[55]

[49] See eg European Commission. Directorate General for Justice and Consumers. and European network of legal experts in gender equality and non-discrimination, *Intersectional Discrimination in EU Gender Equality and Non-discrimination Law* (Publications Office 2016) 30 <https://data.europa.eu/doi/10.2838/241520> accessed 21 June 2022.

[50] ibid; Atrey (n 46).

[51] DT Meyers, 'Intersectional Identity and the Authentic Self? Opposites Attract' in C Mackenzie and N Stoljar (eds), *Relational Autonomy* (Oxford University Press 2000); K Wallace, 'Autonomous "I" of an Intersectional Self' (2003) 17 The Journal of Speculative Philosophy 176.

[52] CHA Kuran and others, 'Vulnerability and Vulnerable Groups from an Intersectionality Perspective' (2020) 50 International Journal of Disaster Risk Reduction 101826; See also, more implicitly, C Mackenzie, 'The Importance of Relational Autonomy and Capabilities for an Ethics of Vulnerability' in C Mackenzie and others (eds), *Vulnerability* (Oxford University Press 2013) 58.

[53] Luna, 'Elucidating the Concept of Vulnerability' (n 2); Luna, 'Identifying and Evaluating Layers of Vulnerability—A Way Forward' (n 2).

[54] Luna, 'Elucidating the Concept of Vulnerability' (n 2).

[55] See eg G Malgieri, 'Vulnerability' in G Comandé (ed), *Elgar Encyclopedia of Law and Data Science* (Edward Elgar Publishing 2022).

5. Vulnerability and the importance of the dignity principle

To understand the definition and protection of vulnerable data subjects, the theoretical overview of the previous sections has elucidated what the notion of the vulnerable individual is. However, it is now necessary to look at how EU law has interpreted and implemented such a concept. Accordingly, in the following sections, I first analyse EU primary law, focusing on the human rights protection discourse from the European Convention on Human Rights (ECHR) and the EU Charter of Fundamental Rights (Section 5). Then, I look at EU secondary legislation (Sections 7 and 8). In general, analysing how other legal fields define vulnerability could give us analogous tools to understand who the vulnerable data subject is. As we will see, there is no consistent definition of the vulnerable person in EU law. However, some common elements, together with the theoretical reflections above, can help us understand the definition of vulnerable data subjects.

I start the analysis of positive law from primary law. Both in the ECHR and the EU Charter of Fundamental Rights, there is no reference to the concept of vulnerability. However, scholars and human rights institutions and organizations refer to it as an imperative to the special protection of socially marginalized groups like women, people with disabilities, children, and ethnic minorities.[56]

Some scholars argue that vulnerability is the rationale for protecting human rights.[57] Other commentators posit that human rights are not grounded on human vulnerability but on human dignity:[58] vulnerability should be considered a condition, not the foundation, of human rights.[59] However, the two concepts (vulnerability and dignity) are inherently linked: the imperative to protect dignity is connected to the duty to care for vulnerable individuals.[60]

Privacy and data protection have a strong link with human dignity.[61] In particular, dignity presupposes the free development of personality through

[56] See in general F Ippolito and SI Sánchez (eds), *Protecting Vulnerable Groups: The European Human Rights Framework* (Bloomsbury Publishing 2015); See also, in the US discourse BS Turner, *Vulnerability and Human Rights* (Pennsylvania State University Press 2006).

[57] Turner (n 56) 6.

[58] The centrality of the dignity principle in the European protection of fundamental rights is evident from art 1 of the EU Charter of Fundamental Rights.

[59] R Andorno, 'Is Vulnerability the Foundation of Human Rights?' in A Masferrer and E García-Sánchez (eds), *Human Dignity of the Vulnerable in the Age of Rights: Interdisciplinary Perspectives* (Springer International Publishing 2016).

[60] ibid 264.

[61] EJ Bloustein, 'Privacy as an Aspect of Human Dignity: An Answer to Dean Prosser' (1964) 39 New York Law Review 962; LA Bygrave, 'Minding the Machine: Article 15 of the EC Data Protection Directive and Automated Profiling' (2001) 17 Computer Law & Security Review 17, 18; JQ Whitman, 'The Two Western Cultures of Privacy: Dignity Versus Liberty' (2004) 113 The Yale Law Journal 72; G González Fuster, *The Emergence of Personal Data Protection as a Fundamental Right of the EU* (Springer International Publishing 2014) 23; L Floridi, 'On Human Dignity as a Foundation for the Right to Privacy' (2016) 29 Philosophy & Technology 307; H Hijmans, *The European Union as Guardian of Internet Privacy: The Story of Art 16 TFEU* (Springer 2016) 40.

self-determination and self-flourishing, two principles that many authors consider the rationale for privacy protection.[62] Similarly, within the German Federal Constitutional Court's doctrine on the existence of a general right to personality, some commentators noted the link between personality, human dignity, and privacy.[63] Moreover, the German Federal Constitutional Court had already suggested that the protection of persons against the processing of personal data fell under the right to human dignity, as mentioned in Article 1(1) of the Fundamental Law, read in conjunction with its Article 2(1), on the free development of personality.[64] Interestingly, in more recent national constitutions in Europe, the concept of dignity and privacy and data protection are often connected.[65] In the Italian Data Protection Law of 1996 (and in the modernized version of 2003), Article 1 declares that the goal of that data protection law was also the protection of dignity.

Considering this connection between data protection and dignity, giving special attention to vulnerable data subjects is even more urgent a matter. Indeed, since the principle of human dignity obliges us to consider and protect the most vulnerable individuals specifically,[66] a dignity-based notion of data protection asks us to consider the specific situation and needs of vulnerable data subjects. Assuming that a rationale for privacy and data protection is human dignity in terms of self-determination and self-flourishing, it is clear that in the case of more vulnerable subjects (cognitively impaired individuals, people from social minorities, etc), the legislator and the interpreter of legislation need to adopt more attentive safeguards that could help reach self-determination and self-flourishing.[67]

[62] B van der Sloot, 'Privacy as Human Flourishing: Could a Shift towards Virtue Ethics Strengthen Privacy Protection in the Age of Big Data?' (2014) 5 Journal of Intellectual Property, Information Technology and Electronic Commerce Law 230; AE Pérez Luño, *Derechos humanos, Estado de Derecho y Constitución* (Tecnos 2010) 324.

[63] See González Fuster (n 61) 26.

[64] Mikrozensus-Urteil, 16 July 1969 (1 BVerfGE 27, Rn. 20). See P De Hert and S Gutwirth, 'Privacy, Data Protection and Law Enforcement. Opacity of the Individual and Transparency of Power' in E Claes and others (eds), *Privacy and the Criminal Law* (Intersentia 2006) 80; see also González Fuster (n 61) 176.

[65] See the Resolution of the Presidium of the Czech National Council of 16 December 1992 on the declaration of the Charter of Fundamental Rights and Freedoms as a part of the constitutional order of the Czech Republic, No 2/1993 Coll. In that Charter, the same Article (art 19) recognizes both a right to human dignity and a right to the protection of private life and protection against the unwarranted collection, publication, or other illicit uses of personal data. Analogously, see art 19(1)–(3) of the 1992 Slovakian Constitution. See also that in the EU Charter of Fundamental Rights, even though the right to dignity (art 1) is separate from the rights to privacy (art 7) and data protection (art 8), Rodotà co-authored an amendment clearly connecting data protection to the protection of identity, human dignity, and confidentiality (see Amendment 373 (CHARTE 4332/00, CONVENT 35, 463).

[66] Andorno (n 59) 264.

[67] C Mackenzie and others (eds), *Vulnerability: New Essays in Ethics and Feminist Philosophy* (1st edn, Oxford University Press 2013) 6–11 affirming that vulnerability is also the higher risk of being harmed in one's own dignity.

6. Vulnerability and human rights: the rise of the concept of vulnerable persons in the ECtHR jurisprudence

The ECtHR recognizes vulnerable situations of particular groups, but it has not developed the notion of vulnerability in the field of private life, privacy, or data protection (Article 8 ECHR). The Court first addressed the idea of vulnerable persons in 1981, referring to children. In *Dudgeons v UK*,[68] the Court referred to 'the moral interests and welfare of certain individuals or classes of individuals who are in need of special protection for reasons such as *lack of maturity, mental disability or state of dependence*'.[69]

The case dealt with criminal laws prohibiting homosexual acts in Northern Ireland. Therefore, the Court, addressing the rationale for such criminal provisions, also focused on the issue of consent and vulnerable individuals and recognized the need 'to provide sufficient safeguards against exploitation and corruption of others, particularly those who are especially vulnerable because they are young, weak in body or mind, inexperienced, or in a state of special physical, official or economic dependence'.[70] In this judgment, the Court adopted the idea of inherent vulnerability based on (*age* as an index of) weakness, inexperience, and dependence.[71] In particular, the category of children's vulnerability qualifies as intrinsically gradual and temporal.[72] However, the Court tends to assume a hybrid definition of vulnerability, both *universal* and *particular*, as the wording 'specially vulnerable' reveals: all individuals are potentially vulnerable, but some are especially vulnerable.[73]

In later judgments, the ECtHR extended the notion of vulnerability to politically and socially disadvantaged groups. For example, in *Chapman v the United Kingdom*, the Court stated that 'the vulnerable position of Gypsies as a minority group means that some special consideration should be given to their needs and their different lifestyle both in the relevant regulatory planning framework and in reaching decisions in particular cases'.[74] The vulnerability of a group is seen here as a source for 'recognising the special needs of minorities and an obligation to protect their security, identity and lifestyle'.[75]

[68] *Dudgeons v UK*, Application No 7525/76 (22 October 1981).
[69] ibid §47. Emphasis added.
[70] ibid §49.
[71] F Ippolito, '(De)Constructing Children's Vulnerability under European Law' in F Ippolito and S Iglesias Sanchez (eds), *Protecting Vulnerable Groups* (Hart Publishing 2015).
[72] G Lansdown, *The Evolving Capacities of the Child* (UNICEF 2005).
[73] L Peroni and A Timmer, 'Vulnerable Groups: The Promise of an Emerging Concept in European Human Rights Convention Law' (2013) 11 International Journal of Constitutional Law 1056.
[74] *Chapman v The United Kingdom*, Application No 27238/95 (18 January 2001), §95.
[75] ibid §93.

The Court further developed the notion of vulnerable groups, extending it to incorporate asylum seekers,[76] people living with HIV, and individuals facing social disadvantage and material deprivation.[77] The partly dissenting opinion of Judge Salò has critically developed the definition of vulnerable persons under the ECtHR jurisprudence: he observed that the concept of vulnerability is not a monolith; there are different grades of vulnerability based on different situations.[78]

These different cases show that the Court sees vulnerability as relational, harm-based, and shaped by the situation of particular communities, ethnic groups, or life situations.[79] As Peroni and Timmer stress, the harms experienced by vulnerable groups can be related to the problem of distribution (limitation of access to services or goods) and recognition (prejudice and stigmatization).[80]

The reference to vulnerability in the ECtHR jurisprudence has three significant legal consequences.[81] First, vulnerability requires establishing positive obligations toward disadvantaged groups and providing tailored measures to recognize their particular needs and situations. For example, in the *Chapman* case, the Court called on British authorities to acknowledge the situation of Roma people in the policy-making process.[82] In other cases, the Court obliged governments to provide special financial assistance to asylum seekers or shelter to people who were evicted by force.[83]

Secondly, the vulnerability of particular groups can also influence the weight of harm in the proportionality test, amplifying the consequences and scope of harm. As stressed in the *Yordanova* case: 'the applicants' specificity as a social group and their needs must be one of the relevant factors in the proportionality assessment that the national authorities are under a duty to undertake'.[84]

The third consequence is related to the margin of appreciation. As was explicitly mentioned in the *Kiyutin v Russia* case, in the situation of vulnerable groups: the 'State's margin of appreciation is substantially narrower, and it must have very weighty reasons for the restrictions in question'.[85]

The notion of vulnerable individuals is also relevant in two specific areas of ECtHR case law: non-discrimination (ie case law about Article 14 of the ECHR)[86]

[76] About the development of the vulnerability notion in the ECtHR case law see M Baumgärtel, 'Facing the Challenge of Migratory Vulnerability in the European Court of Human Rights' (2020) 38(1) Netherlands Quarterly of Human Rights 12.

[77] *M.S.S. v Belgium and Greece*, Application No 30696/09, 21 January 2011; *Kiyutin v Russia*, Application No 2700/10, 10 March 2011; *Yordanova v Bulgaria*, Application No 25446/06, 5 June 2012.

[78] Ippolito (n 71).

[79] Peroni and Timmer (n 6) 1063–64.

[80] ibid 1065–68.

[81] ibid 1076–83.

[82] *Chapman v The United Kingdom*, §96.

[83] *M.S.S. v Belgium and Greece*, §249; *Yordanova v Bulgaria*, §130.

[84] *Yordanova v Bulgaria*, §130.

[85] *Kiyutin v Russia*, 2011, §63.

[86] OM Arnardóttir, 'Vulnerability under Article 14 of the European Convention on Human Rights' (2017) 4 Oslo Law Review 150.

and human trafficking. Although none of the EU secondary laws on non-discrimination mentions 'vulnerable individuals',[87] supranational courts often used the concept of vulnerable individuals in connection with non-discrimination law. This is the case of the ECtHR, in different circumstances. The first relevant case is *Alajos Kiss v Hungary* (2010), where the Court used the notion of vulnerability to identify prohibited grounds of discrimination, such as mental disability.[88] In more general terms, the Court used the notion of vulnerability to 'single out the most disadvantaged subgroups' within the broader categories defined by the discrimination ground in a more analytical framework, giving greater consideration to the contexts of discrimination.[89]

We observe another explicit link between discrimination and the concept of vulnerable individuals in the case law about hate crimes. The Court has emphasized states' obligation to investigate the discriminatory motives of violence. In several rulings, the ECtHR acknowledged that a lack of response to violence violated Article 14 ECHR.[90] This case law mainly focuses on vulnerable groups who are protected as victims of hate crimes, including Roma and Lesbian, Gay, Bisexual, and Transgender (LGBT) individuals.[91] However, vulnerability is not an explicitly required 'factor' of discrimination grounds.[92] The Grand Chamber, in particular, does not build a solid theoretical link between discrimination and vulnerability, trying to avoid using the vulnerability argument for a legal analysis based only on Article 14 ECHR.[93] Thus, as noted, in the anti-discrimination case law, the concept of vulnerability has been limited to a mere guiding principle, an argumentative tool that the Court uses with pragmatism rather than rigour.[94]

The last sub-field in which the ECtHR mentions the concept of vulnerability and proposes an operational definition is human trafficking. In *S.M. v Croatia*,[95]

[87] See the Directive 2000/43/EC against discrimination on grounds of race and ethnic origin; Directive 2000/78/EC against discrimination at work on the grounds of religion or belief, disability, age or sexual orientation; Directive 2006/54/EC equal treatment for men and women in matters of employment and occupation; Directive 2004/113/EC equal treatment for men and women in the access to and supply of goods and services; Directive Proposal (COM(2008)462) against discrimination based on age, disability, sexual orientation and religion or belief beyond the workplace.

[88] ECtHR, *Alajos Kiss v Hungary*, Application No 38832/06 (ECtHR, 20 May 2010), para 42. See, on this point, Baumgärtel (n 76) 18 In another case, *N.B. v Slovakia* (2012), No 29518/10, 12 June 2012, §121, about forced sterilization of a Roma woman at a public hospital who complained that she was discriminated because of her ethnic origin and her sex, the judges made no explicit reference to multiple discrimination, but they argued that 'the practice of sterilisation of women without their prior informed consent affected vulnerable individuals from various ethnic groups'.

[89] *Guberina v Croatia*, Application No 23682/13 (ECtHR, 22 March 2016).

[90] See among others ECtHR, *Opuz v Turkey*, No 33401/02, 9 June 2009 relating to violence against women; ECtHR, *Boacă and Others v Romania*, No 40355/11, 12 January 2016 relating to violence against Roma and ECtHR, *M.C. and A.C. v Romania*, No 12060/12, 12 April 2016 relating to violence against LGBT persons.

[91] For example, see ECtHR, *R.B. v Hungary*, 64602/12, 12 April 2016, para 39.

[92] Baumgärtel (n 76) 18.

[93] See *Biao v Denmark*, Application No 38590/10 (ECtHR, 24 May 2016). Arnardóttir (n 86) 170; Baumgärtel (n 76) 18.

[94] Arnardóttir (n 86) 170; Baumgärtel (n 76) 18.

[95] ECtHR, *S.M. v Croatia*, Application No 60561/14, 19 July 2018

the Court acknowledges that the notion of vulnerability at Article 4(1)(a) of the Council of Europe (CoE) Convention on Trafficking in human beings[96] should be interpreted widely, since according to the Explanatory report, 'the vulnerability may be of any kind, whether physical, psychological, emotional, family-related, social or economic'.[97]

Moreover, 'abuse of a position of vulnerability' refers to an 'abuse of any situation in which the person involved has no real and acceptable alternative to submitting to the abuse'.[98] This definition seems very relevant for the broader scholarly definition of 'decisional vulnerability'.[99] However, this case refers to a specific legal topic (human trafficking): it is unlikely that these considerations might be easily exported to other fields by analogy.

Summarizing, although in the ECHR there is no reference to vulnerable individuals, the Court first addressed the issue of children as vulnerable persons needing special protection. Then, the ECtHR extended the concept of vulnerability to minority ethnic groups ('gypsies') and then to other social groups (eg asylum seekers, people with HIV). Specific references to vulnerability can also be found in the case law on anti-discrimination and human trafficking. The Court tends to accept a hybrid definition of vulnerability, both universal and particular. The situation of vulnerable groups can shape the proportionality test or the interpretation of (positive) obligations of the states. The jurisprudence of the ECtHR shows that the notion of vulnerability is embedded in human rights practice and debate.[100] This conclusion provides some starting points to think about the vulnerability of data subjects, which could be helpful in the next section about how other legal fields in EU law address the notion of vulnerability.

7. The rise of vulnerable individuals in EU secondary law: an overview

As noted, neither the Charter of Fundamental Rights nor the Treaty of the European Union (TEU) and the Treaty on the Functioning of the EU (TFEU) contain explicit references to the concept of human vulnerability. Still, the conceptualization of human dignity and the case law of the ECtHR are two critical bases on

[96] Council of Europe Convention on Action against Trafficking in Human Beings, Warsaw, 16.V.2005, Council of Europe Treaty Series—No 197 <https://www.coe.int/it/web/conventions/full-list/-/conventions/rms/090000168008371d> accessed 20 February 2023.

[97] Explanatory Report to the Council of Europe Convention on Action against Trafficking in Human Beings Warsaw, 16.V.2005 <https://rm.coe.int/16800d3812> accessed 20 February 2023, §83.

[98] ibid §83.

[99] Gennet and others (n 21).

[100] See Baumgärtel (n 76) 18 affirming: 'vulnerability as a legal principle has been employed by the Court with quite some flexibility both in terms of its meaning and in terms of the legal effects that it creates. While this has certainly increased its utility, the Court's approach also displays some striking ambiguities and negative consequences.'

which to develop the legal notion of the vulnerable person in Europe. However, we can observe special recognition of vulnerable individuals in many EU secondary legal texts in different contexts and frameworks. In this section, following a rapid overview of the dawn of the concept of vulnerable individuals in the EU legal secondary framework, I focus on two sectors where the notion of vulnerability is relevant: research regulation and consumer protection.

One of the first legal mentions of personal vulnerability was in the 1983 Council Decision on the European Social Fund.[101] The preamble refers to 'categories of persons who are particularly vulnerable on the labour market (in particular women, the handicapped and migrants)'. The following year, two other Council acts referred to vulnerable persons, always in the field of the labour market (in particular, disabled workers).[102] In the 1990s, the concept of vulnerability was then used in the even more context-dependent case of road users. We may observe the case of the Council Directive on Civil Liability insurances,[103] whose preamble referred to motor vehicle passengers as 'vulnerable category of potential victims'. However, vulnerable groups were mentioned in the preambles only and not in the body of the legislative acts of legal texts for many years. In 1994, the notion of vulnerability was included in an article of a European Directive relating to young workers for the first time.[104]

Over the years, the notion of vulnerability slowly appeared in different legal contexts to describe various groups, as illustrated by Table 3.1.[105] Examples of legal instruments that refer to the vulnerability of particular groups range from employment to biomedical research, from migration policy to social assistance. Those instruments do not always describe vulnerable groups in detail; sometimes, they even refer to the universal and inherent concept of vulnerability, as in the first medical device directive ('the vulnerability of human body').[106]

In our view, these fragmented and heterogeneous references to vulnerable individuals reflect the contextual, relative, and relational nature of vulnerability. Several EU secondary laws propose different manifestations of vulnerability in various specific contexts. Still, two fields of EU law, namely the regulation on clinical trials and consumer protection law, require more attention as they offer insights into the notion of vulnerability that could be imported into the data protection discourse.

As I will argue, the two legal fields analysed below (consumer protection and biomedical research) take two different approaches in recognizing and protecting

[101] Council Decision of 17 October 1983 on the tasks of the European Social Fund, 83/516/EEC.

[102] Council resolution of 27 February 1984 on a second programme of action of the European Communities on safety and health at work, 84/C 67/02, art 17.

[103] Third Council Directive 90/232/EEC of 14 May 1990 on the approximation of the laws of the Member States relating to insurance against civil liability in respect of the use of motor vehicles.

[104] Council Directive 94/33/EC of 22 June 1994 on the protection of young people at work, art 7.

[105] This table is built on the previous work of the author, with a co-author, but it represents a substantial modification of it. See Malgieri and Niklas (n 11) 9.

[106] Council Directive 93/42/EEC of 14 June 1993 concerning medical devices, see the preamble.

Table 3.1 Examples of vulnerable groups in EU secondary law

Vulnerable categories of people	Sectors
- 'elderly and other vulnerable users'[a] - 'vulnerable households, including those affected by energy poverty'[b]	Consumer protection
- 'pregnant workers, workers who have recently given birth or who are breastfeeding'[c] - 'women, migrants and domestic workers, some undeclared workers'[d]	Labour law
- 'prisoners and cognitively impaired patients'[e] - 'frail or older people, people suffering from multiple chronic conditions, and people affected by mental health disorders'[f]	Clinical trials
- 'pregnant women and children'[g]	Public healthcare
- 'children and unaccompanied minors'[h]	Refugees
- 'persons with disabilities, refugees and displaced persons'[i]	Social welfare
- 'blind, visually impaired and aurally challenged pedestrians, cyclists and children'[j]	Road traffic

Adapted from Malgieri and Niklas, 'Vulnerable Data Subjects' (2020) 37 Computer Law and Security Review 105415, Table 1, 9. Adapted here under the terms of the Creative Commons CC-BY License.

[a]Regulation (EU) 2015/751 of the European Parliament and of the Council of 29 April 2015 on interchange fees for card-based payment transactions, art 17(f).

[b]Directive (EU) 2018/2002 of the European Parliament and of the Council of 11 December 2018 amending Directive 2012/27/EU on energy efficiency, recital 23.

[c]Council Directive 92/85/EEC of 19 October 1992 on the introduction of measures to encourage improvements in the safety and health at work of pregnant workers and workers who have recently given birth or are breastfeeding (tenth individual Directive within the meaning of art 16 (1) of Directive 89/391/EEC). See the preamble.

[d]Directive 2014/54/EU of the European Parliament and of the Council of 16 April 2014 on measures facilitating the exercise of rights conferred on workers in the context of freedom of movement for workers, Recital 5 refers to workers as vulnerable persons.

[e]94/913/EC: Council Decision of 15 December 1994 adopting a specific programme of research and technological development, including demonstration, in the field of biomedicine and health (1994–1998), Annex I, § 7.

[f]Regulation (EU) No 536/2014 of the European Parliament and of the Council of 16 April 2014 on clinical trials on medicinal products for human use, recital 15.

[g]Decision No 646/96/EC of the European Parliament and of the Council of 29 March 1996 adopting an action plan to combat cancer within the framework for action in the field of public health (1996–2000), art 8.

[h]Council Directive 2004/83/EC of 29 April 2004 on minimum standards for the qualification and status of third country nationals or stateless persons as refugees or as persons who otherwise need international protection and the content of the protection granted, now repealed by Directive 2011/95/EU, art 20(3).

[i]Regulation (EU) No 231/2014 of the European Parliament and of the Council of 11 March 2014 establishing an Instrument for Pre-accession Assistance (IPA II), art 2(b)(iv).

[j]Regulation (EU) No 540/2014 of the European Parliament and of the Council of 16 April 2014 on the sound level of motor vehicles and of replacement silencing systems, and amending Directive 2007/46/EC and repealing Directive 70/157/EC, recital 20.

vulnerable persons (category-based in the Clinical Trials Regulation EU 536/2014 (CTR) and general recognition in the Unfair Commercial Practices Directive 2005/29/EC (UCPD)). In Chapter 7, I discuss these two models of protection further when considering possible better protection of vulnerable data subjects *de lege ferenda*.

Although analysing these two fields along in detail might appear limited (since I do not investigate the overlap between, eg, labour law and data protection law or administrative law and data protection law in any great depth), this book argues that it is mostly in these fields that the notion of the vulnerable individual is developed to any maturity: the other EU legal fields mentioned earlier that also address vulnerable individuals show no systemic efforts to define the term but instead cast eventual and incidental references to some forms of vulnerability. On the contrary, consumer law and clinical trials legislation are two fields where the notions of average and vulnerable individuals are more fully developed. In addition, these two fields demonstrate two opposing approaches to categorizing individual vulnerability. While consumer law (UCPD) proposes a general notion of vulnerable consumers, the CTR proposes a precise and advanced classification of vulnerable subjects that seems compatible with the layered vulnerability theory that this book adopts. Keeping these two frameworks as reference might be helpful to imagine possible developments of data protection law in the future (see Chapter 8).

8. Vulnerable research subjects in EU law

A legal field that generates substantial discussion about human vulnerability is the regulation of biomedical research. The Clinical Trials Regulation of 2014 deals with this topic at the EU level.[107]

The CTR addresses the question of vulnerable research subjects from different perspectives. Article 10, whose title is 'specific considerations for vulnerable populations', requires that for specific groups (minors, incapacitated subjects, pregnant or breastfeeding women, or 'other specific groups or subgroups'), the researcher give specific consideration to the assessment of the application for authorization[108] of a clinical trial. This provision does not clarify whether this 'specific consideration' should be dedicated to the *decision-making vulnerability* of such research subjects (ie their greater difficulty in giving consent to their involvement in the

[107] 'Regulation (EU) No 536/2014 of the European Parliament and of the Council of 16 April 2014 on Clinical Trials on Medicinal Products for Human Use, and Repealing Directive 2001/20/EC Text with EEA Relevance', Pub L No 32014R0536, 158 OJ L (2014).

[108] As regards authorization procedures that ethics committee should follow for clinical trials see in particular Chapter II (arts 5–9) of the Clinical Trials Regulation.

research)[109] or to the *higher risks of harm* that these subjects might encounter during a medical research project.[110]

Articles 31–33 address decision-making vulnerability. These articles dictate rules for obtaining valid consent from and giving adequate information to minors (Article 31), incapacitated subjects (Article 32), pregnant or breastfeeding women (Article 33). The Member States can even guarantee further protection for other people in a situation of institutional or hierarchical dependency likely to influence their freedom of consent (Article 34).[111] In terms of decision-making vulnerability, Recital 31 incidentally mentions another category of vulnerable subjects that should require specific attention when collecting informed consent: individuals belonging to 'an economically or socially disadvantaged group or in a situation of institutional or hierarchical dependency that could inappropriately influence her or his decision to participate'.

A further reference to vulnerable people is at Recital 15. Here the notion of vulnerability does not refer to decision-making vulnerability but to the weaker health conditions of specific categories of persons that the research should consider. The reference to vulnerable groups in Recital 15 aims to encourage specific medical research for vulnerable people in order to avoid the under-representation of vulnerable groups. In other words, this Recital does not provide any particular safeguard or limitations for protecting vulnerable research subjects. On the contrary, it encourages the involvement of more vulnerable individuals in research projects.[112]

9. Vulnerable consumers in EU law

Before moving to the discussion on the General Data Protection Regulation (GDPR), I analyse now how consumer protection theories have addressed the notion of vulnerable consumers. Considering the potentially fruitful link between consumer protection and data protection (as noted in Chapter 2), I consider this analysis a relevant step to conceptualize vulnerability in the data protection field.

The first explicit application of the concept of vulnerability in the consumer protection field can be found in the Directive 97/55/EC on misleading advertising.[113] Recital 22 allowed Member States to limit comparative advertising, particularly for

[109] Council of Europe, Convention for the protection of human rights and the dignity of human beings with regard to the application of biology and medicine. Oviedo 1997; ETS No 164. Council of Europe. Additional Protocol to the Convention on Human Rights and Biomedicine, concerning biomedical research. Strasbourg 2005. CETS No 195.

[110] Gennet and others (n 21).

[111] Namely: 'persons performing mandatory military service, persons deprived of liberty, persons who, due to a judicial decision, cannot take part in clinical trials, or persons in residential care institutions'.

[112] Gennet and others (n 21) 929.

[113] Directive 97/55/EC of European Parliament and of the Council of 6 October 1997 amending Directive 84/450/EEC concerning misleading advertising so as to include comparative advertising.

advertising that targets *vulnerable consumer groups*.[114] As observed in Table 3.1, consumer law also took into account consumer vulnerability in specific sectors, like energy or e-payments.

In more general terms, the UCPD refers in Article 5(3) to vulnerable groups of consumers as 'people particularly vulnerable to the practice or the underlying product because of their mental or physical infirmity, age or credulity'. The recognition of those vulnerable consumers is based on the idea that they should be afforded a higher level of protection than 'the average consumer' referred to in Article 5(2).[115] However, the meaning of vulnerability in the UCPD is a matter of lively discussion. For example, the European Commission Report of 2016 (mentioned above in Section 4) confirmed the gradual nature of the vulnerability,[116] in particular highlighting that the notion of vulnerable consumers should be assessed on several elements, 'as a result of socio-demographic characteristics, behavioural characteristics, personal situation or market environment'.[117] Additionally, the European Commission Guidance on the implementation of the UCPD has also argued that consumer vulnerability is 'multi-dimensional'[118] and so is 'the impact of personal characteristics on the likelihood of being vulnerable as a consumer'.[119] For example, characteristics like age and gender can increase vulnerability in some dimensions but not in others.[120]

In addition, the UCPD, though defining vulnerable data subjects, does not provide specific safeguards for them or specific vulnerability mitigation measures: vulnerable consumers are relevant only if the seller can reasonable foresee that one particular commercial practice can distort their economic behaviour and, in that case, the 'average' representative of that vulnerable group should be considered to

[114] Surprisingly, this directive has been repealed by 'Directive 2006/114/EC of the European Parliament and of the Council of 12 December 2006 concerning misleading and comparative advertising (codified version)' that has no more reference to vulnerable persons.

[115] European Commission, Staff Working Document Guidance on the Implementation/Application of Directive 2005/29/EC on Unfair Commercial Practices accompanying the Document Communication from the Commission to the European Parliament, the Council, the European Economic and Social Committee and the Committee of the Regions—A comprehensive approach to stimulating cross-border e-Commerce for Europe's citizens and businesses, SWD/2016/0163 final, §2.6.

[116] European Commission, *Consumer Vulnerability across Key Markets in the European Union*, Final report, January 2016 <https://ec.europa.eu/info/sites/info/files/consumers-approved-report_en.pdf> accessed 20 February 2023.

[117] ibid.

[118] SM Baker and others, 'Building Understanding of the Domain of Consumer Vulnerability' (2005) 25(2) Journal of Macromarketing 128, 134–35.

[119] European Commission Staff Working Document Guidance on the Implementation/Application of Directive 2005/29/EC on Unfair Commercial Practices accompanying the Document Communication from the Commission to the European Parliament, the Council, the European Economic and Social Committee and the Committee of the Regions. A comprehensive approach to stimulating cross-border e-Commerce for Europe's citizens and businesses (COM(2016) 320 final), Brussels, 25 May 2016 <https://eur-lex.europa.eu/legal-content/EN/TXT/PDF/?uri=CELEX:52016SC0163&from=EN> accessed 20 February 2023, 43.

[120] ibid 43.

assess the unfairness of a commercial practice (Article 5(3)).[121] In sum, the only protection for vulnerable consumers is to adapt the consumer cognitive benchmark to the characteristics of the vulnerable group that the commercial practice might foreseeably impact.

The discussion about vulnerability in the UCPD also stresses the limitations about the division between 'average' and 'vulnerable' consumers, and focus on temporal, gradual, and contextual-relational aspects.[122] The European Commission has also recently relied on the gradual approach to vulnerability in the Guidelines for the General Product Safety Directive.[123]

In sum, the EU consumer protection framework shows a general recognition of average consumers and vulnerable consumers. Still, while the first concept may be considered unrealistic and inadequate (see Chapter 2), the latter is not adequately developed in terms of legal safeguards and vulnerability mitigation measures.

The European Commission Report on Consumer Vulnerability in the EU

In 2016 the European Commission commissioned a study on consumer vulnerability across key markets in the EU. This report, in its conclusions, proposes five effects of consumers' vulnerability:[124]

1. *heightened risk of negative impacts on well-being*,[125] interpreting vulnerability as an *ex-ante* assessment of the probability of a negative outcome, as a loss of welfare due to choices in markets, and as higher susceptibility to harm and diminished well-being;[126]

[121] JHV Stuyck, 'The Notion of the Empowered and Informed Consumer in Consumer Policy and How to Protect the Vulnerable under Such a Regime' (2007) The Yearbook of Consumer Law 2007 20 <https://repository.ubn.ru.nl/handle/2066/54027> accessed 30 May 2020; L Waddington, 'Reflections on the Protection of "Vulnerable" Consumers Under EU Law' Maastricht Faculty of Law Working Paper No. 2013-2 (2014) 16 <https://papers.ssrn.com/abstract=2532904> accessed 1 March 2020.

[122] European Parliament resolution of 22 May 2012 on a strategy for strengthening the rights of vulnerable consumers (2011/2272(INI)), §1, FW Morgan and others, 'A Framework for Examining the Legal Status of Vulnerable Consumers' (1995) 14(2) Journal of Public Policy & Marketing 275.

[123] Commission Decision of 16 December 2009 laying down guidelines for the management of the Community Rapid Information System RAPEX established under art 12 and of the notification procedure established under art 11 of Directive 2001/95/EC (the General Product Safety Directive) (notified under document C(2009) 9843), Table 1.

[124] European Commission (n 35).

[125] ibid 47.

[126] F Povel, 'Perceived Vulnerability to Downside Risk' (2010) Discussion Papers, No 43, Georg-August-Universität Göttingen, Courant Research Centre—Poverty, Equity and Growth (CRC-PEG), Göttingen <https://econpapers.repec.org/paper/gotgotcrc/043.htm> accessed 23 February 2020; R Burden, *Vulnerable Consumer Groups: Quantification and Analysis* (Office of Fair Trading 1998); NC Smith and E Cooper-Martin, 'Ethics and Target Marketing: The Role of Product Harm and Consumer Vulnerability' (1997) 61(3) Journal of Marketing 1.

2. *having characteristics that limit the ability to maximize well-being,*[127] interpreting vulnerability as characteristics that restrict consumers' ability to maximize their utility and well-being, as consumers of diminished capacity to understand advertising and product effects, and as consumers' certain abiding characteristics;[128]
3. *having difficulty in obtaining or assimilating information,*[129] also called information vulnerability; it refers both to information asymmetries between consumers and suppliers and to the limitations of consumers to acquire or assimilate information;[130]
4. *inability or failure to buy, choose, or access suitable products,*[131] that is, a consumer's incapability to choose or access products and services which they need, or the attitude to choose and access these products without disproportionate effort, including buying unsuitable goods or services and failing to buy suitable goods and services;[132]
5. *higher susceptibility to marketing practices, creating imbalances in market interactions,*[133] in other words vulnerability as the effect of marketing practices and consumers' particular susceptibility. This arises from a combination of consumers' characteristics and the techniques used by marketers to render them particularly vulnerable, powerlessness due to imbalanced market interactions and consumption of marketing messages.[134]

Some of these five dimensions overlap with the others or are causes or consequences of others. As an example, information vulnerability (point 3) can be generated by personal characteristics (point 2). It can generate an inability to buy (point 4) and, in the long term, negatively impact consumer well-being (point 5).

The complexity of consumers' vulnerability factors confirms the contextual nature of vulnerability. The classical distinction between internal and external vulnerability has proved ineffective for consumers, whose vulnerability is at the intersection between internal factors of the consumer (physical and mental competency and sensitivity)[135] and external factors caused by the commercial

[127] European Commission (n 35) 47.

[128] Smith and Cooper-Martin (n 136); S Commuri and A Ekici, 'An Enlargement of the Notion of Consumer Vulnerability' (2008) 28(2) Journal of Macromarketing 183.

[129] European Commission (n 35) 47.

[130] Burden (n 136).

[131] European Commission (n 35) 47.

[132] J Stearn, 'Tackling Consumer Vulnerability an Action Plan for Empowerment' (2012) 11 <https://www.bl.uk/collection-items/tackling-consumer-vulnerability-an-action-plan-for-empowerment> accessed 23 February 2020; C Shultz and M Holbrook, 'The Paradoxical Relationship between Marketing and Vulnerability' (2009) 28 Journal of Public Policy & Marketing 125.

[133] European Commission (n 35) 47.

[134] GG Brenkert, 'Marketing and the Vulnerable' (1998) 7 Business Ethics Quarterly 303; Baker and others (n 128) 134; Stearn (n 142) 11.

[135] Morgan and others (n 132).

counterpart or the structure of the market (informational asymmetry, supply, or vulnerability to pressure, etc).[136]

The hybrid (internal–external) nature of consumer vulnerability is even more evident when microtargeting and data mining allow great knowledge (the so-called information vulnerability, ie an external factor) on inherent vulnerabilities of consumers (cognitive biases,[137] personal vulnerabilities, ie internal factors).[138] In other words, new forms of consumer vulnerability in the algorithmic world (generally based on behavioural advertising) are generated neither merely by an external power imbalance between consumers and individuals, nor by personal characteristics of the consumers alone: the two elements are intrinsically linked. Indeed, the power imbalance is often the source used to discover and exploit internal vulnerabilities.

Layers of relational vulnerability for consumers

As noted in the previous sub-sections, in the consumer protection field, the notion of (consumer) vulnerability is based on (and qualified by) the specific *relationship* between a company and a person. In general terms, we can say that *relational vulnerability* is based both on inherent factors of vulnerability (temporary or permanent physical or mental conditions)[139] and on external factors (eg information asymmetries, a massive amount of personal data that the data controller can infer on data subjects).[140]

Several scholars have focused on different aspects of the vulnerability of consumers in the market (like duration[141] and perception[142]). A significant group of authors focused in particular on vulnerability

136 Cartwright (n 140); European Commission (n 35) 45–46.

137 MG Haselton and others, 'The Evolution of Cognitive Bias' in DM Buss (ed), *The Handbook of Evolutionary Psychology* (John Wiley & Sons, Inc 2015); O Thomas, 'Two Decades of Cognitive Bias Research in Entrepreneurship: What Do We Know and Where Do We Go from Here?' (2018) 68 Management Review Quarterly 107; Association for Psychological Science, 'Cognitive Bias' <https://www.psychologicalscience.org/tag/cognitive-bias> accessed 28 February 2019.

138 Clifford (n 1); ADI Kramer and others, 'Experimental Evidence of Massive-Scale Emotional Contagion through Social Networks' (2014) 111 Proceedings of the National Academy of Sciences 8788.

139 Waddington (n 131) 23, discussing the European Parliament, Report on a strategy for strengthening the rights of vulnerable consumers (2011/2272[INI]), 8 May 2012, A7- 0155/2012, Committee on the Internal Market and Consumer Protection.

140 Cartwright (n 140) 36; European Commission (n 35) 45–46.

141 Vulnerability of consumers can be permanent (eg chronic psychiatric illnesses) or temporary (eg temporary physiological conditions of the human being, such as childhood/elderliness and temporary pathological conditions or transient mental conditions during the day, such as anxiety, dejection, etc). See Baker and others (n 128) 138, identifying personal characteristics as individual characteristics (generally permanent) and individual statuses (generally temporary, like grief, motivation, etc).

142 Scholars distinguished actual vulnerability (higher risks of harms) from perceived vulnerability (self-conception of the individual). See ibid 128; Smith and Cooper-Martin (n 136) 3–4.

sources. In line with Luna's theory of vulnerability, I believe that such sources are groups of 'layers' of vulnerability. However, in more specific terms, economics scholars found different sub-categories of vulnerability sources:

1. Some authors tried to categorize specific internal sources of vulnerability, in other words, *personal characteristics of consumers*;
2. others have focused on the external sources of vulnerability in consumers,[143] *power characteristics of suppliers*;
3. recently, law and economics scholars outlined a third category of sources, called '*vulnerability drivers*'.[144]

In this and the following paragraphs, I explain these three concepts. As regards personal characteristics, Baker distinguishes between individual characteristics and individual states.[145] Individual characteristics can be biophysical, such as addictions, age, disability, gender, race/ethnicity, and cognitive deficiencies; or psychosocial, such as self-concept, social perceptions of appearance, socio-economic status, perceived skills, resource assets, acculturation, fear of being victimized, and perceived health. Biophysical characteristics affect the ability to recognize and protect oneself from persuasion attempts and the ability to understand the implications of marketing messages.[146] In contrast, the psychosocial characteristics affect how consumers experience, respond to, and interpret marketing messages and contexts.[147] On the other hand, individual states are transitionary states that can act at an emotional level. Examples are grief, transition, and motivation.[148] Other scholars have classified personal characteristics as (i) physical sensitivity, (ii) physical competency, (iii) mental competency, and (iv) sophistication level.[149] To offer some examples, belonging to a social or ethnic minority might expose an individual to a higher risk of being discriminated, in a given context and in relationship to a specific data controller. Being very young or being a person with a cognitive disability might offer a higher risk of being mentally manipulated in some specific contexts and by some data controllers. Being an LGBTQI+ person might bring to higher risks of feeling stigmatized in certain relationships with some data controllers.

[143] Baker and others (n 128) 129–31.
[144] European Commission (n 35) 49; see also Baker and others (n 128) 134.
[145] Baker and others (n 128) 130.
[146] GR Laczniak and PE Murphy, *Ethical Marketing Decisions: The Higher Road* (Pearson 1992); TL Rittenburg and M Parthasarathy, 'Ethical Implications of Target Market Selection' (1997) 17(2) Journal of Macromarketing 49.
[147] Stacey Menzel Baker and others, 'Marketplace Experiences of Consumers with Visual Impairments: Beyond the Americans with Disabilities Act' (2001) 20 Journal of Public Policy & Marketing 215.
[148] Baker and others (n 128) 130.
[149] FW Morgan and others, 'A Framework for Examining the Legal Status of Vulnerable Consumers' (1995) 14 Journal of Public Policy & Marketing 267, 272.

As regards the *external factors* (2), these are based on the supplier's potentialities or on the market structure, which generates structural asymmetry between suppliers and consumers. Structural asymmetry can manifest in different ways: for example, information asymmetry between the company and the consumer; supply limitations (consumer group cannot participate in the market even though they wish to, or they have less choice in the market due to their characteristics); difficulties in obtaining redress; etc.[150] We can link all these distinctions to the categories mentioned regarding power imbalances in Section 3 (modal relational, ie one-to-one vulnerability, and modal structural, ie vulnerability based on structural market or societal issues). Suppliers usually exploit these vulnerabilities through *vulnerability drivers*. To offer some examples, if the data subject is a fixed-term employee and the data controller is their employer, the power asymmetry in this data-processing relationship is relevant and can increase the level of vulnerability of the data subject. Indeed, they will have weaker resistance to denying consent to data processing and they risk suffering more adverse effects if they exercise their data protection rights. A similar example is when the data controller is a dominant social media platform collecting large amounts of personal data from its users and the data subject is a user experiencing locked in to that platform: the increased informational asymmetry and power asymmetry in this relationship increase the level of vulnerability of the data subjects (weaker resistance to refuse undesirable data processing practices, reluctance to exercise data protection rights, higher risks that the amount of personal data collected could lead to mental manipulation of the user and discrimination against her, etc).

The last factor to consider (3) is *vulnerability drivers*. They are described as mechanisms through which consumers can become vulnerable and through which their vulnerabilities can be exploited. These drivers might be either mechanisms in which the supplier actively exploits consumers through specific means (eg personalized practices leading to deception, undue influence, aggressive communication),[151] or wider contextual factors that can impact vulnerability too. These can include social, economic, technical, political, geographical, and institutional factors that directly or indirectly influence the level of vulnerability of individuals (see the examples below).

As we will see, we can adapt this analysis to data subjects' vulnerability in the data protection field. We can compare the power relationship between suppliers and consumers with the power relationship between data controllers and data subjects.

It would be helpful to offer some real-life examples that could elucidate how these three factors are interrelated in determining the level of vulnerability of a data subject. We can consider the case of a person depressed because her mother

[150] Cartwright (n 140) 48; European Commission (n 35) 45–46.

[151] Baker and others (n 128) 130.

recently died. Every day, at a particular time of the evening (usually the time when, in the past, she was used to speaking to her mother by phone), she is shown specific expensive clothes ads on her social media proposing happy images of a mother and a daughter spending time together. Even though she had neither the intention nor the need to buy such expensive clothes at the beginning, after some days she bought some clothes by clicking on the ad banner on the social media web page. At the same time, her grief and depression grew and she felt addicted to buying new clothes every time she was sad about her mother's loss. What makes her vulnerable in this situation? Not only her individual characteristics (experiencing grief for her mother's death, feeling lonely at certain times of the day) but also the specific power of the social media platform. She consented to be profiled and to receive personalized ads because she felt the social pressure to have a profile on that social network. At the same time, by collecting a significant amount of information about that user, the social network learned about her weak points (emotions at certain times of the day, recent painful life events, etc) in order to maximize the chances that the ads are effective. Being a dominant social media platform that processes a massive amount of personal data would not be enough to trigger the human vulnerability of the user. However, the fact that a specific advertisement is displayed at a particular time, with specific emotional images, exploiting specific cognitive biases of that consumer, is a 'vulnerability driver' that increases the risks for the data subject.

To give another example, we can consider the case of a young male rider, a worker for a food delivery company, who is bisexual and is asked (for the purpose of 'services optimization') to keep the geolocation of his working phone always 'on', even during work breaks between food deliveries. What determines his level of vulnerability is his individual characteristics (eg being a member of the LGBTQIA+ community, being in precarious economic conditions) but also the potentialities of the counterparty: the data controller is his employer and, even considering that the employment contract at issue is a non-permanent contract, there is a significant power imbalance. Indeed, when the data subject was asked to give consent to continuous geolocation, he felt obliged to accept, even though tracking his positions could reveal that he spent his free time in the gay quarter of the city, enhancing his risk of being discriminated in the workplace for his sexual orientation. The fact that that company is based on an algorithm that 'optimizes' the work shifts in real-time, the fact that the logic of that algorithm is opaque and that riders are asked to be geolocated even when they do not work might be examples of 'vulnerability drivers'. In broader terms, the structural and societal conditions at stake (pervasive tracking of riders, opaque AI-driven organization of the workload, exploitation of precarious employees, general homophobia, biphobia, and transphobia in specific social contexts) can be considered vulnerability drivers. In sum, even though the mere individual characteristics of this data subject are not enough to qualify him as 'vulnerable', and even though the power characteristics of the data controller, in this case, may not be enough to qualify all their employees as vulnerable, the specific encounter between that rider and his employer, combined with specific structural and societal conditions of that encounter (vulnerability drivers) might be sufficient to consider our data subject as being vulnerable in that context.

What appears clear from these examples is that the distinction between these three factors is rarely sharp. The individual characteristics of the data subject 'influence' the power of the data controller and vice versa. The vulnerability drivers depend on the power of the data controller, but they are successful only if the data subject is particularly susceptible to possible adverse effects in a given social context. However, although the borderlines are often blurred, it is important to understand that the factors influencing human vulnerability are not merely 'internal' or 'external' but a complex combination of at least three elements (internal about the data subject, external about the data controller, and internal/external about the structural context in place).

These different levels of analysis are compatible with Luna's theory of layered vulnerability described in the previous sections.[152] Every source is a group of 'layers' of consumers' vulnerability (composed of several sub-layers) which needs to be assessed in a given specific context, considering the specific temporary conditions and the specific relationship between the consumer and their supplier.

10. Conclusions

In this chapter, I observed that the interpretations of human vulnerability are diverse in different scholarly sectors and in different pieces of legislation. Despite the tension between universal vulnerability (everyone is vulnerable) and particular vulnerability (some people are more vulnerable than others), a common ground for vulnerable individuals seems to be power imbalance and the higher risks to fundamental rights and freedoms, on the basis of a structural, institutional, or relational power imbalance.

Focusing on EU law, although we observed specific lists of vulnerable subjects in several sectors, the general picture reveals a highly contextual and relational understanding of vulnerability based on power imbalance and higher risks of harm. Vulnerability can be, thus, defined as the significant likelihood of incurring identifiable *harms* while lacking the ability to protect oneself.

The problematic reference to 'harm' recurs in many parts of this chapter. The link between vulnerability and (higher risks of) harm is, indeed, present in the legal philosophical reflections on human vulnerability and power imbalances,[153]

[152] Luna, 'Elucidating the Concept of Vulnerability' (n 2); Luna, 'Identifying and Evaluating Layers of Vulnerability—a Way Forward' (n 2).

[153] Renner (n 38) 513; Foucault and others (n 40) 130.

in the law and economics analysis of consumer vulnerability,[154] in some interpretations of EU law on clinical research,[155] and even in the scholarly analyses of the ECtHR case law on human vulnerability.[156]

However, at this stage, it is important to clarify that different authors might refer to different concepts of harm. The legal meaning of 'harm' might be often different from many non-legal references to harm. Due to the interdisciplinary nature of this chapter, it is impossible to adopt a universal notion of harm. Harm might refer, for example, to a quantifiable or demonstrable damage, to an abstract interference with protected values and rights, and to a subjective or objective adverse impact on individuals' rights or interests. In the data protection framework, the discussion about 'harms' is heated and far from reaching a consensus.[157] However, I highlight that the analysis in this book does not relate vulnerability to demonstrable harms but to the 'higher risks' of *interference* with data subjects' fundamental rights and freedoms. Chapter 7 will focus largely on this open issue and will conclude that the generic reference to 'harms' should be meant, at least, as a 'legal or similarly significant effect' on data subjects.

Looking at the factors of vulnerability, often scholars have focused on the personal characteristics of the vulnerable individual (cognitive biases, age, being part of a social minority, etc). However, we should observe vulnerability as an 'encounter' between personal characteristics of the subject, the potentialities (the power) of the counterparty, and the specific social or technological mechanisms at issue. In other words, a mature and contextual analysis of individual vulnerability requires an analysis of power structures and dynamics based on architectures of choice and incentive structures.

The intersectional, relative, and contextual notion of vulnerability has been well described by the theory of Luna of 'layered' vulnerability:[158] the layers of

[154] Smith and Cooper-Martin (n 136).

[155] Gennet and others (n 21).

[156] Peroni and Timmer (n 73) 1064–65.

[157] About the difficulty to interpret 'harms' in the risk-based approach of the GDPR see R Gellert, 'We Have Always Managed Risks in Data Protection Law: Understanding the Similarities and Differences between the Rights-Based and the Risk-Based Approaches to Data Protection' (2016) 2 European Data Protection Law Review 481, 482; see also M Macenaite, 'The "Riskification" of European Data Protection Law through a Two-Fold Shift' (2017) 8 European Journal of Risk Regulation 506, 515, who contrasts the 'risk-based' approach (of the GDPR) to the 'harm-based' approach. In the US literature about privacy and data protection, the notion harm is recurring, and often diverse. See L Austin, 'Enough About Me: Why Privacy Is About Power, Not Consent (or Harm)' in A Sarat (ed), *A World without Privacy: What Law Can and Should Do?* (Cambridge University Press 2014); MR Calo, 'The Boundaries of Privacy Harm' 86 Indiana Law Journal 33; Future of Privacy Forum, 'Unfairness By Algorithm: Distilling the Harms of Automated Decision-Making' (2017) <https://fpf.org/2017/12/11/unfairness-by-algorithm-distilling-the-harms-of-automated-decision-making/> accessed 8 February 2020; D Solove and DK Citron, 'Privacy Harms' (2022) 102 Boston University Law Review 793.

[158] Luna, 'Elucidating the Concept of Vulnerability' (n 2); Luna, 'Identifying and Evaluating Layers of Vulnerability—a Way Forward' (n 2).

vulnerability are not fixed attributes of specific individuals or groups. They are features constructed by status, time, and location. The identification and assessment of layers of vulnerability should be based on an analysis of the origins of vulnerability and its effects (ie likelihood and severity of harms). The following chapter will develop these conclusions, looking at the EU data protection framework.

4

The vulnerable data subject in the GDPR

1. Introduction: situating vulnerable individuals in the data protection field

After an analysis of the possible theoretical and legal definitions of vulnerable individuals, it is possible to argue that in the EU there is no unique concept of vulnerable individuals, and that vulnerability is a heterogeneous concept in secondary law. In the previous chapter, I observed that the layered theory of vulnerability would adequately explain the nature of individual vulnerability as hybrid (neither universal nor particular) and contextual and relational. In Chapter 3, I observed how the philosophical literature debated the universal versus particular nature of vulnerability. I also observed how the reflection on structural power imbalance can lead to a contextual and relational nature of vulnerability. Both personal conditions and structural components can cause the risks to an individual stemming from data collection and exploitation to have greater adverse impacts on their fundamental rights and freedoms. In addition, Chapter 3 has elucidated three contextual factors of vulnerability already mentioned in law and economics literature on consumer vulnerability: (i) personal characteristics of the individual; (ii) potentialities or 'power' of their counterpart; (iii) vulnerability drivers.

Nevertheless, the different approaches to vulnerable individuals in various EU laws have in common the link between vulnerability and harm: being vulnerable—according to several EU directives and regulations—basically means being more exposed to power imbalance and its adverse effects (if compared to other individuals) in some particular contexts.[1]

Building on these different theories and ways of understanding vulnerability, this chapter looks at the notion of vulnerability in the data protection discourse and, in particular, in the General Data Protection Regulation (GDPR) (Section 2). After an analysis of the manifestations (Section 3) and the effects (Section 4) of data subjects' vulnerability, this chapter aims to show how the consumer vulnerability literature mentioned in Chapter 3 informs the notion of the vulnerable individual in data protection (Section 5). Consequently, a more systematic analysis of

[1] L Peroni and A Timmer, 'Vulnerable Groups: The Promise of an Emerging Concept in European Human Rights Convention Law' (2013) 11 International Journal of Constitutional Law 1056, 1058, 1064–67; É Gennet and others, 'Does the New EU Regulation on Clinical Trials Adequately Protect Vulnerable Research Participants?' (2015) 119 Health Policy (Amsterdam, Netherlands) 925, 926.

Vulnerability and Data Protection Law. Gianclaudio Malgieri, Oxford University Press. © Gianclaudio Malgieri 2023.
DOI: 10.1093/oso/9780192870339.003.0004

the GDPR provisions related to vulnerable data subjects (Section 6)—and in particular to children (Section 7)—shows the need to analyse vulnerability also from the perspective of power imbalance (Section 8). Such a perspective can be found in the new proposed EU Artificial Intelligence Act (Section 9), which offers additional stimulating elements for protecting vulnerable individuals in the digital environment, complementing the GDPR provisions.

2. Universalistic or particularistic approach to data subjects' vulnerability

The concept of human vulnerability plays a vital role in situating the position of the individual in the context of data processing, in particular, because of its inherent link with the concept of dignity, an essential element in privacy and data protection discourses (see Chapter 2.4). Although the scope of this book is primarily on data protection, this section refers to both data protection and privacy. Even considering the different scope, consequences, and legal implications of the two areas,[2] a combined analysis of privacy and data protection might be helpful for several reasons: the discourse on privacy has meaningful implications for data protection too, especially considering the power relationship between the individual (the person whose private life is under surveillance) and the public or private entity who tries to interfere with the individual's private life. The analogy between this power relationship and the data subject/data controller relationship is relevant. This is true especially in non-EU contexts where, due to terminological, historical, and legislative reasons, the distinction between the two areas is much more blurred than in the EU context but where the scholarly reflections on this field might be very relevant for our purposes.

In general terms, we can see that the manifestations of vulnerability in the privacy and data protection field replicate the same tension, already observed in Chapter 2.2, between the particular and universal definition of individual vulnerability.[3]

According to the *universalistic* approach (everyone is equally vulnerable), privacy and data protection might be seen as a way to mitigate the vulnerability of all individuals when their private life is under surveillance or their personal data are processed. As Calo explains, knowledge and information confer power over

[2] O Lynskey, *The Foundations of EU Data Protection Law* (Oxford University Press 2015) 89–129; G González Fuster, *The Emergence of Personal Data Protection as a Fundamental Right of the EU* (Springer International Publishing 2014) 256; LD Corte, 'A Right to a Rule: On the Substance and Essence of the Fundamental Right to Personal Data Protection' in D Hallinan and others (eds), *Data Protection and Privacy* (Hart Publishing 2020); M Tzanou, 'Data Protection as a Fundamental Right next to Privacy? 'Reconstructing' a Not so New Right' (2013) 3 International Data Privacy Law 88.

[3] G Malgieri and J Niklas, 'The Vulnerable Data Subject' (2020) 37 Computer Law & Security Review.

individuals and make them vulnerable.[4] Therefore, privacy and data protection play a protective function and create barriers for discovering, rendering, and exploiting those vulnerabilities. Under this universalistic starting point, in the data-driven environment, we are all vulnerable.

At the same time, data subjects are different (*particularistic* approach—some people are more vulnerable than others): they have various levels of understanding and awareness, decision-making capacities, propensities to disclose their data, and weaknesses. However, in the data protection discourse, the notion of the data subject has usually been based on a general definition without particular consideration of different categories of subjects.[5] As affirmed in Chapter 2, there is no clarity about whether such a monolithic notion refers to an 'average' data subject (as in the consumer field) or not.[6] Scholars articulate how different situations of specific groups and individuals shape their capabilities, enjoyment, and expectations about privacy and data protection. A typical example here is the case of children.

Children have limited capacity to understand the complexity of data-driven architecture, have less experience and less awareness of risks and rights than adults, and may be easily exploited. For those reasons, processing the data of minors is shaped by specific rules in data protection regimes and is also subject to numerous studies.[7] Nevertheless, inequality between data subjects goes beyond the issue of age.

In other contexts, scholars show that intrusion of privacy can be marked by social differences—race, ethnicity, class, sexual orientation, migration status, or gender.[8] For example, those conditions often act as a justification for particularly onerous forms of surveillance. Furthermore, Gilman argues that privacy laws do not always protect those in less advantaged positions, mirroring existing inequalities and power dynamics.[9] Similarly, analysing the EU context, Blume recognizes that numerous factors like age, mental capacity, literacy, or gender can affect the enjoyment and execution of individual data protection rights.[10]

In sum, there is a significant conundrum in individual vulnerability theories that we can find relevant in the privacy and data protection discourse too, that is,

[4] R Calo, 'Privacy, Vulnerability, and Affordance' (2017) 66 DePaul Law Review 601, 594.

[5] P Blume, 'The Data Subject' (2015) 1(4) European Data Protection Law Review 259.

[6] G González Fuster, 'How Uninformed Is the Average Data Subject? A Quest for Benchmarks in EU Personal Data Protection' (2014) 19 Revista de Internet, Derecho y Política 92–104.

[7] For example recent study by Mariya Stoilova and others shows different expectations and strategies employ to protect their privacy: M Stoilova and others, *Children's Data and Privacy Online* (London School of Economics and Political Science 2019).

[8] M Madden and others, 'Privacy, Poverty and Big Data: A Matrix of Vulnerabilities for Poor Americans' (2017) 95(1) Washington University Law Review; KM Bridges, *The Poverty of Privacy Rights* (Stanford University Press 2017) 1–35; J Gilliom, *Overseers of the Poor: Surveillance, Resistance and the Limits of Privacy* (University of Chicago Press 2001) 1–16.

[9] ME Gilman, 'The Class Differential in Privacy Law' (2012) 77(4) Brooklyn Law Review 1394; ME Gilman and R Green, 'The Surveillance Gap: The Harms of Extreme Privacy and Data Marginalization' (2018) 42 NYU Review of Law and Social Change 296–99.

[10] Blume, 'The Data Subject' (n 5) 258.

the definition of vulnerable subjects between universality (everyone is equally vulnerable) and particularity (some subjects are more vulnerable). If we affirm that all data subjects are universally vulnerable, we may ignore significant differences among them, which may weaken the protection of individuals in an already disadvantaged position. At the same time, more specific protection rules and safeguards can lead to fragmentation of the already complicated legal regime.

However, as observed in Chapter 3, at least one theory could help develop the notion of vulnerability in data protection in a constructive way: Luna's theory of layered vulnerability mentioned above.[11]

3. Data subjects' vulnerability during the data processing or as an outcome of the data processing

Considering the layered and contextual definition of individual vulnerability as a higher risk of harms of fundamental rights, I observe that in the data protection field, we should distinguish two different moments in which vulnerability can manifest itself: (i) vulnerability *during* the data processing and (ii) vulnerability as a *consequence* of the data processing. This distinction is not only about the 'timing' of manifestation but also about its nature: during the data processing the data subjects might be vulnerable to the higher risk of losing control of their personal data (they may be incapable of reading or understanding privacy policies, they may have difficulty in refusing consent and exercising their data protection rights) and so they are vulnerable *to the data processing itself*. In addition, the data subject might be vulnerable to other fundamental rights as a consequence of the data processing (eg discrimination, mental manipulation, freedom of movement). In this case, we can see that there are risks to the vulnerable data subject related not to the data processing itself but to the *outcomes of the data processing*.

Under the first perspective, vulnerability can emerge, for example, in limited capabilities to provide valid consent for data collection, to understand information about data processing, or to execute data protection rights adequately. Those limitations may result from various factors like age, disability, or socio-economic position. Typical examples include children, the elderly, or a person with cognitive diseases or linguistic issues (non-native language speaker, for instance) who may have a problem understanding data protection notices and giving informed consent; employees that feel compelled to consent to the processing of their data by or to their employer; consumers that are locked into monopolistic (or quasi-monopolistic) social networks and give their consent even under undesirable

[11] F Luna, 'Elucidating the Concept of Vulnerability: Layers Not Labels' (2009) 2 International Journal of Feminist Approaches to Bioethics 121; F Luna, 'Identifying and Evaluating Layers of Vulnerability—A Way Forward' (2019) 19 Developing World Bioethics 86.

terms and conditions; users who might be exploited in their cognitive biases (with or without the use of hidden patterns)[12] to accept data protection conditions, etc.

Under the second perspective, the vulnerability in the data protection framework is more related to understanding the risks of harm[13] to which individuals are exposed. As explained by some commentators, data-driven systems can serve as tools of potential discrimination and manipulation or may lead to physical and psychological harms. Different examples from law enforcement, welfare, banking, and housing demonstrate that those technologies can reinforce social inequalities and lead to discrimination in the access to services, goods, or other elements.[14] This discussion often focuses on harmful biases embedded in models, training data, and problematic definitions.[15] Similarly, some controversial examples of personal data-driven research are accused of reproducing inflammatory stereotypes and creating life-threatening situations for marginalized communities.[16]

4. Effects of data subjects' vulnerability

The general definition of vulnerability that seems to arise from different sources is the significant likelihood of incurring identifiable *harm* to fundamental rights and freedoms while substantially lacking the ability or means to protect oneself.[17]

[12] R Ducato and E Marique, 'Come to the Dark Side: We Have Patterns. Choice Architecture and Design for (Un)Informed Consent' (Social Science Research Network 2018) SSRN Scholarly Paper ID 3365952 <https://papers.ssrn.com/abstract=3365952> accessed 31 May 2020; CM Gray and others, 'The Dark (Patterns) Side of UX Design' in *Proceedings of the 2018 CHI Conference on Human Factors in Computing Systems* (ACM 2018).

[13] About the notion of 'harm' and its complex ambiguity in the vulnerability discussion, see the final section of Chapter 3.

[14] J Angwin and J Larson, 'Bias in Criminal Risk Scores is Mathematically Inevitable, Researchers Say' ProPublica, December 2016 <https://www.propublica.org/article/bias-in-criminal-risk-scores-is-mathematically-inevitable-researchers-say> accessed 20 February 2023; V Eubanks, *Automating Inequality: How High-Tech Tools Profile, Police, and Punish the Poor* (St Martin's Press 2018) 1–13; F Pasquale, *The Black Box Society: The Secret Algorithms That Control Money and Information* (Harvard University Press 2015) 1–18; L Edwards and M Veale, 'Slave to the Algorithm? Why a 'Right to an Explanation' Is Probably Not the Remedy You Are Looking For' (2017) 16(1) Duke Law & Technology Review 2–32.

[15] For example S Barocas, 'Data Mining and the Discourse on Discrimination,' in *Proceedings of the Data Ethics Workshop, Conference on Knowledge Discovery and Data Mining (KDD)* (2014) 4; DK Citron, 'Promoting Innovation While Preventing Discrimination: Policy Goals for the Scored Society' Washington Law Review 89 (2014): 1413; OH Gandy, 'It's Discrimination, Stupid!' in J Brook (ed), *Resisting the Virtual Life: The Culture and Politics of Information* (City Lights Books 1995) 35–47; T Zarsky, 'Understanding Discrimination in the Scored Society' (2014) 89(4) Washington Law Review 1375–412.

[16] J Metcalf, '"The Study Has Been Approved by the IRB': Gayface AI, Research Hype and the Pervasive Data Ethics Gap' (*Medium*, 2017) <https://medium.com/pervade-team/the-study-has-been-approved-by-the-irb-gayface-ai-research-hype-and-the-pervasive-data-ethics-ed76171b882c> accessed 19 October 2019.

[17] D Schroeder and E Gefenas, 'Vulnerability: Too Vague and Too Broad?' (2009) 18 Cambridge Quarterly of Healthcare Ethics 113; RE Goodin, *Protecting the Vulnerable: A Reanalysis of Our Social Responsibilities* (University of Chicago Press 1985).

Accordingly, the next question we can pose when analysing individual vulnerability in the data protection framework is: vulnerable to which *risk of harm*?

As already affirmed, there are two types of data subjects' vulnerability that we can identify: processing-based vulnerability (vulnerability *during the data processing*) and effect-based vulnerability (vulnerability to *the outcome* of the data processing). These two types of vulnerability have different effects on data subjects.

As regards vulnerability *during the data processing*, the effects of vulnerability can be, for example:

1. the data subject being incapable of understanding information about the data processing (eg data protection policy notices) or understanding the significance and envisaged effects of some data processing;[18]
2. the data subject being incapable of freely giving their consent to data processing;[19]
3. the data subject being incapable of exercising their data protection rights adequately or understanding the significance and consequences of such rights.[20]

If one of these circumstances applies, the data subject will lose control of their personal data. This would result in an evident interference with the fundamental right to privacy and data protection.

Regarding vulnerability as the *outcome of data processing*, some data subjects might be at higher risk of interference in their fundamental rights and freedoms than others. As Recital 4 GDPR, the Article 29 Data Protection Working Party on the Protection of Individuals with regard to the Processing of Personal Data (WP29),[21] and the European Data Protection Board (EDPB)[22] affirm, the reference to '*the rights and freedoms*' of the data subjects in the GDPR primarily concerns:

1. the right to privacy and data protection, which is already the case in processing-based vulnerability ('during' the data processing),[23] but may also involve other fundamental rights such as:

[18] Recital 38, GDPR.

[19] WP29, Guidelines on Consent, WP259 rev.01, 5.

[20] Recital 38, GDPR.

[21] WP29, Guidelines on Data Protection Impact Assessment (DPIA), WP248, 15.

[22] See eg European Data Protection Board, Letter in reply to Sophie In't Veld, Ref: OUT2020-0004, 29 January 2020, 4.

[23] The reference to 'risk of harm' is problematic, especially if we focus on this first point (risk of harm to the fundamental rights to privacy and data protection), where the demonstrability of the harm might appear more problematic. However, as affirmed in the last section of Chapter 3, this book does not assume that vulnerability depends on demonstrable harms, but to the 'higher risks' of interference with data subjects' fundamental rights and freedoms. Chapter 7will focus largely on this open issue and will conclude that the generic reference to 'harms' (that authors from other disciplines often made when referring to human vulnerability) should be meant as, at least, a 'legal or similarly significant effects' on data subjects.

2. freedom of speech;
3. freedom of thought;
4. freedom of movement;
5. prohibition of discrimination,
6. right to liberty, freedom of conscience, and religion;
7. freedom to conduct a business.

Several violations of these rights may overlap and there might be cascade effects. However, in general terms, vulnerable data subjects are more likely than non-vulnerable subjects to suffer the impact of violations of rights and freedoms.

Chapter 7 will propose a more detailed analysis of the impact of data processing on vulnerable data subject, comparing different levels of effects under the GDPR. This current section has served as a basis for understanding how the two different types of vulnerabilities in the GDPR (processing-based vulnerability, in other words, vulnerability during the data processing; and effect-based vulnerability, that is, vulnerability to the outcome of data processing) differ in terms of the effects they have on data subjects. This analysis of the effects and manifestations of vulnerability will profit from comparing the consumer vulnerability literature mentioned in Chapter 3.

5. How consumer vulnerability literature could inform the analysis on vulnerable subjects in the data protection framework

As observed in Chapter 2, González Fuster suggests looking at the notion of average and vulnerable data subjects in comparison with the concept of average and vulnerable consumers in the EU consumer protection law.[24] Similarly, other scholars call for an integrated approach to data protection and consumer law, particularly for what concerns the analysis of and the reaction to 'consumer vulnerability'.[25] I am aware that the discussion on consumer protection often offers a limited and non-exhaustive approach to the data protection framework. Focusing on the analogy between data subjects and consumers is helpful but may lead to too individualistic and market-oriented perceptions, ignoring more structural perspectives based on societal dynamics and public–private power relations. However, although I am aware of these limitations and weaknesses, consumer

[24] González Fuster (n 6) 99.

[25] N Helberger and others, 'The Perfect Match? A Closer Look at the Relationship between Eu Consumer Law and Data Protection Law' (2017) 54 Common Market Law Review 1427, 1456–458. A similar call for an integrative approach between Data Protection Law and Consumer and Competition Law can be found in I Graef and others, 'Fairness and Enforcement: Bridging Competition, Data Protection, and Consumer Law' (2018) 8 International Data Privacy Law 200.

protection analyses can still provide mature elaborations on the concepts of human vulnerability and power imbalance. One of the challenges for future research is to consider these elaborations via a prudent and critical comparison with the data protection framework.

A first exercise is place the analyses of factors and effects of consumer vulnerability that I made in Chapter 2 Section 8 in context within the data protection framework.

As regards factors (individual characteristics, the power of the supplier, and vulnerability drivers), we can quickly identify that the personal characteristics of consumers and data subjects are similar, and the possible data processing practices of data controllers can generate vulnerability in data subjects (see point 5 of Table 4.1). In sum, we can identify three groups of factors of data subjects' vulnerability:

Table 4.1 How the five effects of consumer vulnerability would arise in the data protection framework

Dimensions of consumer vulnerability (EC Report, 2016)	How these dimensions would arise in the data protection framework
1. *Heightened risk of negative outcomes on well-being*	Some data processing might have negative impact on well-being of the data subjects (more specifically, on their fundamental rights and freedoms)
2. *Having characteristics that limit the ability to maximize well-being*	Personal characteristics of data subjects (age, literacy, mental conditions, etc) might contribute to the negative impacts of data processing on well-being (on their fundamental rights and freedoms)
3. *Having difficulty in obtaining or assimilating information*	Some data subjects (including eg children) might have problems in reading and understanding information policies about data processing
4. *Inability or failure to buy, choose, or access suitable products*	Some data subjects (including eg children) might have problems in making a decision as to whether or not to give consent to data processing or how to exercise data protection rights (eg withdrawing the consent, object, erasure, portability, etc), or to choose services based on data protection by design and by default.
5. *Higher susceptibility to marketing practices, creating imbalances in market interactions*	This dimension could refer to hidden patterns exercised by, and unfair practices of the data controller to unduly induce data subjects to give consent to data processing. In general, higher susceptibility might depend on the personalization of these marketing practices. Such personalization might come from automated profiling. However, this should be considered as a manifestation of negative impact on individual well-being (point 1).

1. the data subject's personal characteristics (eg age, ethnicity, gender, sexual orientation, cognitive capacity, temporary emotions, etc);
2. the data controller's power and potentialities (eg information asymmetries, hierarchical asymmetries, data mining capabilities, predictive capabilities);
3. vulnerability drivers (eg intrusive practices that actively exploit subjects' vulnerabilities; structural or technical factors that indirectly influence vulnerability; geographical or socio-economic contexts; political or institutional factors).

As regards five dimensions of vulnerability identified by the European Commission Study as shown in Section 8 (negative outcome on well-being; personal characteristics; informational vulnerability; inability to buy; choose or access suitable products; higher susceptibility to marketing practices), we can easily consider them also in the data protection field. Table 4.1 shows how the five dimensions might be relevant for the data protection field.

After this comparison, further consideration seems necessary as the data protection field is different from other legal fields. As noted, the EU data protection law[26] focuses on protecting the fundamental rights and freedoms of any individual whose personal data are being processed.[27] This is clear not just in Article 1(2) but also in the risk-based approach (Article 24) and the data protection impact assessment model: the data protection framework is a tool for protecting all fundamental rights and freedoms of data subjects. In other terms, the scope of application of data protection is more comprehensive than in consumer law, which is based on individuals' economic well-being.[28] Accordingly, the analysis of consumer vulnerability can be a relevant starting point to analyse data subjects' vulnerability,[29] but it is intrinsically limited. Put differently, it is impossible to make a pure analogy between the analysis of consumer vulnerability and the analysis of data subjects' vulnerability. What is different is the motivation to protect vulnerable individuals, in other words the reply to the question: 'vulnerable to what?' (as analysed in the previous section).

However, the analysis of consumer vulnerability seems fruitful for the data protection framework. The vulnerability drivers and the effects of vulnerability are also applicable in the data protection framework. This comparison teaches us that the

[26] The complex nature of the fundamental right to data protection emerges from the combined reading of the Treaty on the Functioning of the European Union (which declares the right to personal data protection in art 16), the EU Charter of Fundamental Rights (which addresses the right to personal data protection in art 8) and the GDPR.

[27] See González Fuster (n 2) 163–206; Lynskey (n 2) 131.

[28] M Oostveen and K Irion, 'The Golden Age of Personal Data: How to Regulate an Enabling Fundamental Right?' in M Bakhoum and others (eds), *Personal Data in Competition, Consumer Protection and Intellectual Property Law: Towards a Holistic Approach?* (Springer Berlin Heidelberg 2018).

[29] Helberger and others (n 25) 1458.

analysis of individual vulnerability is multidimensional but is based on many factors (external, internal, drivers) and produces different manifestations. However, the five effects or manifestations of consumer vulnerability (see Table 4.1) can be observed in the data protection field under the two types of data subjects' vulnerability that I identified above: vulnerability to the data processing itself (or 'during' the data processing) and vulnerability to the outcome of the data processing.

As already explained, in the first case, I refer to individuals with reduced decision-making capabilities who might not understand information policies and risks involved in, and their rights regarding data processing. These data subjects might also be unable to give consent because their intellectual capabilities (ie they are children, elderly, mentally unwell) or their particular circumstances (they are in a situation of dependency, such as employees or patients) adversely affect the freedom to consent. In the second case, data subjects (regardless of their decision-making capabilities) might suffer from the outcome of data processing in terms of, for example, stigmatization and discrimination (in the case of automated profiling), manipulation (in the case of commercial micro-targeting), psychophysical damages (in case of a data breach), etc. Here what matters is not the ongoing data processing but the potential impact of the outcome of this data processing.

6. Manifestation of data subjects' vulnerability in the text of the GDPR: first analysis

Building on this analysis, it is necessary to refine our understanding of the notion of data subject vulnerability in the wording of the GDPR and explain why a *layered* approach to vulnerability might be constructive. Accordingly, this section analyses the wording of the GDPR and the interpretations offered by the WP29, now the EDPB.

The question to consider is this: what is the status of vulnerable persons in the GDPR, and how could we solve the dichotomy between universal and particular vulnerability when interpreting the wording of the GDPR?

In the Data Protection Directive (DPD), there was no mention of vulnerability. Moreover, there was no special protection for children and no provisions about the risk of power imbalance in sensitive contexts (eg in the case of consent provision).

Although the GDPR made essential steps forward to protect vulnerable data subjects, the original proposal did not contain any specific reference to vulnerability. In particular, in the original European Commission proposal of the GDPR in 2012, there was no reference to vulnerable individuals, not even in the preamble. The concept of vulnerability was used in Recital 42 for the definition of sensitive data ('personal data which are, by their nature, particularly ... vulnerable in relation to fundamental rights or privacy, deserve specific protection').[30] In the finally

[30] Proposal for a Regulation of the European Parliament and of the Council on the protection of individuals with regard to the processing of personal data and on the free movement of such data (General Data Protection Regulation) 2012.

approved version, this reference was removed, but the legislator added the reference to 'vulnerable data subjects, especially children' among the risk indexes to be considered to assess the level of risk of data processing (Recital 75). In addition, the European Parliament proposed to define children as 'vulnerable consumers' in the preamble of the GDPR (Recital 29).[31] However, this proposal was not adopted in the final text, but the link between children and vulnerability was kept in the consolidated version of Recital 75.

However, the GDPR does not contain an explicit definition of vulnerable data subjects. As said, there is just a slight reference in Recital 75 about relevant risks to consider when performing a Data Protection Impact Assessment: 'where personal data of *vulnerable natural persons, in particular of children*, are processed'. 'In particular' means that children are vulnerable subjects, but it also implies that other data subjects might be considered vulnerable too. The situation of children is addressed in the GDPR through special requirements for consent for information society services (Article 8) and specific transparency duties towards children (Article 12(1)).[32] Considering that children are specifically vulnerable data subjects, one may conclude that the GDPR approach to vulnerability is *particular* and not universal: only some groups (namely, children) are vulnerable. However, as already affirmed, the definition of the data subject is universal and unique[33] and children are just one group at risk; other groups can be vulnerable to similar risks (elderly, people with cognitive impairment, etc).

In Recital 38 the GDPR offers a justification for the *sui generis* protection for children: 'children merit specific protection with regard to their personal data, as they may be less aware of the risks, consequences and safeguards concerned and their rights in relation to the processing of personal data'. In other words, a lack of awareness and understanding about consequences and legal rights (what can be called decision-making vulnerability) justifies the special protection afforded to children. The idea of the decision-making vulnerability of children is then reaffirmed in Recital 65, which emphasizes the problem of consent in the context of

[31] Draft European Parliament legislative resolution on the proposal for a regulation of the European Parliament and of the Council on the protection of individuals with regard to the processing of personal data and on the free movement of such data (General Data Protection Regulation) (COM(2012)0011—C7-0025/2012—2012/0011(COD)) (Ordinary legislative procedure: first reading) <https://www.europarl.europa.eu/doceo/document/A-7-2013-0402_EN.html?redirect#title1> accessed 20 February 2023, Amendment 11.

[32] About the topic of children data protection see, in general, L Jasmontaite and P De Hert, 'The EU, Children under 13 Years, and Parental Consent: A Human Rights Analysis of a New, Age-Based Bright-Line for the Protection of Children on the Internet' (2014) 5 International Data Privacy Law 20–33; A Mantelero, 'Children Online and the Future EU Data Protection Framework: Empirical Evidences and Legal Analysis' (2016) 2 International Journal of Technology Policy and Law 169–81; E Lievens and V Verdoodt, 'Looking for Needles in a Haystack: Key Issues Affecting Children's Rights in the General Data Protection Regulation' (2018) 34(2) Computer Law & Security Review 269–78; S van der Hof, 'I Agree… Or Do I? A Rights-Based Analysis of the Law on Children's Consent in the Digital World' (2017) 34(2) Wisconsin International Law Journal 409–45; S van der Hof and E Lievens, 'The Importance of Privacy by Design and Data Protection Impact Assessments in Strengthening Protection of Children's Personal Data Under the GDPR' (2018) 23 Communications Law 33.

[33] See WP29, Opinion 4/2007 on the concept of personal data, WP136, 21–22.

erasing personal data. Additionally, Recital 58 reveals that the reason for protection is mainly based on children's reduced capacity for understanding. Building on these considerations, one may wonder whether some of the rationales for protecting children in the data protection framework can be considered—by analogy—for other vulnerable adults. The WP29 has remarked in several opinions that vulnerability is not limited to children.

In particular, the WP29 argues that the identifying factor for individual vulnerability is the power imbalance between the data subject and the data controller. Power imbalance means that individuals may be 'unable to easily consent to, or oppose, the processing of their data, or exercise their rights'. The WP29 lists some vulnerable data subjects: children, since 'they can be considered as not able to knowingly and thoughtfully oppose or consent to the processing of their data'; employees; more vulnerable segments of the population requiring special protection ('mentally ill persons, asylum seekers, or the elderly, patients, etc.'); and 'in any case where an imbalance in the relationship between the position of the data subject and the controller can be identified'.[34]

Here the link between *power imbalance* and *vulnerability* of data subjects is clear: when the data controller is in a position of significant power (in particular in terms of hierarchical or institutional superiority; possible impacts on the fundamental rights and freedoms of the data subject; significant information asymmetry based on predictive analytics, etc) towards the data subject, the latter should be considered vulnerable if that power imbalance may result in adverse effects for the subject.

We can find similar wording in the WP29 Opinion on legitimate interests.[35] When data controllers perform the balancing test that is required if they want to process personal data on the basis of legitimate interests,[36] they need to consider the nature and source of the legitimate interest, whether there are additional safeguards available to protect the data subject, and what is the impact on the data subject, considering in particular 'the status of the data controller and data subject, including the *balance of power between the data subject and the data controller*, or whether the data subject is a child or otherwise *belongs to a more vulnerable segment of the population*'.[37] Again, we observe the link between the idea of vulnerability and *power imbalance*. In particular, vulnerability is considered as a contextual notion: 'the question whether the data subject is an employee, a student, a patient, or whether there is otherwise an imbalance in the relationship between the

[34] WP29, Guidelines on Data Protection Impact Assessment (DPIA) and determining whether processing is 'likely to result in a high risk' for the purposes of Regulation 2016/679, WP 248 rev.01, 10.

[35] WP29, Opinion 06/2014 on the 'Notion of legitimate interests of the data controller under Article 7 of Directive 95/46/EC'.

[36] I Kamara and P De Hert, 'Understanding the Balancing Act behind the Legitimate Interest of the Controller Ground: A Pragmatic Approach' in E Selinger and others (eds), *The Cambridge Handbook of Consumer Privacy* (1st edn, Cambridge University Press 2018).

[37] WP29, Opinion 06/2014 on the 'Notion of legitimate interests of the data controller under Article 7 of Directive 95/46/EC', 51. Emphasis added.

position of the data subject and the controller must certainly be also relevant. It is important *to assess the effect of actual processing on particular individuals*.'[38] The WP29 Guidelines on Purpose Limitation under the Data Protection Directive and the WP29 Guidelines on Transparency articulated similar views.[39]

The WP29 has also expanded the understanding of vulnerable groups beyond children when addressing the meaning of 'significant effects' under Article 22, GDPR. In that Opinion, the WP29 clarifies that when assessing the automated decision-making effects on individuals, one factor to consider is whether the controller used 'knowledge of the vulnerabilities of the data subjects targeted'.[40] The notion of vulnerability is highly related to adverse impacts: 'processing that might have little impact on individuals generally may, in fact, have a significant effect for certain groups of society, such as minority groups or *vulnerable adults*'.[41]

The notion of vulnerability in the texts mentioned above seems to refer both to vulnerability *during* the data processing (ie decision-making vulnerability related to the collection of data, the provision of consent, and to the exercise of the data subject rights)[42] and to vulnerability to the *outcome* of the data processing (ie higher risk of harms arising as a result of the data processing).

Apart from the mere decision-making aspect of vulnerability (eg regarding children's vulnerability), the WP29 also engages in the debate about *harm* that particular processing of data may produce. In the Guidelines on the Data Protection Impact Assessments, the vulnerability of data subjects is considered one of the nine factors for identifying cases of high risk of harm caused by data processing under Article 35 GDPR. Recital 75 suggests that the reason why vulnerable data subjects (in general, not only children) require special attention when determining whether a specific instance of data processing poses a high risk of harm to the rights and freedoms of natural persons: risks to rights and freedoms 'may result from personal data processing which could lead to physical, material or non-material damage, in particular ... where personal data of vulnerable natural persons, in particular of children, are processed'.[43] In other words, some subjects should be protected not only because of their limited capacity to understand and give consent to the processing of their data but also of the higher risk of material or non-material damages being imposed on them. The examples might be several: some individuals are more at risk of discrimination during automated data processing (in particular in case of, eg, automated profiling); other data subjects' freedom of thought might be

[38] ibid 41. Emphasis added.

[39] WP29, Opinion 03/2013 on purpose limitation, WP 203, 32; WP29, Guidelines on Transparency under Regulation 2016/679 clarifying requirements of the EU GDPR, WP 260, 9.

[40] WP29, Guidelines on Automated individual decision-making and Profiling for the purposes of Regulation 2016/679, WP 251 rev.01, 22.

[41] ibid 22.

[42] WP29, Guidelines on Data Protection Impact Assessment (DPIA) and determining whether processing is 'likely to result in a high risk' for the purposes of Regulation 2016/679, WP 248 rev.01, 10.

[43] See Recital 75, GDPR.

more easily impaired when their data are processed for direct marketing purposes; other people might incur more significant physical or psychological damages as a result of a data breach, etc. I am aware that children comprise a category that has both vulnerability of decision-making capacity and higher risks of harm. However, we can imagine categories of data subjects who have no such limited decision-making capacity but can still suffer from higher risks of harm from the processing of their data.

In sum, I have analysed how the GDPR addresses the definition of vulnerable subjects and what kind of manifestations of vulnerability are taken into account in the data protection framework. We can observe a tension between a universal notion of vulnerability (since there is no reference to vulnerable groups, merely an open reference to vulnerability in Recital 75) and a particular notion (children alone are mentioned as an example and there are specific safeguards that only concern them).

However, it seems that the GDPR is open to both approaches: particularism and universalism. As Chapters 5 and 6 will argue, the solution to this apparent contradiction is in the notion of 'risk', which is close to Luna's idea of 'layers' of vulnerability. The risk-based approach in the GDPR suggests a layered analysis of vulnerability: everyone is potentially vulnerable, but at varying levels and contexts.

In sum, vulnerability risks *during the data processing* (ie vulnerability as regards decision-making related to the collection of data, and the lack of capability to exercise rights concerning that data) are the declared rationale for protecting the only vulnerable category made explicit (ie children). However, Recital 75 and the WP29 put more significant emphasis on the vulnerability risks arising as an *outcome* of the processing of data.

7. Children as the typical vulnerable data subjects

Children are generally considered the typical vulnerable subject. The European Court of Human Rights (ECtHR) has recognized the inherent vulnerability of children in several cases.[44] Such vulnerability has been justified on two bases: children's dependency on their family, and their consequent limited autonomy. However, considering their particular conditions, scholars noted that children's autonomy—from a legal perspective—is a 'gradated' autonomy, based on their increasing maturity with age.[45]

[44] For a comprehensive analysis of the ECtHR jurisprudence on children's vulnerability see F Ippolito, '(De)Constructing Children's Vulnerability under European Law' in F Ippolito and SI Sanchez (eds), *Protecting Vulnerable Groups* (Hart Publishing 2015).

[45] ibid.

Regarding the digital environment, some scholars emphasized the risks related to children's presence online and the processing of children's personal data even before the advent of the GDPR.[46] These risks induced several commentators to suggest special provisions on children's consent to the processing of data concerning them,[47] while other scholars recommended additional positive obligations on the data processor,[48] including education.[49]

The GDPR, for the first time in the EU legislation, acknowledges that children should have 'specific protection' of their personal data.[50] The preamble of the GDPR clarifies the reasons for this protection: minors 'may be less aware of the risks, consequences and safeguards concerned and their rights in relation to the processing of personal data'.[51] In addition, the GDPR explains that, since children's data processing might result in particularly likely and severe risks to their rights and freedoms, they are 'vulnerable natural persons'.[52] Combining these two considerations in the preamble of the Regulation, we can affirm that the rationale for addressing children differently from other data subjects seems to be at least twofold: (i) they know and understand less than average adults; and (ii) data processing can have a worse impact for children than for their adult counterparts. This dualism was never clearly explained or clarified in the legislative procedure of the GDPR.[53]

This lack of clarity seems quite evident if we observe one of the most important GDPR provisions about children ('parental consent').[54] Article 8(1) introduces the 'parental consent' rule for children who are users of information society services; the processing of personal data of a child under the age of 16 is lawful only if consent is given or authorized by the holder of parental responsibility for the child. This is perhaps one of the most robust vulnerability-aware safeguards in the GDPR. Although it is clear that children are considered vulnerable data subjects who are incapable of autonomously giving valid consent to data processing, the reason for this vulnerability is not specified. Three possible reasons might be: (i) considering their limited age, there is a presumption of 'clear imbalance' between children and controllers, which would make impossible the provision of a 'free' consent; (ii) children are too young to be adequately informed about data processing and

[46] S Livingstone and L Haddon (eds), *Children, Risk and Safety on the Internet: Research and Policy Challenges in Comparative Perspective* (Policy Press 2012).

[47] Jasmontaite and De Hert (n 32); Mantelero (n 32); van der Hof (n 32).

[48] For the notion of 'positive obligations' in the field of children's vulnerability see Ippolito (n 44).

[49] D Rosani, 'Child's Participation Online and the General Data Protection Regulation—A Dialogue between Educational and Legal Sciences Is Urgently Needed' (2018) 6 MerzWissenschaft 41.

[50] Recital (38) of the GDPR

[51] ibid.

[52] Recital (75) of the GDPR.

[53] See Ga González Fuster, 'GDPR: We All Need to Work at It!' (*Better Internet for Kids*, 31 March 2016) <https://www.betterinternetforkids.eu/practice/articles/article> accessed 29 May 2021.

[54] G Malgieri and G González Fuster, 'The Vulnerable Data Subject: A Gendered Data Subject?' (2022) 13(2) European Journal of Law and Technology <https://www.ejlt.org/index.php/ejlt/article/view/843> accessed 7 February 2023.

their consequent limited knowledge makes them incapable of giving 'informed' consent;[55] (iii) the impact of some data processing activities on them might be too severe or too probable, and, thus, the processing of children's data is so risky[56] that consent is not an adequate legal basis on which to allow the processing to occur; (iv) all the previous points.[57]

A clarification on this point would also have helped the national implementation of the GDPR: Article 8(1) of the GDPR allows the Member States to 'provide by law for a lower age for [parental consent] provided that such lower age is not below 13 years'. Considering the different hypotheses on the 'sources' of children's vulnerability, the Member States set a variety of different ages, including 13, 14, 15, and 16 years as the cut-off point.[58]

An unwanted effect of these provisions about parental consent (and of their fragmented implementation) was that some data controllers, artificially rejecting the fact that they target children, might be trying to avoid compliance with child-related rules in the GDPR. The consequence is that many digital services are organized to completely negate the possibility that minors' personal data are processed, depriving them of even the most essential data protection safeguards.[59]

The European Commission has already identified the lack of clarity and the circumvention of rules in its assessment of the first two years of application of the GDPR.[60] In particular, the Commission affirmed that national differences in the age of parental consent create '*uncertainty to children and their parents as to the application of their data protection rights in the Single Market*'[61] and that '*many organisations ignore [the fact] that children may be concerned by their data processing*'.[62] According to the European Commission, it is necessary to explore whether some possible amendments to the GDPR might solve these problems. A parallel solution suggested by the Commission is that Data Protection Authorities (DPAs) adopt specific guidelines to provide tools clarifying and supporting the application of

55 Van der Hof (n 32) 127.

56 Mantelero (n 32).

57 See, in general, Jasmontaite and De Hert (n 32); I Milkaite and E Lievens, 'Status Quo Regarding the Child's Article 8 GDPR Age of Consent for Data Processing across the EU' (*Better Internet for Kids*, 20 December 2019) <https://www.betterinternetforkids.eu/practice/articles/article> accessed 29 May 2021; Lievens and Verdoodt (n 32).

58 Milkaite and Lievens (n 57).

59 Malgieri and González Fuster (n 54) mentioning the case of Kelloggs, Fanta, and Tik Tok. J Grierson, 'Kellogg's UK Prompts Anger by Branding Frosties an Adult Cereal' *Guardian* (1 December 2017) <http://www.theguardian.com/society/2017/dec/01/kelloggs-uk-anger-branding-frosties-adult-cereal-sugar> accessed 29 May 2021.

60 European Commission, *Communication to the Council and to the European Parliament: Data protection as a pillar of citizens' empowerment and the EU's approach to the digital transition—Two years of application of the General Data Protection Regulation*, COM(2020) 264 final, Brussels, 24 June 2020.

61 ibid 16.

62 European Commission, *Commission Staff working document accompanying the Communication to the Council and to the European Parliament: Data protection as a pillar of citizens' empowerment and the EU's approach to the digital transition—Two years of application of the General Data Protection Regulation*, COM(2020) 264 final, Brussels, SWD(2020) 115 final.

data protection rules to children.[63] Some DPAs have already implemented these guidelines.[64]

In sum, the kind of protection that responds to the vulnerability of children is a remarkable novelty of the GDPR. However, at least in the first years of application, this specific protection has been considered to be among the main failures of the GDPR: the legislator intended to protect children but the final effect—in many cases—was ineffective. It is essential to consider these remarks when proposing policy recommendations for reform of the GDPR that takes vulnerability into consideration.

8. Classifying data subjects' vulnerability in relation to power imbalance

After this overview, considering the WP29 definition of vulnerability, we still need to analyse an essential aspect of data subjects' vulnerability in the GDPR: *power imbalance*. Indeed, we observed that the general WP29 definition of data subjects' vulnerability is (apart from a non-exhaustive list of cases) 'any case where an *imbalance* in the relationship between the position of the data subject and the controller can be identified'.[65] Accordingly, this section contextualizes the power imbalance reflections proposed in Chapter 2 into the data protection framework. The questions I address here are: what is the role of power imbalance in the GDPR, and when can power imbalance be considered significant enough to induce data subjects' vulnerability?

In privacy and data protection discussions, the notion of power is pivotal. De Hert and Gutwirth have discussed privacy and data protection in terms of opacity and transparency,[66] suggesting that information asymmetry could be the source of power imbalance in the information society. In legal terms, the first international legal text about data protection, the Council of Europe's Convention 108, in the explanatory report refers to '*information power* ... of the data users in the private and public sector' as one of the issues to mitigate through the Convention.[67]

Scholarly literature in the field of privacy law has also broadly referred to power imbalance. In particular, Daniel Solove theorized privacy as a tool to contrast power

[63] COM(2020) 264 final, p 16.

[64] Information Commissioner Officer (ICO), 'Children and the GDPR' (ICO 2020) <https://ico.org.uk/for-organisations/guide-to-data-protection/guide-to-the-general-data-protection-regulation-gdpr/children-and-the-gdpr/> accessed 28 March 2020.

[65] WP29, Guidelines on Data Protection Impact Assessment, 10. Emphasis added.

[66] P De Hert and S Gutwirth, 'Privacy, Data Protection and Law Enforcement. Opacity of the Individual and Transparency of Power' in E Claes and others (ed), *Privacy and the Criminal Law* (Intersentia 2006).

[67] Council of Europe, Explanatory Report to the Convention for the Protection of Individuals with regard to Automatic Processing of Personal Data Strasbourg, 28 January 1981, 1. Emphasis added.

imbalance, mostly between individuals and public administration.[68] Similarly, Julie Cohen analyses privacy, surveillance, and self-exposure under the perspective of relational power.[69] Austin contrasts the harm paradigm with the power paradigm in the privacy realm.[70] She suggests reconsidering privacy under the notion of power, in particular as a rebalancing tool based on 'power over' (power over something, a spatial power, based on constraining public power in particular in the surveillance field) and 'power to' (power to do something, empowering individuals to undertake actions that they would not have otherwise been able to take).[71] In addition, Ryan Calo assumes such a reconceptualization of privacy in terms of power control. The analysis of power is a basis for his theory of privacy as a mitigation tool for vulnerability.[72] The link between data privacy, power, and vulnerability appears, thus, crucial.[73]

Reconsidering our taxonomy of power imbalance in Section 3, I observe that different fields of law have adopted different approaches to control power imbalance. For example, EU consumer protection law is considered to have a 'relational' approach. Indeed, what triggers consumer protection is not the effects (causes) of specific practices but the roles and contexts between two subjects (the supplier and the consumer).[74] Instead, EU competition law is based on a causal-structural understanding of power: competition rules and sanctions occur when specific effects are caused, considering the structure (of society, of the market, of institutions) in general and not the relationship between two particular parties.[75]

In the EU data protection framework, the approach to power imbalance is hybrid. Indeed, in general terms, the data protection framework has a *causal* understanding of power, given that it is based on the prevention of adverse effects.[76] Indeed, the GDPR focuses on the impact on fundamental rights and freedoms in

[68] DJ Solove, 'Privacy and Power: Computer Databases and Metaphors for Information Privacy' (2001) 53 Stanford Law Review 1393, 1399.

[69] JE Cohen, *Configuring the Networked Self* (Yale University Press 2012) Chapter 6 passim. On the link between privacy and power in the work of the same author, see also JE Cohen, 'Turning Privacy Inside Out' (2019) 20 Theoretical Inquiries in Law 22.

[70] L Austin, 'Enough About Me: Why Privacy Is About Power, Not Consent (or Harm)' in A Sarat (ed), *A World without Privacy: What Law Can and Should Do?* (Cambridge University Press 2014) 131–89 <doi:10.1017/CBO9781139962964.004>.

[71] ibid 189.

[72] Calo (n 4) 601.

[73] Recently, even the European data protection framework has been analysed through the lens of power and power imbalance. Richter tried to introduce a holistic model for regulating personal data in the EU under the perspective of power analysis. See H Richter, 'The Power Paradigm in Private Law' in M Bakhoum and others (eds), *Personal Data in Competition, Consumer Protection and Intellectual Property Law: Towards a Holistic Approach?* (Springer Berlin Heidelberg 2018).

[74] ibid 541.

[75] ibid 544; H Schweitzer, 'Wettbewerbsrecht und Das Problem Privater Macht in F. Möslein (Ed.)' in F Möslein (ed), *Private Macht* (Mohr Siebeck) 464.

[76] Richter (n 73) 556.

general.[77] Consistently, the risk-based approach is based on the expected effects on individuals[78] (*causal*), not on the fixed roles and circumstances.

However, in some cases, the power approach in the GDPR is more *modal*. For example, the restrictive rules for processing special categories of data[79] are not based on a specific impact analysis but on the context and modalities of data processing. More importantly, the notion of valid consent at Article 7(4) (as explained by Recital 43) and the obligation to give adequate and legible information to the data subjects (Articles 12–14) are based on a *modal* approach:[80] in these cases, what matters is not the specific effects of data processing on data subjects but the particular situation, status, or capacity of the data subject (eg being a child, an employee, a patient).

In sum, power imbalance is inherent in any data processing and that data protection law is a tool aimed at rebalancing this power asymmetry. However, the WP29 definition of a data subject's vulnerability is based on the *significant* power imbalance between the data controller and the data subject.[81] Similarly, some DPAs also define human vulnerability as a 'significant power imbalance'.[82] Thus, analysing power imbalance is essential to understand how vulnerability can be assessed and mitigated. In general terms, we observe a notion of *causal vulnerability* in the data protection rules: if some data subjects may be at higher risk of harm to their fundamental rights and freedoms, they are considered vulnerable, and the GDPR imposes special safeguards for them (see eg the Data Protection Impact Assessment (DPIA)). Recital 75 connects the idea of vulnerability to the risks of harm and impact assessment.

However, in some cases, there is no need to predict specific harms in order to protect vulnerable subjects; for example, in the case of information duties and consent provision, what matters is the particular capacity of the data subject (they are children, they are mentally incapacitated, etc) or the contextual relationship between the data subject and the data controller (a patient and a doctor; an employee and an employer, etc). Accordingly, in addition to the causal vulnerability, we can also observe an approach based on *modal* vulnerability.

[77] Article 1(2) of the GDPR, but also Recitals 2–4.

[78] See arts 24, 25, 35, GDPR.

[79] See art 9.

[80] Richter (n 73) 557–58.

[81] Recital 43 refers to a 'clear' power imbalance. See also WP29, Guidelines on DPIA, 10 refers to 'increased power imbalance'.

[82] See Slovenian Information Commissioner, 'The list of the kind of processing operations which are subject to the requirement for a Data Protection Impact Assessment under the Article 35(4) of the General Data Protection Regulation (EU) 2016/679 (GDPR)' <https://www.ip-rs.si/fileadmin/user_upload/Pdf/Ocene_ucinkov/SI_DPIA_list_35-4_35-6_Slovenia_revised_21dec2018_OBJAVA_ZA_WEB.pdf> accessed 20 February 2023. See in similar tone also the Polish Data Protection Agency, 'Proponowany wykaz rodzajów przetwarzania, dla których wymagane jest przeprowadzenie oceny skutków dla ochrony danych' <https://iapp.org/media/pdf/resource_center/poland_blacklist.pdf> accessed 20 February 2023.

In the previous sections, I have identified two manifestations of vulnerability: (i) vulnerability *during* the data processing (difficulty to read information policy, understand risks and rights, and ability to decide freely to provide consent) and (ii) vulnerability to *the outcomes* of data processing (risks of discrimination, manipulation, etc, as outcomes of the data processing).

We can compare these two manifestations of vulnerability to the analysis of the power imbalance mentioned above. Vulnerability *during* the data processing (i) is based on a modal-relational or modal-structural notion of vulnerability: the vulnerable individual is the person with limited control and choice about data protection rights. Vulnerability *to the outcomes* of the data processing (ii) is based on a causal-relational understanding of vulnerability: the vulnerable is the person at higher risks of adverse impacts (harms).

9. The proposed Artificial Intelligence Act: a new approach to vulnerable data subjects?

The previous sections of this chapter analysed the existing data protection provisions about vulnerable data subjects, while Chapter 3—comparing the different theoretical approaches to human vulnerability—proposes a 'layered' approach as an adequate way to address vulnerability issues.

Looking beyond the existing legislation, the proposed EU Artificial Intelligence Act (AIA) seems to refer to a layered approach to individual vulnerability.[83] Article 5 mentions 'people with vulnerabilities', instead of 'vulnerable people', when stating that what shall be prohibited—among other things—is 'the placing on the market, putting into service or use of an AI system that exploits *any of the vulnerabilities of a specific group of persons due to their age, physical or mental disability*,[84] in order to materially distort the behaviour of a person pertaining to that group in a manner that causes or is likely to cause that person or another person physical or psychological harm'.

Mentioning 'people with vulnerabilities' instead of 'vulnerable people' seems, indeed, an appropriate way to overcome the risks of stigmatization or 'labelling' connected to the traditional discussions on individual vulnerability,[85] though keeping the proactive approach of protecting some individuals at higher risks.[86]

[83] European Commission, 'Proposal for a Regulation of the European Parliament and of the Council laying down harmonised rules on Artificial Intelligence (Artificial Intelligence Act) and amending certain union legislative acts (sec(2021) 167 final)', Brussels, 21 April 2021.

[84] Emphasis added.

[85] C Mackenzie and others (eds), *Vulnerability: New Essays in Ethics and Feminist Philosophy* (1st edn, Oxford University Press 2013); Luna, 'Elucidating the Concept of Vulnerability' (n 11).

[86] A Cole, 'All of Us Are Vulnerable, But Some Are More Vulnerable than Others: The Political Ambiguity of Vulnerability Studies, an Ambivalent Critique' (2016) 17 Critical Horizons 260.

Although Article 5 of the Commission Proposal[87] specifies that only vulnerabilities related to age and disability are in the scope of the proposed Regulation, this idea of vulnerabilities as an eventual (and transient) attribute seems to be in line with a 'layered' approach to vulnerable subjects. However, it is unclear and subject to great debate whether this might be a deliberate and conscious choice of those who are responsible for drafting the proposal, or rather—as some authors suggested—an unwanted consequence of the cybersecurity legislation, in which the term 'vulnerabilities' is most common.[88]

Another passage of the AIA proposal also refers to human vulnerability. When updating the list of 'high-risk' AI systems and practices, the European Commission needs to pay attention to a possible 'vulnerable position' in which adversely impacted persons might find themselves in relation to an entity using an AI system, 'in particular due to an imbalance of power, knowledge, economic or social circumstances, or age' (Article 7(2)(e)). For the first time in EU legislation, these provisions would introduce a link between vulnerability and (power, information, economic, etc) *imbalance*. Such a link has already been identified in the data protection discussion.[89]

10. Concluding remarks

The main question of this chapter was whether the GDPR contains a notion of the vulnerable data subject and, if it does, what that definition is. I have already observed that the GDPR seems to have an implicit notion of the average data subject (well informed, circumspect), but this chapter showed that the GDPR also recognizes, implicitly, non-average data subjects.

Although the GDPR does not contain an explicit definition of vulnerable data subjects, there are at least two indirect references to vulnerable individuals: the special protection of children (Articles 8 and 12); and the notion of risk to fundamental rights and freedoms, including *inter alia* the analysis of whether data subjects are vulnerable to the risk of harm to their rights and freedoms (Recital 75).[90]

The rationale for protecting children is their decision-making vulnerability during the data processing, their incapability of understanding information about the processing (the implications, risks, and related rights), their inability to give

[87] Proposal for a Regulation of the European Parliament and of the Council laying down harmonised rules on Artificial Intelligence (Artificial Intelligence Act) and amending certain Union legislative acts. Brussels, 21 April 2021, COM(2021) 206 final 2021.

[88] Malgieri and González Fuster (n 54).

[89] WP29, 'Guidelines on Data Protection Impact Assessment (DPIA) and Determining Whether Processing Is 'Likely to Result in a High Risk' for the Purposes of Regulation 2016/679' (2017) 9; Malgieri and Niklas (n 3) 6–7.

[90] Indirectly, also the *sui generis* protection for special categories of personal data (see art 9) might be seen as a way to protect vulnerable data subjects. See Chapter 5.

valid consent and to exercise the data protection rights. Such a form of decision-making vulnerability concerns not only children but other data subjects too. The following two chapters analyse how a vulnerability-aware interpretation of the GDPR could help extend children's protection to other individuals.

The other rationale for protecting vulnerable data subjects, as suggested at Recital 75, is that these subjects are under higher risk of having their fundamental rights and freedoms harmed. In particular, we need to consider rights and freedoms protected in the EU Charter of Fundamental Rights.

Considering the contextual, relative, relational, and often temporary nature of such violations, it is impossible to enlist a range of vulnerable subjects from the outset. Potentially, any data subject can be vulnerable in a particular context or circumstance (because of, eg, the lack of freedom of consent, manipulation, discrimination, etc). Accordingly, the analysis must focus on the *layered* relationship between the data controller and the data subject. Put differently, what qualifies vulnerability is the specific power imbalance between data subjects and data controllers considering all particular characteristics involved and the higher risk of adverse effects for individuals.

As regards vulnerability layers, in Chapter 3, I have observed how law and economics scholars have analysed the three main groups of factors of consumer vulnerability: personal characteristics of consumers, external characteristics of suppliers, and vulnerability drivers. Table 4.2 contextualizes these three groups of factors in the data protection sphere.

In conclusion, this chapter sought to analyse whether the GDPR contains an (implicit or explicit) notion of vulnerable data subjects. We can reply that the GDPR does indeed contain such a notion (Section 2). Table 4.2 describes this notion, summarizing the main findings about data subjects' vulnerability. The types of vulnerability that I have found here are twofold (Section 3): processing-based vulnerability (ie vulnerability *during* the data processing) and effect-based vulnerability (vulnerability to the *outcomes* of data processing). The identifying criteria of these two types of vulnerability are different: in one case, it is the structural or institutional power imbalance that makes data subjects vulnerable within the exercise of their data protection rights; in the other case, it is the higher risk of adverse effects for some data subjects to make them vulnerable to the outcome of data processing. The two kinds of vulnerability also differ under several other perspectives: different impacts on individuals (see Section 4), different layers of vulnerability (see Section 5), different manifestations in the GDPR (see Section 6 and the particular case of children in Section 7), and different power imbalance structure (see Section 8). Regarding groups of factors, I proposed three elements: mental or social characteristics of the data subjects; hierarchical or information power of the data controller; and effectiveness of vulnerability drivers.

The distinction between the two different types of vulnerability is often blurred. There might be several overlaps between the two groups (eg, an individual

Table 4.2 Classification of the two types of data subjects' vulnerability based on manifestation, power imbalance, effects, factors

		Processing-based vulnerability	*Effect-based vulnerability*
Identifying criterion		*Relational power asymmetry*, eg hierarchical, institutional, mental dependence	Higher risks of *harms*
Manifestations in the Data Protection sphere (§8)		Vulnerability *during* the data processing (eg reading information, provision of consent, exercising data protection rights)	Vulnerability to the *outcome* of data processing (eg scoring, automated decisions)
Classification of vulnerability in relation to **power imbalance** (§9)		*Modal vulnerability*	*Causal vulnerability*
Effects, ie higher risks of (§10)		Limited capacity to: read or understand information about data processing; understand data protection rights and risks; give free and informed consent to the data processing	Discrimination, manipulation, limitations to freedom of speech, stigmatization, physical or psychological damages, etc
Groups of *Factors* of vulnerability (combining Luna's theory with consumer protection analysis)	Data subject's personal characteristics	For example, cognitive issues, linguistic issues, etc	For example, being part of a social minority group, being physically or mentally incapacitated
	Data controller's potentialities	For example, hierarchical or institutional dominance of the data controller on the data subject	For example, augmented information asymmetry (large amount of information held by the data controller and predictive capabilities of the data controller)
	Vulnerability drivers	Elements that the data controller can use to exploit decision-making vulnerability of the data subject (exploitative architectures, socio-economic or institutional factors, etc)	Mechanisms that the data controller can use to manipulate, discriminate, and stigmatize data subject

(*continued*)

Table 4.2 Continued

	Processing-based vulnerability	*Effect-based vulnerability*
Examples of vulnerable data subjects (in specific contexts, even temporarily)	Children, elderly, employees, patients, citizens when dealing with public administrations, mentally disabled persons, speakers of foreigner languages, asylum seekers, consumers affected by aggressive commercial practices, etc	Children, elderly, ethnic minorities, asylum seekers, sexual orientation, disabled persons, consumers affected by aggressive commercial practices, etc
How the GDPR reacts	Specific rules about information policies and transparency duties (Articles 12–15), freedom of consent (Article 7), etc	Risk-based approach, Data Protection by Design and By Default, DPIA

suffering from decision-making vulnerability *during* the data processing might also have higher adverse effects as an *outcome* of the data processing), and many conditions are often just temporary and difficult to detect. Although the notion of vulnerability as anticipated by the proposed EU AIA (Section 9) can be a meaningful step forward, it is necessary to focus further on the implications and possible implementations of the GDPR provisions that have the potential to protect vulnerable individuals. This is the goal of the following three chapters.

5

Data protection principles and vulnerable data subjects

1. Introduction

This chapter and Chapter 6 analyse how the interpretation of the whole text of the General Data Protection Regulation (GDPR) could address specific situations or circumstances of data subjects and, in particular, data subjects' vulnerability. Chapter 2 analysed the definition of the data subject under the GDPR and noticed how such a definition lacks an explicit consideration of different personal conditions of data subjects. In particular, there are no 'categories' of data subjects,[1] and no distinctions between the average data subject and vulnerable ones. However, in trying to improve our understanding of the conditions of data subjects, Chapter 2 compares the notion of the average consumer to a possible 'standard' data subject, also interpreting the wording of the GDPR. That chapter concludes that an 'average' data subject implicitly exists in the GDPR and is generally similar to the average consumer, a subject that is reasonably rational, observant, and circumspect.

However, the GDPR has also several provisions protecting data subjects' vulnerability. To understand whether, why, and how the GDPR also protects vulnerable data subjects, Chapter 3 investigated the general concept of vulnerable individuals in different fields: in philosophical terms, in law and economics literature, and in the practical implementation in EU primary and secondary law (with particular attention to consumer protection law and regulation of research).

Building on that, it has been possible to analyse why and how the notion of vulnerability can also be defined in the field of privacy and data protection. In particular, following references in the GDPR to vulnerability and the Article 29 Working Party (WP29) and European Data Protection Board (EDPB) Opinions, I identified two elements for the definition of vulnerability: power imbalance and higher risk of harm to fundamental rights and freedoms. As noted, these two concepts are not separate.

An analysis of power imbalance reveals that human vulnerability in the data protection field can be of two different types: vulnerability *during* the data processing (processing-based vulnerability) and vulnerability *to the adverse effects* of

[1] As noted in Chapter 6, the only reference to 'categories of data subjects' is in arts 28(3), 30(1)(c), and 33(3)(a), but in the GDPR there is no clarification about which categories to consider and why.

Vulnerability and Data Protection Law. Gianclaudio Malgieri, Oxford University Press.
DOI: 10.1093/oso/9780192870339.003.0005

the data processing (effect-based vulnerability). In the first case, the data subject is vulnerable when making decisions, in other words they cannot freely understand, choose, and control the conditions of data processing concerning them. In the latter case, the data subject may incur significant harmful effects or even harm to their fundamental rights and freedoms due to the specific outcome of the data processing (eg discrimination, algorithmic manipulation, etc).

Building on these considerations, this chapter and the following will focus on the role of vulnerability in the wording of the GDPR. This chapter focuses on the data protection principles while the following examines data protection rights and obligations. Accordingly, the research question that this chapter addresses is:

> When implementing the data protection principles in the GDPR, how should we consider the personal situations of the data subjects, in particular the vulnerable ones (as defined in the previous chapters)?

Among the data protection principles in Article 5 of the GDPR, this chapter focuses primarily on the principles of lawfulness, fairness, purpose limitation, and accuracy. The first three are indeed principles requiring a balancing between the different relative positions of the data subject and the data controllers[2] and, consequently, an analysis of the impact of data processing on the data subject, including an analysis of their vulnerability, as I will explain below. In addition, the accuracy principle is important to guarantee a correct balancing of interests, prevent biases, and actively mitigate specific situations of individual vulnerability.

Section 2 addresses the principle of *fairness*. At first sight, this principle is vague and open to different interpretations. However, the notion of fairness might be interpreted to mitigate the situations of significant power imbalances between data controllers and data subjects and the related conditions of data subjects' vulnerability.

Section 3 analyses the lawfulness concept, including legal bases for processing personal data and special categories of personal data. Two aspects are considered: the appropriate legal basis for processing data and the special protection for sensitive data.

Section 4 focuses on the *purpose limitation* principle. The data controller's duty to have specified, explicit, and legitimate data processing purposes should lead to an assessment of the conditions of the data subjects.

Lastly, Section 5 analyses the accuracy principle, which might both limit biases (eg racial biases, especially in algorithmic decision-making systems) and allow

[2] R Gellert, 'We Have Always Managed Risks in Data Protection Law: Understanding the Similarities and Differences between the Rights-Based and the Risk-Based Approaches to Data Protection' (2016) 2 European Data Protection Law Review 481; R Gellert, *The Risk-Based Approach to Data Protection* (Oxford University Press 2020).

better identification and mitigation of data subjects' vulnerabilities (with appropriate balancing, legal choices, and safeguards).

Among the other principles, transparency and accountability are analysed more fully in Chapter 6 than in the current chapter because transparency is better understood in conjunction with data protection rights (Articles 12–15), while accountability should be addressed in conjunction with accountability duties (Chapter III of the GDPR).

2. The principle of fairness: first locus of the protection of data subjects' vulnerability

The principle of fairness is mentioned in Article 5(1) point (a) of the GDPR as one of the main principles of data processing, in conjunction with lawfulness and transparency.[3] The notion of fairness might help prevent an unfair imbalance of power between data subjects and data controllers, thus mitigating the vulnerability of data subjects. Accordingly, the main questions in this section are: when implementing the fairness principle, should the interpreter consider data subjects' vulnerability? Can the principle of fairness help build a vulnerability-centred interpretation of the GDPR?

The meaning of the fairness principle in the GDPR is still vague, but this principle can have a central role in understanding how the GDPR could consider the contextual vulnerability of data subjects. In a previous work, the author has analysed the meaning of fairness in the GDPR.[4] This section will show how the fairness principle aims to protect data subjects' vulnerability in different contexts.

The idea of fairness can have many possible nuances. Looking at the scholarly literature on data protection fairness in the EU (as shown below), there are at least three possible nuances that we can observe in the interpretation of the fairness principle such as (i) procedural fairness, (ii) fair balancing (aiming to prevent adverse effects), and (iii) good faith. However, before analysing these different nuances, we need to remind ourselves that—as found in Chapter 3—data subjects' vulnerability in the GDPR can have two different dimensions: a power imbalance affecting freedom to make decisions during the data processing (*processing-based vulnerability*), and the higher risks of adverse effects as outcomes of the data processing on data subjects (*effect-based vulnerability*). As this section will explain, the notion of fairness can react to both these dimensions of vulnerability.

[3] D Clifford and J Ausloos, 'Data Protection and the Role of Fairness' (2018) 37 Yearbook of European Law 130 <https://doi.org/10.1093/yel/yey004> accessed 16 December 2018; H Hijmans, *The European Union as Guardian of Internet Privacy: The Story of Art 16 TFEU* (Springer 2016) 56–57.

[4] G Malgieri, 'The Concept of Fairness in the GDPR: A Linguistic and Contextual Interpretation' in *Proceedings of the 2020 Conference on Fairness, Accountability, and Transparency* (Association for Computing Machinery 2020).

The first nuance of fairness: procedural fairness. A way to mitigate processing-based vulnerability?

I begin with procedural fairness. In general terms, there is a link between fairness, *lawfulness*, and *transparency*: these three different principles are mentioned together as three interdependent notions. This link (with lawfulness and transparency) is confirmed in Recital 39, which first declares that 'any processing of personal data should be *lawful* and *fair*',[5] and then affirms that the *transparency* principle 'concerns, in particular, information to the data subjects on the identity of the controller and the purposes of the processing and further information to ensure *fair* and transparent processing'.[6] The other references to 'fairness' in the GDPR are either related to the link between fairness and *lawfulness* or to the link between fairness and *transparency*. However, fairness cannot be reduced to a synonym of transparency or lawfulness but has an independent meaning. That specific meaning can have different nuances if combined with the transparency principle or the lawfulness principle. The notion of fairness in the GDPR seems to refer to a substantial approach to prevent processing-based vulnerability based on a power imbalance in concrete situations, particularly when conflicting interests need to be balanced.

The WP29 also tends to associate the concept of fairness either to lawfulness or to transparency. This is clear in two different opinions: the WP29 Opinion on Consent and the WP29 Opinion on Transparency. As regards the link between fair and lawful, the WP29 Opinion on Consent clarifies that the fairness principle requires the data controller to choose and communicate the legal basis for data processing clearly: for example, sending the message that data will be processed on the basis of consent while some other lawful basis is relied on would be fundamentally *unfair* to individuals.[7] In addition, basing personal data processing on the consent of the data subject does not permit the collection of data that are 'not necessary in relation to a specified purpose of processing', as this would 'be fundamentally unfair'.[8]

Looking at the relationship between fairness and transparency, the WP29 Opinion on Transparency often refers to fairness. In particular, fair transparency seems to require additional efforts compared to merely formal transparency since it also considers 'reasonable expectations' of data subjects. Processing data in a fairly transparent way means processing data in ways that are both expected and foreseen,[9] 'consider[ing] the circumstances and context of each

[5] Emphasis added.
[6] Emphasis added.
[7] WP29, Guidelines on consent under Regulation 2016/679, Adopted on 28 November 2017 as last Revised and Adopted on 10 April 2018, WP259 rev.01, 23.
[8] WP29, Guidelines on consent under Regulation 2016/679, 4.
[9] WP29, Guidelines on transparency under Regulation 2016/679, WP260, 16.

situation'.[10] When considering contexts and circumstances, the level of understanding and involvement of the data subjects (and so their potential *vulnerability*) should also be considered. The Court of Justice of the European Union (CJEU) has also interpreted the notion of fairness in data protection as related to the transparency principle.[11]

According to the WP29, the notion of fairness is also relevant in the case of further processing of personal data. Indeed, the fairness principle requires that the more intrusive (or less expected) the new data processing is, the further in advance data subjects should be provided[12] 'with further information on the compatibility analysis carried out under Article 6(4)'.[13]

In sum, the GDPR usually relates the notion of fairness to specific '*measures*',[14] '*procedures*',[15] or *information duties*[16] that the data controller needs to adopt. That is why Clifford and Ausloos refer to 'procedural fairness':[17] fairness should be practically implemented through specific procedures that can improve the level of transparency and lawfulness of a particular event of data processing in a specific context. Such procedural fairness seems aimed at rebalancing the power asymmetry between the data subject and the data controller: the final goal should be to avoid the *decision-making vulnerability* of data subjects, providing them with adequate information and decision-making tools regarding the data processing.

The second nuance of fairness: fair balancing. A tool against power imbalance?

Analysing the GDPR provisions, Clifford and Ausloos notice that the notion of fairness, in addition to procedural fairness, can have another interpretation, that of fair balancing.[18] While 'procedural fairness' is based on transparency duties, timeliness of communications from the data controller to the data subject, and the duty

[10] ibid 16: 'Data controllers should carefully consider the circumstances and context of each situation where an update to transparency information is required, including the potential impact of the changes upon the data subject and the modality used to communicate the changes, and be able to demonstrate how the timeframe between notification of the changes and the change taking effect satisfies the principle of fairness to the data subject.'

[11] Judgment of 1 October 2015, *Bara and Others* (C-201/14, EU:C:2015:638), §34. See also Opinion of Advocate General Campos Sánchez-Bordona delivered on 17 October 2018 (1) Case C-496/17 *Deutsche Post AG v Hauptzollamt Köln*, §71.

[12] WP29, Guidelines on transparency under Regulation 2016/679, 22.

[13] ibid 21.

[14] Article 6(2) and (3), Recital 45, GDPR.

[15] See Recital 71 of the GDPR.

[16] Articles 13(2) and 14(2), Recitals 39 and 60, GDPR.

[17] D Clifford and J Ausloos, 'Data Protection and the Role of Fairness' (2018) 37 Yearbook of European Law 130.

[18] ibid 177.

of care obligation resting in the data controller, 'fair balancing' is based on proportionality between *interests* and necessity of purposes.[19]

The notion of fair balancing comes from several provisions in the GDPR. Article 6, in paragraphs (2) and (3), refers to measures to ensure (lawful and) fair processing of personal data in specific processing situations, such as the cases described in Chapter IX GDPR, which regulates complex balancing between conflicting interests, for example freedom of expression and information (Article 85), public access to official documents (Article 86), archiving and research purposes (Article 89), and freedom of religious entities to process personal data (Article 91). The idea of fairness as comprising achieving a fair balance between conflicting interests is also confirmed in the jurisprudence of the CJEU, as I show below.

However, within the GDPR, the data controller is asked to choose and adopt their own procedures to make data processing 'fair and transparent' and 'fair and lawful', in particular looking at the 'specific circumstances and context in which the personal data are processed'[20] or the 'specific processing situations'.[21] In other words, one might say that the difference between 'mere' transparency/lawfulness and '*fair*' transparency/lawfulness is the adoption of additional safeguards that could potentially, in specific circumstances, mitigate the *unfair imbalance* between the data controller and the subject.[22] Under this perspective, one might affirm that the two components of fairness (procedures and balancing) are not separate but connected as means to ends: *procedural fairness* leads to a *fair balance*.[23]

The dualism of fairness as procedural fairness and fair balancing has been recently adopted in the Council of Europe's (CoE) Modernized Convention 108.[24] On the one hand, Article 5(4) states: 'personal data undergoing processing shall be: processed *fairly* and in a transparent manner'.[25] On the other hand, the same article at paragraph 1 affirms: 'data processing shall be proportionate in relation to the legitimate purpose pursued and reflect at all stages of the processing *a fair balance between all interests* concerned, whether public or private, and the rights and freedoms at stake'.[26]

[19] ibid 185.

[20] Recitals 60 and 71, GDPR.

[21] Article 6(2) and (3), GDPR.

[22] About the concept of fairness as a balancing see Gellert, 'We Have Always Managed Risks in Data Protection Law' (n 2).

[23] See Clifford and Ausloos (n 17) 177 according to whom fairness in arts 5 and 6 GDPR is an '*ex ante*' assessment on the average data subjects, while data subject rights such as right to object and erasure (arts 17 and 21) are based on an '*ex post*' idea of fairness, tailored on specific circumstances.

[24] Council of Europe, Modernised Convention for the Protection of Individuals with Regard to the Processing of Personal Data, 128th Session of the Committee of Ministers (Elsinore, Denmark, 17–18 May 2018) <https://search.coe.int/cm/Pages/result_details.aspx?ObjectId=09000016807c65bf> accessed 1 June 2019.

[25] Emphasis added

[26] Emphasis added

The relationship between fairness and *interests* is not new in the legal discourse: Bygrave, in his interpretations of the Data Protection Directive (DPD), related the notion of fairness to the consideration of interest and expectations of data subjects.[27] As I show below, the link between fairness and the real interests of the individuals is in line with the Western legal history of the notion of fairness/loyalty.[28]

The Explanatory Memorandum of the CoE's Modernized Convention also considers a notion of fairness as the respect of expectations of data subjects, particularly when it connects the idea of fairness to predictability and legal certainty.[29] Analogously, the Explanatory Memorandum mentions fairness in the *balancing* with the interests of law enforcement authorities processing data under a necessity and proportionality principle.[30]

Moreover, the CJEU has referred to fairness as an interpretative tool for balancing the different interests and rights at stake (fair balancing),[31] that is, not only to balance the interests to data protection with the burden which the data protection obligations represent for the data controller[32] but—more generally—to balance the fundamental right to privacy and the interests requiring free movement of personal data.[33] It is noteworthy that an Advocate General Opinion seemed to propose a low threshold for fair balancing: balancing is 'fair' if it is not based on 'an invidious choice between two such rights'.[34] More recently, the Court in the *Google Spain* case affirmed that a fair balancing requires specific consideration of the factual circumstances and interests at issue.[35]

[27] LA Bygrave, *Data Protection Law: Approaching Its Rationale, Logic and Limits* (Kluwer Law International 2002) 58. See also Clifford and Ausloos, 'Data Protection and the Role of Fairness', 165.

[28] See Section 6.2.

[29] Council of Europe, Explanatory Report regard to Automatic Processing of Personal Data, Strasbourg, 10 October 2018 <https://rm.coe.int/cets-223-explanatory-report-to-the-protocol-amending-the-convention-fo/16808ac91a> accessed 20 February 2023, §49.

[30] ibid § 92.

[31] Case C-275/06 *Productores de Música de España (Promusicae) v Telefónica de España SAU*, [29 January 2008], § 68: 'Member States must, when transposing the directives mentioned above, take care to rely on an interpretation of the directives which allows a fair balance to be struck between the various fundamental rights protected by the Community legal order.' See also Joined Cases C-92/09 and C-93/09, *Volker und Markus Schecke GbR and Hartmut Eifert v Land Hessen* [2009], §88: 'the provisions of European Union law, the validity of which is questioned by the referring court, observe, in so far as they concern the publication of data relating to legal persons, *a fair balance* in the consideration taken of the respective interests in issue'.

[32] Case C-553/07, *College van burgemeester en wethouders van Rotterdam v M.E.E. Rijkeboer*, 7 May 2009, §§64 and 66.

[33] Case C-362/14, *Maximillian Schrems v Data Protection Commissioner*, joined party: Digital Rights Ireland Ltd, §42.

[34] Opinion of Advocate General Sharpston delivered on 15 October 2009 (1) in Case C-28/08 P, *Commission of the European Communities v The Bavarian Lager* Co. Ltd, §95: 'the conflicting interests must be weighed in order to seek a fair balance between those interests and the fundamental rights at stake. However, the ideal solution is clearly one that avoids making an invidious choice between two such rights.'

[35] Case C-131/12, *Google Spain SL, Google Inc. v Agencia Española de Protección de Datos (AEPD), Mario Costeja González*, 13 May 2014, § 81. This has been confirmed in Case C-136/17, *GC and Others v Commission nationale de l'informatique et des libertés (CNIL)* [24 September 2019], §§66 and 76 and

Clifford and Ausloos conclude that even in the reasoning of the Court, fairness gives a level of protection to the inherent asymmetric relationship between data subject and controller and hence, protection also against the potential for *negative consequences* for data subjects stemming from personal data processing even in the absence of a controller intent to deceive.[36]

For our purposes, this second nuance could help redress—as an interpretative tool—the imbalance of power that is the ground of data subjects' vulnerability (especially, but not only, *processing-based vulnerability*).

A particular specification of this second nuance is fairness as a way to mitigate adverse effects, especially for vulnerable data subjects. Indeed, the fairness concept has often been combined to non-discrimination, particularly in algorithmic regulation discourse.[37] The *Oxford English Dictionary* defines 'fair' as 'impartial and just treatment or behaviour without favouritism or *discrimination*'.[38] The relation between discrimination and (un)fairness can also be found in the first international documents on data protection.[39]

In the GDPR,[40] Recital 71 affirms that 'in order to ensure *fair* and transparent processing in respect of the data subject, the controller should use appropriate mathematical or statistical procedures for the profiling, implement technical and organisational measures appropriate to' prevent 'potential risks' for the interests and rights of the data subject, such as '*discriminatory effects* on natural persons on the basis of racial or ethnic origin, political opinion, religion or beliefs, trade union membership, genetic or health status or sexual orientation, or that result in measures having such an effect'.[41]

in the Opinion of Advocate General Bot delivered on 8 September 2016, Case C-398/15 *Camera di Commercio, Industria, Artigianato e Agricoltura di Lecce v Salvatore Manni* (Request for a preliminary ruling from the Corte suprema di cassazione), §99. See also Opinion of Advocate General Sharpston delivered on 15 October 2009, Case C-28/08 P *Commission of the European Communities v The Bavarian Lager Co. Ltd*, §99.

[36] Clifford and Ausloos (n 17) 144.

[37] See eg B Lepri and others, 'Fair, Transparent, and Accountable Algorithmic Decision-Making Processes' (2018) 31 Philosophy & Technology 611; T Douglas, 'Biased Algorithms: Here's a More Radical Approach to Creating Fairness' (*The Conversation*) <http://theconversation.com/biased-algorithms-heres-a-more-radical-approach-to-creating-fairness-109748> accessed 22 January 2019; S Galhotra and others, 'Fairness Testing: Testing Software for Discrimination' in *Proceedings of the 2017 11th Joint Meeting on Foundations of Software Engineering—ESEC/FSE 2017* (ACM Press 2017).

[38] Emphasis added.

[39] In particular, two Resolutions of the Council of Europe from the early 1970s on the protection of privacy in electronic data banks refer to 'unfair discrimination'. See Council of Europe, Committee of Ministers, 'Resolution (73) 22 on the Protection of the Privacy of Individuals vis-à-vis Electronic Data Banks in the Private Sector'; see in particular Annex X, §3. See also Council of Europe—Committee of Ministers, 'Resolution (74) 29 on the Protection of the Privacy of Individuals Vis-a-Vis Electronic Data Banks in the Public Sector' <https://rm.coe.int/CoERMPublicCommonSearchServices/DisplayDCTMContent?documentId=0900001680502830> accessed 20 February 2023, Annex X, § 1.

[40] While in the Data Protection Directive there is no direct link between fairness and non-discrimination, the GDPR seems to refer to that link.

[41] Emphasis added.

Similarly, the WP29 Opinion on automated decision-making also associates unfairness with discrimination: 'profiling may be *unfair* and create *discrimination*, for example by denying people access to employment opportunities, credit or insurance, or targeting them with excessively risky or costly financial products'.[42] The WP29 also gives the example of unfair profiling that 'can lead to some consumers being offered less attractive deals than others': the case of a data broker selling consumers' profiles (based on consumers' scoring) to financial companies for the offer of 'non-traditional' financial services.[43] Similarly, the CNIL (the French Data Protection Authority), in a report on algorithms and artificial intelligence (AI), has concluded that 'a *fair algorithm* should not end up generating, replicating or aggravating any form of *discrimination*'.[44]

As noted, under this nuance, the fairness principle might be used to mitigate vulnerability based on the higher risks of adverse effects for data subjects ('effect-based vulnerability'). I am aware that discrimination might be one of the main adverse effects arising from the outcomes of data processing. However, as I argue in Chapter 7, the notion of harms to fundamental rights and freedoms should be broader than mere discrimination and should encompass all possible 'adverse effects'.

The UK and the French Data Protection Authorities (DPAs) have elaborated on the concept of fairness in the GDPR. In particular, the Information Commissioner's Office (ICO), in a report on Big Data, AI, and data protection,[45] has proposed an original interpretation of the fairness principles.[46] According to the ICO, fairness involves three elements: (i) considerations of *effects* on individuals; (ii) consideration of *expectations* of data subjects; (iii) and *transparency* of data processing. While the link between fairness and transparency is evident in the wording of the GDPR, the connection between fairness and *expectations* is more implicit but not new in the legal discourse.[47] The WP29 Opinion on Transparency

42 WP29 Opinion on Automated Decision-Making, 10. Emphasis added.

43 ibid 10.

44 Comission National Informatique and Libertés, *How Can Humans Keep the Upper Hand? The ethical matters raised by algorithms and artificial intelligence*, Report on the public debate led by the French data protection authority (CNIL) as part of the ethical discussion assignment set by the Digital Republic Bill December 2017 <https://www.cnil.fr/sites/default/files/atoms/files/cnil_rapport_ai_gb_web.pdf> accessed 20 February 2023, 49. Emphasis added.

45 Information Commissioner's Office, *Big Data, Artificial Intelligence, Machine Learning and Data Protection*, 2017, 19–22 <https://ico.org.uk/media/for-organisations/documents/2013559/big-data-ai-ml-and-data-protection.pdf> accessed 20 February 2023.

46 M Butterworth, 'The ICO and Artificial Intelligence: The Role of Fairness in the GDPR Framework' (2018) 34 Computer Law & Security Review 257.

47 LA Bygrave, *Data Protection Law, Approaching Its Rationale, Logic and Limits* (1st edn, Kluwer Law International 2002) 58; Clifford and Ausloos (n 17) 158. See also Council of Europe, Explanatory Report regard to Automatic Processing of Personal Data, Strasbourg, 10 October 2018 <https://rm.coe.int/cets-223-explanatory-report-to-the-protocol-amending-the-convention-fo/16808ac91a> accessed 20 February 2023.

has also associated fairness with the considerations of reasonable expectations of and effects on data subjects.[48] The relevance of expectations and effects is in line with the data subject-centred (and vulnerability-centred) analysis of the GDPR proposed in this book.

The link between *fairness* and *effects* is innovative but consistent with the considerations above. The GDPR seems to refer to fair processing as being based on specific circumstances and situations, looking at the substantial balancing between different parties. In other words, what matters is the effect on the data subject, not the mere compliance to procedural duties. In a report, the French DPA (the CNIL) has proposed a similar approach: the fairness principle should be interpreted as the prevention of unjust 'outcomes' or 'impacts'.[49] In addition, according to the CNIL, the effects should be assessed not only on the data subject but at a collective level.[50] This view is inherently linked to the fair balancing of positions between data controllers and data subjects. Taking, for example, the case of algorithmic platforms, the French Conseil d'État (as rephrased by CNIL) affirms that 'fairness consists of ensuring, in good faith, the search engine optimisation (SEO) or ranking service, without seeking to alter or manipulate it for purposes that are not in the users' interest'.[51] On a more general level, in the algorithmic environment, 'fairness could well represent a solution to the problem of *unbalanced relations* between controllers of algorithms and users'.[52] In sum, the concept of fairness could be a heuristic tool used to prevent adverse effects (discrimination, but not only discrimination) arising as outcomes of the data processing (what I defined as *effect-based vulnerability*).

[48] WP on Transparency, 25: 'the requirements of fairness and accountability under the GDPR require data controllers to always consider the reasonable expectations of data subjects, the effect that the processing may have on them and their ability to exercise their rights in relation to that processing, when deciding at what point to provide the Article 14 information'.

[49] <https://www.cnil.fr/en/algorithms-and-artificial-intelligence-cnils-report-ethical-issues> accessed 20 February 2023.

[50] Commission National Informatique and Libertés, 'How Can Humans Keep the Upper Hand? The Ethical Matters Raised by Algorithms and Artificial Intelligence, Report on the Public Debate Led by the French Data Protection Authority (CNIL) as Part of the Ethical Discussion Assignment Set by the Digital Republic Bill' (2017).

[51] Conseil d'État, Étude annuelle 2014 du Conseil d'État—Le numérique et les droits fondamentaux, Etudes et documents, Conseil d'État, Septembre 2014 <https://www.ladocumentationfrancaise.fr/rapports-publics/144000541-etude-annuelle-2014-du-conseil-d-etat-le-numerique-et-les-droits-fondamentaux> accessed 20 February 2023, 224. Translation by the author. Note that in this case the notion of platform fairness refers to consumer protection law (e-commerce Directive) and not to data protection law. However, see the link between these two fields in I Graef and others, 'Fairness and Enforcement: Bridging Competition, Data Protection, and Consumer Law' (2018) 8 International Data Privacy Law 200.

[52] CNIL, *Can Humans Keep Upper Hand, Report on Ethical Matters Raised by Algorithms and AI* <https://www.cnil.fr/en/how-can-humans-keep-upper-hand-report-ethical-matters-raised-algorithms-and-artificial-intelligence> accessed 20 February 2023.

The third nuance: fairness as good faith. A hybrid way to mitigate the two facets of data subjects' vulnerability?

The third understanding of the fairness principle might be good faith. This interpretation comes from the linguistic comparison between different official translations of the GDPR in several other EU official languages.[53]

The CJEU has affirmed that a correct interpretation of EU law must involve a comparison of the different language versions, all equally authentic expressions of EU legislation.[54] The different translations of the fairness principle in the GDPR reveal different nuances and perspectives. In a previous article,[55] the author has compared some of the most relevant official translations of the GDPR, considering various linguistic families: German, Dutch, French, Spanish, Portuguese, Italian, Romanian, Greek, Polish, Swedish, and Slovenian.[56]

In all these legal traditions, the notion of fairness and good faith have been developed primarily from contract law. The Draft Common Frame of Reference for European Contract Law (DCFR) explicitly addresses this notion: '[t]he expression 'good faith and fair dealing' refers to a standard of conduct characterised by honesty, openness and consideration for the interests of the other party to the transaction or relationship in question'.[57] Even the European Commission (now withdrawn) proposal for a Common European Sales law proposed the same definition of good faith and fair dealing found in the DCFR.[58]

In other EU legal fields, the link between fairness and equity or good faith is more explicit. As an example, the Unfair Terms Directive defines 'unfair' as what is 'contrary to the requirement of *good faith* [and] causes a *significant imbalance* in the parties' rights and obligations arising under the contract, to the detriment of the consumer'.[59] The link between *unfairness*, *good faith*, and *significant imbalance*

[53] Malgieri (n 4).

[54] CJEU Case 283/81 *Srl CILFIT and Lanificio di Gavardo SpA v Ministry of Health* [1982] ECR 3415, §18: 'it must be borne in mind that Community legislation is drafted in several languages and that the different language versions are equally authentic. An interpretation of a provision of Community law thus involves a comparison of the different language versions' (emphasis added). See also CJEU Case 29/69 *Stauder v City of Ulm* [1969] ECR 419, ECLI:EU:C:1969:57, §2. See, largely, M Bajčić, 'Linguistic Comparison within CJEU's Decision-Making: A Debunking Exercise' [2020] 34(2) International Journal for the Semiotics of Law—Revue internationale de Sémiotique juridique 1433.

[55] Malgieri (n 4).

[56] The author chose these languages (among the most representative ones of the European linguistic families) because he could profit from various linguistic support from several national experts of those languages.

[57] Article I-1:103 of the Draft Common Frame of Reference; Principles, Definitions and Model Rules of European Private Law.

[58] See Proposal for a Regulation of the European Parliament and of the Council on a Common European Sales Law, COM/2011/0635 final, art 2(b): 'good faith and fair dealing' means a standard of conduct characterized by honesty, openness and consideration for the interests of the other party to the transaction or relationship in question. On this point see also FJ Zuiderveen Borgesius, *Improving Privacy Protection in the Area of Behavioural Targeting* (Kluwer Law International 2015) 113.

[59] Council Directive 93/13/EEC of 5 April 1993 on unfair terms in consumer contracts 1993 [31993L0013] art 3. Emphasis added. Graef and others (n 51) 204 and 207.

in consumer law is in line with the reflections above about '*bona fide*' and fair balance in Member States' national legal histories[60] and in data protection law.[61]

For our purposes, this third meaning of the concept of fairness might also be relevant to protect vulnerable data subjects: fairness as good faith might be a way to rebalance asymmetric relationships by preventing adverse effects. Thus, fairness as good faith might be both a tool to mitigate processing-based vulnerabilities and a way to prevent effect-based vulnerabilities.

The need for a vulnerability-centred understanding of fairness

We have thus observed that fairness in the GDPR is a complex principle, embedding several different nuances and tasks. In particular, we have observed three perspectives of fairness: procedural fairness, fair balancing (aimed at the prevention of adverse effects), and good faith. All these perspectives might be seen as tools to consider and mitigate data subjects' vulnerability, both in terms of a power imbalance during the data processing (processing-based vulnerability) and as the existence of higher risks of adverse effects from the outcomes of the data processing (effect-based vulnerability).

These nuances involve other data processing principles, like transparency and lawfulness, but also more general concepts like non-discrimination, proportionality, and due balancing. Fairness in the GDPR goes beyond abstract lawfulness ('*summum ius, summa iniuria*'): it is aimed at considering the factual circumstances at stake. Accordingly, fairness implies a consideration of *expectations* of the individuals, *effects* on the data subjects, and *actual interests* of the parties. In particular, the inherent link between fairness and good faith (as shown in the linguistic comparison), even considering the national legal traditions in terms of *bona fide* and equity, seems to suggest that 'fair' should mean prevention of unfairly

[60] See Falco, *La buona fede e l'abuso del diritto: principi, fattispecie e casistica* (Giuffrè Editore 2010) 9. The same link can be found also in other legal systems. See, interestingly, Department of Justice of State of Victoria, *Preventing unfair terms in consumer contracts. Guidelines for businesses* <http://docplayer.net/11137227-Preventing-unfair-terms-in-consumer-contracts-guidelines-for-businesses.html> accessed 20 February 2023, p 4: 'A term is unfair if: it causes a *significant imbalance* in the parties rights and obligations under the contract it is not reasonably necessary to protect a *legitimate interest* of the trader it would cause detriment to the consumer it is contained in a standard-form consumer contract.' Emphasis added. See also Zuiderveen Borgesius, *Improving Privacy Protection* (n 58) 112.

[61] Clifford and Ausloos (n 17) 175. The controller should not deliberately choose a form of compliance which may be legal but would frustrate the data subject's ability to exercise their rights or enjoy protection. Two examples: (i) deliberately choosing to design a system in such a way that data subjects will not have the means to identify themselves to the data controller, in order to come under art 11 and not have to respond to rights requests, even though it would have been easy to enable this; (ii) choosing from a range of possible lawful bases the one which minimizes compliance burden in order to make life easier for the controller. Neither of these are technically in breach of any particular requirement of the GDPR, but they are unfair because they exploit the power imbalance between controller and data subject.

asymmetric relationships between subjects, balancing their substantial interests (or their 'bargaining power').[62]

Accordingly, going back to the research question posed at the beginning of this section, we can reply that the fairness principle, if widely interpreted, might be an adequate tool to protect individual vulnerabilities and prevent the exploitation of data subjects' vulnerability. Indeed, as I showed through its different nuances, fairness is an overarching interpretative principle aimed at preventing situations of significative *power imbalance* that could produce adverse effects for some data subjects.

3. The principle of lawfulness: second locus of the protection of data subjects' vulnerability

In the previous section, we observed how the principle of lawfulness is linked to fairness and individual conditions of data subjects. This section wonders whether in the interpretation of the lawfulness principle we should take into account different data subjects, including paying special attention to vulnerable subjects.

To answer this, I analyse lawful grounds for processing personal data in Article 6 and Article 9 (about the processing of special categories of personal data) of the GDPR to understand whether the assessment of the particular situations/conditions of the data subjects should be a necessary step to implement the lawfulness principle.

Consent in case of vulnerable data subjects: limits and potentialities

For individuals in a situation of vulnerability, the use of consent as a lawful basis (according to Article 6(1)(a)) can be problematic. One might indeed wonder whether consent is an adequate legal basis. If the answer is yes, should consent be accompanied by more tailored information? If not, are there better legal bases for processing personal data of vulnerable data subjects, or should data controllers just avoid processing those data?

As mentioned in the previous chapter, the only vulnerable category with group-specific protection mentioned in the GDPR is children. Their specific protection is mainly based on two elements: consent and information duties of data

[62] On the notion of good faith as a tool for rebalancing asymmetry in bargaining power see GN La Diega, 'Can the Law Fix the Problems of Fashion? An Empirical Study on Social Norms and Power Imbalance in the Fashion Industry' (2019) 14(1) Journal of Intellectual Property Law & Practice 18–24.

controllers.[63] When data processing is based on consent and relates to the offer of information society services, under a certain age (sixteen years, that the Member States can reduce to thirteen years), consent should be given or authorized by the holder of parental responsibility over the child (Article 8).[64] At the same time, transparency duties and any communication within the exercise of data protection rights should be 'in a concise, transparent, intelligible, and easily accessible form, using clear and plain language, *in particular for any information addressed specifically to a child*'[65] (Article 12(1)).

One might wonder whether these safeguards could also be used for other vulnerable data subjects (adults) by analogy. Interestingly, the WP29 Guidelines on consent, when referring to a child's consent in Article 8, affirm: '[c]ompared to the current directive, the GDPR creates an additional layer of protection *where personal data of vulnerable natural persons, especially children, are processed*'.[66] This sentence seems to suggest that special rules for consent were conceived for all vulnerable natural persons: 'especially children' does not mean 'only children'. However, parental consent for information society services is a special rule that cannot be easily applied in different contexts: the only similarity with some 'vulnerable adults' is that legally incapacitated persons might need consent (or authorization to consent) from their legal representatives, according to the national laws.[67] In general terms, we could assume that data controllers should adopt special safeguards when collecting consent from vulnerable adults.

This assumption is in line with the characteristics of consent under Articles 4(11) and 7: freely given, specific, informed, and unambiguous. Consent is freely given only if the data subject is capable of choosing and controlling their consent provision.[68] In particular, the WP29 adds: the 'element of inappropriate pressure or influence upon the data subject (which may be manifested in many different ways) which prevents a data subject from exercising their free will, shall render the consent invalid'.[69] In sum, when the data subject is in a situation where making an

[63] However, children should receive special consideration also in case of processing data under the legitimate interest legal basis (art 6(1)(f)), in case of right to erasure (art 17 as interpreted by Recital 65) in case of automated decision-making (art 22 as interpreted by Recital 71).

[64] L Jasmontaite and P De Hert, 'The EU, Children under 13 Years, and Parental Consent: A Human Rights Analysis of a New, Age-Based Bright-Line for the Protection of Children on the Internet' (2014) 5 International Data Privacy Law 20.

[65] Emphasis added.

[66] WP29, Guidelines on Consent under Regulation 2016/679, 23. Emphasis added.

[67] Article 8(3) GDPR clarifies that special rules for child's consent 'shall not affect the general contract law of Member States such as the rules on the validity, formation or effect of a contract in relation to a child'.

[68] WP29, Guidelines on Consent, 5: 'The element "free" implies real choice and control for data subjects. As a general rule, the GDPR prescribes that if the data subject has no real choice, feels compelled to consent or will endure negative consequences if they do not consent, then consent will not be valid.'

[69] WP29, Guidelines on Consent under Regulation 2016/679, 6.

informed decision is difficult or impossible, in other words, in a state of decision-making vulnerability, consent shall not be valid.

Recital 43 relates the idea of freedom to consent to the notion of *power imbalance*:[70] 'in order to ensure that consent is freely given, consent should not provide a valid legal ground for the processing of personal data in a specific case *where there is a clear imbalance between the data subject and the controller*, in particular where the controller is a public authority' (emphasis added). This concept was marked even more clearly in the EU Commission Proposal for the GDPR, where Recital 43 added a new example of 'clear imbalance': 'this is especially the case where the data subject is in *a situation of dependence* from the controller, among others, where personal data are processed by the employer of employees' personal data in the employment context'.[71] I have already observed how individual vulnerability is defined by the WP29 as power imbalance between controllers and subjects.[72] The emphasis on the 'situation of dependence' of the data subjects is also relevant for our purposes: as affirmed in Chapter 3, vulnerability is often defined as a situation of dependence of individuals.[73]

However, the WP29 explains that imbalances of power are not limited to public authorities but also include the relationship between employees and employers and other situations: 'consent can only be valid if the data subject is able to exercise a real choice, and there is no risk of deception, intimidation, coercion or significant negative consequences (e.g., substantial extra costs) if he/she does not consent. Consent will not be free in cases where there is any element of compulsion, pressure or inability to exercise free will.'[74] In other words, the data controller should not choose consent as a legal basis for processing personal data when the data subject can be in a situation of decision-making vulnerability. The EDPB Opinion on Clinical Trials Regulation also highlights that consent should not be a legal basis for data processing in the case of vulnerable data subjects, in particular when the potential subject is not 'in good health conditions' or 'belongs to an economically or socially disadvantaged group, or is in a situation of institutional or hierarchical dependency that could inappropriately influence her or his decision to participate'.[75]

[70] On this point see also O Lynskey, *The Foundations of EU Data Protection Law* (Oxford University Press 2015) 213–15.

[71] Proposal for a Regulation of the European Parliament and of the Council concerning the respect for private life and the protection of personal data in electronic communications and repealing Directive 2002/58/EC (Regulation on Privacy and Electronic Communications), COM/2017/010 final - 2017/03 (COD). See, on this point also Lynskey (9) 214.

[72] WP29, Guidelines on DPIA, 10: 'Vulnerable data subjects may include … any case where an imbalance in the relationship between the position of the data subject and the controller can be identified.'

[73] See eg E Gilson, *The Ethics of Vulnerability: A Feminist Analysis of Social* 'The Vulnerable Subject: Anchoring Equality in the Human Condition' (2016) 20 Yale Journal of Law & Feminism 12.

[74] WP29, Guidelines on Consent under Regulation 2016/679, 7.

[75] EDPB, Opinion 3/2019 concerning the Questions and Answers on the interplay between the Clinical Trials Regulation (CTR) and the General Data Protection regulation (GDPR) (art 70.1.b), 6.

In sum, as noted in Chapter 4, it is essential to remember that data subjects' vulnerability is not based merely on the personal characteristics of the data subject but on the *encounter* between those characteristics and the *power* of the counterparty: an employer, a doctor, the public administration, and even a market-dominant digital platform or digital service provider.

To determine who are the powerful data controllers, it is necessary to clarify what power means in the data-driven environment. Answering this question, Véliz[76] builds on Forst's definition of power as the 'capacity of A to motivate B to think or do something that B would otherwise not have thought or done'.[77] This is consistent with EU consumer law definitions,[78] and it is, thus, not limited to brute force but also includes (undue) influences.[79] As noted in Chapter 3, in rational choice theory users are considered 'actors' who must choose from a set of choices of possible actions to achieve desired outcomes, but an 'incentive structure' influences them. This structure includes the costs of different actions in the choice set and the estimated likelihood that different actions will lead to desired outcomes.[80]

Weber defines power as the ability 'to carry out one's own will despite resistance'.[81] In our context, even if we might feel personal resistance to give our consent to data processing and even if there is no brute force imposed on us to give our consent, the (social, market, or technological) architecture can make us act in the way that our powerful counterparts wish. In other words, the choice architecture and incentive structures (eg access to a digital service that is considered essential in customers' daily lives or an online platform to which the user becomes addicted, etc) reduces our resistance to surrendering our personal data. If the level of impairment to such resistance is high, we are in a situation of individual vulnerability and data controllers should thus avoid using consent as a legal basis for obtaining our data. In this context, the competition law notion of market 'power' and 'dominance' can help to delineate the borderline between valid and invalid (non-free) consent to data processing, as the recent German Antitrust case on Facebook revealed.[82]

[76] C Véliz, *Privacy is Power: Why and How You Should Take Back Control of Your Data* (Bantam Press 2020) 58.

[77] R Forst, 'Noumenal Power' (2015) 23 Journal of Political Philosophy 111.

[78] See art 5 of the Unfair Consumer Practice Directive.

[79] Véliz (n 98).

[80] KM Dowding, *Power* (Open University Press 1996).

[81] M Weber, *Economy and Society: An Outline of Interpretive Sociology* (University of California Press 1978) 53.

[82] Bundeskartellamt, decision no B6-22/16 of 6 February 2019. OLGDüsseldorf, 26 August 2019, VI-Kart 1/19 (V), *Bundeskartellamt v Facebook*; Bundesgerichtshof, 23 June 2020, KVR 69/19. G Colangelo, 'Facebook and Bundeskartellamt's Winter of Discontent' [2019] Competition Policy International <https://www.competitionpolicyinternational.com/facebook-and-bundeskartellamts-winter-of-discontent/> accessed 4 February 2022; T Höppner, 'Data Exploiting as an Abuse of Dominance: The German Facebook Decision' [2019] Hausfeld Competition Bulletin <https://www.hausfeld.com/sv-se/what-we-think/competition-bulletin/data-exploiting-as-an-abuse-of-dominance-the-german-facebook-decision/> accessed 4 February 2022; O Budzinski and others, 'The Economics of the German Investigation of Facebook's Data Collection' (Ilmenau Economics Discussion Papers 2020) Working

The proceeding brought by the German *Bundeskartellamt* against Facebook Inc. (and its subsequent developments before the District Court of Dusseldorf and the German Federal Court of Justice, and now pending at the CJEU) is of particular interest.[83] In 2019, the German authority deemed Facebook's practice of collection of user and device-related information from sources outside Facebook account—an abuse of dominant position, arising as a direct consequence of the violation of the GDPR on data subjects' consent. In particular, the use and implementation of unlawful terms of use and data protection notices was considered an abuse of a dominant position according to the German antitrust law (GWB),[84] since the exploitation of users' diminished consent to data processing was both a manifestation of the power Facebook has in the social network market, and a tool for the company to strengthen its dominant position in the provision of personalized advertisements still further.[85]

The Court bases its decision in the appraisal of the dominance that Big Techs acquired in the market and its implications on the power relationships in the digital environment.[86] According to the German authority, the volume of data that Facebook obtained from consumers can be an indirect manifestation of the company's monopolistic power, given that it constitutes an extra profit that Facebook obtained as a result of its dominant position on the German social media market.

In sum, in many situations, vulnerability can be induced by the business model of the data controller. The classic example is when a data subject consents to data processing in exchange for services or other counter-performances.[87] Article 7(4) clarifies that when assessing whether permission is freely given,

Paper 139 <https://www.econstor.eu/handle/10419/217207> accessed 4 February 2022; A Witt, 'Excessive Data Collection as a Form of Anticompetitive Conduct—The German Facebook Case' (2021) 66 Antitrust Bulletin 276; A Witt, 'Data, Privacy and Competition Law' (Social Science Research Network 2021) SSRN Scholarly Paper ID 3989241 <https://papers.ssrn.com/abstract=3989241> accessed 30 January 2022.

[83] Bundeskartellamt, decision no B6-22/16 of 6 February 2019. OLGDüsseldorf, 26 August 2019, VI-Kart 1/19 (V), *Bundeskartellamt v Facebook*; Bundesgerichtshof, 23 Jun 2020, KVR 69/19.

[84] *Gesetz gegen Wettbewerbsbeschränkungen*.

[85] P Këllezi, 'Data Protection and Competition Law: Non-Compliance as Abuse of Dominant Position' [2019] Sui-generis 343 <https://sui-generis.ch/article/view/sg.114> accessed 20 February 2023. G Malgieri and A Davola, 'Data-Powerful' [2022] (Social Science Research Network 2022) SSRN Scholarly Paper ID 4027370 <https://papers.ssrn.com/sol3/papers.cfm?abstract_id=4027370> accessed 30 April 2022.

[86] H Richter, 'The Power Paradigm in Private Law' in M Bakhoum and others (eds), *Personal Data in Competition, Consumer Protection and Intellectual Property Law: Towards a Holistic Approach?* (Springer Berlin Heidelberg 2018) 565. See also F Pasquale, 'Privacy, Antitrust, and Power' (2014) 20 George Mason Law Review 1009; LM Khan, 'Amazon's Antitrust Paradox' (2016) 126 Yale Law Journal 710.

[87] G Malgieri, '"User-Provided Personal Content" in the EU: Digital Currency between Data Protection and Intellectual Property' (2018) 32(1) International Review of Law, Computers & Technology 118.

utmost account shall be taken of whether, among other things, the performance of a contract, including the provision of a service, is conditional on consent to the processing of personal data that is not necessary for the performance of that contract. In other terms, personal data should not be considered as digital currency,[88] although recently the CJEU Advocate General seemed quite lenient on this point.[89]

Even though the GDPR does not explicitly affirm that impairing data subjects' freedom of choice through material benefits is a form of *induced vulnerability*, other pieces of EU legislation make this point. This is the case of, for example, the Clinical Trials Regulation, whose Recital 31 explains that 'in order to certify that informed consent is given freely, the investigator should take into account all relevant circumstances which might influence the decision of a potential subject to participate in a clinical trial, in particular whether the potential subject belongs to an economically or socially disadvantaged group or is in a situation of institutional or hierarchical dependency that could inappropriately influence her or his decision to participate'.[90]

However, consent should be avoided not for every vulnerable data subject but only when data subjects are affected by their vulnerability in decision-making,[91] in particular when even transparency provisions tailored to cater to the vulnerable subject are incapable of mitigating this vulnerability.

In other cases, for instance when the subject is not suffering from cognitive vulnerability (processing-based vulnerability), consent is not only possible but is recommended: this is why the WP29 Guidelines on Purpose Limitation affirm that further processing of data (re-purposing of data processing) for vulnerable data subjects should be possible only upon consent.[92] In that context, the focus of the WP29 is presumably not on a subject's vulnerability when it comes to making decisions but on effect-based vulnerability (eg the risk that re-purposing might lead to discrimination or other adverse effects).[93]

[88] R Robert and L Smit, 'The Proposal for a Directive on Digital Content: A Complex Relationship with Data Protection Law' (2018) 19 ERA Forum 159; V Janeček and G Malgieri, 'Commerce in Data and the Dynamically Limited Alienability Rule' (2020) 21(5) German Law Journal 924.

[89] Opinion of Advocate General Szpunar delivered on 21 March 2019, Case C-673/17 *Bundesverband der Verbraucherzentralen und Verbraucherverbände—Verbraucherzentrale Bundesverband e.V. v Planet49 GmbH*, §§97–99.

[90] É Gennet and others, 'Does the New EU Regulation on Clinical Trials Adequately Protect Vulnerable Research Participants?' (2015) 119 Health Policy (Amsterdam, Netherlands) 925.

[91] About the distinction between decisional vulnerability and other forms of vulnerability see Chapter 4.

[92] WP29, Opinion 03/2013 on purpose limitation, 32.

[93] ibid 32: 'further processing of personal data concerning health, data about children, other vulnerable individuals, or other highly sensitive information should, in principle, be permitted only with the consent of the data subject'.

Other lawful bases for processing data of (vulnerable) data subjects

As noted, consent is not always an adequate lawful ground for processing personal data of vulnerable individuals, particularly in the case of decision-making vulnerability of data subjects. In that case, the data controller should choose another legal basis to obtain a subject's data under Article 6.[94]

Suppose the data processing is necessary for the performance of a contract to which the data subject is party or to take steps at the request of the data subject before entering into a contract. In that case, the data controller can process data under Article 6(1)(b).[95] However, several vulnerable persons have limited contractual capacity (eg minors, persons with mental disabilities, etc).[96] The appropriateness of contracting with a vulnerable person and the adequacy of measures to protect vulnerable contracting parties concerns contract law (and consumer law, where appropriate) and not merely data protection law.[97] In other words, in the case of Article 6(1) point (b), the principle of lawfulness is respected when the data processing is strictly necessary for the performance of (or for entering into) a contract:[98]: additional requirements (eg whether it is appropriate and lawful to conclude specific contracts with certain vulnerable individuals) are regulated by contract law in each EU Member State.[99]

[94] About the limits of consent see in general G Fortuna-Zanfir, 'Forgetting about Consent. Why the Focus Should Be on "Suitable Safeguards" in Data Protection Law' in S Gutwirth and others (eds), *Reloading Data Protection* (Springer 2014); BW Schermer and others, 'The Crisis of Consent: How Stronger Legal Protection May Lead to Weaker Consent in Data Protection' (2014) 16 Ethics and Information Technology 171; B Custers and others, 'Consent and Privacy', *The Routledge Handbook of the Ethics of Consent* (Routledge 2019).

[95] See eg EDPB, Guidelines 2/2019 on the processing of personal data under Article 6(1)(b) GDPR in the context of the provision of online services to data subjects, adopted on 9 April 2019.

[96] The regulation of contractual capacity limitations is different in each legal system. At an international level the UN Convention on the Rights of Persons with Disabilities (2006) recognizes access to consumer goods and service. The EU Consumer Law has taken into account such concepts. See eg E Varney, 'Redefining Contractual Capacity? The UN Convention on the Rights of Persons with Disabilities and the Incapacity Defence in English Contract Law' (2017) 37(3) Legal Studies 493–519; see also I Eskytė, 'Disabled People's Vulnerability in the European Single Market: The Case of Consumer Information' (2019) 42(4) Journal of Consumer Policy 521–43.

[97] EDPB, Guidelines 2/2019, at 5 mention as an example the case of contract with children: 'As mentioned, as a matter of lawfulness, contracts for online services must be valid under the applicable contract law. An example of a relevant factor is whether the data subject is a child. In such a case (and aside from complying with the requirements of the GDPR, including the 'specific protections' which apply to children), 9 the controller must ensure that it complies with the relevant national laws on the capacity of children to enter into contracts.'

[98] The strict interpretation of the 'necessity' criterion can be found in WP29, Opinion 06/2014 on the notion of legitimate interests of the data controller under Article 7 of Directive 95/46/EC, WP217, adopted on 9 April 2014, 16: 'The provision must be interpreted strictly and does not cover situations where the processing is not genuinely necessary for the performance of a contract, but rather unilaterally imposed on the data subject by the controller.'

[99] See EDPB, Guidelines 2/2019 on the processing of personal data under Article 6(1)(b) GDPR in the context of the provision of online services to data subjects, 4: 'contracts and contractual terms must comply with the requirements of contract laws and, as the case may be for consumer contracts, consumer protection laws in order for processing based on those terms to be considered fair and lawful'.

When the processing is necessary for compliance with a legal obligation to which the controller is subject, it is lawful according to Article 6(1)(c). Similarly, when the processing is necessary for the performance of a task carried out in the public interest, it is lawful according to Article 6(1)(e). These two types of processing must be based on Member State or Union law. These national or EU laws allowing data processing should have specific safeguards to protect vulnerable persons according to the lawfulness and fairness principles. Article 6(2) clarifies thus: 'Member States may maintain or introduce more specific provisions to adapt the application of the rules of this Regulation with regard to processing for compliance with or compliance with points (c) and (e) of paragraph 1 by determining more precisely specific requirements for the processing and other measures to ensure *lawful and fair processing*.'[100] In addition, Article 6(3) specifies that the legal basis may contain specific provisions to adapt the application of the GDPR, 'inter alia: the general conditions governing the lawfulness of processing by the controller; the types of data which are subject to the processing; *the data subjects concerned*; ... and processing procedures, including measures to ensure lawful and fair processing'. The mention of 'the data subjects concerned' (among other aspects that Member States should consider when regulating specific data processing in accordance with Article 6(1)(c) and (e)) seems also to refer to the needs and conditions of different types of data subjects, including the vulnerable. Accordingly, *measures to ensure lawful and fair processing* in national laws should also consider the particular situations of vulnerable subjects.

The legal basis of vital interests (Article 6(1)(d)) is explicitly considered for the situation of vulnerability of data subjects (eg in case of a health emergency), but its scope is very limited to exceptional conditions 'of life and death'.[101]

Legitimate interests and vulnerable data subjects

If it is not possible to process data on the basis of a contract, legal obligations, and vital interests, the data controller might consider processing data on the basis of legitimate interest (Article 6(1)(f)) or public interest (Article 6(1)(e)). However, in such cases, the controller is asked to balance their interests and the data subject's.[102] Such balancing test should be conducted on the basis of four steps: (i) assessing the controller's legitimate interest, (ii) impact on the data subjects, (iii) provisional

[100] Emphasis added.

[101] WP29, Opinion 06/2014 on the notion of legitimate interests, 20: 'this legal ground should have a limited application. First, the phrase "vital interest" appears to limit the application of this ground to questions of life and death, or at the very least, threats that pose a risk of injury or other damage to the health of the data subject.'

[102] ibid 33. See also I Kamara and P De Hert, 'Understanding the Balancing Act behind the Legitimate Interest of the Controller Ground' in E Selinger and others (eds), *The Cambridge Handbook of Consumer Privacy* (Cambridge University Press 2018) 321–52. doi:10.1017/9781316831960.019.

balance, and (iv) additional safeguards applied by the controller to prevent any undue impact on the data subjects.[103]

For what concerns the impact on the data subject (point (ii)), the WP29 suggests a series of sub-criteria: assessment of impact; nature of the data and the way data are processed; reasonable expectations of the data subject; and *status of the data subject* and the controller.[104] These sub-criteria are linked to each other. For example, the assessment of impact depends on the other criteria and, in particular, on the status of the data subject. Interestingly, the notion of 'status of the data subject' refers to the distinction between average and vulnerable data subjects that sits at the heart of the research question of this book. Indeed, the WP29 affirms: 'while the balancing test should in principle be *made against an average individual, specific situations should lead to a more case-by-case approach*: for example, it would be relevant to consider whether the data subject is a child or otherwise *belongs to a more vulnerable segment of the population* requiring special protection, such as, for example, the mentally ill, asylum seekers, or the elderly'.[105] In addition, the WP29 clarifies that the question whether the data subject 'is an employee, a student, a patient, or whether there is otherwise an imbalance in the relationship between the position of the data subject and the controller must certainly be also relevant'.[106]

This part of the WP29 Opinion seems relevant for this book for at least three reasons: (i) it clarifies that the data controller willing to use legitimate interests as a legal basis for data processing needs to undertake a preliminary Data Protection Impact Assessment (DPIA), regardless of whether they are subject or not to the duty of DPIA at Article 35;[107] (ii) in this impact assessment, utmost importance must be given to the status of the data subject[108] and, in particular, if there are vulnerable data subjects, specific safeguards should be adopted to comply with Article 6(1)(f); (iii) the notion of the data subject is based on the dualism of average versus vulnerable data subjects. In addition, this Opinion seems to propose two different notions of vulnerability: one intrinsic, such as the 'mentally ill', asylum seekers, or the elderly; and another more contextual, for example an employee, a student, a patient, or whether there is another kind of imbalance in the relationship. Interestingly, this is the first and only time in which the WP29 considers students as a vulnerable category. Lastly, the Opinion mentioned above clarifies that vulnerability should be considered on a case-by-case approach,[109] without easy generalizations being made.

[103] WP29, Opinion 06/2014, 33.

[104] On these points, see J Ausloos, *The Right to Erasure in EU Data Protection Law* (Oxford University Press 2020) 320–22.

[105] WP29, Opinion 06/2014, 39–40. See also WP29, Opinion 03/2013 on purpose limitation, 51.

[106] WP29, Opinion 06/2014 on the notion of legitimate interests, 40.

[107] See Ausloos (n 126) 308, 320 (fn 198) who clarifies the distinction between the risk analysis and the impact assessment in art 35 and the balancing exercise under art 6(1)(f).

[108] ibid 321.

[109] ibid 40: 'specific situations should lead to a more case-by-case approach'.

Even the CJEU has clarified that the considerations of legitimate interests for data processing depend on the status of the data subject, that is, on the particular situation of the subject.[110]

In sum, the status and conditions of data subjects are relevant for the lawfulness principle. Indeed, the data controller needs to assess the level (or 'layer') of their data subjects' vulnerability to choose the lawful basis for processing data. If the data subject is vulnerable, the data controller needs to understand the source of this vulnerability. In case of vulnerabilities in making decisions, the data controller should not use consent as a legal basis. Among the other possible lawful bases, legitimate interest is an option (in particular if the data processing is not necessary for a contract, for a legal obligation, for a public task, or a public interest). However, in that case, the data controller needs to perform a balancing test, assessing the impact of data processing by looking at the data subject's particular situation. It might be that the data processing will impose too great an impact on the data subject—particularly in the case of vulnerable data subjects—and that the data controller cannot find any suitable measures to mitigate such an imbalance of power. In such cases, the data processing should not be started or continued, according to the lawfulness and fairness principles.

Sensitive data: a concept for protecting (more) vulnerable data subjects?

When talking about data subjects' vulnerability and lawfulness principle, another sub-question seems necessary to answer the general research question of this book: do the notion and the *sui generis* protection of special categories of data take into account different data subjects and, in particular, vulnerable individuals? In other words, I wonder whether the definition of sensitive data is conceived, in part, for the protection of vulnerable people.

First, we need to understand what sensitive data ('special categories of personal data') means under the GDPR. Article 9(1) states as follows: 'Processing of personal data revealing racial or ethnic origin, political opinions, religious or philosophical beliefs, or trade union membership, and the processing of genetic data, biometric data for the purpose of uniquely identifying a natural person, data concerning health or data concerning a natural person's sex life or sexual orientation shall be prohibited.' Article 9(2) provides some exceptions to this prohibition.[111]

[110] CJEU, Case C-131/12 *Google Spain SL, Google Inc. v Agencia Española de Protección de Datos (AEPD), Mario Costeja González* [13 May 2014], §§ 76 ('the balancing to be carried out … thus enables account to be taken in a more specific manner of all the circumstances surrounding the data subject's particular situation'), 98 ('it should be held that, having regard to the sensitivity for the data subject's private life of the information contained in those announcements'). See also CJEU C-398/15, *Camera di Commercio, Industria, Artigianato e Agricoltura di Lecce v Salvatore Manni* [9 March 2017], §47.

[111] See below in this section.

To understand whether sensitive data were conceived to protect vulnerable data subjects, we need to look at the justification of sensitive data protection in the different data protection regimes until the GDPR. Justifications for the concept of sensitive (or special categories of personal) data appear in the first international legal formulations of sensitive data protection, where one can find justification for the *sui generis* protection for sensitive data.[112] Common reasons for the existence of sensitive data often revolve around the need to prevent harmful forms of discrimination or related phenomena. The United Nations, for example, issued Guidelines for the Regulation of Computerized Personal Data Files in 1990, justifying further protection for sensitive data because such data are 'likely to give rise to *unlawful or arbitrary discrimination*'.[113]

Similarly, almost thirty years later, the GDPR[114] also contains a justification for the augmentation of requirements for sensitive data processing. In particular, Recital 51 explains that such data are 'by their *nature*, particularly sensitive in relation to fundamental rights and freedoms', and thus they 'merit specific protection as the context of their processing could create *significant risks to the fundamental rights and freedoms*'.[115] In addition, Recital 71, when addressing the right not to be subject to automated decisions with legal or similarly significant effects on individuals, explains that one crucial concern is the possibility of discrimination based on sensitive data: 'discriminatory effects on natural persons on the basis of racial or *ethnic origin, political opinion, religion or beliefs, trade union membership, genetic or health status or sexual orientation, or that result in measures having such an effect*'.[116] In sum, the GDPR provides specific protection for some types of personal data because their processing could produce significant risks to fundamental rights and freedoms,[117] which include (but are not limited to) discriminatory effects.[118]

[112] See, interestingly, the first reflections on the difficulty to define sensitive data (especially considering different cultures and legal traditions) in N Lindop (ed), *Report of the Committee on Data Protection* (HMSO 1978) 20. See also P Quinn and G Malgieri, 'The Difficulty of Defining Sensitive Data—The Concept of Sensitive Data in the EU Data Protection Framework' (2021) 22(8) German Law Journal 1583.

[113] UN General Assembly, 'Guidelines for the Regulation of Computerized Personal Data Files, Available' (1990) §5 <https://www.refworld.org/docid/3ddcafaac.html> accessed 20 February 2023, Emphasis added.

[114] This was unlike its predecessor Directive 95/46/EC which did not give any justification/rationale for the existence of the concept of sensitive data.

[115] Emphasis added.

[116] Emphasis added.

[117] On the concept of 'risks to rights', including discrimination, see N van Dijk and others, 'A Risk to a Right? Beyond Data Protection Risk Assessments' (2016) 32(2) *Computer Law & Security Review* 286–306.

[118] See, in general, R Gellert and others, 'A Comparative Analysis of Anti-Discrimination and Data Protection Legislations' in B Custers and others (eds), *Discrimination and Privacy in the Information Society: Data Mining and Profiling in Large Databases* (Springer 2013); FJ Zuiderveen Borgesius, 'Strengthening Legal Protection against Discrimination by Algorithms and Artificial Intelligence' (2020) 0 The International Journal of Human Rights 1.

Beyond the GDPR, looking at other parallel data protection frameworks might be useful. Indeed, the Council of Europe Modernized Convention 108 on Automatic Processing of Personal Data, for example, provides a more detailed justification of sensitive data protection in its Explanatory Report.[119] In general, it also acknowledges that sensitive data processing 'may lead to encroachments on interests, rights and freedoms'.[120] The Explanatory Report argues that this 'can for instance be the case where there is a potential *risk of discrimination* or *injury to an individual's dignity or physical integrity*, where the data subject's most intimate sphere, such as his or her sex life or sexual orientation, is being affected, or where processing of data could affect the presumption of innocence'. Accordingly, 'to prevent *adverse effects for the data subject*' this processing 'should only be permitted where appropriate safeguards, which complement the other protective provisions of the Convention, are provided for by law'. In sum, the CoE's Convention Report does not only mention discrimination, it adopts a broader approach. It recognizes that the processing of sensitive data is more likely to have adverse effects on data subjects, especially discrimination, *but also* injury to dignity or physical integrity, thus affecting their most intimate sphere, their presumption of innocence, etc. The new proposed e-privacy Regulation (in the first version of the Commission Proposal)[121] also shows a broad justification for protecting 'sensitive information'.[122]

This overview shows how the notion of sensitive data, in the broader data protection framework, is conceived for protecting situations of significant risks to fundamental rights and freedoms, which includes discrimination[123] but also more in general physical, psychological, social, or economic harms. Considering that the definition of data subject's vulnerability adopted in Chapter 4 refers to a permanent or temporary status of higher exposure to risks to fundamental rights and freedoms, we can affirm that the rationale of sensitive data protection seems to be, at least in part, the general protection of *vulnerable* data subjects. Thus, the *sui generis* protection of special categories of data partly aims at safeguarding vulnerable data

[119] Council of Europe, Explanatory Report—CETS 223—Automatic Processing of Personal Data (Amending Protocol), 10 October 2018 <https://rm.coe.int/cets-223-explanatory-report-to-the-protocol-amending-the-convention-fo/16808ac91a> accessed 20 February 2023.

[120] Council of Europe, Explanatory Report, Section 55.

[121] Proposal for a Regulation of the European Parliament and of the Council concerning the respect for private life and the protection of personal data in electronic communications and repealing Directive 2002/58/EC (Regulation on Privacy and Electronic Communications), COM/2017/010 final—2017/03 (COD).

[122] Recital 2 states: 'the content of electronic communications may reveal highly sensitive information about the natural persons involved in the communication, from personal experiences and emotions to medical conditions, sexual preferences and political views, *the disclosure of which could result in personal and social harm, economic loss or embarrassment*'. Here the term discrimination is not even mentioned, while the broad perspective (personal, social and economic harm or embarrassment) is preferred.

[123] Lynskey (n 92) 197–202.

subjects. However, we can still wonder *how* this protection mitigates individual vulnerability and whether this approach is effective or not.

Looking at Article 9(1), it emerges that vulnerable subjects that could receive higher safeguards from sensitive data protection are, at least, the following categories: ethnic minorities, sexual orientation minorities (LGBTQIA+ community), political minorities, sick persons, persons at risk of genetic illnesses, workers in terms of their participation in trade unions, etc. These groups of data subjects are more vulnerable to discrimination[124] but also to other risks to their autonomy, dignity, and integrity (eg sick people may have reduced decisional freedom or higher risks regarding their integrity; similarly, workers, etc). Although the protection for special categories of data seems broad under this perspective, it is not comprehensive in terms of all situations in which data subjects might find themselves to be vulnerable. Even if the interpretation of those categories of sensitive data is contextual[125] and thus relatively extensive,[126] the presence of a closed list of vulnerable situations does not help extend the notion of vulnerability beyond the traditional categories.[127] In particular, considering that there is no reference to, for example, commercial preferences, economic conditions, educational background, age, performance at work or school, etc, several forms of data subjects' vulnerability are excluded from the scope of sensitive data protection.

However, is this special protection adequate to protect (at least some) vulnerable data subjects? The rules about sensitive data are based on several different tools: stricter lawful conditions for processing such data (general prohibition with a close list of exemptions at Article 9(2)) and for using them as a basis for automated decision (ie automated decisions based on sensitive data can just be based on explicit consent or the substantial public interest, under Article 22(4)).[128] In addition, when the processing of special categories of data is 'on a large scale', there is a duty to appoint a Data Protection Officer (Article 37(1)(c)) and to perform a Data Protection Impact Assessment (Article 35(3)(b)).

Article 9(2) provides that the processing of special categories of data is forbidden unless a specific exception applies (eg there is the explicit consent of the

[124] Fineman (n 95).

[125] S Simitis, *Revisiting Sensitive Data, Review of the answers to the Questionnaire of the Consultative Committee of the Convention for the Protection of Individuals with regard to Automatic Processing of Personal Data* (ETS 108) (Strasbourg, 24–26 November 1999). Council of Europe study <https://rm.coe.int/16806845af> accessed 23 January 2023.

[126] K McCullagh, 'Data Sensitivity: Proposals for Resolving the Conundrum' (2007) 2(4) Journal of International Commercial Law and Technology 190.

[127] On the distinction between unlawful data processing because based on protected grounds and morally problematic data processing see Lynskey (n 92) 201. Similarly, on the distinction between discriminatory biases and morally problematic biases, see M Hildebrandt, 'The Issue of Bias: The Framing Powers of ML' in M Pelillo (ed), *Machine Learning and Society: Impact, Trust, Transparency* (MIT Press 2021).

[128] Article 22(4): 'Decisions referred to in paragraph 2 shall not be based on special categories of personal data referred to in Article 9(1), unless point (a) or (g) of Article 9(2) applies and suitable measures to safeguard the data subject's rights and freedoms and legitimate interests are in place.'

data subject; the controller is carrying out obligations or guaranteeing rights in the field of employment law; the processing is in the vital interests of the data subjects, etc). As regards the data subject's explicit consent, as noted previously, if the data subject is in a situation of decision-making vulnerability, the data controller should look for another exception under Article 9(2). If such an alternative is not possible, the controller should not proceed with that data processing.

These tools might appear a first attempt to cope with data subjects' vulnerability: limiting the processing of such data to well-circumscribed situations only and providing additional accountability duties (having a Data Processing Officer (DPO) and conducting a DPIA) might contribute to adequate protection. However, the limited list of sensitive data compared to all potential data subjects' vulnerabilities weakens this special protection (see Chapter 8).

4. The purpose limitation principle: third locus of the protection of data subjects' vulnerability

The purpose limitation principle might well be relevant for the protection of vulnerable data subjects. According to Article 5(1)(b), personal data must be 'collected for specified, explicit and legitimate purposes and not further processed in a manner that is incompatible with those purposes'.[129] The notion of *legitimate* purpose seems related to the lawfulness principle (a purpose is lawful if it respects one of the legal grounds at Article 6), but, as the WP29 clarifies, the requirement of legitimacy means that the purposes must be 'in accordance with the law' in the broadest sense (any source and field of law) and 'within the confines of law, other elements such as ... the general context and facts of the case, may also be considered ... This will include the nature of the underlying relationship between the controller and the data subjects, whether it be commercial or otherwise.'[130] Also, in this case, it seems that the nature of the relationship between subjects and controllers and, in particular, the type of imbalance (and so *the type of data subjects* at issue) is relevant.

If, for example, the data controller deals with vulnerable data subjects, the controller will not only need to assess the data processing under a fairness and lawfulness perspective but also under a purpose limitation (and more specifically, a purpose legitimacy) perspective. For example, the determination regarding clarity and granularity of purpose of data will be more critical when vulnerable data subjects are involved.

129 For archiving, research, and statistical purposes there is an exemption in art 5(1), point b: 'further processing for archiving purposes in the public interest, scientific or historical research purposes or statistical purposes shall, in accordance with Article 89(1), not be considered to be incompatible with the initial purposes ('purpose limitation')'.

130 See WP29, Opinion 03/2013 on purpose limitation, 20.

These last considerations are particularly relevant in the processing of data beyond the reason for which they were collected initially, in other words, for secondary purposes. Article 6(4) clarifies that where the processing for a purpose other than that for which the personal data have been collected is not based on the data subject's consent or a Union or Member State law, 'the controller shall, in order to ascertain whether processing for another purpose is compatible with the purpose for which the personal data are initially collected, take into account' a series of factors: the link between the initial and new purposes; the context of data collection and 'the relationship between data subjects and the controller'; the nature of personal data; the possible consequences of the intended further processing; the existence of appropriate safeguards.

Regarding the relationship between data subjects and the controller, the WP29[131] suggests considering, *inter alia*, 'the status of the data controller and data subject, including the balance of power between the data subject and the data controller, or whether the data subject is a child or otherwise belongs to a more vulnerable segment of the population.... It is important to assess the effect of actual processing on particular individuals.'[132] In other words, if the data subject is vulnerable (with regards to the relationship with their data controller), the compatibility test of Article 6(4) will need to take this vulnerability condition into account.

That is why the same opinion of the WP29 suggests as a general rule that 'further processing of personal data concerning ... data about children, other vulnerable individuals, or other highly sensitive information should, in principle, be permitted only with the consent of the data subject'.[133]

This seems to contradict our previous conclusions about the general inappropriateness of using consent as a lawful basis for processing data of vulnerable data subjects.[134] However, this contradiction can be resolved only if we take into account the notion of vulnerability as layered vulnerability,[135] considering the difference between processing-based and effect-based vulnerability. Suppose the vulnerability is effect-based and not involving the data subject's decision-making. In that case, there are no obstacles to asking for data subjects' consent. Quite the contrary, consent might also be preferable to prevent adverse outcomes of the data processing. In contrast, if the data subject's vulnerability affects their decision-making (what I called in general also *processing-based vulnerability*, ie affecting the decision-making capacity of the subject, for example persons with mental

131 WP29, 'Opinion 03/2013 on purpose limitation' referred to the Data Protection Directive, but it proposed the same compatibility test that now has been formalized in art 6(4) of the GDPR. Accordingly, we can take that Opinion as a valid interpretation of rules regulating further purposes.

132 WP29, Opinion 03/2013 on purpose limitation, 51.

133 WP29, Opinion 03/2013 on purpose limitation, 32.

134 See Section 3.1.

135 F Luna, 'Elucidating the Concept of Vulnerability: Layers Not Labels' (2009) 2 International Journal of Feminist Approaches to Bioethics 121; F Luna, 'Identifying and Evaluating Layers of Vulnerability—A Way Forward' (2019) 19 Developing World Bioethics 86.

disabilities, children, etc), consent might not be an appropriate legal basis. In this case, even a secondary use of data should not be based on consent since the data subject might not be able to give that consent freely. Accordingly, the data controller will be asked to perform a compatibility test under Article 6(4). As observed above, this compatibility test will need to be particularly strict in the case of vulnerable individuals. The result is that, in many cases, for data subjects affected by decision-making vulnerability, the data controller could not (or at least not easily) process data on the basis of secondary uses.

5. The accuracy principle

The accuracy principle (Article 5(1)(d)) might also be relevant to mitigate data subjects' vulnerability. According to this principle, the data controller should only process personal data that are accurate and, where necessary, kept up to date; consequently, 'every reasonable step must be taken to ensure that personal data that are inaccurate, having regard to the purposes for which they are processed, are erased or rectified without delay'.

Despite the ambiguous nature of this principle for privacy and data protection, as discussed in the scholarly debate,[136] we can observe the relevance of this principle for this research under two different perspectives: (i) inaccurate data might be the effect of biased and discriminatory data processing affecting vulnerable groups; (ii) the lack of accurate information about the individual vulnerabilities of certain data subjects (ages, mental, or linguistic vulnerabilities, etc) might lead data controllers to implement the other principles and rights of the GDPR inadequately.

As regards point (i), data inaccuracies might be both the source and the effect of discriminatory data processing. Racial biases are one example, but the data accuracy principles might prevent many other forms of discrimination. This is true in particular in the field of automated decision-making, where, as Recital 71 affirms, inaccuracies in automated profiling is a relevant risk that controllers should face since they might lead to discriminatory effects.

As regards point (ii), the data controller can adequately balance their interests with the data subject's interest (when, for example, choosing the legal basis for processing data under Articles 6 or 9 or when guaranteeing the exercise of data subjects' rights, for example the right to object) only if the controller is accurately informed about the conditions of data subject's vulnerability. When assessing the validity of consent as a legal basis for data processing concerning vulnerable data subjects (in case of processing-based vulnerability) or when performing the

[136] See eg G González Fuster, 'Inaccuracy as a Privacy-Enhancing Tool' (2010) 12 Ethics and Information Technology 87; J Chen, 'The Dangers of Accuracy': (2018) 4 European Data Protection Law Review 36.

balancing test required to process data on the basis of legitimate interests, accurate data on the personal condition of data subjects are essential to allow the data controller to protect the subject adequately. Similarly, the data controller can shape their communication to the data subject appropriately if they are aware of the data subject's specific condition. As an example, in the case of very young children, the accuracy of data about age is very relevant to tailor adequate transparency duties (under Articles 13–15) and to decide whether and how the consent is an adequate lawful basis: as affirmed by WP29, specific safeguards for children should be proportional to the degree of physical and psychological development of the child at issue;[137] accordingly, the more accurate is the information about age and maturity, the more effective can be the safeguards adopted by the data controller. We can imagine similar examples for any other type of processing-based or effect-based vulnerability.

I am aware that acquiring more data about (vulnerable) data subjects—particularly special categories of data—just to protect them might appear in contradiction with the data minimization principle. However, at a certain level of granularity, such additional and accurate information might be vital to protect specific situations of vulnerability adequately. Chapter 8 analyses explicitly this data minimization paradox.

6. Conclusions

This chapter has analysed how the implementation of the data protection principles in the GDPR should consider the special situations of the data subjects, particularly when these situations might qualify as vulnerability (as defined in Chapter 3). I have focused on the principles of fairness, lawfulness, and purpose limitations. Indeed, these principles require a strict balancing between the relative positions of the data subject and the data controllers[138] and, consequently, an examination of the impact of data processing on data subjects, including an assessment of their vulnerability.

The analysis of fairness (Section 2) has revealed that such a principle—if widely understood through a contextual and linguistic interpretation—might help protect individual vulnerabilities and prevent the exploitation of data subjects' vulnerability. Indeed, as I showed through the three different possible interpretations of fairness in the data protection framework (procedural fairness; fair balancing aimed at the prevention of adverse effects; and good faith), fairness is an overarching interpretative principle aimed at preventing situations of significative

[137] WP29, Opinion 2/2009 on the protection of children's personal data (General Guidelines and the special case of schools), WP 160, Adopted on 11 February 2009, 6.

[138] Gellert, 'We Have Always Managed Risks in Data Protection Law' (n 2).

power imbalance that could produce *adverse effects* for some vulnerable data subjects.

Section 3 analysed the concept of lawfulness, including lawful bases for processing personal data and special categories of personal data. Two aspects were considered. First, the choice between consent and legitimate interest (or other legal bases) as a consequence of an assessment of the data subject's vulnerability. For some subjects, particularly those affected by processing-based vulnerability (decision-making vulnerability during the data processing), consent is not an appropriate legal basis, while the legitimate interest (following a strict balancing test) might be preferable. Second, the rationale for the higher protection of special categories of personal data (sensitive data) is also the mitigation of specific forms of data subjects' vulnerability. However, as that section argues, such protection is not always adequate.

Section 4 focused on purpose limitation. The data controller's duty to adhere to lawful and specific data processing purposes should also inspire an assessment of the particular conditions of the data subjects, especially in the case of secondary use of data. Lastly, Section 5 addressed the accuracy principle, which might both prevent discriminatory biases and permit the identification and mitigation of data subjects' vulnerabilities (with appropriate balancing, legal choices, and safeguards).

In conclusion, when interpreting all the principles mentioned above, it seems necessary to consider the specific, individual conditions of data subjects, particularly the data subjects' vulnerability. These principles impose on the data controller the requirement to assess the data subjects' specific circumstances and implement the data protection rules accordingly. To understand how such rules might be implemented in practice, Chapter 6 analyses the system of rights and duties of the GDPR. In contrast, Chapter 7 will propose a vulnerability-based implementation of the whole data protection framework based on the DPIA model.

6
Data protection rights and duties and vulnerable data subjects

1. Introduction

This chapter discusses data protection rights and duties under the perspective of data subjects' personal conditions, in particular considering data subjects' vulnerabilities. Based on the analysis developed in Chapter 5 on the protection of vulnerable data subjects in the General Data Protection Regulation (GDPR) principles, this chapter covers the other provisions of the GDPR, and poses the following question: when implementing the data protection rights and duties in the GDPR, how should we consider the situation of the data subjects, in particular their vulnerabilities?

As regards data protection rights in the GDPR, Section 3 of this chapter focuses mainly on transparency rights (the right to receive information about data processing cited in Articles 13 and 14, and the right to access to information about the data processing and the personal data processed, cited in Article 15), Section 4 addresses the right to erasure (Article 17), Section 5 the right to object (Article 21), and Section 6 the 'particular situation' relevant for that right. Section 7 addresses the right not to be subject to automated decision-making (Article 22). When interpreting and implementing these rights in practice, the vulnerability of data subjects is a relevant element to consider.

As regards the data controller's duties covered in the GDPR, I dedicate particular attention (Sections 8 and 9) to the references to 'categories of data subjects' in the records of data processing activities and the security measures for data processing (including measures in case of a data breach), to the risk-based approach (Section 10), to the principle of data protection by design (Section 11), and the Data Protection Impact Assessment (DPIA) (Sections 12–14). As argued in this chapter, at least in these cases, data subjects' personal situations or conditions are relevant. In particular, for some accountability duties (record of data processing and data breach notifications), the data controller needs to identify the 'categories of data subjects'. In other cases (risk-based approach, data protection by design, DPIA), the data controller needs to perform an analysis of risks for data subjects. As I argue, this analysis should include the level of vulnerability of the data subject in a given situation.

Vulnerability and Data Protection Law. Gianclaudio Malgieri, Oxford University Press. © Gianclaudio Malgieri 2023.
DOI: 10.1093/oso/9780192870339.003.0006

2. Data subjects' rights in the GDPR: towards a vulnerability-based interpretation?

The following investigation focuses on whether the current interpretation and application of data subjects' rights take into account individual vulnerabilities, among other factors. The GDPR provides several data protection rights in its Chapter 3: the right to receive transparent information about the data processing (Articles 12–14), the right to access to information about the data processing and the personal data processed (Article 15), the right to rectification (Article 16), the right to erasure (Article 17), the right to restriction of processing (Article 18), the right to data portability (Article 20), the right to object (Article 21), and the right not to be subject to automated decision-making (Article 22).

A detailed analysis of all these rights[1] is beyond the scope of this chapter, which instead addresses the rights where the balancing of powers and interests between the data controllers and the data subjects has been considered to be crucial both in the case law and in the literature. The analysis will aim to elucidate the role played by the data subjects' conditions (and especially, their level of vulnerability) in the interpretation and implementation of these rights based on difficult balancing acts. In particular, this chapter covers transparency rights (Articles 13–15), the right to erasure, the right to object, and the right not to be subject to automated decision-making.

3. Transparency rights and the types of the data subject

Articles 12–15 focus on the right of data subjects to receive adequate information about data processing. Article 12 provides general rules about the application of transparency rights that can be found in the following articles. Article 13 deals with *ex-ante* information duties of data controllers to data subjects in case personal data are 'collected from the data subject'. In contrast, Article 14 addresses *ex-ante* information duties if personal data are 'not obtained from the data subject'. Lastly, Article 15 provides data subjects with a right to obtain confirmation from the controller as to whether personal data concerning them is being processed, access to the personal data, and information about the data processing.[2]

As noted in Chapter 2, this set of rights is based on the idea that the data subject, when well informed, can adequately exercise all their data protection rights, such as the right to give and revoke their consent, to object, to rectify, to erase, and to

[1] See HU Vrabec, *Data Subject Rights under the GDPR* (Oxford University Press 2021).

[2] See, in particular, European Data Protection Board, 'Guidelines 01/2022 on Data Subject Rights—Right of Access—Version 1.0. Adopted on 18 January 2022'.

exercise data portability.[3] In other words, the idea of the legislator was to empower data subjects, through a system of enhanced transparency.[4] However, it is clear that individual cognitive capacities depend on several variables. Thus, one may wonder who the well-informed data subject is and whether the data processing policy information is clear and detailed, taking into account the specific data subject at issue.[5]

Under the Data Protection Directive (DPD), the right to information did not explicitly imply that the provided information had to be readily understandable to the individual data subject. In practice, it was accepted that information could be given in a standardized form.[6] In the GDPR, on the contrary, much more attention is paid to whether the information supplied to the data subject is comprehensible to that subject. In particular, Article 12 states that this information must be provided in a 'transparent, intelligible and easily accessible form, using clear and plain language, in particular for any information addressed specifically to a child'. The use of the wording '*in particular* for ... a child' seems to suggest that the child is not the data subject who may have limited cognitive capacities.

Recital 58 further clarifies that the information provided should also be 'easy to understand'. This requirement is essential when the data subject is a child too.[7] Recital 60 adds that, according to the fairness and transparency principles,[8] the controller should provide the data subject with any further information necessary 'taking into account the specific circumstances and context' in which the personal data are processed. The reference to the specific *context* also seems to suggest requirement for a case-by-case analysis of the data subject at stake and their cognitional capacity.[9] In other words, developing the analogy from the case where the data subject is a child, all vulnerable situations should be taken into account when providing information on data processing activities. The Article 29 Data Protection Working Party on the Protection of Individuals with regard to the Processing of Personal Data (WP29) Guidelines on Transparency confirm this interpretation of information duties, in particular for vulnerable adults.[10]

[3] See CJEU, Case C-533/07 *College van burgemeester en wethouders van Rotterdam v M.E.E. Rijkeboer* [2009], ECR I-03889, Opinion of AG Ruiz-Jarabo Colomer, delivered on 22 December 2008, para 29: right to access is a 'true subjective dimension of the directive [since] it enables individuals to react in defence of their interests'.

[4] G González Fuster, 'How Uninformed Is the Average Data Subject? A Quest for Benchmarks in EU Personal Data Protection' (2014) 19 IDP Revista de Internet, Derecho y Política 92; O Lynskey, *The Foundations of EU Data Protection Law* (Oxford University Press 2015) 214.

[5] M Hildebrandt, 'The Dawn of a Critical Transparency Right for the Profiling Era' in J Bus (ed), *Digital Enlightenment Yearbook* (IOS Press 2012).

[6] P Blume, 'The Data Subject' (2015) 1 European Data Protection Law Review 258, 259.

[7] See Recital 58: 'given that children merit specific protection, any information and communication, where processing is addressed to a child, should be in such a clear and plain language that the child can easily understand'.

[8] González Fuster (n 4) 102.

[9] ibid.

[10] WP29 on Transparency, 9: 'if a data controller is aware that their goods/services are availed of by (or targeted at) other vulnerable members of society, including people with disabilities or people who

In its recent guidelines on the right to access, the European Data Protection Board (EDPB) has explicitly recognized the need to consider the special needs of children and other vulnerable data subjects when implementing the right to access, in particular the intelligibility and accessibility of the communications from the data controller to the data subject.[11] The reference to children in Article 12(1) must be extended analogically to other people 'with special needs', for example 'by proactively providing easily accessible elements to facilitate the exercise of these rights'.[12]

In sum, it seems that the GDPR conceives transparency rights mainly in terms of the 'average' data subject, who can easily understand data processing characteristics and react accordingly. This idea of the 'average' data subject is thus similar to the notion of the average consumer (see Chapter 2). When provided with more information, the decision of the average data subject will be considered to be well-informed and thus rational.[13] However, through a systematic interpretation of the GDPR, such as the one presented here, it is possible to observe that the data controller—when implementing transparency duties—needs to take into account the specific situations of data subjects, particularly considering whether the subject is cognitively vulnerable.

4. The right to erasure and the vulnerable subjects

Another data protection right that is worth examining is the right to erasure ('right to be forgotten').[14] According to Article 17 of the GDPR, the data subject shall have the right to obtain from the controller the erasure of personal data concerning them without undue delay when the data are no longer necessary for the original purposes stated, where the processing is unlawful, when the subject withdraws the consent or successfully exercises the right to object to the processing of their data, when the erasure of that data is required by law, or when 'personal data have been collected in relation to the offer of information society services' directly to a child.

Recital 65 further explains that this right is relevant, in particular, where the data subject has given their consent as a child and is not fully aware of the risks involved

may have difficulties accessing information, the vulnerabilities of such data subjects should be taken into account by the data controller in its assessment of how to ensure that it complies with its transparency obligations in relation to such data subjects'.

[11] EDPB (n 2) 44: 'the controller should take special care to ensure that people with special needs, such as elderly people, children, visually impaired persons or persons with cognitive disabilities can exercise their rights, for instance by proactively providing easily accessible elements to facilitate exercise of these rights'.

[12] ibid.

[13] González Fuster (n 4).

[14] See, in general, J Ausloos, *The Right to Erasure in EU Data Protection Law* (Oxford University Press 2020).

by the processing, and later wants to remove such personal data, especially if it is available and visible on the Internet. The data subject should be able to exercise that right, even though they are no longer children.

By reading this recital, it seems clear that one of the rationales of the right to erasure is to remove any effect of the data processing where the data subject was not fully conscious of the significance of the data processing. Other vulnerable individuals might also not be fully aware of the risks involved in processing their data. As affirmed in Chapter 3, these data subjects are in a position of cognitive vulnerability (what I defined 'vulnerability during the data processing'), subjects who did not provide free, conscious, and informed consent. In this case, the exercise of the right to erasure would afford them some protection from the harm of data exploitation.

In sum, even though in Article 17 there is no explicit reference to the particular conditions and circumstances of the data subjects (or to data subjects' vulnerability), it seems clear that the existence of this new right is also a way to offer stronger protection to at least some vulnerable data subjects, in particular children and cognitively vulnerable adults and, as Ausloos argues, to mitigate power imbalance between subject and controller.[15] Before the approval of the GDPR, the Court of Justice of the European Union (CJEU) in *Google Spain*[16] had already addressed the right of data subjects to have their personal data delisted by search engines.[17] The Court explicitly considered the particular situation of data subjects in that specific context, finding that search engines could indeed cause data subjects to become more exposed and thus more vulnerable than they would otherwise be.[18] That is why some authors argue that the right to erasure can be an adequate tool to strengthen the autonomy of data subjects,[19] in particular for more vulnerable subjects whose autonomy and informational self-determination might be more easily impaired than those of the 'average' subject.[20]

[15] ibid Chapter 5.

[16] E Frantziou, 'Further Developments in the Right to Be Forgotten: The European Court of Justice's Judgment in Case C-131/12, Google Spain, SL, Google Inc v Agencia Espanola de Proteccion de Datos Recent Developments' (2014) 14 Human Rights Law Review 761; L Siry, 'Forget Me, Forget Me Not: Reconciling Two Different Paradigms of the Right to Be Forgotten' (2014) 103 Kentucky Law Journal 311.

[17] See EDPB, Guidelines 5/2019 on the criteria of the Right to be Forgotten in the search engines cases under the GDPR (part 1), Adopted on 2 December 2019 <https://edpb.europa.eu/sites/edpb/files/consultation/edpb_guidelines_201905_rtbfsearchengines_forpublicconsultation.pdf> accessed 20 February 2023.

[18] CJEU Case C-131/12 *Google Spain SL and Google Inc v Agencia Española de Protección de Datos (AEPD) and Mario Costeja González* [2014], §81. See, in particular, on this point Frantziou (n 16) 769.

[19] C Bartolini and L Siry, 'The Right to Be Forgotten in the Light of the Consent of the Data Subject' (2016) 32 Computer Law & Security Review 218, 223.

[20] About the potentiality of the right to erasure to rebalance the imbalance of vulnerable subjects, see also, interestingly, A Trites, 'Black Box Ethics: Why the Rights to Explanation and to Be Forgotten Are Ethically Critical Components for Vulnerable Populations' (PhD Thesis, Université Saint-Paul/Saint Paul University 2019) <http://ruor.uottawa.ca/handle/10393/39126> accessed 10 May 2020.

5. The right to object and 'the particular situation' of vulnerable data subjects

Another right that we must consider when considering different data subjects is the right to object, as regulated by Article 21 of the GDPR. I focus in particular on the right to object for three reasons.

First, as aforementioned, one manifestation of vulnerability is decision-making vulnerability, the incapability of understanding and deciding whether to accept certain conditions. In that case, it is unfair or unlawful if the data controller uses consent as a legal basis to pursue the processing of data. Instead, they should choose other legal bases under Article 6 GDPR; for example—if no other lawful basis can apply—public interest or legitimate interest or refrain from processing those data. However, the data subject would not have the right to revoke the consent in these cases. Accordingly, the right to object is an important opportunity for data subjects to stop that data processing and it is also a key safeguard, counterbalancing the legitimate interest adequacy test of the data controllers.

Secondly, the right to object is the critical *ex-post* tool for guaranteeing fair data processing. Indeed, the right to object is an actual specification of the fairness principle because it contributes to the fair balancing of power between the position of the data controller and the position of the data subject.[21] Considering that fairness is tightly linked to the protection of data subjects' vulnerability, the right to object is a relevant element to consider.

Thirdly, the wording of Article 21 GDPR—also in the previous form of Article 14 of the Data Protection Directive, as interpreted by the CJEU, for example in the *Google Spain* case[22]—seems to refer to different types of data subjects, and this makes the right to object a particularly interesting provision for our purposes.

The right to object is the only data protection right that the wording of the GDPR explicitly relates to the 'grounds relating to' the 'particular situation' of the data subject. What does 'particular situation' mean in this case? Can we consider the status of the data subject and their permanent or temporary condition of vulnerability as a particular situation of the data subject?

The text of the GDPR is not clear on this point, neither in the body of the Articles nor in the Recitals. The Explanatory Memorandum of the EC Commission proposal for the GDPR only declares that the right to object 'is based on Article 14 of Directive 95/46/EC, with some modifications, including as regards the burden of proof and its application to direct marketing'.[23]

[21] D Clifford and J Ausloos, 'Data Protection and the Role of Fairness' (2018) 37 Yearbook of European Law 130, 177–81.

[22] *Google Spain* (n 18) §§76 and 90; these considerations have been then confirmed in CJEU Case C-136/17 *GC and Others v Commission nationale de l'informatique et des libertés (CNIL)* [2019], §§51–52.

[23] Proposal for a Regulation of The European Parliament and of the Council on the protection of individuals with regard to the processing of personal data and on the free movement of such data (General Data Protection Regulation), COM(2012) 11 final, Explanatory Memorandum, page 9.

Indeed, as regards the burden of proof, while according to Article 14 of the Directive, the data subject had to base their request 'on compelling legitimate grounds relating to his [or her] particular situation', under the new Article 21 GDPR, a data subject can object to data processing 'on grounds relating to his or her particular situation'. They thus no longer have to demonstrate 'compelling legitimate grounds'.[24] As the EDPB also confirms, this provision changes the burden of proof, providing a presumption in favour of the data subject[25] by obliging, on the contrary, the controller to demonstrate 'compelling legitimate grounds for the processing'.[26]

However, we still need to understand what a 'particular situation' means and if it can refer to different types of data subjects (including vulnerable ones). The notion of 'particular situation' was unclear even in the DPD (Article 14).[27]

The CJEU in *Google Spain* clarified the meaning of 'particular situation' in the provision on the right to object. The Court affirmed that '[t]he balancing to be carried out' according to the right to object 'enables account to be taken in a more specific manner *of all the circumstances surrounding the data subject's particular situation*'.[28] In that case, the notion of 'compelling legitimate grounds relating to their particular situation' was a matter of disagreement between Google (who considered that sentence to mean that the right to object cannot be exercised 'merely because [data subjects] consider that that processing may be prejudicial

[24] EDBP, Guidelines 5/2019 on the criteria of the Right to be Forgotten in the search engines cases under the GDPR (part 1), adopted on 2 December 2019, version for consultation, 7–8. See also, on this point, the Explanatory Memorandum of the CoE's Modernized Convention 108, §78, according to which it is the data controller that will have to demonstrate on a case-by-case the compelling legitimate grounds basis and 'failure to demonstrate such compelling legitimate grounds while pursuing the processing could be considered as unlawful'.

[25] See the opposite opinion of N Purtova, 'Default Entitlements in Personal Data in the Proposed Regulation: Informational Self-Determination Off the Table … and Back on Again?' (2014) 30 Computer Law & Security Review 6, 16.

[26] ibid 8. However, the Commission proposal extended the scope of the right to object also to data processing based on vital interests (art 6(1) point (d)). This proposal was then rejected by the Parliament, see European Parliament legislative resolution of 12 March 2014 on the proposal for a regulation of the European Parliament and of the Council on the protection of individuals with regard to the processing of personal data and on the free movement of such data (General Data Protection Regulation) (COM(2012)0011—C7-0025/2012—2012/0011(COD)) (Ordinary legislative procedure: first reading).

[27] Although the Commission proposal proposed that wording in the GDPR as well, the European Parliament erased the sentence 'on grounds relating to their particular situation' in their first reading of the GDPR (European Parliament legislative resolution of 12 March 2014 on the proposal for a regulation of the European Parliament and of the Council on the protection of individuals with regard to the processing of personal data and on the free movement of such data (General Data Protection Regulation) (COM(2012)0011—C7-0025/2012—2012/0011(COD)) (Ordinary legislative procedure: first reading)). It was then the Council to reintroduce it in its subsequent position, which was then approved in the final text. See Position of the European Council at first reading with a view to the adoption of a Regulation of the European Parliament and of the Council on the protection of natural persons with regard to the processing of personal data and on the free movement of such data, and repealing Directive 95/46/EC (General Data Protection Regulation), adopted by the Council on 8 April 2016.

[28] *Google Spain* (n 18) §76. Emphasis added. See also C-398/15, *Camera di Commercio, Industria, Artigianato e Agricoltura di Lecce v Salvatore Manni* [9 March 2017], §47.

to them')[29] and Mr Costeja González and the Spanish and Italian governments (who affirm that the data subject may object to the data processing where: (i) it is prejudicial to them, and (ii) their fundamental rights to the protection of those data and to privacy override the legitimate interests of the operator).[30] The Court seems to reply that the right to object cannot be based on a 'standard' notion of the data subject, while the controller should consider all different types of data subjects, via a case-by-case analysis. In particular, the Court affirms that what should be analysed is 'the sensitivity for the data subject's private life' of the consequences of that data processing.[31] However, the CJEU clarifies that it is not necessary that the data processing 'causes prejudice to the data subject'.[32] Accordingly, what is relevant for the exercise of the right to object is the *risk* of prejudicial effects that data subjects can suffer (I mentioned the link between vulnerability and risks of harms in Chapter 3, but I develop this link in detail in this chapter and Chapter 7).

More recently, the EDPB[33] has clarified that in the case of 'delisting requests' made to search engines, the particular situation must be taken into account when undertaking the balance between personal rights and the right to information, in addition to the classic criteria for handling delisting requests (that the data subject played a role in public life; the data have no relation to the subject's professional life; the information is hate speech or unverified personal opinion or it refers to minor crimes that happened in the past). The EDPB also offers some examples of the 'particular situation' mentioned in Article 21: 'for example, a search result creates *detriment* for a data subject when applying for jobs, or undermines his or her reputation in his or her personal life'.[34] As observed above, vulnerability can be defined as the higher exposure to the risk of harm to fundamental rights and freedoms of data subjects.[35] Thus, one can broadly interpret the 'particular situation' in Article 21 as also encompassing situations of vulnerability. Considering the WP29 definition of vulnerability as an unfair imbalance of power between the data subject and the controller,[36] the right to object effectively constitutes a manifestation of the fairness principle, rebalancing the position of the data subjects, that is empowering data subjects to challenge an *ex-ante* balancing test based on Article 6(1) GDPR.[37]

29 *Google Spain* (n 18) §90.
30 ibid §91.
31 ibid §98.
32 ibid §96.
33 EDBP, Guidelines 5/2019 on the criteria of the Right to be Forgotten in the search engines cases under the GDPR (part 1), adopted on 2 December 2019, version for consultation, 7–8.
34 ibid 7–8. Emphasis added.
35 It is not maybe a coincidence that an example concerns job seekers. The WP29 has often defined workers as vulnerable data subjects. See eg WP29 Guidelines on DPIA, 10.
36 ibid 10.
37 Clifford and Ausloos (n 21).

6. The right to object and 'the particular situation' in the different Member States

Before the adoption of the GDPR, the Member States used to have three different approaches to the scope of the right to object.[38] The first approach was neutral: several Member States simply transposed the concept of 'particular situation of the data subject' into their national law. This is the case in Germany,[39] Belgium,[40] Portugal,[41] and the Netherlands.[42]

The second approach did not give weight to the phrase 'particular situation', preferring to limit the right to object to the 'legitimate reasons' of the data subject. This is the case in France[43] and Italy.[44]

The third approach was the one adopted in the United Kingdom and Ireland. The UK Data Protection Act 1998, in Part II, Section 10(1) stated that an individual is entitled to require the data controller to cease, or not to begin, processing, or processing for a specified purpose or in a specified manner, any personal data in respect of which he is the data subject, on the ground that, for specified reasons (i) the processing of those data or their processing for that purpose or in that manner *is causing or is likely to cause substantial damage or substantial distress to him or to another*, and (ii) that damage or distress is or would be unwarranted.[45] Similarly, the Irish Data Protection Act 1988 (as amended in 2003), in Article 6A.1 provided that the data subjects could exercise their right to object 'for specified reasons' if '(a) the processing of those data or their processing for that purpose or in that manner is causing or likely to cause substantial damage or distress to him or her *or to another person*, and (b) the damage or distress is or would be unwarranted'.[46]

As affirmed in Chapter 4, the notion of vulnerability adopted in this book is the susceptibility to a higher risk of harm to one's interests. Accordingly, the first

[38] Under the GDPR, Member States have limited margin of manoeuvre in specifying the Regulation. The right to object cannot be modified, in its nature and scope, by Member States. Instead, under the DPD, Member States had lower harmonization duties.

[39] Bundesdatenschutzgesetz (2001), §20(5): 'wegen seiner besonderen persönlichen Situation'.

[40] 08/12/1992 | Loi relative à la protection de la vie privée à l'égard des traitements de données à caractère personnel (M.B., 18 mars 1993)—Version consolidée (01/08/2007), art 12, §1er: 'Toute personne a en outre le droit de s'opposer, pour des raisons sérieuses et légitimes tenant à une situation particulière.'

[41] Lei da Protecção de Dados Pessoais, Lei no 67/98 <https://dre.pt/web/guest/legislacao-consolidada/-/lc/123536794/201909121410/73736604/element/diploma?consolidacaoTag=Comunica%C3%A7%C3%A3o+Social&did=34450175> accessed 20 February 2023, art 12º: 'se opor em qualquer altura, por razões ponderosas e legítimas relacionadas com a sua situação particular'.

[42] Wet bescherming persoonsgegevens <https://wetten.overheid.nl/BWBR0011468/2018-05-01> accessed 20 February 2023, art 40: 'in verband met zijn bijzondere persoonlijke omstandigheden'.

[43] Loi no 78-17 du 6 janvier 1978 relative à l'informatique, aux fichiers et aux libertés, art 38: 'pour des motifs légitimes'.

[44] Codice in materia di trattamento dati personali, D.lgs. 196/2003, art 7(4), lett. a): L'interessato ha diritto di opporsi, in tutto o in parte: a) per motivi legittimi al trattamento dei dati personali che lo riguardano.

[45] UK Data Protection Act 1998. Emphasis added.

[46] Irish Data Protection Act 1988 as amended in 2003. Emphasis added.

approach (the neutral one) and the second ('legitimate reasons') do not link the idea of 'particular situations' to the concept of data subjects' vulnerability. In contrast, the third approach clearly defines 'particular situation' as a situation of vulnerability, in the sense of higher risks of 'substantial damages'. While the first two approaches allow for more flexibility for the data subjects to challenge problematic data processing operations, the third approach constrains the exercise of the right to object to specific cases and requirements. In addition, the reference to 'damages' might be a high burden of proof for data subjects.

7. The right not to be subject to automated decision-making and the vulnerable data subject

Another data protection right to mention is the right not to be subject to automated decision-making, pursuant to Article 22 of the GDPR. This book analyses this right because profiling and automated decision-making can be sources of inducement or exploitation of individual vulnerabilities. The use of algorithmic decision-making systems, particularly automated profiling, increases the power asymmetry between the data controller and the data subject.[47]

In addition, and as we will see in Chapter 7, the wording of Article 22, referring to (legal or similarly) significant effects on individuals, seems to conform to a multi-layered definition of data subjects (including vulnerable ones). I clarify these points below. The issue requiring clarification now is whether the regulation of automated profiling takes into account different data subjects, including the vulnerable ones.

> Article 22(1) states: 'the data subject shall have the right not to be subject to *a decision based solely on automated processing, including profiling, which produces legal effects concerning him or her or similarly significantly affects him or her*'. This right shall not apply in only three cases:
>
> a. the decision 'is necessary for entering into, or performance of, a contract between the data subject and a data controller';
> b. 'is authorised by Union or Member State law to which the controller is subject and which also lays down *suitable measures to safeguard the data subject's rights and freedoms and legitimate interests*';[48] or
> c. 'is based on the data subject's explicit consent' (Art. 22(2)).

[47] See, in general, AD Selbst, 'Disparate Impact in Big Data Policing' (2018) 52 Georgia Law Review 109.

[48] Emphasis added.

> In cases 1 and 3, 'the data controller shall implement suitable measures to safeguard the data subject's rights, and freedoms and legitimate interests, at least the right to obtain human intervention on the part of the controller, to express his or her point of view and to contest the decision' (Article 22(3)).[49] In addition, Recital 71 explains that such suitable safeguards 'should include specific information to the data subject and the right to obtain human intervention, to express his or her point of view, to obtain an explanation of the decision reached after such assessment and to challenge the decision'.[50]

Automated decisions can be based on sensitive data[51] only if the data subject has given explicit consent to process such data or the processing is necessary for reasons of substantial public interest, and if suitable measures to safeguard the data subject's rights and freedoms and legitimate interests are in place (Article 22(4)).

The interpretation of the automated decision-making regulation in the GDPR has triggered lively debate in legal circles. In particular, several scholars have interpreted this set of provisions as a new right to algorithm explanation,[52] while others have argued against the existence of the right to explanation in the GDPR.[53] Other scholars have preferred a contextual interpretation of Articles 13 to 15 and 22, suggesting that the scope of those provisions is not so limited and that they actually can provide individuals with more transparency and accountability.[54] Even the EDPB, in its recent guidelines on the right of access, explains that according to Article 15 the data controller must guarantee transparency on the specific

[49] Emphasis added.

[50] Emphasis added.

[51] For 'sensitive data' we refer in this chapter to 'special categories of personal data' according to art 9(1). This exemption does not apply in case of point (a) or (g) of art 9(2) (ie sensitive data given with explicit consent of data subject or processing necessary for reason of substantial public interest) when 'suitable measures to safeguard the data subject's rights and freedoms and legitimate interests are in place'.

[52] B Goodman and S Flaxman, 'European Union Regulations on Algorithmic Decision-Making and a "Right to Explanation"' (2017) 38 AI Magazine 50; Ben Wagner, 'Efficiency vs. Accountability?—Algorithms, Big Data and Public Administration—Centre for Internet & Human Rights' (December 2016) <https://cihr.eu/efficiency-vs-accountability-algorithms-big-data-and-public-administration/> accessed 27 May 2022; 'Researchers: GDPR May Create "Right to Explanation" on Algorithmic Decision-Making' <https://iapp.org/news/a/researchers-gdpr-may-create-right-to-explanation-on-algorithmic-decision-making/> accessed 27 May 2022. For a general analysis of explanation in artificial intelligence T Miller, 'Explanation in Artificial Intelligence: Insights from the Social Sciences' (2019) 267 Artificial Intelligence 1. See also F Cabitza and others, 'Quod Erat Demonstrandum?—Towards a Typology of the Concept of Explanation for the Design of Explainable AI' (2023) 213 Expert Systems with Applications 118888.

[53] S Wachter and others, 'Why a Right to Explanation of Automated Decision-Making Does Not Exist in the General Data Protection Regulation' (2017) 7(2) International Data Privacy Law 76–99.

[54] AD Selbst and J Powles, 'Meaningful Information and the Right to Explanation' (2017) 4(1) International Data Privacy Law 233–42; G Malgieri and G Comandé, 'Why a Right to Legibility of Automated Decision-Making Exists in the General Data Protection Regulation' (2017) 7(4) International Data Privacy Law 243–65. See also M Kaminski, 'The Right to Explanation, Explained' (2019) 34 Berkeley Technology Law Journal 189.

automated decisions taken in relation to the data subject who is requesting access to the data.[55]

Before these guidelines, WP29 had already clarified several elements of automated decision-making provisions in the GDPR.[56] More precisely, the WP29 affirmed that the scope of Article 22 should not be interpreted restrictively. In particular, decisions based 'solely on automated means' had to include any decision in which the human intervention is not meaningful.[57] The 'legal effects or similarly significant effects' should also have been considered in a broad sense: even online marketing or price discrimination, under some conditions, could be regarded as significant effects relevant under Article 22.[58] When addressing the scope of 'legal effects or similarly significant effects', the WP29 explains: 'for data processing to significantly affect someone, the effects of the processing must be sufficiently great or important to be worthy of attention'.[59]

> Consequently, the WP29 enlisted three alternative factors that can determine if the effect is significant, namely, 'the decision must have the potential to:
>
> - significantly affect the circumstances, behaviour or choices of the individuals concerned;
> - have a prolonged or permanent impact on the data subject; or
> - at its most extreme, lead to the exclusion or discrimination of individuals'.[60]

In other words, these three parameters refer to *internal effects* (affecting behaviour/choices), *duration of effects* (prolonged or permanent impact), and *external effects* (exclusion/discrimination). Chapter 7 analyses the link between significant effects and the concept of data subjects' vulnerability in more detail. Can these effects be considered sources of vulnerability of data subjects and, thus, can Article 22 be considered a particular form of protection for vulnerable data subjects?

The first element to consider is that Recital 71 clarifies that automated decision-making having legal or similarly significant effects on data subjects '*should not concern a child*'. The WP29 Guidelines propose a singular and arguable interpretation of this recital. They clarify that, since this phrase is only in the preamble and not

[55] EDPB (n 2) 39: 'If possible, information under Art. 15(1)(h) has to be more specific in relation to the reasoning that lead to specific decisions concerning the data subject who asked for access.'

[56] WP29, 'Guidelines on Automated individual decision-making and Profiling for the purposes of Regulation 2016/679', WP251rev.01, adopted on 3 October 2017, as last revised and adopted on 6 February 2018; L Edwards and M Veale, 'Slave to the Algorithm? Why a "Right to an Explanation" Is Probably Not the Remedy You Are Looking For' (2017) 16 Duke Law & Technology Review 18.

[57] WP29 (n 56) 21.

[58] ibid 21–22.

[59] See the critical view of M Veale and L Edwards, 'Clarity, Surprises, and Further Questions in the Article 29 Working Party Draft Guidance on Automated Decision-Making and Profiling' (2018) 34 Computer Law & Security Review 398–404, 401 and 404.

[60] WP29 (n 56) 22.

in the body of the GDPR, it should not represent an absolute prohibition of automated decision-making related to children. However, in the light of that recital, the WP29 recommends that controllers should not rely on the exceptions in Article 22(2) (contract, Member States' or Union law, explicit consent) to justify profiling of minors.[61]

If in exceptional cases it is necessary to perform automated decisions on children, for example for the protection of their welfare, 'suitable safeguards should be in place', as required by Article 22(2)(b) and 22(3). The WP29 affirms that such safeguards must therefore be appropriate for children.[62] The controller must ensure that these safeguards effectively protect the rights and the legitimate interests of the children whose data they are processing. In other words, there should be vulnerability-tailored safeguards.

Lastly, the WP29 emphasizes that particular attention should be given to automated decisions that influence children's choices and behaviours. Since 'children represent a *more vulnerable group of society*', data controllers should, in general, avoid profiling them for marketing purposes. Children can be particularly 'susceptible' in the online environment and more easily influenced by behavioural advertising. However, the approach of the WP29 is layered: the age and maturity of the child should be taken into due account, 'since it may affect their ability to understand the motivation behind this type of marketing or the consequences'.[63]

The analogy between children and other vulnerable individuals seems particularly appropriate in this case. Children are protected against automated decision-making because they 'represent a more vulnerable group of society' since they are particularly susceptible and easily influenced because of their 'age and [lack of] maturity'. Accordingly, following the rationale declared in the WP29 Guidelines, other vulnerable groups of society—if susceptible and able to be relatively easily influenced (because of their advanced age, mental health conditions, etc)—should be adequately protected against profiling.

The WP29 seems to refer to these other groups of *vulnerable adults* also in the Guideline sections dedicated to behavioural advertising and direct marketing. The WP29 clarifies that, although in principle these marketing practices do not produce legal or similarly significant effects, they might be considered to affect the data subject significantly 'depending upon the particular characteristics' of the case (similar to the 'particular situations' of the right to object), including, *inter alia*, 'using knowledge of the *vulnerabilities* of the data subjects targeted'. Indeed, as the WP29 argues, some kinds of data processing that could have a limited impact on

[61] ibid 22.

[62] ibid 22.

[63] ibid 28. See also the WP29 Opinion 02/2013 on apps on smart devices (WP202), adopted on 27 February 2013, 26: 'data controllers should not process children's data for behavioural advertising purposes, neither directly nor indirectly, since this will be outside of the scope of the child's understanding and therefore exceed the boundaries of lawful processing'.

individuals generally may significantly affect specific groups of society, 'such as minority groups or *vulnerable adults*'.[64]

When mentioning marketing, manipulation, and individual vulnerabilities, the WP29 seems to refer to cognitive biases that all consumers can experience at different times, to different degrees, and at different stages.[65] Accordingly, even though here the idea of vulnerable adults is associated with 'minority groups', it is reasonable to adopt a broader notion of vulnerable data subjects, including the specific power and information imbalance between data controllers (having more and more capabilities to infer and exploit individual biases) and data subjects (generally affected by many cognitive biases, according to the most recent developments of behavioural economics studies).[66]

8. Accountability and vulnerable data subjects: the risk-based approach in the GDPR

Having analysed the different individual circumstances of data subjects (and their vulnerabilities) under the perspective of data protection rights, I look now at the data controllers' accountability duties.[67] The question is: when the data controller implements their accountability duties, do they need to consider the individual situation of different types of data subjects, particularly vulnerable ones?

Accordingly, this section discusses first the concept of 'categories of data subjects' in the accountability duties of the GDPR, the notion of the general controller's responsibility, and the risk-based approach compared to vulnerability theory (Article 24); the notion of data protection by design and by default (Article 25); the security measures of the processing (Article 32); and the Data Protection Impact Assessment (DPIA) (Article 35) as the most typical and fruitful provisions considering the individual data subject's particular situation, status, and risk of coming to harm, including the vulnerable data subject.

[64] WP29 (n 56) 22.

[65] MG Haselton and others, 'The Evolution of Cognitive Bias' in DM Buss (ed), *The Handbook of Evolutionary Psychology* (John Wiley & Sons, Inc 2015); Association for Psychological Science, 'Cognitive Bias' <https://www.psychologicalscience.org/tag/cognitive-bias> accessed 28 February 2019; O Thomas, 'Two Decades of Cognitive Bias Research in Entrepreneurship: What Do We Know and Where Do We Go from Here?' (2018) 68 Management Review Quarterly 107.

[66] A Reyna, 'The Psychology of Privacy—What Can Behavioural Economics Contribute to Competition in Digital Markets?' (2018) 8 International Data Privacy Law 240.

[67] When referring to 'accountability duties', I refer to all data protection obligations for data controllers and data processor, in particular Chapter IV of the GDPR (arts 24–43). The principle of accountability, as established at art 5(2), states that the controller shall be responsible for, and be able to demonstrate compliance with the data protection principles at art 5(1). When implementing the accountability principle, data controllers have a certain room of manoeuvre, but they need to respect the provisions contained in arts 24–43.

The 'categories' of data subjects in the accountability duties

As affirmed in Chapter 2, in the GDPR and the previous DPD (as well as in the Council of Europe's Convention 108 and its Modernized version), there is one single notion of the data subject, without any explicit reference to different kinds of data subjects. Beneath the surface, though, this is not entirely true if we consider some of the accountability duties in the GDPR.

In particular, in three cases, the data controller is explicitly asked to identify 'categories of data subjects'. Article 28(3), regulating the contract (or other legally binding acts) between the processor and the controller, requires that this act should clarify—*inter alia*—'categories of data subjects'. Similarly, Article 30, point (c), requires that the data controller needs to add 'a description of the categories of data subjects' within the registry of data processing activities. Lastly, Article 33(3), point (a), regulating the content of the data breach notification to the Data Protection Authority (DPA), specifies that in this notification, the data controller should communicate, among other details, 'the categories and approximate number of data subjects concerned'.

However, the GDPR does not explain what the phrase 'categories of data subjects' means. I note that this is the only reference in the Regulation to a possible plurality of data subjects' types. In the Guidelines about data breach notification, the WP29 explains that the concept of 'categories of data subjects' refers to the various types of individuals whose personal data have been affected by a breach.[68] The WP29 also specifies that 'depending on the descriptors used, this could include, amongst others, children *and other vulnerable groups*, people with disabilities, employees or customers'.[69] This clarification is relevant because the WP29 mentions vulnerable individuals and lists four examples of vulnerability: children, disabled people, employees, and customers. As argued in Chapter 3, there are different taxonomies and layers of vulnerability. In addition, I identified two types of vulnerability in the data protection framework: processing-based (ie decision-making vulnerability during data processing)[70] and effect-based (ie the higher risk that the outcome of data processing may harm the data subject).[71] From our perspective, the four examples proposed by the WP29 represent different types of vulnerability. While 'disabled' individuals might be at higher risk of adverse effects (physical harms or discrimination), employees might suffer from vulnerability in their

68 WP29 Guidelines on Personal data breach notification under Regulation 2016/679, adopted on 3 October 2017, as last revised and adopted on 6 February 2018, WP250rev.01, 14.

69 Emphasis added.

70 On this concept see É Gennet and others, 'Does the New EU Regulation on Clinical Trials Adequately Protect Vulnerable Research Participants?' (2015) 119 Health Policy (Amsterdam, Netherlands) 925.

71 H Richter, 'The Power Paradigm in Private Law' in M Bakhoum and others (eds), *Personal Data in Competition, Consumer Protection and Intellectual Property Law: Towards a Holistic Approach?* (Springer Berlin Heidelberg 2018) 532.

decision-making capabilities (because of the power imbalance between themselves and their employers; they could also suffer from other adverse effects like discrimination). Also, children and customers might be affected by both processing-based and effect-based vulnerability: there might be both a risk of greater harm and a lack of decision-making freedom (due to, for example, manipulation via hidden data patterns or cognitive biases).

However, it is right to clarify that the rationale for mentioning vulnerable groups in the data breach notification (as well as in the data processing records and the contract between the data controller and the data processor) is 'limiting damage to individuals'.[72] Accordingly, the WP29 argues that if the types of data subjects may indicate *a risk of particular damage* occurring as a result of a data breach (eg identity theft, fraud, financial loss, a threat to professional secrecy), then it is essential that the notification to the data subject indicates these categories. To put it differently, this requirement needs to describe the likely consequences of the breach.

In other words, the WP29 clarifies that the notion of categories of the data subject—and in particular, the notion of vulnerable data subjects—should be based on the concept of 'higher risks of harms'. This is in line with many conceptualizations of human vulnerability described in Chapter 3,[73] and confirms that the harm-based understanding of vulnerability[74] is crucial in the GDPR.

In sum, when the GDPR refers to 'categories of the data subject' (in the contract with the data processor, in data processing records, and in data breach notifications), the data controller should assess the individual situation of data subjects. According to Luna's theory,[75] this assessment may consist of evaluating the higher risks of harm to vulnerable data subjects, analysing the 'layers' of this vulnerability in specific conditions and contexts.

The risk-based approach and the layers of data subjects' vulnerability

Another aspect one needs to consider when assessing the data controller's duties is the risk-based approach. Article 24(1) states that

> taking into account the nature, scope, context and purposes of processing as well as the risks of varying likelihood and severity for the rights and freedoms

[72] WP29, Guidelines on Personal data breach notification under Regulation 2016/679 (n 68) 14.

[73] RE Goodin, *Protecting the Vulnerable: A Reanalysis of Our Social Responsibilities* (University of Chicago Press 1985); D Schroeder and E Gefenas, 'Vulnerability: Too Vague and Too Broad?' (2009) 18 Cambridge Quarterly of Healthcare Ethics 113.

[74] Richter (n 71) 532.

[75] F Luna, 'Elucidating the Concept of Vulnerability: Layers Not Labels' (2009) 2 International Journal of Feminist Approaches to Bioethics 121; F Luna, 'Identifying and Evaluating Layers of Vulnerability—A Way Forward' (2019) 19 Developing World Bioethics 86.

of natural persons, the controller shall implement appropriate technical and organisational measures to ensure and to be able to demonstrate that processing is performed in accordance with this Regulation. Those measures shall be reviewed and updated where necessary.

This provision emphasizes the shift from a more rights-based approach to a more risk-based approach in the data protection framework.[76] It states that the compliance duties should not be the same for all data processing. Accountability duties are strongly related to the level of risks that a specific event of data processing can create for the data subjects at issue.[77] Similar considerations also apply to Article 32 about the controller's and processor's duty to implement appropriate technical and organizational measures to ensure a level of security appropriate to the risk.

The shift from the rights-based to the risk-based approach in data protection law has triggered vivid debate about whether it is admissible to abandon a rights-based structure when protecting a fundamental right like the right to personal data protection,[78] and how to balance the need for uniform compliance (in terms of rights and duties) with contextual risk-based analysis.[79]

The WP29[80] implicitly replies to these fundamental questions explaining that while compliance is generally binary (ie a yes/no question), the quantity and intensity of measures necessary to reach such compliance is scalable.[81] Indeed, general data protection principles are scalable: this is an inherent property of lawfulness, transparency, fairness, purpose limitation, data minimization (or necessity), data quality, storage limitation, and accountability. These principles require a balancing

[76] R Gellert, *The Risk-Based Approach to Data Protection* (Oxford University Press 2020); M Macenaite, 'The "Riskification" of European Data Protection Law through a Two-Fold Shift' (2017) 8 European Journal of Risk Regulation 506; K Demetzou, 'GDPR and the Concept of Risk' in E Kosta and others (eds), *Privacy and Identity Management. Fairness, Accountability, and Transparency in the Age of Big Data: 13th IFIP WG 9.2, 9.6/11.7, 11.6/SIG 9.2.2 International Summer School, Vienna, Austria, August 20–24, 2018, Revised Selected Papers* (Springer International Publishing 2019); See also the critical approach of R Gellert, 'We Have Always Managed Risks in Data Protection Law: Understanding the Similarities and Differences between the Rights-Based and the Risk-Based Approaches to Data Protection' (2016) 2 European Data Protection Law Review 481.

[77] Demetzou, 'GDPR and the Concept of Risk' (n 76).

[78] Gellert, 'We Have Always Managed Risks in Data Protection Law' (n 76); Gellert, *The Risk-Based Approach to Data Protection* (n 76) 185 ff.

[79] J Bracy, 'Demystifying the Risk-Based Approach' (30 April 2014) <https://iapp.org/news/a/demystifying-the-risk-based-approach/> accessed 5 February 2023.

[80] WP29, 'Statement on the Role of a Risk-Based Approach in Data Protection Legal Frameworks' (2014) 2.

[81] Opinion of the European Data Protection Supervisor on the Communication from the Commission to the European Parliament, the Council, the Economic and Social Committee and the Committee of the Regions, 'A comprehensive approach on personal data protection in the European Union', 14 January 2011, 22–23. See also Gellert, 'We Have Always Managed Risks in Data Protection Law' (n 76) 486; Macenaite, 'The "Riskification" of European Data Protection Law through a Two-Fold Shift' (n 76) 517, 525; C Quelle, 'The "Risk Revolution" in EU Data Protection Law: We Can't Have Our Cake and Eat It, Too' in R Leenes and others (eds), *Data Protection and Privacy: The Age of Intelligent Machines* (Hart Publishing 2017).

test[82] in which the data controller needs to analyse the current context, the peculiarity of data subjects at issue, the actual impact of that data processing on them, etc.[83] If data subjects are, for example, particularly vulnerable to some risks, the data controller needs to take this into account in the balancing test and, accordingly, choose the appropriate lawful ground for data processing under Article 6 (or 9), appropriate transparency safeguards, appropriately delimit the purpose and assess the opportunity for secondary use of that data, etc.[84]

As affirmed above, individual vulnerability in the data protection framework is influenced by the position and potentialities of the data controller (for instance, in terms of computational capacity to collect and predict data, influence behaviours, and take significant decisions on individuals); the more powerful the data controller, the more 'vulnerable' the data subject will be. Accordingly, the condition of the data subject is co-determined mainly by the condition of the data controller, by the controller's power and the specific vulnerability drivers used in processing the data. The link between vulnerability and risk is also semantic, as the first definition of 'risk' in data protection reveals ('exploitation of vulnerability of personal data supporting assets').[85]

Accordingly, the risk-based approach seems fruitful for our study of vulnerability. When assessing the risks to fundamental rights and freedoms of the data subjects, the data controller should consider situations in which specific data processing could affect particular individuals. This is explicitly requested by the WP29, which declares that 'origin, nature, particularity and severity of the risks' should be appreciated '*from the perspective of the data subjects*'.[86] Indeed, this approach has been defined as 'subjective, individual-centred' in the literature.[87]

Maceinate[88] clarifies that individuals exposed to the same risks 'will not experience the same harm': some 'will be able to cope with risks while others not'.[89]

[82] Gellert, *The Risk-Based Approach to Data Protection* (n 76) 64 ff; Gellert, 'We Have Always Managed Risks in Data Protection Law' (n 76) 487.
[83] See the critical view of B van der Sloot, 'Editorial' (2017) 3 European Data Protection Law Review 1. See also the reply of R Gellert, 'On Risk, Balancing, and Data Protection: A Response to van Der Sloot' (2017) 2 European Data Protection Law Review 180; see also the counterarguments of B van der Sloot, 'Ten Questions about Balancing' (2017) 3 European Data Protection Law Review 187.
[84] See eg the case study in K Demetzou, 'Data Protection Impact Assessment: A Tool for Accountability and the Unclarified Concept of "High Risk" in the General Data Protection Regulation' (2019) 35(6) Computer Law & Security Review 105342.
[85] CNIL, 'Privacy Impact Assessment (PIA)—Methodology (how to carry out a PIA)' (2015) 6 <https://www.cnil.fr/sites/default/files/typo/document/CNIL-PIA-1-Methodology.pdf> accessed 5 February 2023. See also I Böröcz, 'Risk to the Right to the Protection of Personal Data: An Analysis Through the Lenses of Hermagoras' (2016) 2 European Data Protection Law Review 467.
[86] WP29 (n 35) 22. Emphasis added. See also, on this point, K Demetzou, 'Risk to the "Rights and Freedoms"—A Legal Interpretation of the Scope of Risk Under the GDPR' in R Leenes and others, *Data Protection and Privacy* (Bloomsbury 2020).
[87] Macenaite, 'The "Riskification" of European Data Protection Law through a Two-Fold Shift' (n 76) 536.
[88] ibid 538.
[89] ibid.

This is why she critically questions whether—since most privacy harms are non-physical and thus hardly measurable and are subjective (best known to the individuals themselves)—the burden for evaluating risks and preventing harm is rightly placed on the data controllers. However, she concludes: 'frameworks for a specific type of data subjects, such as children, the elderly and other groups of individuals requiring special protection, could also be considered as they could address the particular needs and rights of these data subjects'.[90]

Indeed, as mentioned earlier, vulnerable persons are often defined as persons with higher risks (in terms of occurrence, likelihood, and severity of the impact)[91] to their rights and freedoms.[92] As observed in Chapter 5, a risk-based notion of vulnerability is broad and needs further specification. The question to ask is: vulnerable regarding which right and freedom? Under a GDPR perspective, the question becomes: which fundamental rights and freedoms should be considered under the risk-based approach (eg Articles 24, 25, 35)?

Article 1(2) of the GDPR states that the Regulation protects fundamental rights and freedoms of natural persons. In more detail, Recital 4 clarifies that the scope of the GDPR is protection of the respect for private and family life; home and communications; the protection of personal data; freedom of thought, conscience, and religion; freedom of expression and information; freedom to conduct a business; the right to effective remedy and a fair trial; and cultural, religious, and linguistic diversity. Similarly, the WP29 enumerates 'other fundamental rights such as freedom of speech, freedom of thought, freedom of movement prohibition of discrimination, right to liberty, conscience and religion'. Moreover, when addressing the notion of risk to fundamental rights, Recital 75 gives relevant examples of situations to be considered including: risk to discrimination, identity theft or fraud, financial loss, damage to the reputation, loss of confidentiality of personal data protected by professional secrecy, unauthorized reversal of pseudonymization or any other significant economic or social disadvantage, the deprivation of rights and freedoms, or the prevention from exercising control over one's own personal data. From these provisions it seems clear that there are two different elements of a 'risk to a right' to be considered: (i) interference with rights and (ii) harms or damages.

To understand the relationship between these two elements, it is necessary to clarify the notion of risk. The concept of risk, and even more of 'risk to a right', is controversial in the scholarly debate.[93] Some commentators have accepted the French DPA, the CNIL's idea of risk as a feared event concerning data security, integrity, and confidentiality.[94] Others have juxtaposed the traditional idea of risk

[90] ibid 540.

[91] Luna, 'Identifying and Evaluating Layers of Vulnerability—A Way Forward' (n 75).

[92] Goodin (n 73).

[93] N van Dijk and others, 'A Risk to a Right? Beyond Data Protection Risk Assessments' (2016) 32 Computer Law & Security Review 286; Böröcz (n 85).

[94] CNIL, 'Privacy Impact Assessment (PIA)—Methodology (how to carry out a PIA)' (n 85). See Böröcz (n 85).

from 'business management risks' to the data protection-friendly 'risk of non-compliance'.[95] Others have preferred the meaning of risk as 'interference with fundamental rights'.[96] The notion of risk in the data protection framework has been qualified as based on three structural elements, namely: event (violation of a principle of data protection[97] or infringement of a fundamental right[98]); outcome of the event (consequences in terms of harms);[99] and risk factors (likelihood and severity).[100] The same event can give rise to different outcomes, depending on risk factors, which are also determined by the specific power (im)balance between data controllers and data subjects in a given situation and, thus, depend on the particular data subject at issue.

In other words, the risk-based approach in the GDPR needs to consider individual vulnerabilities of data subjects or—in other terms—the notion of risk strictly depends on the situation of relational vulnerability suffered by a specific data subject in a particular data processing context. This approach is explicitly accepted by the WP29, which declared that the 'origin, nature, particularity and severity of the risks' should be appreciated '*from the perspective of the data subjects*'.[101] Indeed, this approach has been defined 'subjective, individual-centred'.[102]

Indeed, as affirmed in Chapter 3, I accept the notion of layered vulnerability as the most suitable theory of vulnerability. In her work on layers of vulnerability, Luna tried to operationalize the concept and propose a method to identify and assess different layers of vulnerability. In particular, she suggests evaluating vulnerability risks on two factors: *the harmfulness of effects* and their *likelihood*.[103]

As noted by Éloïse Gennet and colleagues, Luna's theory adopts a risk-based definition of vulnerable persons. As noted, in the GDPR, the notion of risks to fundamental rights and freedoms is central. In particular, according to the risk-based approach in the GDPR (Article 24), the data controller is obliged to implement

[95] R Gellert, 'Understanding the Notion of Risk in the General Data Protection Regulation' (2018) 34 Computer Law and Security Review 279. See also R Gellert, 'Why the GDPR Risk-Based Approach Is about Compliance Risk, and Why It's Not a Bad Thing' in E Schweighofer and others (eds), *Trends und Communities der Rechtsinformatik—Trends and Communities of legal informatics: Tagungsband des 20. Internationalen Rechtsinformatik Symposions—IRIS 2017—Proceedings of the 20th International Legal Informatics Symposium* (Austrian Computer Society 2017) 527–32.

[96] Demetzou, 'Data Protection Impact Assessment' (n 84) 10.

[97] Gellert, 'Understanding the Notion of Risk in the General Data Protection Regulation' (n 95); Gellert, 'We Have Always Managed Risks in Data Protection Law' (n 76).

[98] Demetzou, 'GDPR and the Concept of Risk' (n 76).

[99] Gellert, 'Understanding the Notion of Risk in the General Data Protection Regulation' (n 95).

[100] Demetzou, 'Data Protection Impact Assessment' (n 84). See also Recitals 76, 77, 90 and arts 24(1), 25(1), and 32(1) of the GDPR.

[101] WP29 (n 35) 21. Emphasis added. See also, on this point, Demetzou, 'Risk to the "Rights and Freedoms"' (n 86).

[102] Macenaite, 'The "Riskification" of European Data Protection Law through a Two-Fold Shift' (n 76) 536.

[103] Luna, 'Identifying and Evaluating Layers of Vulnerability—A Way Forward' and 'Elucidating the Concept of Vulnerability: Layers Not Labels' (both n 75).

appropriate technical and organizational measures to ensure compliance with the data protection principles, 'taking into account the nature, scope, context and purposes of processing as well as the *risks of varying likelihood and severity* for the rights and freedoms of natural persons'.[104] When assessing such risks of varying likelihood and severity for rights and freedoms, the controller should consider situations in which a specific data processing could cause damage to particular (vulnerable) individuals. Indeed, as mentioned earlier, vulnerable persons are often defined as persons at higher risk (in terms of likelihood and severity)[105] to damages to their rights and freedoms.[106] Moreover, the notion of severity and likelihood seems perfectly in line with the two criteria for evaluating vulnerability layers in Luna's theory (harmful effects and likelihood).

9. Data protection by design

According to the data protection by design principle (hereafter DPbD) in Article 25(1),[107] the controller shall, both at the time of the determination of the means for processing and at the time of the processing itself, implement appropriate technical and organizational measures which are designed to implement data protection principles. The controller should take into account 'the nature, scope, context and purposes of processing as well as the risks of varying likelihood and severity for rights and freedoms of natural persons' but also 'the state of the art [and] the cost of implementation'.

It is interesting to compare this to Article 24, which describes the 'responsibility of the data controller', referring also to technical and organizational measures to ensure and to be able to demonstrate that processing is performed in accordance with this Regulation. The difference between Article 24 and Article 25 is that, in the first case, the data controller should ensure compliance with the GDPR, and in the latter, she should also 'implement' data protection principles (according to what is proportional to the state of the art and the costs of implementation). In both cases, the attention to vulnerable data subjects and the implementation of specific safeguards to protect their rights and freedoms (ie to mitigate factors of vulnerability) are required.[108]

[104] Emphasis added.
[105] Luna, 'Identifying and Evaluating Layers of Vulnerability—A Way Forward' (n 75).
[106] Goodin (n 73).
[107] In fact, art 25 addresses also the data protection by default (at para 2). However, for the purposes of this book, I focus in particular on the first one, since it is risk-based and more relevant to consider individual vulnerability of data subjects.
[108] S van der Hof and E Lievens, 'The Importance of Privacy by Design and Data Protection Impact Assessments in Strengthening Protection of Children's Personal Data under the GDPR' (2018) 23 Communications Law 33.

Van der Hof and Lievens argue that, since the DPbD principle encourages a proactive approach towards the protection of individuals, it is necessary to adopt a vulnerability-centred implementation of data protection by design in relation to data processing activities that involve vulnerable subjects' personal data (and more specifically children).[109]

Indeed, since the role of DPbD is to enhance the effectiveness of the data protection principles considering their scalability, it is clear that specific consideration of the condition of the data subjects at issue is highly needed.

10. Data Protection Impact Assessment and the vulnerable data subjects

To understand whether and how the data controller should take into account vulnerable data subjects under the risk-based approach of the GDPR, the last provision to be considered is Article 35 regulating the DPIA.

The GDPR does not give a clear definition of DPIA. Still, the WP29 describes it as a 'process designed to describe the processing, assess the necessity and proportionality of a processing and to help manage the risks to the rights and freedoms of natural persons resulting from the processing of personal data (by assessing them and determining the measures to address them)'.[110]

In the previous sections, I have observed that the concept of risk plays a vital role in the GDPR approach to accountability. In general, depending on the level of the risk (likelihood and severity), data controllers need to implement safeguards to ensure compliance with data protection principles (Article 24) and implement technical and organizational measures to enhance such principles (Article 25). The data controller already needs to perform a risk analysis and impact assessment to implement such safeguards and measures. In addition, as explained above, an impact assessment is necessary for many other data protection duties, such as choosing lawful grounds for processing data. However, the DPIA is an additional and more substantial requirement, in instances of data processing 'likely to result in a high risk to the rights and freedoms of natural persons'. Since risks are scalable, variable, and measurable (under the factors of likelihood and severity), data controllers should understand what types or events of processing has 'high risks' and, in those cases, implement an additional requirement, which is to conduct a DPIA.

Article 35(3) gives insights about what types of events of processing should be considered at 'high risk', highlighting in particular three cases: (i) evaluating

[109] ibid.

[110] WP29 (2017), Guidelines on Data Protection Impact Assessment (DPIA), 4.

individual personal characteristics systematically and extensively based on automated profiling, producing decisions with legal or similarly significant effects; (ii) processing special categories of data (including data relating to criminal convictions) on a large scale; (iii) systematically monitoring publicly accessible areas on a large scale.

Gellert notices that while only case (i) refers to an actual impact of individuals, the three examples refer to the same factors: type of processing, new technology, and type of data.[111] Demetzou differently summarizes these factors in the phrase the 'purpose, nature, [and] scope of the processing'.[112]

However, these are not the only cases of 'high-risk' data processing: the three data processing examples are simply relevant cases in which the likelihood and severity of adverse impact on individuals are likely to be high.

The WP29—building on Recital 75 and other provisions of the GDPR—identifies ten risk indicators: evaluation or scoring of individuals; automated decision-making; systemic monitoring; the processing of special categories of data or other data of particularly sensitive nature; large-scale nature of data processing; the combination of different datasets; *vulnerable data subjects*; innovative technologies; data transfers across the EU borders; data processing preventing data subjects from exercising a right or using a service.[113] In some cases, processing where only one of these criteria is present will require a DPIA.[114]

In Chapter 4, I already analysed what the WP29 means when referring to 'vulnerable data subjects', ie situations of 'increased power imbalance between the data subject and the data controller, meaning the individual may be unable to consent to, or oppose, the processing of his or her data'.[115] The examples include employees in relation to human resources management; children; more vulnerable segments of the population requiring special protection, including the mentally ill, asylum seekers, and the elderly; a patient or in any case where an imbalance in the relationship between the position of the data subject and the controller can be identified.[116]

However, this definition is still vague and open to different interpretations. That is why we should investigate in more detail the threshold analysis of individual vulnerability relevant under Article 35. In other words, since all data subjects are vulnerable to a certain extent, what is the minimum level of vulnerability that triggers the special protection of the DPIA? And what should a vulnerability-centred DPIA look like?

[111] Gellert, 'Understanding the Notion of Risk in the General Data Protection Regulation' (n 95) 286.
[112] Demetzou, 'Data Protection Impact Assessment' (n 84) 6.
[113] WP29 (n 35) 9.
[114] van der Hof and Lievens (n 108).
[115] WP29 (n 35) 9.
[116] ibid 9.

11. Data subjects' vulnerability as a risk factor in different national DPIA lists

To answer those questions, Chapter 7 will offer a detailed analysis. Now, however, it might be helpful to compare different national approaches to DPIAs. This is made possible by Article 35(4), according to which national DPAs should establish and make public a list of the kinds of processing operations which are subject to the requirement for a data protection impact assessment in their own countries (the so-called blacklist).

In the following sub-sections, I identify four different approaches to data subjects' vulnerability according to the national DPAs lists (see Table 6.1). In the first group, DPAs do not even mention the concept of vulnerability. In the second group, DPAs consider the processing of personal data of vulnerable subjects as a high risk factor in combination with another factor. In the third group, DPAs consider that the mere fact of processing personal data of vulnerable data subjects makes the data processing at high risk.

First group: the Member States with a minimalist approach to vulnerability as a high risk for data protection

All Member States have developed their own lists of data processing needing a specific DPIA. Many of them do not mention the concept of vulnerable data

Table 6.1 The four different approaches to data subjects' vulnerability in national DPAs lists about DPIA

	How DPAs consider data subjects vulnerability in their DPIA lists	Member States
First Group	DPAs do not mention vulnerability among the high-risk factors	Belgium, Portugal, Bulgaria, Estonia, and the United Kingdom
	DPAs just mention children or employees (but they do not name them as vulnerable subjects)	Slovakia, Luxembourg, the Netherlands, Cyprus, Croatia, Norwich.
Second Group	DPAs consider that processing personal data of 'vulnerable data subjects' (broadly understood) is at high risk just when in combination with another factor (monitoring, automated profiling, etc)	Finland, Hungary, France, Germany, Lithuania, Romania
Third Group	DPAs consider that processing personal data of vulnerable data subjects is at high risk without any other factor needed	Italy, Spain, Malta
Fourth Group	DPAs explain what vulnerability means, giving a general definition	Slovenia, Poland, Ireland, Czech Republic, Greece

subjects: this is the case of Belgium,[117] Portugal,[118] Bulgaria,[119] Estonia,[120] and the United Kingdom.[121]

Other national DPAs consider vulnerable subjects only as regards workers and children. Many countries just mention the monitoring of employees: Slovakia,[122] Luxembourg,[123] the Netherlands,[124] and Cyprus.[125] The situation of the Croatian DPIA list is similar, where the only addition in terms of vulnerable data subjects concerns the risk factor of 'automated decision making on *children*'.[126] The Norwegian DPIA list is similar, but in addition to monitoring employees, it also mentions the case of video surveillance in kindergarten.[127] However, this final list indirectly also mentions consumers as vulnerable data subjects, in particular when it mentions as high-risk data processing: 'collecting and combining personal data from third parties in order to decide whether the data subject shall be offered, continue to receive, or shall be denied a product, service or offer'.

[117] Autorité de Protection des Données, Liste des types d'opérations de traitement pour lesquelles une AIPD est requise <https://www.autoriteprotectiondonnees.be/sites/privacycommission/files/documents/Liste_des_traitements_AIPD.pdf> accessed 5 February 2023.

[118] Aviso (extrato) no 17575/2018 <https://www.cnpd.pt/bin/decisoes/regulamentos/DR_Regulamento_1-2018_lista_de_AIPD.pdf> accessed 5 February 2023. English translation available at <https://edpb.europa.eu/sites/edpb/files/files/file1/2018-09-25-opinion_2018_art._64_pt_sas_dpia_list_en.pdf> accessed 5 February 2023.

[119] Bulgarian DPA, List of processing operations requiring data protection impact assessment (DPIA) pursuant to Art 35, paragraph 4 of Regulation (EU) 2016/679. English version available at <https://iapp.org/media/pdf/resource_center/bulgaria_blacklist.pdf> accessed 5 February 2023.

[120] Data Protection Inspectorate, List of cross-border processing operations which are subject to the requirement for a data protection impact assessment. English version available at <https://www.eurocloud.at/news/detail/news/the-estonian-data-protection-authority-issued-guidance-on-the-definition-of-large-scale-processing/> accessed 5 February 2023.

[121] ICO, Examples of processing 'likely to result in high risk' <https://iapp.org/media/pdf/resource_center/UK_ico_blacklist.pdf> accessed 5 February 2023.

[122] Urad Na Ochranu Osobnych Udajov, Slovak list of processing operations which are subject to the requirement for a data protection impact assessment. English version available at <https://iapp.org/media/pdf/resource_center/slovakia_blacklist.pdf> accessed 5 February 2023. 'Monitoring employee work on the ground of serious reasons based on the particular nature of the employer's activities (hereinafter "employee monitoring processing").'

[123] CNDP, Délibération 34/2019 du 6 mars 2019 de la Commission nationale pour la protection des données portant adoption de la liste des types d'opérations de traitement pour lesquelles une analyse d'impact relative à la protection des données est requise: 'Les opérations de traitement qui consistent en ou qui comprennent un contrôle régulier et systématique des activités des employés—à condition qu'elles puissent produire des effets juridiques.'

[124] Autoriteit Persononsgegevens, Besluit inzake lijst van verwerkingen van persoonsgegevens waarvoor een gegevensbeschermingseffectbeoordeling (DPIA) verplicht is, Autoriteit Persoonsgegevens <https://www.autoriteitpersoonsgegevens.nl/sites/default/files/atoms/files/stcrt-2019-64418.pdf> accessed 5 February 2023. English translation available at <https://edpb.europa.eu/sites/edpb/files/files/file1/2018-09-25-opinion_2018_art._64_nl_sas_dpia_list_en.pdf> accessed 5 February 2023.

[125] Office of the Commissioner for Personal Data Protection, Indicative list of processing operations subject to DPIA requirements under Article 35(4) of the GDPR. English version available at <https://iapp.org/media/pdf/resource_center/cyprus_blacklist.pdf> accessed 5 February 2023.

[126] AZOP, Odluka o uspostavi i javnoj objavi popisa vrsta postupaka obrade koje podliježu zahtjevu za procjenu učinka na zaštitu podatak. English translation available at <https://iapp.org/media/pdf/resource_center/croatia_blacklist.pdf> accessed 20 February 2023.

[127] Datatilsynet, The Norwegian Supervisory Authority's List of Processing Operations Subject to the Requirement of a Data Protection Impact Assessment. English version available at <https://edpb.europa.eu/sites/edpb/files/decisions/no_dpia_list_en_gb_20190316.pdf> accessed 20 February 2023.

In sum, the Member States mentioned above do not place specific emphasis on vulnerable data subjects in their lists for 'high-risk' data processing. They consider vulnerability either implicitly or referring to some particular vulnerable groups (children, workers, consumers).

Second group: the Member States where vulnerability combined with another risk factor determines the high risk of data processing

Some other Member States have many references to data processing concerning vulnerable individuals, but there is no further definition. Finland considers as high risk all forms of data processing concerning *vulnerable individuals* when the processing involves genetic data, location data, or when the data controller has not provided the (vulnerable) data subject with information notices because she used an exemption at Article 14(5).[128] Similarly, the Hungarian DPA mentions biometric data processing of vulnerable subjects' data and further processing (or secondary purposes or use of that data) involving vulnerable subjects.[129] The French list also mentions genetic data and health data processing for vulnerable subjects but also data processing related to workers.[130]

The German list refers to biometric and genetic data processing of vulnerable individuals, extensive evaluation of workers, and profiling of consumers (similar to the Norwegian example).[131]

The Lithuanian list refers to the use of new technologies targeting vulnerable data subjects, video surveillance of vulnerable individuals (including employees' monitoring), and biometric data processing concerning vulnerable subjects.[132] Similarly, the Latvian list mentions only surveillance on vulnerable subjects, but

[128] List compiled by the Office of the Data Protection Ombudsman of processing operations which require data protection impact assessment (DPIA), updated 21 December 2018 <https://tietosuoja.fi/en/list-of-processing-operations-which-require-dpia> accessed 5 February 2023.

[129] Nemzeti Adatvédelmi és Informacioszabadsag Hatosag, List of Processing Operations Subject to DPIA 35(4) GDPR. English version available at <https://www.naih.hu/list-of-processing-operations-subject-to-dpia-35-4--gdpr.html> accessed 5 February 2023.

[130] CNIL, Délibération no 2018-327 du 11 octobre 2018 portant adoption de la liste des types d'opérations de traitement pour lesquelles une analyse d'impact relative à la protection des données est requise <https://www.legifrance.gouv.fr/jo_pdf.do?id=JORFTEXT000037559521> accessed 5 February 2023.

[131] Datenschutz Konferenz, Liste der Verarbeitungstätigkeiten, für die eine DSFA durchzuführen ist, 18 July 2018. English translation available at <https://www.lda.bayern.de/media/dsfa_muss_liste_dsk_de.pdf> accessed 5 February 2023.

[132] Director of the State Data Protection Inspectorate, Order on the approval of the list of data processing operations subject to the requirement to perform data protection impact assessment 14, March 2019. English translation available at <https://iapp.org/media/pdf/resource_center/lithuania_blacklist.pdf> accessed 5 February 2022.

interestingly it introduces imprisoned people among vulnerable subjects.[133] The Romanian list mentions large-scale data processing of vulnerable subjects but also the monitoring of vulnerable subjects and automated decisions made about them.[134]

In sum, this second group of Member States considers data subjects' vulnerability a relevant factor in the lists at high risk, but in combination with another factor (monitoring, biometric data processing, etc). The DPAs of these Member States either refer to specific examples of vulnerability (workers, imprisoned people) or simply name 'vulnerable' data subjects in general.

Third group: the Member States where vulnerability is a significant risk factor, even considered alone

The third group of DPAs gives more importance to vulnerable data subjects as a risk factor that should lead to the performance of a DPIA. These DPAs affirmed that the mere presence of vulnerable data subjects in data processing is sufficient to require a DPIA without any further risk criterion.

This is the case in Italy, where the mere fact of processing data of vulnerable subjects 'non occasionally' is considered to produce high risk for individuals.[135] The Spanish list takes a similar approach.[136] In addition, the Spanish DPA clarifies what 'vulnerable subjects' means (to qualify the data processing as high-risk processing): 'data processing regarding vulnerable subjects or those who are at risk of social exclusion, including the data of persons aged under 14, older people with any kind of disability, the disabled, persons who access social services, and the victims of gender-related violence, as well as their descendants and persons who are in their guardianship or custody'. In addition to the traditional categories of

[133] Datu Valsts Inspekcija, List of processing operations requiring data protection impact assessment pursuant to Article 35(4) of the GDPR. English version available at <https://edpb.europa.eu/sites/edpb/files/decisions/lv_sa_dpia_final_list_20181212.pdf> accessed 5 February 2022.

[134] DECIZIE no 174 din 18 octombrie 2018 privind lista operațiunilor pentru care este obligatorie realizarea evaluării impactului asupra protecției datelor cu caracter personal <https://iapp.org/media/pdf/resource_center/romanian_dpa_blacklist.pdf> accessed 5 February 2022. English version available at <https://iapp.org/media/pdf/resource_center/romanian_dpa_blacklist_english.pdf> accessed 5 February 2022.

[135] Garante per la Protezione dei Dati Personali, Elenco delle tipologie di trattamenti, soggetti al meccanismo di coerenza, da sottoporre a valutazione d'impatto <https://www.garanteprivacy.it/documents/10160/0/ALLEGATO+1+Elenco+delle+tipologie+di+trattamenti+soggetti+al+meccanismo+di+coerenza+da+sottoporre+a+valutazione+di+impatto> accessed 5 February 2022. In fact, the Italian DPA, after EDPB Opinion 12/2018 (25 September 2018), clarified that the wording 'non-occasionally' needs to be considered as 'large-scale' data processing.

[136] AEDP, List of the types of data processing that require a data protection impact assessment under Art 35.4. English version available at <https://www.aepd.es/media/criterios/listas-dpia-en-35-4.pdf> accessed 5 February 2022.

vulnerable subjects, victims of gender-related violence are also considered vulnerable.[137] Also, the criterion is more socially oriented ('risk of social exclusion'), and 'accessing social services' is an index of vulnerability.[138]

Similarly, the DPA of Malta considers as a risk factor the mere processing of data concerning vulnerable persons, and it also redefines vulnerability in a more socially centred way: not only children and employees but also 'individuals receiving any form of social assistance' are considered vulnerable data subjects.[139]

In sum, this third group of Member States considers at 'high risks' all kinds of data processing of vulnerable data subjects, without any additional risk factor (eg monitoring, profiling, etc). Although the DPAs of the Member States mentioned above give the utmost consideration to data subjects' vulnerability, there is no clear definition of who a vulnerable data subject is.

Fourth group: the Member States where the notion of vulnerability is better clarified and conceptualized

The last group of DPAs also accepts individual vulnerability as an essential risk factor for the scope of the DPIA. Still, they also offer more insights into the general notion of vulnerability and the threshold analysis regarding vulnerability.

The Slovenian DPIA list is an emblematic example.[140] It does not refer to 'vulnerability' but it rephrases the primary rationale of individual vulnerability in the WP29 Guidelines: 'imbalance of power'. In particular, the following must be considered to be of high risk: 'processing of personal data of vulnerable (groups of) individuals, where there is a significant imbalance of power between data controllers and individual, such as: processing of personal data of employees in conjunction with at least one other criterion, children, individuals with fully or partially limited legal capacity, asylum seekers, migrants, elderly, patients, etc.'. Here the emphasis is wholly on *power imbalance*. In addition, 'migrants' are defined independently from the status of asylum seekers.[141]

[137] See on this point eg E Gilson, *The Ethics of Vulnerability: A Feminist Analysis of Social Life and Practice* (1st edn, Routledge 2014) 148–77.

[138] AEDP, List of the types of data processing that require a data protection impact assessment (n 136).

[139] Office for the Information and Data Protection Commissioner, Data Protection Impact Assessment <https://idpc.org.mt/en/Pages/dpia.aspx> accessed 5 February 2022. However, another risk factor is also the monitoring of employees.

[140] Information Commissioner, The list of the kind of processing operations which are subject to the requirement for a Data Protection Impact Assessment under the Article 35(4) of the General Data Protection Regulation (EU) 2016/679 (GDPR). English version available at <https://www.ip-rs.si/fileadmin/user_upload/Pdf/Ocene_ucinkov/SI_DPIA_list_35-4_35-6_Slovenia_revised_21dec2018_OBJAVA_ZA_WEB.pdf> accessed 20 February 2023.

[141] On these distinction in the Human Rights case law see F Ippolito and SI Sánchez, *Protecting Vulnerable Groups: The European Human Rights Framework* (Bloomsbury Publishing 2015).

The approach the Polish DPIA list takes is similar.[142] The criterion is whether the assessment of the data subject or the provision of services to the data subject 'depend[s] on entities or persons which have authoritative and/or assessment-related power'. In particular, the list mentions the case of subjects assessed on the basis of age or gender, personalized systems used when offering jobs, and whistleblowing systems.

The Irish DPIA list[143] clarifies that processing the data of vulnerable data subjects is a high risk activity, and the notion of vulnerability means 'audiences that may have particular or special considerations related to their inherent nature, context or environment' (including minors, employees, the 'mentally ill', asylum seekers, the aged, and those suffering incapacitation).

Lastly, one of the most advanced categorizations of individual vulnerability in the data protection framework can be found in the Czech DPIA list for high-risk data processing.[144] First of all, it does not refer to vulnerability as an absolute concept inherent to specific individuals but it rightly mentions vulnerability as a contextual and relational property of specific data processing: 'processing including personal data exposing data subjects to vulnerability-provoking environment'.[145]

The Czech DPA clarifies that vulnerability can be considered a high-risk data processing criterion if the processing focuses *solely* on subjects from a specified group. In addition, the DPA document mentions three layers of vulnerability: (i) permanent vulnerability, (ii) timely-limited vulnerability, and (iii) situational vulnerability. The first category (permanent vulnerability) refers to 'members of a specified group pursuant nationality, religion, sexual orientation, physical or mental handicap, conviction for criminal offence, etc.'. The second category (time-limited vulnerability) refers to members 'of a specified group depending on whether they are migrants, ill people, old people, children, teenagers, etc.'. The third category (situational vulnerability) includes data subjects who deal with public administration, employees interfacing with their employers, health or social services recipients and their interactions with social service providers, and consumers of medicaments or erotic aids.

The innovative aspect of this definition is that for the first time, a DPA proposes a taxonomy of the data subject's vulnerabilities (based on vulnerability duration and data processing context), and also that this DPA reveals the contextual nature

[142] Proponowany wykaz rodzajów przetwarzania, dla których wymagane jest przeprowadzenie oceny skutków dla ochrony danych <https://iapp.org/media/pdf/resource_center/poland_blacklist.pdf> accessed 20 February 2023.

[143] Data Protection Commission, List of types of data processing which require a DPIA. English version available at <https://www.dataprotection.ie/sites/default/files/uploads/2018-11/Data-Protection-Impact-Assessment.pdf> accessed 5 February 2023.

[144] Office for Personal Data Protection of the Czech Republic, List of processing operations subject to data protection impact assessment. English version available at <https://iapp.org/media/pdf/resource_center/czech_blacklist.pdf> accessed 20 February 2023.

[145] On the notion of risk as 'environment' see also van Dijk and others (n 93).

of vulnerability and mentions—among other vulnerable subjects—consumers, although in restricted fields like the healthcare and erotic market.[146]

The Greek list of data processing requiring a DPIA is atypical. Even though vulnerable individuals are not explicitly mentioned, the DPA clarifies that the criteria for carrying out a DPIA are grouped in three categories: (i) types and purposes of the processing; (ii) types of personal data and/or *categories of data subjects*; (iii) additional characteristics and/or means of the processing. In other words, the categories of data subjects are a relevant criterion to understand the level of risk of the data processing.

12. The content of a DPIA: towards a vulnerability-centred implementation

According to Article 35(7), the DPIA is based on several steps: a systematic description of the processing, an assessment of necessity and proportionality, an assessment of risks, and a description of measures envisaged to mitigate such risks.[147]

It is not easy to interpret what the *necessity and proportionality* assessment means in this context. The WP29 affirmed that necessity and proportionality at Article 35 should be based on the assessment of compliance with data protection principles.[148] Building on this, commentators have argued that the data controller needs to perform a balancing test for most of the data protection principles:[149] that is, when understanding whether a given data processing is fair; when choosing the lawful ground for processing data; when determining the purposes (and eventually deciding to process for secondary purposes); when replying to data subjects' requests; when informing the data subject (a balancing between the right of subjects to know versus the right of the data controller to keep information secret).[150] The result of all these balancing tests should turn into a *justification*[151] of that data processing about the respect of data protection principles (in particular, lawfulness, fairness, transparency, purpose limitation, data minimization, and of course accountability).

[146] On the link between erotic market and vulnerability see Gilson (n 137) 177.

[147] D Kloza and others, 'Data Protection Impact Assessments in the European Union: Complementing the New Legal Framework towards a More Robust Protection of Individuals' <https://cris.vub.be/files/32009890/dpialab_pb2017_1_final.pdf> accessed 5 February 2023.

[148] WP29 (n 35) Annex II, 21.

[149] Gellert, 'We Have Always Managed Risks in Data Protection Law' (n 76). See also the critical reply of Sloot (n 83); See the counterarguments of Gellert, 'On Risk, Balancing, and Data Protection: A Response to van Der Sloot' (n 83).

[150] G Malgieri, 'Trade Secrets v Personal Data: A Possible Solution for Balancing Rights' (2016) 6 International Data Privacy Law 102.

[151] About the interpretation of necessity and proportionality as justification see ME Kaminski and G Malgieri, 'Algorithmic Impact Assessments under the GDPR: Producing Multi-Layered Explanations' (2019) University of Colorado Law Legal Studies Research Paper 6, 19–28. About the notion of justification in case of automated data processing see M Hildebrandt, *Law for Computer Scientists and Other Folk* (Oxford University Press 2020) 301; ME Kaminski, 'Binary Governance: Lessons from the GDPR's Approach to Algorithmic Accountability' (2019) 92 Southern California Law Review 15.

In sum, and according to the accountability principle, the controller should determine the measures for protecting vulnerable individuals.[152] Each step should be linked to an identified risk.[153] I have repeatedly referred to vulnerable subjects under different risk factors. Data controllers may suggest specific mitigation measures for specific vulnerable individuals: for example in cases of decision-making vulnerability, the data controller could implement specific forms of consent collection and specific information disclosure measures; in cases where individuals might be easily discriminated against, the data controller could implement periodical audits against discrimination, etc.

However, especially in the context of highly vulnerable data subjects, it has been noted that those measures must be revised or adjusted based on physical, emotional, educational, and other needs. Since in these cases the risk factors could vary over time, they must be assessed and analysed in both the short and long term.[154]

Chapter 7 will develop the DPIA model as a tool to assess individual vulnerability and offer specific examples of risk mitigation measures.

13. Conclusion: a vulnerability-attentive analysis of the GDPR

This chapter analysed the relevance of data subjects' vulnerability in the interpretation of the GDPR data subjects' rights and accountability duties. In particular, I focused on the notion of vulnerable data subjects, meaning—as proposed in Chapter 4—individuals at higher risk of harm being done to their fundamental rights and duties.

In the previous chapter, in the analyses of the principles, I observed that the principle of fairness should be interpreted to rebalance power relations between controllers and subjects. In other terms, and according to our definition of vulnerable subjects, one of the rationales of the fairness principle is the mitigation of data subjects' vulnerability in specific contexts. Other principles (in Article 5 GDPR) are also based on an assessment of the status of the data subject and of their level of vulnerability. This is the case of the lawfulness principle (choosing the correct lawful basis under Articles 6 and 9 implies an evaluation of the particular situation of the data subject at issue), but also of the transparency principle (the amount of information should be data subject-centred) and the purpose limitation principle (determining the purpose must be based on the particular needs and vulnerability of the subject).

152 Kaminski (n 151).

153 Demetzou, 'Data Protection Impact Assessment' (n 84).

154 Van der Hof and Lievens, 'The Importance of Privacy by Design and Data Protection Impact Assessments in Strengthening Protection of Children's Personal Data under the GDPR'; KC Montgomery and J Chester, 'Data Protection for Youth in the Digital Age: Developing a Rights-Based Global Framework' (2015) 1(4) European Data Protection Law Review 277–91.

In this chapter, it was observed that the provisions about data protection rights also reveal that the personal situation of data subjects (especially data subjects' vulnerability) should be adequately considered when implementing such rights in practice. An average, well-informed data subject does not exist in reality: the data controller should consider different levels of cognitive vulnerabilities when implementing transparency duties according to Articles 12–15.

As shown in this chapter, the right to erasure (Article 17) was probably also conceived for more vulnerable subjects: Recital 65 mentions this right as a safeguard for children who are not fully aware of data processing risks. The reference to children was even stronger in the original Commission Proposal.[155] We might draw an analogy with other vulnerable subjects who are cognitively vulnerable: the right to erasure can mitigate impairment of autonomy and self-determination of these data subjects.

Another relevant right that this chapter considered is the right to object (Article 21). It has been considered one of the tools that can mitigate (on an *ex-post* basis) the unfair asymmetry between the controller and the subject. In addition, this right can be exercised on the basis of the 'particular situation' of the data subject. I have shown that some states explicitly relate this 'particular situation' to data subjects' vulnerability. The last right I considered was the right not to be subject to automated decisions (Article 22). Since this right applies where automated decisions produce legal or similarly significant effects on individuals, I observed how important the data subject's particular characteristics are, especially their exposure to harms and damages (ie their vulnerability).

As regards controllers' duties and responsibilities, the obligation to analyse the 'categories of data subjects' (at Articles 28(3), 30(1)(c), 33(3)(a)) is meaningful for our research of data subjects' conditions. Furthermore, the risk-based approach is fruitful for our layered analysis of the human vulnerability. In addition, the concept of vulnerable subjects is relevant for the evaluation of (high) risks in data protection. Several DPAs have clarified that vulnerability in the data protection field is contextual and depends on power imbalance, which is directly proportional to the level of risk for individuals.

In conclusion, to reply to the research question of this chapter, we can affirm that the GDPR provisions about data protection rights and duties, if correctly interpreted and implemented, take into account data subjects' personal conditions, including individual vulnerabilities. The next chapter will explore how a vulnerability-aware interpretation of those provisions could improve mitigation of individual vulnerabilities.

[155] In the Commission proposal the reference to children was at the first paragraph of art 17. See European Commission Proposal for the General Data Protection Regulation, COM (2012)11 final, art 17: 'The data subject shall have the right to obtain from the controller the erasure of personal data relating to them and the abstention from further dissemination of such data, *especially in relation to personal data which are made available by the data subject while he or she was a child*' (emphasis added).

7

Assessing (and mitigating) layers of data subjects' vulnerability

Using the DPIA as a model

1. Introduction

In the previous chapters, we analysed the notion of the data subject. In particular, Chapters 2, 3, and 4 explored the two possible notions of the average and vulnerable data subjects. Then, in Chapter 4, we analysed the General Data Protection Regulation (GDPR) provisions that are most relevant for vulnerability to understand how the EU data protection framework takes into account the status and the specific circumstances of the data subject, including situations of vulnerability. We thus concluded that the GDPR contains a notion of the 'average' data subject (comparable to the average consumers). At the same time, it includes several provisions that could lead to a layered, contextual, temporary, causal, and modal notion of the vulnerable data subject.

The aim of this chapter is to develop a vulnerability-aware implementation of the GDPR. In particular, building on the notion of *layered* vulnerability (from Luna's theory) as outlined in Chapters 3 to 5, we analyse how risk assessment tools in the GDPR could be used in practice as a model to take into account the specific conditions of the data subject and mitigate permanent or temporary situations of vulnerability. Accordingly, the question that this chapter aims to address is: how to use the GDPR provisions as a tool to mitigate the negative impacts that result from data processing of vulnerable data subjects?

To answer this question, this chapter follows the data protection impact assessment (DPIA) model in Article 35 GDPR. In the previous chapters, we observed that data subjects' vulnerability means a higher risk of their fundamental rights and freedoms being harmed. We also observed that vulnerability should be understood as a concept comprising several layers. Accordingly, an assessment of these layers might coincide with an analysis of risks of harm to fundamental rights and freedoms.[1] Accordingly, in this chapter, we propose an analysis of vulnerability layers based on the risk assessment model proposed for DPIA by Article 35 GDPR.

[1] See É Gennet and others, 'Does the New EU Regulation on Clinical Trials Adequately Protect Vulnerable Research Participants?' (2015) 119 Health Policy (Amsterdam, Netherlands) 925, highlighting the link between layer assessment (proposed by Luna) and risk assessment in the EU law.

Vulnerability and Data Protection Law. Gianclaudio Malgieri, Oxford University Press. © Gianclaudio Malgieri 2023.
DOI: 10.1093/oso/9780192870339.003.0007

As also explained in Chapter 6, the DPIA is a process in which, before starting a data processing activity that risks harming the fundamental rights and freedoms of data subjects, the data controller conducts an assessment of the impacts of the envisaged processing operations on the protection of personal data (Article 35(1)). The assessment shall contain at least:

> (a) a systematic description of the envisaged processing operations and the purposes of the processing, including, where applicable, the legitimate interest pursued by the controller; (b) an assessment of the necessity and proportionality of the processing operations in relation to the purposes; (c) an assessment of the risks to the rights and freedoms of data subjects referred to in paragraph 1; and (d) the measures envisaged to address the risks, including safeguards, security measures and mechanisms to ensure the protection of personal data and to demonstrate compliance with [the GDPR] taking into account the rights and legitimate interests of data subjects and other persons concerned. (Article 35(7))

This chapter is structured as follows. After the introduction, Section 2 examines the concept and possible manifestations of *risks (of interference with) fundamental rights and freedoms*, especially in the case of vulnerable data subjects. This is necessary to then analyse the impacts of such interferences and the level of risks. In other words, Section 2 analyses the rights and freedoms protected in the GDPR and the attacks thereon that can lead to individual vulnerability. This chapter uses the phrase 'interference with fundamental rights and freedoms' when addressing the notion of risk in Article 35. Even though the GDPR does not mention the word 'interference', I assume that the term—derived from the human rights jurisprudence—is implicit in the notion of 'risk to a right', and it will be helpful to analyse the notion of risks in this context.[2]

After clarifying (in Section 2) how difficult an assessment based on the concept of risks of interference with fundamental rights and freedoms is, a way to proceed with my vulnerability analysis is to assess the severity and likelihood of the impact of such interferences that render data subjects vulnerable. To determine the impact of such interferences Recital 90 specifies two parameters: the likelihood and the severity of the risks. Section 3 analyses the *severity* of these violations, while Section 4 their *likelihood*. Consequently, Section 5 addresses the assessment of

See more in general on layers assessment F Luna, 'Identifying and Evaluating Layers of Vulnerability—A Way Forward' (2019) 19 Developing World Bioethics 86.

[2] The concept of interference is more appropriate than the term 'harm' because not all interference with fundamental rights can lead to quantifiable harms. Analogously, the concept of interference is more appropriate than 'violation': the first is a gradual notion, while the latter is a yes-or-no notion. For the purpose of this book, when I address the concept of risk, I prefer to use a neutral and gradual notion of interference with fundamental rights and freedoms. See N van Dijk and others, 'A Risk to a Right? Beyond Data Protection Risk Assessments' (2016) 32 Computer Law & Security Review 286.

the proportionality and necessity requirements (as required by Article 35(7)(b)). Lastly, Section 6 proposes possible risk mitigation measures (as required by Article 35(7)(d)) based on a vulnerability-aware interpretation of the GDPR, and Section 7 describes the situation in which data processing (involving vulnerable individuals) should not start or continue at all (the backstop scenario).

As shown below, a vulnerability-aware interpretation of the GDPR is possible and should be encouraged in order to protect vulnerable data subjects. Several provisions might be interpreted to take into account and mitigate vulnerability layers of data subjects.

2. Risks to 'fundamental rights and freedoms': which ones?

Following the DPIA structure in order to analyse different layers of vulnerability, I start by addressing what 'risk to fundamental rights and freedoms' means (Article 35(1)). In other words, if the definition of vulnerability is the higher risk of having one's fundamental rights and freedoms being adversely affected,[3] it is worth understanding what this risk to fundamental rights and freedoms means. Then, in the following sections, I assess the severity and likelihood of such risks.[4]

As Recital 4 argues, and as also explained by the Article 29 Data Protection Working Party on the Protection of Individuals with regard to the Processing of Personal Data (WP29)[5] and the European Data Protection Board (EDPB),[6] the reference to '*the rights and freedoms*' of data subjects in the GDPR primarily concerns:

1. the right to privacy and data protection, but this may also involve other fundamental rights, such as:
2. freedom of speech, expression, and information;
3. freedom of thought;
4. freedom of movement;
5. the prohibition of discrimination;
6. the right to liberty, freedom of conscience, and religion;
7. the freedom to conduct a business;
8. the right to effective remedy and to a fair trial;
9. the right to cultural, religious, and linguistic diversity.

[3] See largely Chapter 3. See in particular RE Goodin, *Protecting the Vulnerable: A Reanalysis of Our Social Responsibilities* (University of Chicago Press 1985); D Schroeder and E Gefenas, 'Vulnerability: Too Vague and Too Broad?' (2009) 18 Cambridge Quarterly of Healthcare Ethics 113.

[4] See Recital 90 GDPR.

[5] WP29, Guidelines on Data Protection Impact Assessment (DPIA), WP248, 15.

[6] See eg EDPB, Letter in reply to Sophie In't Veld, Ref: OUT2020-0004, 29 January 2020, 4.

In Chapter 4, I clarified that there are at least two different kinds of vulnerability in the data processing field: processing-based vulnerability (during the data processing) and effect-based vulnerability (to the outcome of data processing). This chapter look at the fundamental rights and freedoms that are at higher risk of interference for each of them.

As regards vulnerability *during the data processing* (what I call processing-based vulnerability), the sources of vulnerability can be:

- incapability of understanding information about data processing (eg data protection notices). This incapability can be triggered or amplified by cognitive issues of the data subject, or their immaturity, or their illiteracy, and by the lack of transparency and opacity of the data processing.
- incapability of understanding the risks, significance, and envisaged effects of some data processing.[7] Once again, this incapability can be triggered or amplified by cognitive issues, immaturity, or illiteracy of the data subject, lack of transparency and opacity of data processing.
- incapability to give valid consent to data processing.[8] This incapability can be triggered or amplified by imbalance of power; knowledge; economic, or social circumstances; cognitive issues; immaturity; illiteracy; lack of transparency and opacity of data processing; manipulative techniques used (eg hidden patterns).
- incapability of exercising data protection rights adequately or understanding the significance of these rights and the consequences of their being exercised or harmed.[9] This incapability can be triggered or amplified by imbalance of power, knowledge, economic or social circumstances, cognitive issues, immaturity, or illiteracy. It can also be amplified by lack of transparency and the opacity of data processing, and data controllers' malicious attempts to obstruct the exercise of data protection rights in specific contexts.

The fundamental rights and freedoms that might be at issue in processing-based vulnerability imply interference with autonomy, dignity, and informational self-determination, and, therefore, these rights include privacy[10] and data protection.[11]

[7] Recital 38 GDPR.

[8] WP29, Guidelines on Consent, WP259 rev.01, 5.

[9] Recital 38 GDPR.

[10] Here the two fundamental rights (privacy and data protection) are mentioned together, as in the EDPB, Letter in reply to Sophie In't Veld, Ref: OUT2020-0004, 29 January 2020, 4. Although—as clarified in the previous chapters of this book—they are separate rights, processing based-vulnerability interferes with principles (informational self-determination, autonomy, dignity) that are in essence of both rights.

[11] See O Lynskey, *The Foundations of EU Data Protection Law* (Oxford University Press 2015) 195 discussing whether data protection should be a source of harm itself or should always lead to harms to other fundamental rights. About the link between harm and data processing see R Gellert and others, 'A Comparative Analysis of Anti-Discrimination and Data Protection Legislations' in B Custers and

If the data subject is asked to give consent that is not valid (ie is not freely given, specific, informed, and unambiguous) or if they are limited in their capability to exercise data protection rights, their fundamental right to data protection (but also to privacy) might be seriously impaired.[12] In addition, processing-based vulnerability might affect other fundamental rights like the right to non-discrimination when the data controllers do not properly accommodate (or obstruct the exercise of) data protection rights of some data subjects (with the effect of discriminating them) or when the opacity of data processing limits the possibility to object to certain (discriminatory) data processing outcomes. Similarly, processing-based vulnerability might affect the right to a fair trial, especially when limited transparency of data processing and the difficulty to exercise data subject rights adversely affect the interests of the data subject in legal claims.

Looking at effect-based vulnerability (vulnerability to the *outcome of data processing*), potentially all other fundamental rights and freedoms might be infringed (points 3–5 above), such as, for example, freedom of speech, freedom of thought, freedom of movement, the prohibition of discrimination, freedom to conduct a business, the right to liberty, and freedom of conscience and religion. However, having identified the main data subjects' rights and freedoms at issue, the *manifestation of the interference* with these rights is not easy to pinpoint.[13]

Recital 75 GDPR seems to enlist some risks of interference with those rights and freedoms when addressing the DPIA and, in particular, the notion of high risk to fundamental rights and freedoms. Recital 75 explains:

> The risk to the rights and freedoms of natural persons, of varying likelihood and severity, may result from personal data processing which could lead to physical, material or non-material damage, in particular: where the processing may give rise to discrimination, identity theft or fraud, financial loss, damage to the reputation, loss of confidentiality of personal data protected by professional secrecy, unauthorised reversal of pseudonymisation, or any other significant economic or social disadvantage; deprivation of their rights and freedoms or prevented from exercising control over their personal data.

Apart from the terminological ambiguity between 'damages' and more general interferences with fundamental rights (eg 'discrimination'),[14] there is no bilateral correspondence between rights and freedoms (as enlisted by Recital 4 and by WP29 and the EDPB) and their violations as described in Recital 75. First, there

others (eds), *Discrimination and Privacy in the Information Society: Data Mining and Profiling in Large Databases* (Springer 2013) 65.

[12] See eg Lynskey (n 11) 254.
[13] van Dijk and others (n 2).
[14] Lynskey (n 11) 194.

is no corresponding violation of freedom of thought and of speech (eg manipulation or similar impairment of mental freedom, censorship, etc) mentioned in Recital 75. On the other hand, some risks in Recital 75 do not correspond to any of the fundamental rights and freedoms mentioned by the WP29 and the EDPB. In particular, Recital 75 refers to 'physical, material or non-material damage', while, in the list in Recital 4 (and in the WP29 list), there is no reference to the right to life[15] and physical and mental integrity.[16] For this reason, in the following analysis, I consider more generally the rights and freedoms as enlisted in the EU Charter of Fundamental Rights.[17]

As many scholars argue, there is no general clear statement of the notion of interference with fundamental rights and freedoms in the GDPR, and this constitutes a problem for the effectiveness of the accountability principle: the more the notion of interference (and 'harm') is unclear, the more arbitrary the power of data controllers in determining how to implement data protection rules.[18]

Lynskey tries to classify the main data protection harms, distinguishing between tangible and intangible harms arising from data processing.[19] In the first category, she identifies discrimination, identity fraud, and physical harms. In the second category, she mentions powerlessness, inhibition, and control (arising from surveillance), and the erosion of the individual's ability to self-representation. She clarifies that she does not propose an exhaustive taxonomy of harms but she tries to understand whether such harms can justify the data protection regime.[20]

As I understand, there are no explicit official institutional documents on the list of possible interference with fundamental rights and freedoms. Still, there are at least two documents that—in different contexts and with different purposes—attempt to classify different kinds of harms in the data protection framework: the

[15] See art 2 of the EU CFR.

[16] See art 3 of the EU CFR.

[17] The EU CFR includes different categories of rights including: the right to life (art 2); the right to integrity of the person (art 3); the right to liberty and security (art 6); the right to the respect for private and family life (art 7); protection of personal data (art 8); the right to marry and the right to found a family (art 9); freedom of thought, conscience, and religion (art 10); freedom of expression and information (art 11); freedom of assembly and of association (art 12); freedom of the arts and sciences (art 13); the right to education (art 14); freedom to choose an occupation and right to engage in work (art 15); freedom to conduct a business (art 16); the right to property (art 17); the right to asylum (art 18); protection in the event of removal, expulsion, or extradition (art 19); equality (art 20), non-discrimination (art 21), etc.

[18] A Cavoukian and others, *The Unintended Consequences of Privacy Paternalism* (Information and Privacy Commissioner 2014) 14 <https://collections.ola.org/mon/28003/326077.pdf> accessed 20 February 2023; DJ Solove, 'Privacy Self-Management and the Consent Dilemma' (2013) 126 Harvard Law Review 1880, 1891; L Bergkamp, 'EU Data Protection Policy. The Privacy Fallacy: Adverse Effects of Europe's Data Protection Policy in an Information-Driven Economy' (2002) 18 Computer Law & Security Review 31, 41 affirming: 'it is remarkable that governments have been able to adopt and implement such onerous, expensive, and paradoxical data protection regimes without any plausible evidence of harm or threatened harm, entirely based on some vague notion of "fundamental right" and hypothetical risks'.

[19] Lynskey (n 11) 196–227.

[20] ibid 192.

National Institute of Standard and Technology (NIST) Impact Assessment report[21] and the Future of Privacy Forum's report on Harms from Algorithmic Unfairness.[22] Although they are based on a different legal system (the United States), some considerations held in those documents might be critically applied *mutatis mutandis* to the EU data protection framework.

These two reports try to identify and classify the 'risks' and the related 'harms' that data processing techniques can bring to data subjects. However, in the list of harms held in the NIST Impact Assessment report, several harms are very vague, such as 'dignity loss' (can it be considered reputational damage, or should it have a broader understanding?). In addition, other violations, like 'loss of trust', seem not to directly correspond to specific fundamental rights and freedoms under the EU legal framework.[23] Even the list of harms in the Future of Privacy Forum's report seems problematic: there are no references to violations affecting freedom of speech, freedom of thought, etc, and the only general reference to liberty appears closely related to the perspective taken in criminal proceedings.[24]

In addition, this analysis is generally problematic for two main reasons: (i) the definition of interference with fundamental rights is not clear, and several harms resulting from those interferences seem to overlap; (ii) harms can have cascading effects, producing secondary or further harms so that it is difficult to connect each harm to the specific fundamental right(s) at issue.

Looking at the (i), it is problematic to understand what harm *per se* is and what, on the other hand, is a consequence of harm or a prerequisite of harm (see the example below). In other words, it is not easy to understand the borderline between not-yet-harmful effects, harm *stricto sensu*, and cascade effects. Focusing on the cascade effect (ii), every interference with fundamental rights can have primary and secondary (or further) manifestations.

To give an example, if a data subject is exposed to personalized behavioural advertisements based on the exploitation of cognitive biases, this might lead to mental manipulation,[25] in other words harm to freedom of thought.[26] However, at

[21] NIST, NIST Privacy Framework: A Tool For Improving Privacy Through Enterprise Risk Management, Version 1.0, 16 January 2020 <https://www.nist.gov/system/files/documents/2020/01/16/NIST%20Privacy%20Framework_V1.0.pdf> accessed 5 February 2022.

[22] Future of Privacy Forum, 'Unfairness By Algorithm: Distilling the Harms of Automated Decision-Making' (2017) 4–5 <https://fpf.org/2017/12/11/unfairness-by-algorithm-distilling-the-harms-of-automated-decision-making/> accessed 8 February 2020.

[23] On the notion of trust in Europe, see in general A Fuchs and others, 'A Formal Notion of Trust—Enabling Reasoning about Security Properties', 4th IFIP WG 11.11 International on Trust Management (TM), June 2010, Morioka, Japan. pp 200–15.

[24] Future of Privacy Forum (n 22).

[25] D Susser and others, 'Online Manipulation: Hidden Influences in a Digital World' (2019) 4 Georgetown Law Technology Review 1; TZ Zarsky, 'Privacy and Manipulation in the Digital Age' (2019) 20 Theoretical Inquiries in Law 157; G Malgieri, 'In/Acceptable Marketing and Consumers' Privacy Expectations: Four Tests from EU Data Protection Law' (2021) 40(2) Journal of Consumer Marketing 209 <https://doi.org/10.1108/JCM-03-2021-4571> accessed 2 January 2022.

[26] On the link between freedom of thought and privacy see N Richards, *Intellectual Privacy: Rethinking Civil Liberties in the Digital Age* (1st edn, Oxford University Press 2015).

the same time, this could produce economic harms to the data subject if they are induced to buy goods or services that were not suitable for them,[27] or even psychological harms if the personalized advertisement exploits particular aspects of the data subject's psyche, etc.[28]

Another example is a data subject who feels pressure from their employer and colleagues because of, for example, their sexual orientation (inferred, for example, from the processing of personal data about their marital status and the name of their partner processed for tax-related reasons). We might qualify this situation as discrimination, but if there is no actual unfair treatment by the employer of the data subject at issue,[29] this situation might qualify as, for example, limitation to the freedom of speech of the data subject if they do not feel free to express their views and personality at work, or it could even lead to psychological harm.

In its guidelines on impact assessment, the European Network and Information Security Agency (ENISA) emphasized the challenge to also consider possible 'secondary adverse effects' to the rights and freedoms of individuals when assessing the impact of data processing on data subjects under the GDPR.[30] Nevertheless, doing so is not easy in practice[31] since it is far from easy to understand the correlations between different effects and assess their actual impact.

Although an assessment based on the concept of 'interference' with fundamental rights and freedoms might appear very difficult to undertake, Recital 90 GDPR indicates that we need to analyse two criteria in order to assess the risk to fundamental rights and freedoms in the data protection frameworks: severity and likelihood. Accordingly, a way to proceed with the vulnerability analysis is to assess the severity and likelihood of the impact of these risks that may render data subjects vulnerable.

This does not mean that this book prefers to take a risk-based approach and rejects a right-based approach: the two systems are interrelated and not antithetic. Any impact needs to be related precisely to a fundamental right, but the severity and likelihood of this impact can vary (from minimum to very significant effects). Stated in other terms, the vulnerability threshold has two components:

[27] J Trzaskowski, 'Behavioural Economics, Neuroscience, and the Unfair Commercial Practises Directive' (2011) 34 Journal of Consumer Policy 377.

[28] See R Calo, 'Digital Market Manipulation' (2013) 82 George Washington Law Review 995, 1029, making the example of online behavioural advertising based on the information of the death of a parent.

[29] On the notion of disparate impacts, see S Barocas and AD Selbst, 'Big Data's Disparate Impact' (2016) 104 California Law Review 671.

[30] ENISA, *Guidelines for SMEs on the security of personal data processing*, December 2016, 14 <https://www.enisa.europa.eu/publications/guidelines-for-smes-on-the-security-of-personal-data-processing>, accessed 5 February 2022.

[31] See also ISO 31000:2018(en), Risk management—Guidelines <https://www.iso.org/obp/ui/#iso:std:iso:31000:ed-2:v1:en> accessed 20 December 2022, which—in addition to likelihood and 'nature and magnitude of consequences'—considers also other element for risk analysis, such as: complexity and connectivity; time-related factors and volatility; the effectiveness of existing controls; sensitivity and confidence levels.

1. *interference with a fundamental right or freedom*: that is, the impact needs to be relatable to one or more specific fundamental rights as protected in the EU Charter of Fundamental Rights.
2. *severity and likelihood of the effects* produced by such an interference.

Thus, bearing in mind that the interference with fundamental rights can lead to unlikely and minimal effects or even to very likely and significant effects, the following sections will analyse the severity and likelihood of possible interferences to fundamental rights in order to qualify a subject as being in a vulnerable position.

In other words, any impact on data subjects must be clearly related to a fundamental right cited in the EU Charter of Fundamental Rights. This is a necessary requirement in order to avoid the accusation that the vulnerability threshold is based on trivial impacts. Once the link with one or more fundamental right is clarified, it is then necessary to analyse the severity and likelihood of that interference with a subject's fundamental rights.

3. Analysing the severity of risks: from mere effects to damages

This section addresses the severity assessment. Severity means the possible intensity of the *effects* of interference with fundamental rights and freedoms of the data subjects. In other words, a key element to consider is the envisaged effects.

Accordingly, this section proposes a taxonomy of (risks of) *effects* of envisaged processing operations, considering how severely these potential effects might affect the data subject. When analysing these (risks of) effects, one can observe that what influences their severity is neither solely the characteristics of the data subject nor the characteristics of the data controller taken alone. The combination of the two types of subjective characteristics influences the final effect.

To conduct this analysis, this section takes into account the wording of the GDPR and other related pieces of legislation in the EU and Member States, but also Court of Justice of the European Union (CJEU) decisions, EDPB opinions, etc.

In the wording of the GDPR there are several degrees of severity of effects of data processing on the data subject: (mere) effects, substantial significant effects, legal or similarly significant effects, damages.[32] As Figure 7.1

[32] As shown below, the notion of damage has a different legal nature if compared to the other kinds of effects. In private law terms, the notion of damage refers to any harm justifying pecuniary and non-pecuniary compensation. For the scope of this book, the notion of damage relates to a more severe harm if compared to other effects. Indeed, if a harm gives rise to a right to compensation, that harm is presumably more impactful than other effects. However, as argued below, I am aware that—according to the legal framework at issue—also other requirements need to apply (violation of legal provisions; causality between action and harm; fault of the counterpart; etc.). In other words, although higher severity

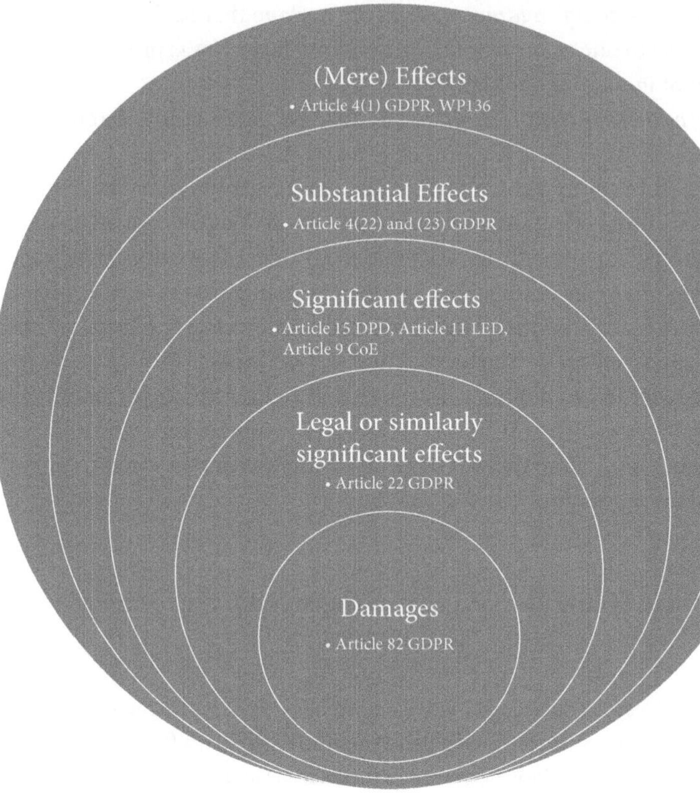

Figure 7.1 The severity of risks could be analysed through different levels of impactful 'encounters' between the data controller and the data subject in the data protection framework: what is the threshold for the legally relevant vulnerability of the data subject?

shows,[33] the different levels of effects are concentric. 'Damages' are included in the notion of 'similarly significant effects', which are included in the broader group of 'significant effects', which are part of the more comprehensive notion of 'effects'.

In the following sub-sections, I examine each of these different *effects*, representing different levels of severity of impact on data subjects. To conduct this analysis, I discuss the definitions of the different levels of effects, their legal recognitions, and their legal implications. The ultimate aim of this analysis is to

of impact is not the only qualifying requirement for 'damages', we argue that the notion of damage refers to more severe harms if compared to other 'effects' in the GDPR wording.

[33] As explained below, Figure 7.1 includes also 'significant effects', wording that is not present in the GDPR but that was in the Data Protection Directive and is in other satellites of the data protection framework (eg in the Law Enforcement Directive).

understand which of these effects can be considered the *severity threshold* between tolerable and intolerable *interferences* with the fundamental rights and freedoms of the data subject (as analysed in the previous section). For the purposes of this book, that severity threshold also determines the borderline between vulnerable and non-vulnerable data subjects. In Chapter 4, I affirmed that all data subjects share some layers of vulnerability. Still, some people share more layers or more burdensome layers than others. Finding the severity threshold mentioned above would help to understand what is the minimum level of vulnerability that the data protection legal framework takes into account to require special protection.

In other words, as observed in Chapters 4 and 6, considering the risk-based approach in the GDPR and the GDPR's aim to protect fundamental rights of individuals, data subjects' vulnerability in the GDPR means a higher risk of interference with fundamental rights and freedoms. But what does 'higher risk of interference' mean? How *severe* should this interference be for a data subject to be considered vulnerable? In the GDPR, there are several examples of interference with fundamental rights and freedoms—the above-mentioned '*effects*' of data processing on the data subject—with different degrees of severity. The following sections analyse different degrees of severity in the GDPR (from mere effects to damages) in order to identify the vulnerability threshold. The subsequent analysis takes a positivist approach, based on a literal interpretation of the GDPR and related legal texts. It assumes that the different mentions of 'effects' (as an impactful 'encounter' between data controllers and data subjects) in the GDPR are relevant legal indicators of the impact of data processing on data subjects at different levels of severity (and, thus, legal indicators of varying levels of vulnerability).[34]

Examining the text of the GDPR (and other legal texts in the data protection framework), it is possible to observe the following different levels of effect: mere effects (Article 4(1) as interpreted in *Nowak*),[35] substantial effects (Article 4(22) and (23)), significant effects (Article 11 of the Law Enforcement Directive (LED), the European Data Protection Regulation (EUDPR), Article 9 Council

[34] I am aware that these effects are not manifestations of risk in the data protection framework (see the ten risk indicators in the WP29 Guidelines on DPIA, as addressed in Chapter 6). However, the aim of this section and of the following sub-sections is not to assess risk indicators but to analyse the severity of (risks of) effects of data processing on individuals from a literal analysis of the GDPR wording. Indeed, following the analysis in Chapter 4, the notion of data subject's vulnerability strictly depends on the adverse effects to fundamental rights and freedoms of the data subject. Accordingly, I take the different mentions of effects in the GDPR as relevant legal indicators of the severity of impact of data processing on data subjects.

[35] CJEU, Case C-434/16 *Peter Nowak v Data Protection Commissioner* [20 December 2017], para 35. Emphasis added. The CJEU seems to endorse the position previously taken by the WP29 in WP136, supra, pp 9– 12. See on this point LA Bygrave and L Tosoni, 'Article 4(1). Personal Data' in C Kuner and others (eds), *The EU General Data Protection Regulation (GDPR)—A Commentary* (Oxford University Press 2020) 110.

Table 7.1 Different degrees of severity of data processing effects on the data subjects, with identifying factors, relevance in the data protection framework and legal consequences

Different degrees of effects on the data subjects	Definition, factors (non-exhaustive list based on the authoritative interpretations of the articles of the GDPR or of related laws)	Relevance in the data protection framework	Legal significance in the data protection framework
(Mere) effects	- *incidental* adverse effects; - purely beneficial effects; - purely subjective effects.	Definition of personal data (Article 4(1)) as interpreted by the CJEU	The GDPR applies.
Substantial effects	- influence on individual delicate spheres (health, well-being, economic circumstances, reputation); - limitation of rights and opportunities; - significant changes of subjects' behaviour; - unwanted and unanticipated consequences in subjects' lives.	Article 4(22)(b) and 4(23)(b)	Territorial scope of DPAs' activities and definition of cross-border processing.
Significant effects	- Objective and also subjective effects, but with some inter-subjective relevance (ie a certain number of other subjects believe these effects are relevant); - both positive and negative effects that can have relevant impact in the long-term; - even effects which are not manifest in the external situation.	Article 15 DPD, Article 11 LED, Article 9 CoE 108+	Prohibition of automated decision-making producing such effects in the criminal law fields (and before the GDPR, for all data processing), unless an exception (with safeguards) applies.
Legal or similarly significant effects	- Impacts on data subjects' status, rights and duties; - significant effects on circumstances, behaviour, or choices; - prolonged or permanent impact; - exclusion or discrimination of individuals; - significant effects in delicate areas (credit, health, education, employment); - online manipulation.	Article 22 GDPR (Article 35(3) GDPR)	Prohibition of automated decision-making producing such effects, unless an exception (with safeguards) applies

Damages	- Injury or loss as a consequence of an interference with fundamental rights and freedoms, which are:
	  - quantifiable or measurable,
	  - caused by negligence or intention,
	  - with proximity of the data controller to the damage.
		Article 82 GDPR	Liability of the data controller: right to compensation.

of Europe (CoE) 108+),[36] legal or similarly significant effects (Articles 22(1) and 35(3)),[37] and damages (Article 82). The borderlines between these different levels of effects are not always clear. Table 7.1 identifies characteristics distinguishing them from one another. Each of these layers is included in the previous layer (as Figure 7.1 reveals) but is more specific than the last (ie damage is a specific and very severe form of legal or similarly significant effect; legal or similarly significant effects are a specifically severe form of 'significant effects', and so on).

The significance of the legal recognition of these different effects in the data protection framework are diverse: from the mere application of the GDPR to the restoration of damages. What matters here is that these different levels of effects are all codified in the text of the GDPR (or in other legal texts in the data protection framework) and should be considered gradual steps from the least to the most impactful 'encounter' between data subjects and controllers.

Every layer of vulnerability is relevant. Still, only from the level of 'legal or similarly significant effects' can one speak about the legally relevant vulnerability of the data subject under the GDPR. Indeed, looking at legal or similarly significant effects seems to offer a balanced compromise between subjective and objective perception and can include the exploitation of not only effect-based but also processing-based vulnerability.

Suppose the controller uses manipulative, hidden patterns to obtain the consent of a data subject (in cases of data processing of a sensitive or intrusive nature) who is incapable of providing consent (decisional vulnerability). This instance might not qualify as risking damage to the data subject, but does qualify as a legal or similarly significant effect (an abuse of autonomy of the subject). In addition, many forms of effect-based vulnerability may not escalate to quantifiable losses but they are still relevant. This might be the case of, for example, commercial manipulation as an outcome of intrusive profiling. The definition of 'similarly significant effect' by the WP29 seems to consider the three main factors of vulnerability that I identified in Chapter 4: data subjects' characteristics, data controller's power/potentialities, and vulnerability drivers.[38]

[36] Even though such a notion is not in the GDPR (where arts 22 and 35[3] simply refer to 'legal or similarly significant effects'), the broader data protection framework has several mentions of 'significant effects'. In particular, the previous Data Protection Directive and the Law Enforcement Directive (hereinafter LED). Similarly, also the Council of Europe's Modernized Convention 108 refers to 'significant effects'. Article 29 Working Party (WP29), 'Opinion 4/2007 on the Concept of Personal Data, WP 136' 3; L Tosoni, 'Article 4(22). Supervisory Authority Concerned' in C Kuner and others (eds) (eds), *The EU General Data Protection Regulation (GDPR)—A Commentary* (Oxford University Press) 276.

[37] LA Bygrave, 'Minding the Machine: Article 15 of the EC Data Protection Directive and Automated Profiling' (2001) 17 Computer Law & Security Review 17, 19; M Martini, 'DS-GVO Art. 22 Automatisierte Entscheidungen Im Einzelfall Einschließlich Profiling' in BP Paal and D Pauly (eds), *Datenschutz-Grundverordnung* (Beck-online 2017) 29.

[38] See WP29, wp251rev.01, 22: 'the intrusiveness of the profiling process, including the tracking of individuals across different websites, devices and service; the expectations and wishes of the individuals concerned; the way the advert is delivered; or using knowledge of the vulnerabilities of the data subjects targeted'.

4. Analysing the likelihood of risks

As Recital 90 of the GDPR indicates, it is necessary to consider two criteria to analyse the risk to fundamental rights and freedoms: severity and likelihood. As already affirmed, we can observe an analogy between the analysis of risk to fundamental rights and the analysis of data subjects' vulnerability. The previous sections analysed the severity of impact, while this section examines the *likelihood* of impact. In her theory of vulnerability layer assessment, Luna considers two factors: harmfulness (severity) and the likelihood of manifestations of vulnerability.[39] In every case in which the GDPR refers to risks, it mentions 'likelihood and severity' as factors for assessing the degree of risks.[40]

A risk is often expressed as a function of the likelihood that an adverse outcome (threat) occurs multiplied by the magnitude of the negative outcome (impact), should it happen.[41] Likelihood is also defined as risk occurrence probability. It can be 'low' (the threat is unlikely to materialize), 'medium' (it is possible that the threat materializes), or 'high' (the threat is likely to materialize).[42]

Some authors criticize the introduction of the 'likelihood' criterion in the GDPR risk assessment as excessive 'quantification' of the analysis of risk to fundamental rights and freedoms of the data subject.[43] Also, while the severity of impact might be more easily estimated, the likelihood can never be wholly predicted.[44]

However, for our purposes, I see significant advantages in using this notion of likelihood: the distinction between 'average' and vulnerable data subjects is precisely the *higher likelihood* of incurring adverse impacts within the processing of their data or as an outcome of that processing. Indeed, several general definitions of vulnerability that I noted in Chapter 4 refer to this higher probability of incurring an identifiable significant effect while substantially lacking the ability or means to protect oneself.[45]

Accordingly, the question should be: what is the minimum likelihood level of incurring significant risks on fundamental rights and freedoms that should trigger special consideration and protection of data subjects' vulnerability? As a preliminary answer, it is possible to affirm that the level of likelihood should be from medium to high and, in general, higher than for the average data subjects.

[39] Luna (n 1) 91.

[40] See arts 24, 25, 32; Recitals 75–77, 90.

[41] European Network and Information Security Agency, *Guidelines for SMEs on the Security of Personal Data Processing* (ENISA 2016) 11 See also ISO 31000:2018 (en), §6.4.3.

[42] ibid 24 and 29.

[43] van Dijk and others (n 2) 7.

[44] I Böröcz, 'Risk to the Right to the Protection of Personal Data: An Analysis Through the Lenses of Hermagoras' (2016) 2 European Data Protection Law Review 467, 476.

[45] Schroeder and Gefenas (n 3); Goodin (n 3).

As observed in Chapter 4, the three groups of vulnerability factors are: (i) personal characteristics of the data subjects, (ii) data controller's characteristics and potentialities, and (iii) vulnerability drivers. Considering that an accurate and correct estimation of the likelihood of 'effects' is well-nigh impossible, Data Protection Authorities (DPAs) (or even codes of conducts)[46] might suggest how the occurrence of these vulnerability factors could influence the likelihood of specific vulnerability manifestations. Although a careful analysis of the relationship between factors and likelihood must be conducted on a case-by-case basis, we can consider some examples to elucidate the issue.

We can analyse the two examples offered in Chapter 3 about manifestations of human vulnerability. The first case referred to a woman who is depressed because of her mother's death and is targeted with manipulative clothes ads that exploit her grief so that she becomes addicted to shopping. The risk to fundamental rights and freedoms here might be interference with the mental integrity of the data subject, her freedom of thought, and her right to personal data protection (she felt compelled to consent to share personal data that she did not want to because of she was locked in to the social media network mentioned). As explained, all three groups of factors contribute to generating this situation of vulnerability: the personality of the data subject and her condition of grief; the potentiality of the data controller (computability power, lock-in effect); and the manipulative techniques of ads. However, how much do these factors contribute to the likelihood that the risk to the data subjects' fundamental rights occurs? In this scenario, we can assume that—although all factors jointly contribute to the manifestation of vulnerability—the likelihood of the risk is mostly based on the personal grief of the data subject and on specifically tailored targeting practices that exploit such grief. In other words, all consumers targeted by commercial practices online share some layers of vulnerability, but the 'likelihood' that those layers are significant in terms of risks to fundamental rights and freedoms is determined by the grief of the data subject and the commercial exploitation of it. In sum, the likelihood that a data subject who is targeted on social media on the basis of their personal grief might be interfered in their fundamental rights (freedom of thoughts, moral integrity) is *high*. Each vulnerability factor contributes to this 'high' likelihood, but some factors (the grief, the available data, the manipulative techniques) might have a higher relevance in this calculation.

The second case made in Chapter 3 referred to a bisexual male rider of a food delivery company who was asked to consent to share geolocation data through his work smartphone, even during work breaks. The risks to the data subjects' fundamental

[46] According to art 40, the Member States, the supervisory authorities, the EDPB, and the European Commission shall encourage the drawing up of codes of conduct intended to contribute to the proper application of the GDPR, taking account of the specific features of the various processing sectors and the specific needs of micro, small, and medium-sized enterprises.

rights and freedoms here might be his risk of discrimination based on sexual orientation (eg poorer work conditions being imposed on him or his being fired), and the risk to his privacy and personal data protection, based on the extortion of consent to certain undesired surveillance practices. In this case, all three factors contribute to generating this vulnerability situation: the sexual orientation of the data subject and his precarious social and economic conditions; the potentiality of the data controller (being the employer in a temporary employment contract, collecting a massive amount of data of the employees); and the 'vulnerability drivers' (biphobia in certain social contexts, opaque AI-driven organization of the workload, exploitation of precarious employees). In this scenario, we can assume that—although all factors are interrelated and jointly contribute to the manifestation of vulnerability—the likelihood of the risk (of discrimination or of interference with data protection and privacy) is mostly based on the sexual orientation of the data subject and the intrusive data processing requests of the employer. In other words, other riders at the same company share a common level of vulnerability, but the 'likelihood' that those layers can coalesce to form a particular manifestation of vulnerability depends on the bisexuality of the employee and on the specific data collection requests. In sum, the likelihood that a bisexual rider who is constantly tracked by his employer might be at risk of having his fundamental rights interfered with (non-discrimination, personal data protection, privacy) is *from medium to high*. Each vulnerability factor contributes to this 'high' likelihood, but some factors (sexual orientation, the data processing requests, the precarious work conditions) might have a greater relevance in this calculation.

5. Mitigation measures: a vulnerability-aware application of the data protection safeguards

Article 35(7) requires an assessment of the necessity and proportionality of the data processing (as discussed in Chapter 6). Although the exact scope and meaning of the provision are still unclear,[47] the WP29 Guidelines on DPIA indicate that carrying out a necessity and proportionality test means determining 'measures envisaged to comply with the Regulation', including measures contributing to the proportionality and the necessity of the processing (eg the principles of purpose limitation, lawfulness, data minimization, data storage limitation), and measures

[47] D Kloza and others, 'Data Protection Impact Assessments in the European Union: Complementing the New Legal Framework towards a More Robust Protection of Individuals', d.pia.lab. Policy Brief No. 1/2017, 2 <https://cris.vub.be/files/32009890/dpialab_pb2017_1_final.pdf> accessed 2 February 2022; D Kloza and others, 'Towards a Method for Data Protection Impact Assessment: Making Sense of GDPR Requirements', d.pia.lab. Policy Brief No. 1/2019, 6 <https://cris.vub.be/ws/portalfiles/portal/48091346/dpialab_pb2019_1_final.pdf> accessed 2 February 2022.

contributing to the rights of the data subjects.[48] Chapter 6 connected this provision to a need to *justify* the data processing under the data protection principles.

In addition, Article 35(7)(d) requires that the last DPIA step is to identify 'measures envisaged to address the risks, including safeguards, security measures and mechanisms to ensure the protection of personal data'. This might be the final step of an operational vulnerability-aware application of the GDPR rules. This section analyses whether and how different data protection rights and safeguards can effectively mitigate data subjects' vulnerability.

In general terms, a way to mitigate individual vulnerability might be to analyse the kind of vulnerabilities at stake and propose specific mitigation measures for each group. Chapter 4 mentioned three vulnerability factors: the data subjects' personal characteristics, the data controller's characteristics (power and potentialities), and vulnerability drivers. For example, focusing on the data subjects' personal characteristics, the data controller might analyse the expectations, wishes, needs, and mental capabilities of the data subject concerned (or of the potential group(s) of data subjects concerned), and shape information duties and transparency rights accordingly. Focusing on the data controller's potentialities, the data controller should perform a self-assessment of, for example, the intrusiveness of profiling and tracking operations and understand how to mitigate it (eg informing the data subject more thoroughly of what the data collected about them will be used for, ensuring that the purpose limitation principle is well respected, etc). Focusing on vulnerability drivers, the data controller should assess whether some of the data processing practices used could be considered unfair and how any eventual asymmetry could be rebalanced (through the supply of better information, through self-restraint on the retrieval and use of information on individual vulnerabilities, etc).

Chapters 5 and 6 discussed the most relevant principles, rights, and duties in the GDPR to see how data subjects' personal conditions (and, in particular, data subjects' vulnerability) are relevant in interpreting the data protection rules. This section summarizes how a vulnerability-aware interpretation of those provisions might appear in practice. Therefore, the following paragraphs are recommendations on how to interpret the existing GDPR provisions in case of vulnerable data subjects.

I begin with the *principles* in Article 5 GDPR. The principle of *fairness* (Article 5(1)(a)) is pivotal in determining whether there is an excessive power imbalance between the data controller and the data subject.[49] It is an overarching interpretative

[48] See WP29, WP248, Annex 2, 21. The link between 'necessity and proportionality' and the data protection principles (art 5) is evident also in WP29, WP259rev.01, 3.

[49] See in general D Clifford and J Ausloos, 'Data Protection and the Role of Fairness' (2018) 37 Yearbook of European Law 130; I Graef and others , 'Fairness and Enforcement: Bridging Competition, Data Protection, and Consumer Law' (2018) 8 International Data Privacy Law 200; G Malgieri, 'The Concept of Fairness in the GDPR: A Linguistic and Contextual Interpretation' in M Hildebrandt and others (eds) *Proceedings of the 2020 Conference on Fairness, Accountability, and Transparency* (Association for Computing Machinery 2020) 154.

principle that should lead to the self-regulation of data controllers in carrying out practices that exploit individual vulnerabilities (eg not asking for consent from data subjects incapable of giving valid consent; not using knowledge of individual vulnerabilities to target data subject through online behavioural advertising).

The principle of *lawfulness* (Article 5(1)(a)) is central in determining whether consent is a reasonable basis for obtaining data from a given individual or if, on the contrary, the data subject is in a position of processing-based vulnerability and another lawful basis should be applied. In this last case, the legitimate interest might be an adequate lawful basis after a strict balancing test.[50] This balancing test should also analyse existing safeguards to mitigate the impact on individuals. A central safeguard might be to insist on dynamic and legible information about the data processing or a guarantee that the data subject (or their representatives) can always exercise the right to object easily and without any obstruction. In this case, the right to object has the same effect as the withdrawal of consent (in analogous cases where consent is the lawful basis): when the vulnerable data subject objects, the data shall no longer be processed. Something similar is already provided in Article 21(2) for data processing for direct marketing purposes (including profiling) based on legitimate interests.[51] This provision reveals that behavioural targeting already constitutes a sensitive situation in terms of data subjects' vulnerability, and the GDPR suggests some mandatory rules to mitigate it.[52] In other words, in case of vulnerability in terms of making decisions, the advantage of not using consent but legitimate interest as a lawful basis is that the data controller must perform a balancing test[53] and propose relevant safeguards, including the easy blocking of data processing at the request of the data subject or their representative. Beyond consent and alternative lawful bases, an interpretation of the lawfulness principle that is attentive to the potential vulnerability of the data subject should mean that the data controller should avoid processing vulnerable data subjects' personal data *at all*. In particular, when the level of data subjects' vulnerability is so high that the

[50] See I Kamara and P De Hert, 'Understanding the Balancing Act behind the Legitimate Interest of the Controller Ground: A Pragmatic Approach' in E Selinger and others (eds), *The Cambridge Handbook of Consumer Privacy* (1st edn, Cambridge University Press 2018) 352.

[51] Article 21: '(2) Where personal data are processed for direct marketing purposes, the data subject shall have the right to object at any time to processing of personal data concerning him or her for such marketing, which includes profiling to the extent that it is related to such direct marketing. (3) Where the data subject objects to processing for direct marketing purposes, the personal data shall no longer be processed for such purposes.'

[52] FJ Zuiderveen Borgesius, *Improving Privacy Protection in the Area of Behavioural Targeting* (Kluwer Law International 2015).

[53] It is true that a balancing test is required under the GDPR even in cases of consent and in all cases of high risks. See in general on this J Ausloos, *The Right to Erasure in EU Data Protection Law* (Oxford University Press 2020) 326–30 However, the balancing test under art 6(1)(f) is made explicitly mandatory by WP29 and the CJEU case law. In addition, in terms of accountability duties and related sanctions in case of non-compliance, the balancing test under art 6(1)(f) has a stronger binding value. See, similarly, S Gutwirth, 'Short Statement about the Role of Consent in the European Data Protection Directive' <https://works.bepress.com/serge_gutwirth/80/> accessed 19 June 2022.

data controllers can find no adequate lawful bases to justify the processing of their data, the only way is not to start (or not to continue) the data processing. Several scholars have recently suggested that what is necessary is not only to mitigate risks of certain data processing but to avoid some kinds of data processing from the outset.[54]

The principle of *transparency* (Article 5(1)(a)) is relevant for both cases of vulnerability (processing-based and effect-based). For processing-based vulnerability, transparency duties of the data processor for vulnerable individuals might be aimed at presenting information in a particular intelligible form, easily understandable by certain minorities of data subjects affected by cognitive vulnerabilities. For effect-based vulnerability, transparency would help reduce the adverse effects of the data processing (eg discrimination, manipulation, etc), informing the data subject and allowing them for example, to contest unfair decisions or protect herself against manipulative practices.[55]

As regards the principle of *purpose limitation* (Article 5(1)(b)), the data controller checks that purposes for collecting and using data are legitimate (eg exploiting individual vulnerabilities is illegitimate), and that the combination of different databases is not too intrusive (intrusiveness of tracking and profiling might be a factor of vulnerability in terms of the data controller's potentialities). Also, in the case of secondary use of data (Article 6(4)), the data controller should take into account the personal situation of the data subjects and avoid secondary use as much as possible in the case of vulnerable data subjects.

As regards the *accuracy principle* (Article 5(1)(d)), the data controller checks that no discriminatory biases are in the data processing through, for example, continuous auditing of eventual algorithmic decision-making systems. At the same time, the data controller needs to check that all information about potential vulnerability characteristics of the data subject is correct, accurate, and up to date (eg age, eventual cognitive issues, country of origin, etc), while respecting the data minimization principle and the lawfulness principle. This means that the data controller does not need to acquire sensitive information for the purpose of protecting the vulnerable subject. Still, if that sensitive information is processed (lawfully and respecting data minimization), it must be as accurate as possible.

As regards *data subjects' rights*:

[54] G Malgieri and J Niklas, 'The Vulnerable Data Subject' (2020) 37 Computer Law & Security Review 14; a similar argument can be found in J Powles and H Nissenbaum, 'The Seductive Diversion of "Solving" Bias in Artificial Intelligence' *Medium* (7 December 2018) <https://onezero.medium.com/the-seductive-diversion-of-solving-bias-in-artificial-intelligence-890df5e5ef53> accessed 26 May 2021 who claim the necessity of reducing risky (discriminatory) data processing practices rather than trying to make them fairer (eg acting on biases).

[55] See, on this point, M Hildebrandt, 'The Dawn of a Critical Transparency Right for the Profiling Era' in J Bus (ed), *Digital Enlightenment Yearbook* (IOS Press 2012).

1. The *right to access* (Article 15) must be tailored to the personal situations of the (group(s)) of vulnerable data subjects. The vulnerable data subject must be made aware of the significance and envisaged effects of data processing activities[56] in a way that is intelligible to that specific person. In other words, the data controller should analyse the level of literacy and maturity of the data subject and their potential cognitive issues, and shape the communications with the data subjects accordingly. While communications from the data controller to the data subject should be intelligible in general, where the data subject is in a situation of processing-based vulnerability, communications should take this into account. At the same time, communications should be specific enough to enable the data subject (especially those who are potentially in a situation of effect-based vulnerability) to understand eventual risks to their rights and freedoms (eg group profiling that might bring risks of discrimination; knowledge about vulnerabilities that might bring the risk of manipulation of the data subject, etc). In sum, as the EDPB recommends, the data controller should proactively provide easily accessible elements to facilitate the exercise of the right to access in the case of vulnerable data subjects.[57]
2. The rights to *erasure* (Article 17), *rectification* (Article 18), and *portability* (Article 20) must be easy for vulnerable individuals to exercise (with active tools to encourage the full exercise of these rights), considering their specific conditions and personal situations. Although the exercise of these rights should be easy for any data subject, it is important that in the case of processing-based vulnerabilities, their exercise is simplified (considering the specific cognitive needs of the subject) and even solicited on a periodical basis. Where a data subject may possess effect-based vulnerabilities, the data controller should solicit the exercise of these rights on a periodical basis: when the data subject is at risk of discrimination, manipulation, or of interference with other fundamental rights, cooperation between the data controller and the data subject aimed at fairness, accuracy, and collection of the minimum data for the purpose(s) described is necessary and can be facilitated by a mature exercise of these rights.
3. The *right to object* (Article 21) must be made easy to exercise, without any obstruction, especially if the data subject was not able to give consent. Considering that subjects incapable of providing consent might be also incapable of objecting to the data processing, the data controller should set specific simplified tools to exercise the right to object. A good example might be

[56] The right to receive information about the significance and envisaged consequences of data processing is already regulated at arts 13(2)(f), 14(2)(g), 15(1)(h).

[57] EDPB, 'Guidelines 01/2022 on Data Subject Rights—Right of Access—Version 1.0. Adopted on 18 January 2022, 44:' The controller should take special care to ensure that people with special needs, such as elderly people, children, visually impaired persons or persons with cognitive disabilities can exercise their rights, for instance by proactively providing easily accessible elements to facilitate exercise of these rights.'

to explore ways in which the right to object can be exercised by data subjects' representatives (eg labour unions, associations).

4. Automated decision-making must be *avoided* as much as possible where subjects are vulnerable (see the analogy with Recital 71 stating that automated decision-making should *not* be imposed on children) unless there is:
   a. explicit consent of the data subject, but never in case of data subjects whose capacity to make informed decisions is impaired;
   b. a contractual basis, but not when the envisaged consequences of automated decision-making might be more adverse than the non-execution of the contract;
   c. Member States' law, with relevant safeguards (to be also applied to points a) and b)), for example:
      i. the right to make a new decision, taking into account vulnerability factors and mitigating them;[58]
      ii. the right to express one's view made easy for the data subject; for example permitting the exercise of this right by representatives of (group(s) of) vulnerable subjects;[59]
      iii. the right to contest an automated decision made by the data controller affecting the data subject. The data subject should have easy tools to contest automated decisions, and they should receive clear replies which explain what steps were taken as a consequence of the contestation and why a new decision was (or was not) taken;[60]
      iv. the right to receive more explanation:[61] general, group-based (based on the affinity characteristics of transient vulnerable groups), individual.[62]

As regards the *accountability duties*:

1. suitable measures to protect fundamental rights and freedoms (Article 24), including security measures (Article 32), must be tailored to different layers of vulnerability detected in the assessment phase;

[58] A Roig, 'Safeguards for the Right Not to Be Subject to a Decision Based Solely on Automated Processing (Article 22 GDPR)' (2018) 8 European Journal of Law and Technology 1.

[59] About the potential role of data subjects' representatives see S Delacroix and ND Lawrence, 'Bottom-up Data Trusts: Disturbing the "One Size Fits All" Approach to Data Governance' (2019) 9(4) International Data Privacy Law 236.

[60] G Malgieri, 'Automated Decision-Making in the EU Member States: The Right to Explanation and Other "Suitable Safeguards" in the National Legislations' (2019) 35(5) Computer Law & Security Review 105327.

[61] ME Kaminski and G Malgieri, 'Multi-Layered Explanations from Algorithmic Impact Assessments in the GDPR' in M Hildebrandt and others (eds), *Proceedings of the 2020 Conference on Fairness, Accountability, and* Transparency (Association for Computing Machinery Press 2020) 68.

[62] KN Ramamurthy and others, 'Model Agnostic Multilevel Explanations' in H Larochelle and others (eds), *Proceedings of the 34th International Conference on Neural Information Processing Systems (NIPS'20)* (Curran Associates Inc. 2020) 5968.

2. the principle of data protection by design (Article 25) must contribute to a system of fairness by design,[63] permitting the contestation of any decision (both an individual's decision and a data governance decision) by data subjects, and by their representatives;[64]
3. the DPIA (Article 35(9)) must involve as many representatives of groups of vulnerable data subjects as possible,[65] checking the impact on vulnerable groups of the population at different intervals, re-performing the DPIA to check if the vulnerability layers have been effectively mitigated;
4. in prior consultation with the DPAs (Article 36), it might be advisable that the data controller, in dialogue with the DPA, discusses possible vulnerable individuals and how to mitigate their layers of vulnerability. The DPAs might release specific lists of risk mitigation measures for different vulnerable subjects.[66]

6. When vulnerability layers cannot be mitigated: the backstop scenario

Article 36 (as interpreted through Recital 94) describes when the data controller needs to consult DPAs before processing data. Such prior consultation is necessary if the DPIA reveals that the data processing could result (in the absence of safeguards, security measures, and mechanisms to mitigate the risk) in high risk to the rights and freedoms of natural persons, and the data controller thinks that the residual risk cannot be mitigated by reasonable means in terms of available technologies and costs of implementation.

Once consulted, the DPA could give specific indications about safeguards to adopt in particular situations, but may also 'use any of its powers referred to in Article 58' (Article 36(2)), including the power to impose a temporary or definitive limitation including a ban on the data processing (Article 58(2), point f). In other words, if the assessment (the 'vulnerability layers' assessment) reveals high risks that could not be mitigated through reasonable efforts on behalf of the data processor, a system of cooperative governance[67] between controllers and DPAs should

[63] On the point of 'fairness by design' and contestability see M Hildebrandt, *Law for Computer Scientists and Other Folk* (Oxford University Press 2020) 353.

[64] See, in general, L Jasmontaite and others, 'Data Protection by Design and by Default' (2018) 4 European Data Protection Law Review 168.

[65] See on the involvement of data subjects in the DPIA process Kaminski and Malgieri (n 61) 26.

[66] Information Commissioner Officer (ICO), 'Children and the GDPR' (ICO 2020) <https://ico.org.uk/for-organisations/guide-to-data-protection/guide-to-the-general-data-protection-regulation-gdpr/children-and-the-gdpr/> accessed 28 March 2020.

[67] The concept of cooperative governance in data protection refers to the fact that not only regulators but also companies (data controllers) share the tasks and responsibility of determining the modalities of data processing activities. The concept of 'cooperative responsibility' in the digital world can

take place. However, DPAs could also prohibit certain data processing where specific forms of vulnerabilities of certain data subjects cannot be rebalanced.

In some contexts, indeed, the data subjects' vulnerability might be so pronounced that data controllers could find no adequate safeguards to mitigate them. In these situations, the only way to proceed is not to start (or not to continue) the data processing.[68] Several scholars have recently suggested that what is necessary is not only to mitigate risks of specific data processing but also to avoid some kinds of data processing from the outset. For example, discussing AI systems and their possible discriminatory outcomes, Powles argues that instead of solving the problem of biases, we need to wonder if particularly harmful data-driven systems should be used at all.[69]

In general terms, the mere application of the data protection principles in Article 5 could lead the data controllers to avoid some data processing activities. In particular, the principle of fairness (Article 5(1)(a))[70] could serve as a barrier against data processing that exploits vulnerable data subjects.[71] The natural consequence of such a principle is that the data controller cannot exploit the contextual situation of data subject's vulnerability.[72] In some cases, this may not be possible simply by implementing suitable safeguards as required at Articles 24, 25, and 35. There might be no safeguards to rebalance the asymmetry between data controllers and vulnerable data subjects.[73]

be first found in N Helberger and others, 'Governing Online Platforms: From Contested to Cooperative Responsibility' (2018) 34 The Information Society 1; looking at the GDPR, the concept of cooperative governance is a consequence of the accountability principle. About this, see ME Kaminski, 'Binary Governance: Lessons from the GDPR's Approach to Algorithmic Accountability' (2019) 92 Southern California Law Review 1529.

[68] See eg EDPB, Letter in reply to Sophie In't Veld, Ref: OUT2020-0004, 29 January 2020, 4.

[69] J Powles, 'The Seductive Diversion of 'Solving' Bias in Artificial Intelligence', 2018 <https://medium.com/s/story/the-seductive-diversion-of-solving-bias-in-artificial-intelligence-890df5e5ef53> accessed 5 February 2022.

[70] Similarly, the principle of legitimacy of purposes (art 5(1) point b) could serve as a barrier against the exploitation of vulnerable data subjects.

[71] See the centrality of the notion of fairness in the vulnerability discourse: F Luna, 'Elucidating the Concept of Vulnerability: Layers Not Labels' (2009) 2 International Journal of Feminist Approaches to Bioethics 121, 126.

[72] D Clifford and J Ausloos, 'Data Protection and the Role of Fairness' (2018) 37 Yearbook of European Law 130; I Graef and others, 'Fairness and Enforcement: Bridging Competition, Data Protection, and Consumer Law' (2018) 8 International Data Privacy Law 200; M Butterworth, 'The ICO and Artificial Intelligence: The Role of Fairness in the GDPR Framework' (2018) 34 Computer Law & Security Review 257; G Malgieri, 'The Concept of Fairness in the GDPR: A Linguistic and Contextual Interpretation' in M Hildebrandt and others (eds), *Proceedings of the 2020 Conference on Fairness, Accountability, and Transparency* (Association for Computing Machinery Press 2020) 154.

[73] This might be the case of researchers, whose research goal is explicitly based on the exploitation of vulnerable situations (eg understanding the sexual orientation of people in specific countries where homosexuality is criminalized, etc). Or cases where any safeguards might be useless: see Luna (n 1) 94, making the example of fertile women in countries where abortion is illegal who will not be able to adhere to and use birth control measures owing to their partners' refusal or because it may lead to intrafamily violence, etc.

An example of this is intrusive and personalized behavioural advertising based on exploiting highly sensitive information, for example, offering self-defence goods to women who were victims of sexual assault. Another problematic example might be using hidden or 'dark' patterns[74] to extort consent for data processing, especially if the controller targets children or people with mental disabilities, for example. In these cases, the most appropriate solution would be not to begin the data processing at all, unless the data controller rejects the main component of their data processing model (eg avoid targeting individuals based on information gathered about sexual assault or mental weaknesses that expose individuals to such dark patterns).

In sum, if the data controller envisions that the data processing might involve vulnerable data subjects and that no mitigation measure could prevent the inducement or exploitation of an individual's vulnerability, the controller should refrain from starting or continuing such data processing.

7. Conclusions

This chapter investigated how the GDPR provisions can be a tool to mitigate data subjects' vulnerability. In the previous chapters, we observed how the notion of vulnerability might be defined as the higher risk of harm to one's fundamental rights and freedoms. I also observed that such a notion is based on different layers. Accordingly, an assessment of such layers might coincide with analysing risks to fundamental rights and freedoms.[75] That is why this chapter recommends analysing vulnerability layers based on the risk assessment model proposed for the DPIA by Article 35 GDPR.

Accordingly, we first analysed the notion of risk to fundamental rights and freedoms: Section 2 examined the possible *interference with fundamental rights* in the case of vulnerable data subjects. Then, to assess the impact of rights violations, Section 3 analysed the *severity* of these violations, while Section 4 looked at the *likelihood*. Consequently, Section 5 proposed possible risk mitigation measures based on a vulnerability-aware interpretation of the GDPR and Section 6 described the situation in which the data processing (involving vulnerable individuals) should not start (or continue) at all (the backstop scenario).

[74] See eg CM Gray and others, 'The Dark (Patterns) Side of UX Design' in R Mandryk and others (eds), *Proceedings of the 2018 CHI Conference on Human Factors in Computing Systems* (ACM 2018), paper 534, 1.

[75] See Gennet and others (n 1) highlighting the link between layer assessment (proposed by Luna) and risk-assessment in the EU law. See more in general on layers assessment Luna (n 1).

Looking at the *interference with fundamental rights and freedoms*, Chapter 4 observed how there might be at least two manifestations of vulnerability in the data protection field: processing-based vulnerability (during the data processing) and effect-based vulnerability (to the outcomes of the data processing). In these two different kinds of vulnerabilities, there are different rights and freedom at issue. In the case of processing-based vulnerabilities, the fundamental right to privacy and data protection (implying adverse effects on individual autonomy, dignity, and informational self-determination, but also on non-discrimination, right to a fair trial, etc) might be at issue. In the case of effect-based vulnerability, it is possible to consider additional fundamental rights and freedoms, for example freedom of speech, freedom of thought, freedom of movement, etc. It is difficult to determine the concrete circumstances of manifestations of these interferences in practice. However, what is easier is to analyse the impact of such violations under two perspectives: severity and likelihood of effects.

Looking at the *severity* of the impacts, this chapter observed that the GDPR mentions different severity 'levels' of data processing effects on data subjects. Accordingly, even accepting that all data subjects are potentially vulnerable, I wondered about the lowest layer of vulnerability that should trigger special protection. In other words, I wondered about the minimum impact that is legally relevant under the perspective of a vulnerable data subject. Looking at the GDPR from a positivist and literal perspective, this chapter identified the following levels of 'effects': mere effects, substantial effects, significant effects, legal or similarly significant effects, and damages. Considering their definitions and legal implications, I noticed that the relevant level of effect that should trigger vulnerability-aware protection is 'legal or similarly significant effects'. Indeed, those kinds of effects are neither purely subjective (or emotional) nor too difficult to prove in practice. I seems clear that when there is a high risk of *damage*, the data subject is probably vulnerable. Still, the notion of 'damage' (under Article 82) requires an infringement of the GDPR and a compensable loss (together with rigid liability rules). In contrast, the notion of legal or similarly significant effects is more comprehensive. Indeed, this concept can encompass several situations of both processing-based vulnerabilities (like abusing the vulnerability that a data subject may possess regarding making informed decisions and giving consent to their data being processed) and effect-based vulnerabilities (such as commercial manipulation by the data controller) that would not be otherwise easily quantifiable as damages.

Looking at the *likelihood* of risks of harm, we observed that it is not easy to predetermine the likelihood that violations to fundamental rights and freedoms may occur. However, in general terms, in the case of vulnerable subjects, such likelihood is higher than in average situations. This estimation should be on a case-by-case basis.

As regards *mitigation measures*, this chapter suggested how a vulnerability-aware interpretation of different data protection rules could take into account various groups of vulnerability layers, considering some suitable safeguards that data controllers and DPAs could implement to mitigate risks of both processing-based vulnerability (during the data processing) and of effect-based vulnerability to the outcome of data processing.

8
The limitations and the alternatives of a vulnerability-based interpretation of the GDPR

1. Introduction

The previous chapter proposed an assessment of vulnerability layers via the Data Protection Impact Assessment (DPIA) model. That model allowed us to show a vulnerability-aware interpretation of the General Data Protection Regulation (GDPR). This chapter offers possible criticisms of such a model, the potential solutions to the problems it presents, and some alternative models to it. In other words, the research questions of this chapter are: what are the limits of a vulnerability-aware interpretation of the GDPR? How can these limits be overcome, *de lege lata* or *de lege ferenda*?

The possible drawbacks of a comprehensive approach to data subjects' vulnerability and the consequent vulnerability-aware interpretation of the GDPR can be several, including (i) limiting the autonomy of data subjects ('paternalism'); (ii) the lack of legal certainty and foreseeability; (iii) the risk of an individualistic approach; (iv) the limits of analogical interpretation; and (v) the inconvenience and ineffectiveness of an extensive interpretation of several GDPR provisions.

Paternalism might be a risk when adopting such a protective model that assumes a ubiquitous (though layered) vulnerability of data subjects and proposes limiting consent and data protection rights to enlarge accountability duties of data controllers (Section 2). The issue of foreseeability depends on the difficulty of predicting whether and what kind of vulnerable subjects will be involved in certain data processing activities: adopting a harm-based (and extensive) notion of vulnerability would require an *ex-post* approach that is difficult to embed in the data processing from the outset. The alternative might paradoxically be to profile data subjects by default in order to understand who is vulnerable and why, but this would jeopardize the effectiveness of, for example, the data minimization principle (Section 3). A corollary of this issue is the risk that *every* data subject is identified as vulnerable: such an inflationary effect would make the definition of vulnerability useless and ineffective.

Vulnerability and Data Protection Law. Gianclaudio Malgieri, Oxford University Press. © Gianclaudio Malgieri 2023.
DOI: 10.1093/oso/9780192870339.003.0008

The risk of taking a too individualistic approach to vulnerability is based on the difficulty to conceive effective subject-based protection without looking at the more significant structural and collective problems (which are often the primary sources of vulnerability) (Section 4). The issue of legal interpretation depends on the wording of the GDPR. There is just one explicit category of vulnerable data subjects in the Regulation's text: children. Exporting rules tailored to children to vulnerable adults by analogy might overestimate the importance of the category of 'vulnerable' data subjects, only explicitly named in Recital 75 of the GDPR (Section 5). This last criticism includes the difficulty of leveraging several data protection principles, rights, and duties to our purposes. The vulnerability-based interpretation of the fairness principle might be considered too speculative. Similarly, the lawfulness principle (limiting the use of consent as a legal basis and applying it strictly in processing sensitive data) and the transparency principle might be ineffective in dealing with the difficult challenge of protecting people with processing-based or effect-based vulnerability. Even data protection rights, like the right to object or not to be subject to automated decision-making, might be ineffective as safeguards that could be useful in rebalancing the power asymmetry suffered by vulnerable subjects (Section 6). This chapter tries to analyse and respond to these criticisms and it proposes solutions to overcome those limitations. However, I am aware that some structural issues cannot be easily resolved, and further research is needed.

After analysing the relevant potentialities and the limits of a vulnerability-based interpretation of the GDPR, *de lege lata*, a final step is to look at alternative models *de lege ferenda*. Section 7 proposes two models: a category-based approach based on a fixed list of vulnerable categories explicitly mentioned in the law, with related rules and safeguards, or a general definition of vulnerable data subjects in the law. I investigate the pros and cons of both approaches, and I explain our preference for the second. Such a preference does not mean that the current set of principles and rules is inadequate to mitigate the layers of vulnerability of data subjects. However, higher legal clarity in the definition of vulnerable data subjects and related safeguards could help solve several interpretational problems analysed below (eg legal foreseeability, limits of analogical interpretation, etc).

2. The risks of paternalism in a vulnerability-based approach to data protection

One of the main criticisms that we can level at a vulnerability-aware approach to data protection is the risk of limiting the autonomy of the data subject (the 'paternalism' argument).

Solove, looking at both the US and EU legislation in 2013, criticized the 'paternalism' of default rules in data protection law (as opposed to the data subjects' consent), arguing that the choices regarding whether one's data ought to be processed are not always clear.[1] Some people might not be concerned about the processing of their data, and they might be willing to be profiled, targeted, tracked to gain advantages (free services online, optimized personalization of content provision, etc). Thus, according to Solove, cost-benefit analysis does not unambiguously counsel against disclosure. In other words, the individual data subject is in the best position to weigh the risks and benefits.[2]

In addition, privacy is inherently contextual.[3] Although self-management of personal data (based on consent and individual rights) can have severe structural and cognitive pitfalls,[4] many authors argue that the only individual who can clarify their own expectations in a given context is the data subject, through their consent and related rights,[5] revealing what they consider appropriate in a given situation.[6] On the contrary, according to some commentators, limiting the opportunities of data subjects to choose how their data are processed, something that would strengthen accountability duties of the data controller, would give data controllers an advantage; they would by default be permitted to interpret data protection rules in their own interests.[7]

Similarly, Cavoukian and others argue that shifting data protection from consent and individual rights to accountability duties of data controllers is unduly paternalistic because it weakens self-determination, participation, and control of the data subject in the data protection framework.[8] Every reduction of the role of consent and individual rights, according to Purtova, threatens one of the legal rationales of the data protection framework: informational self-determination.[9]

In addition, limiting consent in order to strengthen accountability duties would place the entire burden of checking data protection compliance on to regulators and enforcers (eg Data Protection Authorities (DPAs)), who would be asked to take on the difficult task of proving data protection harms.[10] The full protection

[1] DJ Solove, 'Privacy Self-Management and the Consent Dilemma' (2013) 126 Harvard Law Review 1880, 1895.

[2] B Bergemann, 'The Consent Paradox: Accounting for the Prominent Role of Consent in Data Protection' in Marit Hansen and others (eds), *Privacy and Identity Management. The Smart Revolution: 12th IFIP WG 9.2, 9.5, 9.6/11.7, 11.6/SIG 9.2.2 International Summer School, Ispra, Italy, September 4–8, 2017, Revised Selected Papers* (Springer International Publishing 2018) 125.

[3] H Nissenbaum, 'Privacy as Contextual Integrity' (2004) 79 Washington Law Review 39.

[4] Solove (n 1) 1895–96.

[5] A Cavoukian and others, 'The Unintended Consequences of Privacy Paternalism' (Information and Privacy Commissioner 2014) 7–8 <https://collections.ola.org/mon/28003/326077.pdf> accessed 20 February 2023.

[6] See C Quelle, 'Not Just User Control in the General Data Protection Regulation. On the Problems with Choice and Paternalism, and on the Point of Data Protection' in Anja Lehmann and others (eds), *Privacy and Identity Management. Facing up to Next Steps, 11th IFIP International Summer School* (Springer International Publishing 2017) 508.

[7] N Purtova, 'Default Entitlements in Personal Data in the Proposed Regulation: Informational Self-Determination Off the Table . . . and Back on Again?' (2014) 30 Computer Law & Security Review 6, 18.

[8] Cavoukian and others (n 5) 5–6.

[9] Purtova (n 7) 16.

[10] Cavoukian and others (n 5) 11.

would thus be shifted on to an *ex-post* approach: the harm-based approach would protect individuals only *eventually* and *after* the causation of harm. This is even more problematic if we consider that there is no normative clarity regarding the notion of *harm* in the data protection field,[11] evident if we observe that some authors declare that 'the imbalance between data subjects and controllers is not ultimately harmful'[12] and claim that it may often be beneficial.[13] Accordingly, some commentators argued that every limitation imposed on the scope of the consent and individual rights must be an exception rather than the rule.[14]

To reply to these remarks, first of all it is useful to remember that if the data controllers rely on consent as a lawful basis for data processing, they are not absolved from the GDPR data protection principles (in Article 5) and requirements (eg Articles 24, 25, 35).[15] In addition, I offer here two different kinds of considerations: general ones on the data protection framework, and more specific ones on the layered vulnerability proposal. In general terms, the idea that the data subject should express their will and expectations through standard ways (eg giving their consent) relies on the notion of the data subject that Chapter 2 identified as the 'average' data subject, a reasonably rational, informed, circumspect individual. Julie Cohen defines this rational person as 'the liberal self', an idealized data subject critically independent from relational ties.[16] Other scholars criticize the individualistic, self-sufficient and rationalist idea of a liberal subject.[17] The real subjects are different—they argue; their needs and interests are dynamic and contextual; and they are dependent on relational ties,[18] susceptible to cognitive biases and, as shown in Chapter 3, vulnerable in many circumstances. Considering such a dynamic subjectivity, individuals can only express their wills and expectations somewhat poorly, through pre-formulated declarations (eg consent), considering the increasing power imbalance in the relationship with the data controller. Such an asymmetry renders the subject often unaware of the risks involved or incapable of balancing their own expectations with potential benefits. In other words, basing

[11] R Gellert, 'Understanding the Notion of Risk in the General Data Protection Regulation' (2018) 34 Computer Law and Security Review 279, 281; Cavoukian and others (n 5) 11–12; Solove (n 1) 1891.

[12] Bergemann (n 2) 125.

[13] K.-H. Ladeur, 'Datenschutz—Vom Abwehrrecht Zur Planerischen Optimierung von Wissensnetzwerken. Zur "Objektiv-Rechtlichen Dimension" Des Datenschutzes' (2000) 24 Datenschutz Datensicherheit DuD 12.

[14] Purtova (n 7) 17.

[15] See S Gutwirth, 'Short Statement about the Role of Consent in the European Data Protection Directive' <https://works.bepress.com/serge_gutwirth/80/> accessed 19 June 2022.

[16] J Cohen, 'What Privacy Is For' (2013) 126 Harvard Law Review 1904, 1904, 1910–11. On the paradox of consent and control in the data protection framework see also J van Hoboken, 'The Privacy Disconnect' in RF Jørgensen (ed), *Human Rights in the Age of Platforms* (MIT Press 2019) 266.

[17] M Fineman, 'The Vulnerable Subject: Anchoring Equality in the Human Condition' (2016) 20 Yale Journal of Law & Feminism 25.

[18] Cohen (n 16) 1911; M Sax, *Between Empowerment and Manipulation: The Ethics and Regulation of For-profit Health Apps* (Kluwer Law International 2021) 71.

data protection on control tools ('notice-and-consent') seems ineffective and anachronistic.[19]

Control rights and accountability duties also have different justifications regarding fundamental rights. Quelle argues that the ground for protecting fundamental rights can be based either on 'will' or on 'interests'.[20] Under the perspective of *interests*, Zuiderveen Borgesius notes that since paternalism means protecting the individual's own interests (regardless of their will), data protection cannot be considered purely paternalistic since it aims to protect not only individual interests but also collective ones.[21] However, the anti-paternalistic view (based on data protection as a tool of control) is grounded not on interests but on theories of *will*.[22] According to this perspective, fundamental rights are seen not as the protection of one's interests but as granting the rights-holder control (or authority) over the duty of another.[23] As commentators have remarked, this theory leaves incompetent or non-autonomous individuals (ie and *vulnerable* data subjects) without any protection.[24] Moreover, the foundation principle of will theories seems to be *freedom*, but the data protection rights in Europe are primarily based on the principle of *dignity*.[25] As some authors noted, the principle of dignity—together with solidarity—is also the founding rationale for protecting individual vulnerability (see Chapter 3).[26] In other words, focusing on individual 'will' risks undermining

[19] JE Cohen, 'Turning Privacy Inside Out' (2019) 20 Theoretical Inquiries in Law 20–22.

[20] Quelle, 'Not Just User Control in the General Data Protection Regulation' (n 6) 518.

[21] FJ Zuiderveen Borgesius, *Improving Privacy Protection in the Area of Behavioural Targeting* (Kluwer Law International 2015) 182–83; see, also, D Kennedy, 'Distributive and Paternalist Motives in Contract and Tort Law, with Special Reference to Compulsory Terms and Unequal Bargaining Power' (1982) 41 Maryland Law Review 563, 572 affirming that paternalism implies a disagreement (in terms of values or moral vision) between the decision-maker and the individual party.

[22] Quelle, 'Not Just User Control in the General Data Protection Regulation' (n 6) 518; Other seminal works have focused on the tension between autonomy (and control rights) versus dignity (accountability duties). See eg N Purtova, *Property Rights in Personal Data: A European Perspective* (Kluwer Law Intl 2011) 172–175; O Lynskey, *The Foundations of EU Data Protection Law* (Oxford University Press 2015) 229–53; R Gellert, *The Risk-Based Approach to Data Protection* (Oxford University Press 2020) 75–79; J Ausloos, *The Right to Erasure in EU Data Protection Law* (Oxford University Press 2020) 65–68.

[23] See HLA Hart, *Essays on Bentham: Jurisprudence and Political Philosophy* (Oxford University Press) 50; see also L Wenar, 'Rights' in EN Zalta (ed), *The Stanford Encyclopedia of Philosophy* (Metaphysics Research Lab, Stanford University 2020) §2.2.2 according to which 'to have a right is to have the ability to determine what others may and may not do, and so to exercise authority over a certain domain of affairs'.

[24] Quelle, 'Not Just User Control in the General Data Protection Regulation' (n 6) 518.

[25] LA Bygrave, 'Minding the Machine: Article 15 of the EC Data Protection Directive and Automated Profiling' (2001) 17 Computer Law & Security Review 17, 18; see also P De Hert and S Gutwirth, '"Privacy, Data Protection and Law Enforcement. Opacity of the Individual and Transparency of Power"' in E Claes and others (eds), *Privacy and the Criminal Law* (Intersentia 2006) 81 explaining that even the German notion of data protection (the first formulation in Europe of data protection) was based on dignity.

[26] R Andorno, 'Is Vulnerability the Foundation of Human Rights?' in A Masferrer and E García-Sánchez (eds), *Human Dignity of the Vulnerable in the Age of Rights: Interdisciplinary Perspectives* (Springer International Publishing 2016) 264.

the protection of dignity, which is a foundational principle in fundamental rights protection in Europe,[27] particularly for protecting vulnerable data subjects.

I can now respond in detail to potential criticisms of paternalism to our vulnerability-based interpretation of the GDPR. First, our model does not suggest disregarding tools of control (eg the provision of consent, the right to withdraw the consent, the right to access, the right to object, etc). In Chapter 4, I identified two different forms of vulnerability: (processing-based) vulnerabilities which occur during the data processing, and (effect-based) vulnerabilities which occur as a result of the data processing. Data subjects are affected by decision-making vulnerabilities[28] in the first case alone, making them incapable of giving valid consent. In other words, not all forms of data subjects' vulnerabilities require the reduction in the use of tools of control (and, thus, autonomous choices) over the data subjects: only when the data subject is in a situation of decision-making vulnerability (eg cognitive issues, maturity issues, meaningful power imbalance) would it be necessary to 'protect' them through accountability and default rules which stretch over the choices they may make. On the contrary, in the case of effect-based vulnerability (eg individuals at risks of discrimination, manipulation, stigmatization, etc), control rights might be among the adequate safeguards used to enhance the protection of data subjects.[29] This is the case, for example, of the provision of consent (and also when data is to be used in ways that move beyond its original purpose), the right to object, and the right to contest automated decisions:[30] all control tools that could limit the power of data controllers to produce adverse outcomes for data subjects (in case of, eg, discriminatory effects, limitations of individual freedoms or rights, etc).

In addition, enhancing the responsibility and the accountability of data controllers, especially where they are dealing with vulnerable data subjects, does not mean leaving the whole data protection system wide open to the arbitrary choices made by data controllers. The accountability principle in the GDPR is built on a well-balanced system of co-governance,[31] where DPAs can examine the data controller's

[27] See art 1 of the EU Charter of Fundamental Rights and the preamble of the Protocol No 13 of the ECHR.

[28] About the notion of decisional vulnerability see É Gennet and others, 'Does the New EU Regulation on Clinical Trials Adequately Protect Vulnerable Research Participants?' (2015) 119 Health Policy 925, 928.

[29] See eg WP29, Opinion 03/2013 on purpose limitation, 32. See Chapter 4.

[30] WP29, Opinion 03/2013 on purpose limitation, 32: 'further processing of personal data concerning health, data about children, other vulnerable individuals, or other highly sensitive information should, in principle, be permitted only with the consent of the data subject'. Similarly, also the right to object, art 21 GDPR is conditional to the 'specific condition' of the GDPR (that could refer also to situations of vulnerability): the right to objects might be a tool that enhance the 'control' of data subjects and in case of vulnerability.

[31] ME Kaminski, 'Binary Governance: Lessons from the GDPR's Approach to Algorithmic Accountability' (2019) 92 Southern California Law Review 1529. See also the concept of 'reflexive governance' in data protection in G González Fuster and P Paepe, 'Reflexive Governance and the EU Third Pillar: Analysis of Data Protection and Criminal Law Aspects' in E Guild and F Geyer (eds), *Security versus Justice? Police and Judicial Cooperation in the European Union* (Ashgate 2008) 129.

activity, checking the fair implementation of the data protection principles.[32] Furthermore, as the GDPR clarifies in many provisions, the data controller needs to consider the interests, wishes, and expectations of data subjects (especially of vulnerable ones) when implementing accountability duties. In particular, the controller needs to take into account the expectation of data subjects to have their data and themselves treated fairly (Article 5(1)(a)),[33] in the balancing test required to process data on the basis of legitimate interests (Article 6(1)(f)),[34] in the purpose compatibility assessment that the data controller needs to perform when data are to be used for secondary purposes (Article 6(4)),[35] and in the duty to seek the views of the data subjects in the DPIA process (Article 35(9)).[36] Moreover, the data subject can interact with the data controllers in many instances. For instance, the right to object (Article 21) allows the data subject to question the balancing test that the controller has performed when processing personal data on the basis of legitimate interests.[37] The right to contest automated decision-making, to have a human intervention in the automated decision-making process, and in particular the right to express one's point of view (Article 22(3)) are also meaningful examples.[38] In addition, in the DPIA process, the data controller needs to seek the views of the data subjects or their representatives on the intended processing of their data (Article 35(9)). Furthermore, it seems wise to affirm that these views should also be permitted to be made by representatives of the data subjects.[39]

[32] See arts 57–58 GDPR.

[33] See the Information Commissioner's Office, 'Big Data, Artificial Intelligence, Machine Learning and Data Protection' (2017) 19–22 <https://ico.org.uk/media/for-organisations/documents/2013559/big-data-ai-ml-and-data-protection.pdf> accessed 20 December 2022. See M Butterworth, 'The ICO and Artificial Intelligence: The Role of Fairness in the GDPR Framework' (2018) 34 Computer Law & Security Review 257; G Malgieri, 'The Concept of Fairness in the GDPR: A Linguistic and Contextual Interpretation' in *Proceedings of the 2020 Conference on Fairness, Accountability, and Transparency* (Association for Computing Machinery 2020). See also Comission National Informatique and Libertés, Algorithms and Artificial Intelligence, CNIL's Report on Ethical Issues, 25 May 2018 <https://www.cnil.fr/en/algorithms-and-artificial-intelligence-cnils-report-ethical-issues> accessed 20 December 2022.

[34] See WP29, Opinion on Legitimate Interest, 36 according to which the data controller needs to check the impact on the data subject 'and their reasonable expectations about what will happen to their data'. See also I Kamara and P De Hert, 'Understanding the Balancing Act behind the Legitimate Interest of the Controller Ground: A Pragmatic Approach' in E Selinger and others (eds), *The Cambridge Handbook of Consumer Privacy* (1st edn, Cambridge University Press 2018).

[35] In this case the data controller needs to consider both the controller-subject relationship and context and the effects of the data processing on the data subject.

[36] See ME Kaminski and G Malgieri, 'Multi-Layered Explanations from Algorithmic Impact Assessments in the GDPR' in M Hildebrandt and others (eds) *Proceedings of the 2020 Conference on Fairness, Accountability, and Transparency* (Association for Computing Machinery 2020) 68.

[37] D Clifford and J Ausloos, 'Data Protection and the Role of Fairness' (2018) 37 Yearbook of European Law 130.

[38] See A Roig, 'Safeguards for the Right Not to Be Subject to a Decision Based Solely on Automated Processing (Article 22 GDPR)' (2018) 8 European Journal of Law and Technology 1. See also G Malgieri, 'Automated Decision-Making in the EU Member States: The Right to Explanation and Other "Suitable Safeguards" in the National Legislations' (2019) 35(5) Computer Law & Security Review 105327.

[39] Although art 80 provides for a limited scope of activity of data subjects' representatives, see the proposal of S Delacroix and ND Lawrence, 'Bottom-up Data Trusts: Disturbing the "One Size Fits All" Approach to Data Governance' (2019) 9(4) International Data Privacy Law 236.

The last criticism is the lack of clarity about what 'harm' means in the data protection field and the consequent impossibility to perform an objective cost-benefit analysis that could protect the individuals *from themselves* without the risk of undue paternalism.[40] In addition, the notion of harm imposes an *ex-post* approach, putting the whole burden on data subjects to check and prove violations of their data protection rights.

Chapter 7 discussed the notion of risk of harm (based on interference) to fundamental rights and freedoms in the GDPR. After identifying the fundamental rights and freedoms at risk during data processing,[41] I analysed the severity and the likelihood of risks of 'effects' of data processing on data subjects in order to identify the benchmark of data subjects' vulnerability. Chapter 7 thus concluded that (even considering that the notion of damage has many restraints) we should consider the risk of incurring 'legal or similarly significant effects' as a benchmark for understanding whether the data subject is in a vulnerable position. This approach widens the scope of 'harm'[42] (which would be otherwise limited to the rigid requirements of the notion of 'damage') and offers adequate balancing between subjective expectations of individuals and foreseeable, objective, adverse consequences on individuals.[43]

Lastly, several examples of vulnerability-aware approaches already exist in EU law. For example, the Unfair Terms Directive (93/13/EEC) assumes that the consumer is inherently vulnerable and may be unable to accept some contractual clauses with their supplier, even if they explicitly wanted to.[44] Accordingly, acknowledging individual vulnerability does not mean violating individuals' autonomy paternalistically but instead protecting the autonomy of individuals from abuses by their counterpart (the supplier, the data controller), who is usually in a more powerful position than they.[45]

[40] Cavoukian and others (n 5) 11–12; Solove (n 1) 1891.

[41] See WP29, Guidelines on Data Protection Impact Assessment (DPIA), WP248, 15. See also eg European Data Protection Board, Letter in reply to Sophie In't Veld, Ref: OUT2020-0004, 29 January 2020, 4.

[42] See Cavoukian and others (n 5) 12 suggesting to 'adopting a broader definition of harm may be helpful'.

[43] LA Bygrave, 'Article 22. Automated Individual Decision- Making, Including Profiling' in C Kuner and others (eds), *The EU General Data Protection Regulation (GDPR)—A Commentary* (Oxford University Press) 534.

[44] Zuiderveen Borgesius (n 21) 182–83; on the Unfair Terms Directive approach to vulnerability and imbalance see also D Clifford and others, 'Pre-Formulated Declarations of Data Subject Consent—Citizen-Consumer Empowerment and the Alignment of Data, Consumer and Competition Law Protections' (2019) 20 German Law Journal 679, 687; I Graef and others, 'Fairness and Enforcement: Bridging Competition, Data Protection, and Consumer Law' (2018) 8 International Data Privacy Law 200, 204.

[45] See a similar view in P Blume, 'The Data Subject' (2015) 1 European Data Protection Law Review 258, 264.

3. Lack of legal certainty and foreseeability?

Another limit of a vulnerability-based interpretation of data protection law is the difficulty for the data controller to predict with accuracy whether vulnerable people will be involved in certain data processing activities and what kind of vulnerable data subjects they are. This difficulty creates a problem of legal certainty and foreseeability for data controllers that need to implement the data protection rules. In other words, adopting our layered and harm-based notion of vulnerability requires an *ex-post* assessment that is impossible to conduct before starting the data processing.[46]

As previously said, Cavoukian and others noted that, if we shift from control tools to stronger accountability, we risk focusing only on redress after the fact, abandoning the effort to *prevent* violations.[47] On the contrary, implementing general safeguards 'by design' (in accordance to Articles 24, 25, and 32 GDPR) might render it difficult—if not impossible—to consider different individual manifestations of vulnerabilities of data subjects.[48] Put differently, how can a data controller know how many and which kind of vulnerable data subjects will be involved in a given data processing? In addition, data subjects' vulnerability can be temporary and transient, as argued in Chapter 3. In other words, this problem would be less severe under the traditional approach to vulnerability based on the identification of historically vulnerable groups (older people, asylum seekers, sexual orientation minorities, etc), whose needs can be foreseen.

At first sight, the data controllers have two alternatives: they can ignore vulnerable data subjects, taking into account a test based on what is assumed to be a 'reasonable' person,[49] or they can profile every data subject involved in the data processing in order to understand who is vulnerable and why.

The first option, considering the 'average' data subject, is the same solution adopted in consumer law. Indeed, the Unfair Commercial Practice Directive takes the average consumer (and not possible vulnerable ones) as a benchmark for understanding whether given commercial practices (see Article 5 in conjunction with Recital 18) are unfair.[50] This solution would lead to ignoring the situation of

[46] See, in a similar tone, L Kammourieh and others, 'Group Privacy in the Age of Big Data' in L Taylor and others (eds), *Group Privacy: New Challenges of Data Technologies* (Springer International Publishing 2017) 51.

[47] Cavoukian and others (n 5) 11.

[48] Quelle, 'Not Just User Control in the General Data Protection Regulation' (n 6) 510 affirming that it is 'unlikely that a general set of rules will meet the anticipated wishes of every data subject, as they are bound to differ'.

[49] Cavoukian and others (n 5) 9.

[50] R Incardona and C Poncibò, 'The Average Consumer, the Unfair Commercial Practices Directive, and the Cognitive Revolution' (2007) 30 Journal of Consumer Policy 21; G González Fuster, 'How Uninformed Is the Average Data Subject? A Quest for Benchmarks in EU Personal Data Protection' (2014) 19 IDP Revista de Internet, Derecho y Política 92 In the UCPD Vulnerable subjects are considered only if the commercial practice reasonably foreseeably distorts the commercial behaviour of a vulnerable group (art 5[3]).

vulnerable data subjects in implementing data protection principles. As previously mentioned, this solution would be not only incompatible with the risk-based approach (Article 24) and the principle of data protection by design (Article 25) but also with the rationale of data protection as a fundamental right based on the principle of dignity.[51]

As an alternative, before starting the data processing (or immediately after collecting personal data), the data controller should analyse all data subjects' personal conditions or, at least, those of relevant groups of data subjects (eg through clusters or affinity profiling)[52] before starting the data processing (or immediately after collecting personal data) in order to detect potential data subjects' vulnerabilities. In particular, the data controller would need to process additional sensitive information, often including special categories of data such as sexual orientation, ethnic origins, mental health conditions, etc, to understand whether the data subject is potentially vulnerable or not, regardless of the purpose for which the data controller processes the data. The paradoxical consequence might be that a data controller who merely needs to process personal data for billing purposes, for example, would be collecting much more information (about age, mental status, etc) about the data subject for the purposes of providing the subject with vulnerable-tailored information policies under Article 13. Yet, this practice is in contradiction with the rationale of Article 11(1), according to which 'the controller shall not be obliged to … process additional information in order to identify the data subject for the sole purpose of complying with this Regulation'.[53] Even though that article refers explicitly only to identification and to the data storage limitation principle, that is, to the duty to process personal data only for the limited period of time necessary for the declared purpose, the general rationale seems broader: the controller should never process more data for the sole purpose of complying with the GDPR. Recital 57 argues that the controller cannot refuse to take additional information provided by the data subject 'in order to support the exercise of his or her rights', but this clarification cannot justify undertaking a vulnerability assessment of *all* data subjects just to perform a vulnerability-attentive implementation of the GDPR on some.

In sum, the two solutions mentioned are inadequate to solve the issue that the data controller faces, namely to predict whether vulnerable data subjects might be involved in data processing activities and what kind of vulnerable data subjects they are. To solve this issue, I propose to look at how data subjects' vulnerability arises according to the different groups of vulnerability layers. Chapter 4 identified three groups: data subjects' personal conditions, vulnerability drivers, and

[51] Andorno (n 26) 264–65.

[52] See the concept in S Wachter, 'Affinity Profiling and Discrimination by Association in Online Behavioural Advertising' (2020) 35 Berkeley Technology Law Journal 367.

[53] This article implements the data storage limitation principle at art 5(1)I GDPR.

data controllers' potentialities. We might identify at least three different situations in which the data controller could be aware of processing data of vulnerable data subjects:

1. the data controller specifically targets vulnerable data subjects;
2. the data controller uses acquired knowledge about individual vulnerabilities;
3. the data controller processes personal data on a very large scale such that the data might include those on vulnerable data subjects.

In the first case mentioned (1), the data processing is targeted specifically at certain types of data subjects at higher risk of harm to their fundamental rights in a particular situation, for example children, the elderly, patients, employees, mentally disabled people, asylum seekers. I derive the criterion of the *special addressee* from Article 12(1) GDPR, which provides that data controllers should implement particularly legible transparency duties if the information is 'addressed specifically to a child'. Such a criterion is also common in EU consumer law. In particular, the Unfair Commercial Practice Directive at Article 5(2)(b) provides that a criterion to determine the unfairness of commercial practices should be to consider the consumer 'whom it reaches or to whom it is addressed'. Here, what counts is the personal situation of the data subject that the data controller aims to involve (eg age, mental conditions, nationality, etc: the first group of vulnerability layers identified in Chapter 4).

In the second case mentioned (2), the data processing is not specifically aimed at data subjects at higher risk of harm. Still, the data controller—in their business model—makes use of the information collected about the vulnerabilities of individuals. An example might be data controllers performing microtargeting to supply hyper-personalized digital content (including behavioural advertising) to exploit cognitive biases. Common microtargeting could not be considered a vulnerability driver. On the contrary, a vulnerability driver might be the personalization of content based on specific 'knowledge' about an individual's vulnerabilities.[54] We can include, for example, information about sexual life or sexual orientation, very strong emotional statuses (anxiety, dejection, grief) arising from particular (even temporary) situations, etc.[55] In sum, what counts here is not the conditions of the data subject taken alone but the vulnerability driver in play (the second group of vulnerability layers identified in Chapter 4).

In the third case (3), the data processing is neither explicitly addressed to vulnerable groups of individuals nor based on the exploitation of knowledge about individual vulnerabilities. The data processing is based on the broad power of the

[54] See WP29, Opinion on Profiling, 22.

[55] See, in the consumer field, SM Baker, and others, 'Building Understanding of the Domain of Consumer Vulnerability' (2005) 25(2) Journal of Macromarketing 128, 138.

data controller in terms of intrusiveness (including the tracking of individuals across different websites, devices, and services),[56] wide availability of other data, powerful data-mining capabilities, etc. It is extremely likely in this case that personal data of subjects at higher risks of harm to their fundamental rights will be processed simply because that individual is one of a great many individuals whose data is being processed. Here, the data subject's vulnerability depends on the significant (information) asymmetry between the controller and the data subject. Even though the occurrence of data subjects' vulnerability seems hypothetical in this case, the precautionary principle[57] imposes on the data controller the requirement to take a vulnerability-aware approach. Big companies who have the capacity (in terms of financial and human resources) to conduct large-scale data collection and processing should be required to implement vulnerability-aware measures that would safeguard data subjects. In other words, what counts here are the capabilities of the data controller (the third group of vulnerability layers identified in Chapter 4).

Using this three-step test (Is the data processor deliberately targeting vulnerable individuals? Is the data controller deliberately exploiting known vulnerabilities of the data subject? Is the data controller likely to have data on vulnerable individuals, collected due to large-scale data processing such as data mining?) in order to determine whether the data controller should implement vulnerability-based safeguards in the data processing would have many advantages. It would mitigate the lack of legal foreseeability while respecting the data minimization principle, the precautionary principle, and the dignity of vulnerable data subjects. Indeed, if the controller reasonably believes (or suspects) that one of these three situations to be in play, it is highly likely that they are going to process the data of vulnerable data subjects. In these cases, the controller would neither face problems of foreseeability, nor they would need to pre-profile the potential data subjects to detect their vulnerabilities. If one of the three cases occurs, the data controller would be probably required to perform a DPIA, where they could assess data subjects' vulnerability layers (following a model similar to the one proposed in Chapter 6) and adopt adequate safeguards accordingly.

The inflation risk: is everyone vulnerable?

A corollary of the foreseeability issue is that adopting a contextual definition of vulnerability based on the high risk to fundamental rights and freedoms in a specific

[56] See WP29, Opinion on Profiling, 22.

[57] About the application of the precautionary principle to the EU Data Protection Framework see R Gellert, 'Data Protection: A Risk Regulation? Between the Risk Management of Everything and the Precautionary Alternative' (2015) 5 International Data Privacy Law 3.

situation might lead to the conclusion that *everyone is vulnerable*. Indeed, if we adopt an extensive interpretation of the phrase 'high risk to fundamental rights', it might be very easy to consider all data subjects vulnerable. In this scenario, the definition of the data subject's vulnerability would lose any usefulness and relevance.

Chapter 7 identifies a clear severity threshold to delimit vulnerable subjects (ie data subjects whose layers of vulnerability are significant enough to trigger special protection) from non-vulnerable ones (ie data subjects whose vulnerability layers are not significant enough to trigger special protection). That borderline is the risk of 'legal or similarly significant effect' to the rights and freedoms of the individual. Our vulnerability threshold has two components: (i) interference with a fundamental right or freedom; (ii) severity (and likelihood) of the effects produced by such an interference.

Regarding the first point, the impact of the data processing activities should be precisely relatable to one or more specific fundamental rights or freedoms as protected in the EU.[58] Regarding the second point, a mere risk of non-significant effects is not sufficient to legally qualify data subjects as vulnerable.

It is impossible to predict all situations of 'legal or similarly significant effects' in the data protection framework and connect them to the list of EU fundamental rights and freedoms. However, we can find an example, looking at the field of cybersecurity risk, where the fundamental right at stake is the right to data protection (Article 8 Charter of Fundamental Rights (CFR)). The European Network and Information Security Agency (ENISA) proposes four different degrees of 'effect' as a consequence of data breaches.[59] Such effects are categorized as follows:

1. low, when individuals may encounter 'a few minor inconveniences, which they will overcome without any problem (time spent re-entering information, annoyances, irritations, etc.)';
2. medium, when individuals may encounter 'significant inconveniences, which they will be able to overcome despite a few difficulties (extra costs, denial of access to business services, fear, lack of understanding, stress, minor physical ailments, etc.)';
3. high, when individuals may encounter 'significant consequences, which they should be able to overcome albeit with serious difficulties (misappropriation of funds, blacklisting by financial institutions, property damage, loss of employment, subpoena, worsening of health, etc.)';

[58] N van Dijk and others, 'A Risk to a Right? Beyond Data Protection Risk Assessments' (2016) 32 Computer Law & Security Review 286.

[59] ENISA, Guidelines for SMEs on the security of personal data processing, December 2016 <https://www.enisa.europa.eu/publications/guidelines-for-smes-on-the-security-of-personal-data-processing> accessed 20 February 2023, 20.

4. very high, when individuals may encounter 'significant, or even irreversible consequences, which they may not overcome (inability to work, long-term psychological or physical ailments, death, etc.)'.[60]

Point 1 (low risk) cannot be considered to cause significant effects on individuals and, thus, cannot be considered sufficient to trigger special vulnerability-based protection. Looking at points 2 and 3, what might help decide what is within and what is outside the scope of data subjects' vulnerability is the likelihood of that impact in practice. Looking at the specific context at issue, medium impact (2) with high likelihood might be considered within the significant effect threshold, similarly to high impact (3) with medium likelihood.[61] Similar scales can be proposed for different contexts and fundamental rights and freedoms.

4. The risk of an individualistic approach versus group-based vulnerability: lessons from 'group privacy' literature

Another possible criticism is that our vulnerability approach might be too *individualistic* and may ignore the fact that most vulnerabilities are structural and group-based. In particular, homogenous groups of vulnerable individuals may experience very similar risks to their fundamental rights and freedoms. For example, we can consider discrimination based on race, gender, sexual orientations; cognitive impairment based on age, mental illnesses, or socio-economic conditions (such as foreign nationality, language spoken, or relative wealth); or freedom limitations based on particular hierarchical structures (workers, soldiers, prisoners, etc). Addressing their vulnerability on an individualistic case-by-case basis may lead to ignoring structural and societal problems (social injustices, racial biases, etc), which are the primary source of many forms of vulnerability.[62] Indeed, as several authors highlighted, the power imbalance between the powerful person and the vulnerable one is not merely relational but structural.[63]

In addition, some forms of group approximation are necessary to apply several of the safeguards proposed and analysed in previous chapters: the representative

[60] ibid.

[61] See Recital 75, GDPR. See also See also ISO 31000:2018(en), Risk management—Guidelines <https://www.iso.org/obp/ui/#iso:std:iso:31000:ed-2:v1:en> accessed 20 December 2022. Similarly, see the matrix of likelihood-impact in ENISA, Guidelines for SMEs, 31. See also D Kloza, *The Concept of Impact Assessment in European Privacy and Personal Data Protection Law* (PhD Thesis, VUB 2020).

[62] RE Goodin, *Protecting the Vulnerable: A Reanalysis of Our Social Responsibilities* (University of Chicago Press 1985); F Ippolito and SI Sánchez, *Protecting Vulnerable Groups: The European Human Rights Framework* (Bloomsbury Publishing 2015).

[63] M Foucault and others, *Microfisica del potere. Interventi politici* (Einaudi 1977) 130; See, also, H Richter, 'The Power Paradigm in Private Law' in M Bakhoum and others (eds), *Personal Data in Competition, Consumer Protection and Intellectual Property Law: Towards a Holistic Approach?* (Springer Berlin Heidelberg 2018) 534.

of data subjects (Article 80) should represent vulnerable 'groups', not simply individuals; collective actions of redress against the same data controller (Articles 77–82) taken by groups of homogenous vulnerable individuals should be encouraged to mitigate vulnerabilities. Similarly, when seeking the view of data subjects under Article 35(9), the data controller should contact representatives of groups of vulnerable subjects, as suggested by WP29.[64] Lastly, when giving more detailed explanations of automated decision-making systems (under Article 22 and Recital 71), Chapter 6 proposed that data controllers provide a group-based explanation (in addition to a general and—eventually—an individual explanation), which might address different groups of data subjects impacted by automated decision-making systems, including vulnerable groups.

In reply to these remarks, it is essential to clarify that the previous chapters do not adopt an individualistic perspective of vulnerability and do not underestimate the importance of group-based protection. Indeed, the last chapters are in line with the European Data Protection Board's (EDPB) interpretation[65] of Article 35 (and of the GDPR accountability provisions in general) regarding basing the analysis of duties and safeguards on the subjects, considering their expectations, their needs, their interests, and the effects the data processing will have on them.[66]

Addressing vulnerability on an intersectional and layered—that is, contextual and relational—basis does not mean rejecting any form of group-based vulnerability. It means considering groups under the smaller perspective of 'layers'. Vulnerability layers are based not on an *ex-ante* label (being part of a specific vulnerable group)[67] but on three parameters: characteristics of data subjects, potentialities of data controllers, and vulnerability mechanisms (which include specific social and institutional structural issues, which might be common to homogenous 'groups'). Vulnerability comes from an encounter between subjects' peculiarities, data controllers' power/potentialities, and specific (technological or structural) mechanisms.

The reason why this book does not focus on *traditionally* vulnerable *groups* (children, the elderly, workers, people with disabilities, LGBTQIA+, etc) as such is that I want to overcome *an ex-ante* labelled approach to vulnerability: that approach might lead to stigmatizing the person or enhancing a condition of so-called pathogenic vulnerability.[68] Defining human vulnerability using only a group perspective does not help identify why, how, and towards whom vulnerability occurs. Nevertheless, considering layers (more than groups) of vulnerable subjects is still

64 See WP29, wp 240, 13.

65 WP29 Guidelines on DPIA, 21.

66 M Macenaite, 'The "Riskification" of European Data Protection Law through a Two-Fold Shift' (2017) 8 European Journal of Risk Regulation 506, 536.

67 F Luna, 'Elucidating the Concept of Vulnerability: Layers Not Labels' (2009) 2 International Journal of Feminist Approaches to Bioethics 121.

68 See W Rogers and others, 'Why Bioethics Needs a Concept of Vulnerability' (2015) 5(2) International Journal of Feminist Approaches to Bioethics 25.

important: different individuals might suffer from similar vulnerability risks in many cases,[69] experiencing similar personal limitations leading to similar unfair effects. A complete taxonomy of these 'new' layers would appear incomplete and quite possibly useless. Still, we should consider the possibility that similar individuals experience homogenous risks to their fundamental rights and freedoms in these layers. *Layers*, unlike *groups*, are homogenous according to three perspectives: similar personal conditions of the data subjects, similar data controllers' characteristics, and similar vulnerability mechanisms (and, in general, similar risks to fundamental rights and freedoms). On the contrary, traditional groups might prove to be static clusters that often consider just one parameter (usually, the data subjects' conditions, for example age, sexual orientation, etc), ignoring the encounter with a specific type of data controller.

The layered approach can be complemented by *group privacy* literature.[70] Considering the individual dimension alone is not enough. At the same time, considering only traditionally recognized minorities or vulnerable groups is also inadequate: groups depend on the harms, the interests, and the purposes that technology (and organizational models) determine. As affirmed, group privacy is not based on fixed groups[71] but on variable geometries, contextual or 'spheric' privacy.[72] This is precisely what our layered approach proposes.

On the one hand, most forms of individual vulnerabilities are structural. They must be addressed at a collective level because focusing merely on the individual level of vulnerability might be ineffective and used as an excuse to avoid addressing the problem at a structural level.[73] On the other hand, groups are not static and fixed, especially in the age of AI and Big Data.[74] New technologies and new organizational practices 'frame' new groups every second, on the basis of different properties and with varied impacts.[75] Members of these dynamic groups could not only be unaware of being part of that particular group (the so-called passive groups) but they could also refuse to identify themselves within specific vulnerable groups.[76]

Considering groups instead of individuals can be helpful in some areas (refugee law, genocide conventions, religious freedoms), but not in the case of performing a comprehensive analysis of risks to fundamental rights and freedoms of those groups/individuals. For the purposes of this book, the problem is not only a structural problem of a social minority that the State could and should help through

[69] A Cole, 'All of Us Are Vulnerable, But Some Are More Vulnerable than Others: The Political Ambiguity of Vulnerability Studies, an Ambivalent Critique' (2016) 17 Critical Horizons 260.

[70] Taylor and others (eds) (n 46).

[71] L Taylor and others, 'Introduction: A New Perspective on Privacy' in Taylor and others (eds) (n 46).

[72] Kammourieh and others (n 46) 51.

[73] MA Fineman, 'The Vulnerable Subject and the Responsive State' 60 Emory Law Journal 26.

[74] Taylor and others (n 71) 7.

[75] L Taylor, 'Safety in Numbers? Group Privacy and Big Data Analytics in the Developing World' in Taylor and others (eds) (n 46).

[76] Kammourieh and others (n 46) 39.

positive actions.[77] In the accountability framework proposed by the GDPR, it is the 'impact' and the policies of private (powerful) parties that matter. Such an impact depends not only on structural social problems but also on how technologies (and business models) frame groups.[78]

In other words, from group privacy and a layered vulnerability perspective, the issue is not simply about which social characteristics increase the level of risk for certain minorities. The problem here is to determine which social characteristics, in which contexts, in the relationship with which kind of data controllers, make the level of risk for individuals' rights and freedoms unbearable.

The DPAs should give more guidance and examples of vulnerable 'sub-groups' and specific mitigation measures. They could collect the view of vulnerable individuals' representatives and eventually create an intense debate in the prior consultation phase (Article 36). National DPAs have tried to suggest some 'sub-groups',[79] but what is essential is to contextualize each sub-group within a specific situation, that is, looking at dynamic layers, not simply at static groups.

Some preliminary examples of layers might be the following ones: young homosexual Facebook users exposed to particular masculinity-based ads; women of fertility age seeking a job in small or medium companies in countries where maternity leave (or similar maternity benefits) are not adequately regulated by law; victims of sexual rape receiving Gmail announcements containing self-defence weapons advertising; long-term prisoners asked to give consent to data processing for clinical and psychological research led by a private pharmaceutical company, etc.[80]

5. The problem of interpretation: too much attention to a hidden concept in the GDPR?

Another main issue in my proposal relates to legal interpretation. Indeed, there is just one explicit vulnerable category of data subjects in the text of the GDPR, namely children. Transposing child-based safeguards on to vulnerable adults by analogy might lead to overestimating the importance of the category of 'vulnerable' data subjects as proposed by the GDPR. Indeed, vulnerable people are explicitly mentioned only in the preamble, in Recital 75, not in the body of the law.

It is possible to summarize this issue in two points: (i) the technical limitations of analogical interpretation and (ii) the risk of overestimating a hidden concept in the GDPR.

77 Fineman (n 73).
78 Taylor (n 75) 14.
79 See Chapter 5, Section 13.
80 See eg similar examples in F Luna, 'Identifying and Evaluating Layers of Vulnerability—a Way Forward' (2019) 19 Developing World Bioethics 86, 92–94.

Focusing on point (i), the analogical interpretation of children-related safeguards may be problematic. I remind readers that the measures dedicated to children in the GDPR are the following: a strict balancing test must be performed in the case of legitimate interest (Article 6(1)(f));[81] the special minimum age for autonomous consent where information society services are to be provided (Article 8); data processing information policies must be designed to be understood by children (Article 12(1)); exercise of the right to erasure must be easily accomplished (Recital 65); limited use of automated decision-making (Recital 71);[82] and special consideration among vulnerable data subjects as a risk factor for a DPIA (Recital 75).[83]

Overall, the analogical interpretation is possible if there is a general principle (emerging from the rationale of specific provisions) that requires the data controller to cover *lacunae iuris* extending the scope of some existing provisions.[84] Accordingly, it is necessary to wonder, what is the rationale for the special protection of children? As Recital 33 indirectly explains and as the WP29 has often clarified, the rationale lies in their heightened vulnerability when compared to adults.[85] Accordingly, data subjects with similar vulnerability layers should receive similar protection according to an analogical interpretation. In some legal traditions, analogical interpretation is forbidden in the case of 'exceptional rules'.[86] Exceptional rules mean derogations from duties or prohibition, which do not seem to be the case where rules related to children are concerned. In addition, all child-related provisions mentioned above do not refer *only* to children, but 'in particular'[87] to

[81] Article 6(1)(f): 'processing is necessary for the purposes of the legitimate interests pursued by the controller or by a third party, except where such interests are overridden by the interests or fundamental rights and freedoms of the data subject which require protection of personal data, *in particular where the data subject is a child*'. Emphasis added.

[82] As affirmed in Chapter 5, the prohibition of automated decision-making for children is only in the preamble (Recital 71) and not in the body of the GDPR text. The WP29 has clarified that this means that the data controller should limit as much as possible automated decisions on children and that the criterion to assess the occurrence of 'legal or similarly significant effects' should be stricter: possibly much more forms of online advertising can have such effects on children, depending on their level of maturity (see WP, Opinion on profiling, 29).

[83] See also, in general, S van der Hof and others, 'The Child's Right to Protection against Economic Exploitation in the Digital World' (2020) 28 International Journal of Children's Rights 833.

[84] K Langenbucher, 'Argument by Analogy in European Law' (1998) 57 The Cambridge Law Journal 481; R Alexy, *Theorie der Grundrechte* (1. Aufl., [Nachdr.], Suhrkamp 2006) 75–77; G Lamond, 'Precedent and Analogy in Legal Reasoning' in EN Zalta (ed), *The Stanford Encyclopedia of Philosophy* (Metaphysics Research Lab, Stanford University 2016).

[85] See Recital 33 GDPR. See also eg WP29, Opinion on Profiling, 29: '*Because children represent a more vulnerable group of society*, organisations should, in general, refrain from profiling them for marketing purposes.' Emphasis added.

[86] See eg art 14 of the implementing provisions of the Italian Civil Code.

[87] Article 6(1)(f) ('except where such interests are overridden by the interests or fundamental rights and freedoms of the data subject which require protection of personal data, *in particular* where the data subject is a child'); Article 12(1) ('the controller shall take appropriate measures to provide any information ... in a concise, transparent, intelligible and easily accessible form, using clear and plain language, *in particular* for any information addressed specifically to a child'); Recital 75 ('where personal data of vulnerable natural persons, *in particular* of children, are processed'). All emphases added.

children (apart from Article 8, which is explicitly only for minors). As affirmed by the WP29, it is necessary to note the term 'in particular':[88] it means that children are a relevant category in those provisions but that the interpreter is required to extend those protections to other categories of data subjects.

Which other categories of data subjects should be considered then? The categories that have similar needs and risks: other vulnerable subjects with similar processing-based or effect-based vulnerability based on the specific context (eg elderly, mentally disabled people, but even consumers in certain conditions, etc). However, we must be aware that children are a misleading example: they are one of the few categories affected at the same time by both processing-based vulnerability (during the data processing) and effect-based vulnerability (to the outcome of data processing). However, we should not fall into this ambiguity: being incapable of taking free and fully informed decisions (what Chapter 4 calls 'processing-based vulnerability') is different from being more likely to be harmed by the outcome of the data processing (what Chapter 4 calls 'effect-based vulnerability').[89]

Returning to point (ii) above, since there is no article of the GDPR mentioning vulnerable data subjects, and children are the only special category of data subjects explicitly mentioned, one might wonder why the GDPR gives so much importance to a hidden concept like the data subject's vulnerability? Considering the previous chapters, I can reply that the specific importance given to vulnerable data subjects in the interpretation of the GDPR is grounded on several reasons: fundamental rights, essence of data protection, and the structure of the GDPR.

I have already observed that the rationale for protecting individual vulnerability is based on fundamental rights and especially on the dignity principle.[90] This is also confirmed by the European Court of Human Rights, which—as shown in Chapter 3—has developed a robust case law about vulnerable persons, accepting a comprehensive, layered, and contextual concept of vulnerability.[91] In the field of privacy and data protection, the protection of dignity[92] and, more specifically, the need to mitigate individual vulnerabilities seem the founding rationales for protecting natural persons.[93] We know that one of the goals of the data protection

[88] See eg WP29, Guidelines on Transparency, WP260rev.01, 10.

[89] Richter (n 63) 533–33. See largely Chapter 3.

[90] Andorno (n 26).

[91] L Peroni and A Timmer, 'Vulnerable Groups: The Promise of an Emerging Concept in European Human Rights Convention Law' (2013) 11 International Journal of Constitutional Law 1056; Ippolito and Sánchez (n 62).

[92] Bygrave (n 25) 18; De Hert and Gutwirth (n 25) 81; L Floridi, 'On Human Dignity as a Foundation for the Right to Privacy' (2016) 29 Philosophy & Technology 307; JQ Whitman, 'The Two Western Cultures of Privacy: Dignity Versus Liberty' (2004) 113 The Yale Law Journal 72. See also G Gonzalez Fuster, *The Emergence of Personal Data Protection as a Fundamental Right of the EU* (Springer International Publishing 2014) 23, referring to the link between 'dignity' principle and data protection in the German Federal Constitutional Court case law and in the Italian legislation about data protection.

[93] R Calo, 'Privacy, Vulnerability, and Affordance' (2017) 66 DePaul Law Review 591.

framework is to rebalance power asymmetries that exist between the data subject and the data controller[94] but—as explained in Chapter 4—there are different levels of vulnerability that we should consider. Children constitute a clear example, but many more cases need to be considered.

Even the structure of the GDPR seems to consider different levels of subjects' vulnerability: the risk-based approach (which is a central principle in the GDPR as compared to the DPD)[95] requires the data controllers to analyse different levels of risks to fundamental rights and freedoms and, accordingly, to implement adequate safeguards. As affirmed in Chapter 4, a legal definition of vulnerability might be that a vulnerable individual is at higher risk of harm being caused to their fundamental rights and freedoms than an 'average' individual.[96] In other words, the notion of vulnerability would be a data-subject-centred notion in the interpretation and implementation of the risk-based approach. This goal is explicitly requested by the WP29, which declared that the 'origin, nature, particularity and severity of the risks' should be appreciated '*from the perspective of the data subjects*'.[97] This approach has been defined as 'subjective, individual-centred'.[98]

This is confirmed by Recital 75, which mentions data subject vulnerability as a typical case of higher risk being done to an individual's fundamental rights and freedoms. Recital 43 (about freedom of consent) also implicitly refers to vulnerability when mentioning a 'clear imbalance between the data subject and the controller'. These Recitals illustrate the two different dimensions of vulnerability that Chapter 3 identified: processing-based vulnerability (incapability to give consent, understand risks, or exercise data protection rights) and effect-based vulnerability (the higher risks of harms arising from the data processing).

Furthermore, even though data subjects' vulnerability is just mentioned in a recital of the GDPR, the WP29 (and now the EDPB) have used and developed the notion of vulnerable data subjects in many opinions and guidelines,[99] and now, even DPAs are developing and employing such a notion.[100]

[94] See Lynskey (n 22) 213–15.

[95] Macenaite (n 66).

[96] See eg D Schroeder and E Gefenas, 'Vulnerability: Too Vague and Too Broad?' (2009) 18 Cambridge Quarterly of Healthcare Ethics 113; Goodin (n 62).

[97] WP29 Guidelines on DPIA, 21. Emphasis added. See also, on this point, K Demetzou, 'Risk to the "Rights and Freedoms"—A Legal Interpretation of the Scope of Risk Under the GDPR' in R Leenes and others (eds), *Data Protection and Privacy* (Bloomsbury 2020).

[98] Macenaite (n 66) 536.

[99] See WP29, Guidelines on Transparency, WP260rev.01, 10; WP29, Opinion on legitimate interest, WP217, 40–41; WP29, Opinion on purpose limitation, WP203, 25 and 32; WP29 Guidelines on DPIA, WP248, 9; WP29, Guidelines on Profiling, WP251rev.01, 22. See indirectly also EDPB, Opinion 3/2019 concerning the Questions and Answers on the interplay between the Clinical Trials Regulation (CTR) and the General Data Protection regulation (GDPR) (art 70.1.b)), 23 January 2019, 6 referring to the 'clear imbalance between the data subject and the controller'.

[100] See Chapter 3.

6. Interpretational issues in a vulnerability-aware implementation of the GDPR

Another limitation of this research might be the too extensive (vulnerability-friendly) interpretation of the GDPR principles and rules: is it legally possible to interpret some provisions (eg children-related provisions) to improve the protection of vulnerable data subjects (eg reinforced rules on consent or even a ban of certain data processing activities in the case of vulnerable subjects)? Also, are those provisions, even if extensively interpreted, adequate to mitigate individual vulnerability?

I start with the principles at stake. Chapter 5 focuses primarily on fairness, lawfulness, and transparency in dealing with data subjects' vulnerability. With regard to *fairness*, one might argue that this principle is too vague and too general to adequately address the challenge of mitigating risks to the fundamental rights and freedoms of vulnerable persons. Indeed, in other fields (eg consumer law), the concept of fairness is often clarified through blacklists of unfair practices (see, eg the case of Unfair Commercial Practice Directive),[101] while in the data protection field, the concept is open to different interpretations. The problem is that in fields and sectors where no specific guidelines or policies already exist to clarify the meaning of fairness in practice, who determines what fairness means in practice is the data controller.

To reply to this criticism, it is important to recall that fairness is merely an interpretational principle that should lead to a contextual implementation of other principles (in particular, lawfulness and transparency) and of data protection rights and duties. At the same time, this principle allows the DPAs to forbid practices that are formally lawful and transparent but that—in practice—might abuse individual vulnerabilities.[102] The fairness principle, in other words, is not sufficient to protect vulnerable data subjects alone. However, combining this principle with other principles could be a helpful tool. In particular, considering fairness together with transparency, the data controller must mitigate the risks posed by decision-making vulnerability (through, for example, vulnerability-tailored implementation of

[101] See Commission Staff Working Document Guidance on the Implementation/Application of Directive 2005/29/EC on Unfair Commercial Practices Accompanying the document Communication from the Commission to the European Parliament, the Council, the European Economic and Social Committee and the Committee of the Regions. A comprehensive approach to stimulating cross-border e-Commerce for Europe's citizens and businesses, Brussels, 25 May 2016, SWD(2016) 163 final. See also the previous version: Commission Staff Working Document, Guidance on the Implementation/Application of Directive 2005/29/EC on Unfair Commercial Practices, Brussels, 3 December 2009, SEC(2009) 1666, Annex I.

[102] On the concept of fairness as an interpretational tool to mitigate also vulnerability see Malgieri (n 33); see, also, on the concept of unfair data processing practices, from a non-EU perspective: Future of Privacy Forum, 'Unfairness by Algorithm: Distilling the Harms of Automated Decision-Making' (2017) <https://fpf.org/2017/12/11/unfairness-by-algorithm-distilling-the-harms-of-automated-decision-making/> accessed 8 February 2020.

transparency duties). On the other hand, considering fairness in combination with lawfulness, the data controller should focus on effect-based vulnerability to the outcome of data processing (eg preventing all discriminatory, manipulative, or similar harmful practices). For more details on the different nuances of this principle, see Chapter 4.

As regards the *lawfulness* principle, Chapter 4 observed that the implementation of this principle might be relevant to protect vulnerable data subjects, in particular considering the new requirements about freedom of consent in the GDPR, the strict balancing test in cases where legitimate interest is used as a legal basis for processing data of vulnerable data subjects and the higher restrictions for processing sensitive data. Even in this case, however, one might formulate several criticisms for each point.

The new equilibrium between stricter parameters for valid (freely given) consent (Article 7 GDPR) and a stricter balancing test in case of legitimate interests (Article 6(1)(f) GDPR) might have the disadvantage of surrendering the power to make all decisions about the data processing to the data controller[103] and thus place vulnerable data subjects in an even weaker position. I already addressed this discussion in Section 2, where I replied to the criticisms of paternalism. Here I shall add that more cautious use of consent should not mean that the data controller can ignore individual wishes and expectations: the balancing test in case of legitimate interests should be tailored to individual particularities of the data subjects, who will always be in a position to question such a balancing test by exercising the right to object (Article 21).

One might argue that a data subject who is cognitively vulnerable and, thus, incapable of freely giving consent would also be unable to exercise the right to object freely (in cases where the data controller processed data on the basis of legitimate interest). In fact, as argued—*mutatis mutandis*—by behavioural economics experts in similar fields (consumer law), from a cognitive perspective giving consent is different from exercising the right to object.[104] While the first is a reply to an (often unsolicited) request that might be based on cognitive biases and might be sudden or unexpected, the second is an *ex-post* activity of the data subject who has reflected on the significance and consequences of processing their data. In addition, it would be easier for the DPA that is checking compliance with the GDPR principle in the case of vulnerable data subjects to question the validity of a balancing test under Article 6(1)(f) instead of the validity of consent. Proving freedom of consent can

[103] On the issue of shifting the relevant decisions from the data subject to the data controller see Solove (n 1) 1903; Cavoukian and others (n 5) 11. For a critical view on accountability duties see also C Quelle, 'Enhancing Compliance under the General Data Protection Regulation: The Risky Upshot of the Accountability- and Risk-Based Approach' (2018) 9 European Journal of Risk Regulation 502, 524–25.

[104] As regards the behavioural studies analysis of withdrawing consent in consumer law see E Bacciardi, *Il recesso del consumatore nell'orizzonte delle scienze comportamentali* (Giappichelli 2019).

be burdensome. It should imply an after-the-fact objective evaluation of the expression of the data subject's *will* at the specific moment that consent was given. Instead, assessing what was an inadequate balancing test would be a more objective *ex-ante* evaluation on the parties' *interests*,[105] something that DPAs might be better equipped to deal with (eg through specific national or international guidelines).

Purtova argues that the right to object does not offer adequate protection because the individual has the whole 'burden' to justify their objection, explaining their personal circumstances. This would favour the processing party, because 'it would be sufficient for the controller to simply restate the same interest in order to override the objection and continue processing'.[106] However, the right to object constitutes a more context-aware assessment based on an individual's characteristics, interests, and grounds (and vulnerability layers).[107] As Clifford and Ausloos argue, the right to object is not a formalistic right that places the whole burden of proof on the individual (that will be probably unsuccessful to prove the validity of their request). Still, it is an essential manifestation of the fairness principle in providing data subjects with further protections, empowering them to challenge an *ex-ante* balancing test based on Article 6(1)(f) GDPR.[108] In other words, the 'burden' on the data subject (to justify why their particular—or vulnerable—situation is relevant for the requirement to block the processing) is an '*ex-post* empowerment' opportunity placed at the disposal of the data subject that 'explicitly imposes a re-balancing exercise' at a more granular and context-dependent level.[109]

Another possible criticism of our vulnerability-friendly interpretation of the GDPR is the ineffectiveness of sensitive data protection (Article 9(1)) to deal with vulnerable individuals. This criticism can be based on several grounds. First, having a *numerus clausus* of sensitive information does not help cover all possible situations (even temporary) of data subjects' vulnerability. Second, this *numerus clausus* does not include several categories of personal data that could be relevant for protecting long-term vulnerability statuses (eg economic status, age) and short-term vulnerability conditions (eg emotions).[110] To offer some examples: gender identity is not included in the Article 9(1) list. This may result in inadequate protection of, for example, transgender and non-binary data subjects against discrimination.[111] Economic conditions of data subjects are also excluded from the scope

[105] About the preference for the 'interest' theories on the 'will' theories see Quelle, 'Not Just User Control in the General Data Protection Regulation' (n 6).

[106] Purtova (n 7) 16.

[107] Clifford and Ausloos (n 37) 173.

[108] ibid.

[109] ibid; On the burden on the data subjects see also B Van Alsenoy, *Data Protection Law in the EU: Roles, Responsibilities and Liability* (Intersentia Uitgevers NV 2019) 602–04.

[110] D Clifford, 'Citizen-Consumers in a Personalised Galaxy: Emotion Influenced Decision-Making, a True Path to the Dark Side?' in L Edwards and others (eds), *Future Law: Emerging Technology, Regulation and Ethics* (Edinburgh University Press 2020).

[111] European Commission, Directorate General for Justice and Consumers, *Trans and Intersex Equality Rights in Europe: A Comparative Analysis* (Publications Office 2018) 9.

of Article 9(1): any form of social discrimination based on economic conditions cannot be limited through the *sui generis* protection of sensitive data. Third, it is easy to circumvent the list of special categories of sensitive data through proxies[112] and, thus, adverse effects like discrimination would still be possible.[113]

Many of these remarks are well founded, but the protection of special categories of personal data may still be of value for our purposes. Indeed, replying to the first two criticisms, the *numerus clausus* of sensitive information is a limited list, but it includes relevant personal characteristics that can correspond to the main vulnerable aspects of data subjects. An example of this is that 'age' is missing from the list, but all elderly people are not all vulnerable subjects and not vulnerable 'because of their age', but probably because of their mental conditions, that can often be considered a 'health condition'.[114] In addition, I am aware that the special protection of sensitive data is not sufficient to protect vulnerable individuals if taken alone. Still, such protection is just one of the complementary tools that could help mitigate power imbalance and prevent adverse effects.

Replying to the last criticism (the easy circumvention of the sensitive data list through proxies), we can affirm that the correct interpretation of special categories of data is contextual:[115] Article 9(1) affirms that any data 'revealing' sensitive information[116] should be included in the definition of special categories of data. Accordingly, the interpretation should be comprehensive and include proxies or indirect references to sensitive information. Also, Recital 71 refers—as a risk that should be mitigated within a DPIA—to the discriminatory effects taken on the basis of special categories of data '*or that result in measures having such an effect*'. This further confirms that indirect discrimination might be eventually protected under the notion of sensitive data.[117]

Moreover, it is important to remark that the protection of special categories of data is not based solely on the prohibition of processing and some exceptions to that prohibition (Article 9(2)), but also on other specific safeguards, that is, the

[112] AD Selbst, 'Disparate Impact in Big Data Policing' (2018) 52 Georgia Law Review 109.

[113] Wachter (n 52).

[114] About the extensive notion of health data see eg G Malgieri and G Comandé, 'Sensitive-by-Distance: Quasi-Health Data in the Algorithmic Era' (2017) 26 Information & Communications Technology Law 229, passim.

[115] K Mccullagh, 'Data Sensitivity: Proposals for Resolving the Conundrum' (2007) 2 Journal of International Commercial Law and Technology 190.

[116] However in art 9(1) the verb 'revealing' refers only to racial or ethnic origin, political opinions, religious or philosophical beliefs, or trade union membership, but does not refer to the other sensitive information (genetic data, biometric data for the purpose of uniquely identifying a natural person, data concerning health, or data concerning a natural person's sex life or sexual orientation). However, the definition of 'data concerning health' in art 4(15) includes 'personal data … which reveal information about his or her health status'.

[117] See FJ Zuiderveen Borgesius, 'Strengthening Legal Protection against Discrimination by Algorithms and Artificial Intelligence' (2020) 24(10) The International Journal of Human Rights 1572, 1582 affirming: '[w]hile the right to the protection of personal data and data protection law are largely untested as non-discrimination tools, they offer possibilities to fight illegal discrimination'.

limited possibility to conduct automated decision-making based on those data (unless there is the explicit consent of the data subject or the processing is necessary for reasons of substantial public interest and specific safeguards are in place, Article 22(4)); the need to perform a DPIA (Article 35(3)(b)) and to designate a Data Protection Officer (DPO) (Article 37(1)(c)) where processing of special data on a large scale is undertaken.[118]

Another criticism of our vulnerability-based approach to the GDPR is from the perspective of the transparency principle. Information rights (Articles 13–15) are often fallacious for several reasons: the data subject is generally uninterested in reading such information, which is often too general or too technical[119] and vulnerable individuals are probably incapable of understanding it or cannot adequately infer all risks and implications of data processing from the mere reading of such information.[120]

To reply to this criticism, it is important to remember that Article 12 imposes a duty of legibility on every communication from the data controller to the data subject.[121] This duty is not based on an 'average' data subject standard but on individual characteristics, including the eventual individual vulnerability of data subjects.[122] According to this principle, together with the principle of data protection by design (Article 25), the data controller should also implement specific transparency by design techniques that could effectively help rebalance the information asymmetry,[123] both in cases of modal and causal vulnerability. The goal of these specifically tailored information policies might also be eventually to prevent specific biases based on personal vulnerabilities. Also, the incapability of cognitively vulnerable subjects to understand risks posed by the data processing should be mitigated by the controller's duty to inform—at least in cases of automated decision-making—the data subject about the envisaged consequences of data

[118] The processing of special categories of personal data is also an exception to several duties exemption in the GDPR: see about the controller's and processor's duty to have a representative in the Union art 27(2)(a) and about records of processing art 30(5).

[119] See the limit of transparency in sensitive areas like algorithmic decision-making, M Ananny and K Crawford, 'Seeing without Knowing: Limitations of the Transparency Ideal and Its Application to Algorithmic Accountability' (2018) 20 New Media & Society 973. On the notion of transparency fallacy see L Edwards and M Veale, 'Slave to the Algorithm? Why a "Right to an Explanation" Is Probably Not the Remedy You Are Looking For' (2017) 16 Duke Law & Technology Review 18, 65–67.

[120] Blume (n 45) 260.

[121] On the notion of legibility see in general R Mortier and others, 'Human-Data Interaction: The Human Face of the Data-Driven Society' [2014] arXiv:1412.6159 [cs] <http://arxiv.org/abs/1412.6159> accessed 21 October 2019. The notion of legibility has been introduced in the GDPR discourse by G Malgieri and G Comandé, 'Why a Right to Legibility of Automated Decision-Making Exists in the General Data Protection Regulation' (2017) 7 International Data Privacy Law 243.

[122] Article 12(1) explicitly mention particular legibility for children. By analogy, this should be applied also to other forms of modal vulnerabilities. See on this point WP29, Guidelines on Transparency, WP260rev.01, 10.

[123] A Rossi and G Lenzini, 'Transparency by Design in Data-Informed Research: A Collection of Information Design Patterns' (2020) 37 Computer Law & Security Review 105402.

processing (Articles 13(2)(f), 14(2)(g), and 15(1)(h)).[124] Hildebrandt considered this a revolutionary novel requirement of the GDPR which could mitigate at least subliminal influences on the process of identity building that would primarily affect vulnerable subjects.[125]

Another criticism might be that the GDPR does not adequately protect vulnerable individuals where automated decision-making is taking place. Some commentators criticize the limited scope of several GDPR measures, including the right not to be subject to such processing and the related safeguards where one of the exceptions applies, namely the right to contest, the right to make a new decision with human intervention rather than via automation, the right to express one's own view (Article 22(3)), and also the right to receive an explanation of the data processing and the duty to perform an audit of the algorithms (Recital 71).[126] Several authors have often considered these rights inadequate to deal with data subjects' vulnerability for several reasons: (i) transparency fallacy (as already discussed above);[127] (ii) the constraints of automated decision-making definition;[128] and (iii) the risk that vulnerable data subjects may not exercise Article 22(1) and (3) rights and the risk that these rights, even when exercised, could not practically change the automated decisions and the related adverse effects that generate vulnerability.[129]

In a previous work, Comandé and I have already argued that the alleged constraints in the definitional requirement of automated decision-making should be interpreted extensively.[130] Moreover, the right to have human involvement should be substantial: in compliance with the accountability principle in Article 5(2), the data controller should prove how the data subjects' view is taken into account and how the decision has been eventually changed accordingly.[131] In addition, focusing on the vulnerability harms, the sole application of 'empowering' rights might not

[124] AD Selbst and J Powles, 'Meaningful Information and the Right to Explanation' (2017) 7 International Data Privacy Law 233.

[125] M Hildebrandt, 'The Dawn of a Critical Transparency Right for the Profiling Era' in J Bus (ed), *Digital Enlightenment Yearbook* (IOS Press 2012) 51.

[126] See generally Roig (n 38).

[127] Edwards and Veale (n 119) 65.

[128] S Wachter and others, 'Why a Right to Explanation of Automated Decision-Making Does Not Exist in the General Data Protection Regulation' (2017) 7 International Data Privacy Law 76; Edwards and Veale (n 119).

[129] For a critic on the effectiveness of art 22 protections for children see S van der Hof and others, 'The Protection of Children's Personal Data in a Data-Driven World: A Closer Look at the GDPR from a Children's Rights Perspective' in T Liefaard (ed), *Monitoring Children's Rights in the Netherlands: 30 Years of the UN Convention on the Rights of the Child* (Leiden University Press 2019) 105–12; for a critic on consent and individual rights for some vulnerable groups in the AI context see P Peña and J Varon, 'A Feminist Anti-Colonial Critique on Consent to Resist AI Systems' (2021) 10(4) Internet Policy Review 1.

[130] Malgieri and Comandé, 'Why a Right to Legibility of Automated Decision-Making Exists in the General Data Protection Regulation' (n 121).

[131] See the UK Data Protection Act 2018, s 14(4). See also the Irish Data Protection Act 2018, s 57(1). Malgieri (n 38) 9.

be sufficient. What is necessary is an algorithmic impact assessment, as already suggested by Recital 71[132] combined with Article 35(3)(a), and as already required explicitly in law by some Member States.[133] Such assessment should also consider individual vulnerabilities and combine the exercise of individual rights with a systemic multi-stakeholder analysis of impacts. External experts and representatives of potential data subjects (including special groups, like vulnerable subjects) should be involved. There should be a cyclic reassessment.[134]

In sum, in this section, I analysed how several elements of our proposed vulnerability-based interpretation of the GDPR are problematic and how our model replies to those limits or criticisms. However, considering the GDPR interpretational and practical issues for protecting vulnerable data subjects, one might wonder whether the GDPR amplifies data subjects' vulnerability instead of mitigating it.

Is the GDPR perpetuating vulnerability itself? Inputs for further research

As explained in previous chapters, the GDPR has the potential to protect vulnerable data subjects. However, it is important not to underestimate the existing drawbacks and limitations of the GDPR, which sometimes could even amplify data subjects' vulnerabilities.

As also discussed in Chapters 5 to 7, it is possible to underline several critical issues in the GDPR for what concerns the protection of vulnerable data subjects: (i) the limited approach to the DPIA in practice; (ii) the lack of transparency duties related to the DPIA, and the weak forms of data subjects' participation in the DPIA; (iii) the limited scope of 'data subjects representatives'; and (iv) the risk of obtaining limited protection for explicitly vulnerable data subjects (eg children).

First, this book devoted particular attention to the DPIA as an essential tool to assess and prevent vulnerabilities of data subjects. However, the DPIA—both in the text of the GDPR and in its application—has severe limitations. First, the ambitious goal to analyse the impact of data processing on fundamental rights and freedoms has appeared too complex in practice due to the lack of clear and

[132] See Recital 71: 'In order to ensure fair and transparent processing in respect of the data subject, taking into account the specific circumstances and context in which the personal data are processed, the controller should use appropriate mathematical or statistical procedures for the profiling, implement technical and organisational measures appropriate to ensure' the mitigation of data processing risks.

[133] See the case of Slovenia in Malgieri (n 38) 18.

[134] Kaminski and Malgieri, 'Multi-Layered Explanations from Algorithmic Impact Assessments in the GDPR' (n 36); D Reisman and others, 'Algorithm Impact Assessment: A Practical Frameworks for Public Agency Accountability' (AI Now Institute 2018); HL Janssen, 'An Approach for a Fundamental Rights Impact Assessment to Automated Decision-Making' (2020) 10(1) International Data Privacy Law 76.

consistent guidance by data protection authorities.[135] Existing DPIA models have had a limited approach,[136] mainly focusing on cybersecurity rather than on fundamental rights in the broad sense.[137] In addition, Article 35(9) limits the involvement of data subjects in the DPIA process to cases 'where appropriate' and the Article 29 Working Party Guidelines on this provision have proposed a minimal approach.[138] Moreover, data controllers are not obliged to disclose the DPIA report to the public, not even in summaries and not even to the impacted data subjects.[139]

Second, the protection of vulnerable data subjects should also be based on adequate safeguards to guarantee that their data protection (substantial and procedural) rights are effective. The role of data subjects' representatives (Article 80) could be beneficial for this purpose. However, as noted, the GDPR limits the data subject's representation to the procedural rights of Articles 77–79, while the representative of—even vulnerable—data subjects has no power to exercise other rights, for example, the right to object on behalf of a group of data subjects who would be incapable of exercising their rights, due to cognitive vulnerability or to the power imbalance between themselves and the data processor.[140] As has also been suggested in the consumer protection law sector,[141] we should find the best solutions towards an 'inclusive' access to remedies to protect vulnerable people.[142] In addition to procedural remedies, we should shape the substantive structure of data subjects' rights in a way that is accessible to vulnerable data subjects. This might include creative forms of the direct and delegated exercise of data protection rights.

Third, children are the only explicitly mentioned 'vulnerable data subject' in the GDPR (Recital 75). However, as explained in Chapter 4, the special protection of children (and its fragmented implementation) has brought several unexpected drawbacks. Some data controllers have artificially negated the fact that they target children to avoid compliance with children-related rules in the GDPR. The paradoxical consequence is that several digital services are organized to completely

[135] European Commission, Commission Staff working document accompanying the Communication to the Council and to the European Parliament: Data protection as a pillar of citizens' empowerment and the EU's approach to the digital transition—Two years of application of the General Data Protection Regulation, COM(2020) 264 final, Brussels, SWD(2020) 115 final, 10.

[136] A Kasirzadeh and D Clifford, 'Fairness and Data Protection Impact Assessments' in M Fourcade and others (eds), *Proceedings of the 2021 AAAI/ACM Conference on AI, Ethics, and Society* (Association for Computing Machinery 2021).

[137] K Bock and others, 'Das PIA-Tool der CNIL im aufsichtsbehördlichen Praxistest' (2019) 3 PinG Privacy in Germany 15.

[138] ME Kaminski and G Malgieri, 'Algorithmic Impact Assessments under the GDPR: Producing Multi-Layered Explanations' (2020) 11(2) International Data Privacy Law 130.

[139] ibid 130–31.

[140] Delacroix and Lawrence (n 39) 247–48.

[141] C Riefa and S Saintier (eds), *Vulnerable Consumers and the Law: Consumer Protection and Access to Justice* (Routledge 2020).

[142] C Riefa and S Saintier, 'The Way Forward: For an "inclusive" Access to Justice to Protect Vulnerable Consumers' in ibid.

refute the possibility that minors' personal data are processed, depriving them of even the most basic data protection safeguards.[143] In sum, the application of vulnerable-aware provisions in the GDPR leads to increased existing vulnerabilities. Considering this issue, we should conclude that any vulnerability-aware reform of the GDPR should take into utmost account the risk of rules circumvention and the related paradox this entails.

In sum, the GDPR is a powerful tool to mitigate data subjects' vulnerabilities, but it also contains many drawbacks and limitations that could even consolidate or reinforce existing vulnerabilities. Accordingly, more research is necessary for this field. In particular, we can anticipate two possible solutions: some policy recommendations to reform the GDPR (see the Section 7) and a more mature implementation of the GDPR provisions as they are. This second goal could be possible through robust guidelines on the protection of vulnerable data subjects (including children), elucidating transparency rules and the conditions for the validity of consent. In addition, explanatory guidelines would be necessary to clarify the practical implications of the fairness principle and comprehensive implementation of the DPIA rules.[144]

Several practices could overcome the problems mentioned in this section (under-representation, transparency, and consent fallacy, etc). For example, a serious system of *participatory design* would be highly beneficial. Involving independent experts and representatives of vulnerable individuals and groups in the design of technologies and business models impacting them[145] would be an important step to guarantee the autonomy and protection of vulnerable people.

There are different ways in which data subjects (individually, in groups, or through representatives) can participate in data processing decision-making or in the design of data-driven technologies. The GDPR already suggests some (vague) room for participation. First, the already mentioned data controller's duty (in Article 35(9)) to 'seek the views of data subjects or their representatives on the intended processing' is an example, but it has many limits, both in the text of the GDPR[146] and in its interpretation.[147] Second, the data subject's right to 'express

[143] G Malgieri and G González Fuster, 'The Vulnerable Data Subject: A Gendered Data Subject?' (2022) 13 European Journal of Law and Technology 1 mentioning the case of Kellogg's, Fanta, and Tik Tok. J Grierson, 'Kellogg's UK Prompts Anger by Branding Frosties an Adult Cereal', *Guardian* (1 December 2017) <http://www.theguardian.com/society/2017/dec/01/kelloggs-uk-anger-branding-frosties-adult-cereal-sugar> accessed 29 May 2021.

[144] Kaminski and Malgieri, 'Algorithmic Impact Assessments under the GDPR' (n 138).

[145] S Costanza-Chock, *Design Justice: Community-Led Practices to Build the Worlds We Need* (MIT Press 2020).

[146] See Chapter 7.

[147] See WP29, 'Guidelines on Data Protection Impact Assessment (DPIA) and Determining Whether Processing is "Likely to Result in a High Risk" for the Purposes of Regulation 2016/679' (2017) 13 suggesting very limited ways to implement the duty to seek the views of data subjects in art 35(9), eg internal studies and surveys. See the critics to these guidelines in Kaminski and Malgieri, 'Algorithmic Impact Assessments under the GDPR' (n 138).

his or her point of view' in cases of automated decision-making (Article 22(3)): although it is not clarified how this participation should be made possible, this safeguard is separate and distinct from 'the right to contest'. While the right to contest might be seen as an *ex-post* right, the right to 'express one's point of view' in cases of automated decision-making could be seen perhaps as an *ex-ante* right of the data subject to be involved in the decision-making process before a decision is produced.

Beyond the GDPR, participation of groups of individuals in business decision-making is a growing reality. In particular, if transparency and consent are not the solutions, relying only on business-driven decisions might be the way to water down accountability in self-referential loops. That is why, the participation of individuals might be key. There are already mechanisms for both individual and community participation in algorithmic design systems.[148] In particular, there are at least two occasions in which groups of individuals could participate in the decision-making process: during the AI engineering step and before the 'adoption' of AI systems in particular social contexts. The first case refers to the inclusion of representatives of diverse groups during the design and engineering of a new AI system; the second case refers to the consultation of different stakeholders when a certain AI system is adopted in a given context (workplace, hospital, public administration, school, etc). A context where this participative decision-making can already work is the workplace, where trade union representatives might be involved whenever a new AI system that will potentially affect workers is adopted.

7. Policy recommendations: how to alter the data protection law to improve the protection of vulnerable data subjects

Throughout this book, I have demonstrated that a vulnerability-based interpretation of the GDPR is not only possible but also preferable. Section 4 of this chapter underlined that in the wording of the GDPR, the explicit mention of vulnerable data subjects is just marginal (in a recital). Chapter 2 clarified that there is no single notion of the data subject: neither the average nor the vulnerable one(s). Undoubtedly, an explicit definition of vulnerable data subjects (beyond the mere example of children) in the GDPR would be beneficial.

Accordingly, it might be interesting to propose more explicit normative definitions to identify different data subjects and improve the protection of vulnerable

[148] See Costanza-Chock, *Design Justice* (n 145) 85; J Gregory, 'Scandinavian Approaches to Participatory Design' (2003) 19 International Journal of Engineering Education 62. See a catalogue of possible participatory design initiative, 'ActionCatalogue' <http://actioncatalogue.eu/> accessed 19 June 2022; see also, Algorithmic Justice League, 'CRASH Project, Formerly Algorithmic Vulnerability Bounty Project (AVBP)' <https://www.ajl.org/avbp> accessed 19 June 2022, addressing vulnerable subjects' participation in order to prevent algorithmic-driven harms.

subjects.[149] Therefore, this section will take a step further, replying to the question: how is it possible to improve and reform data protection law to protect vulnerable data subjects better? In other words, under a *de lege ferenda* perspective, I will try to propose different models for improving the legal consideration of vulnerable subjects.

In this book, I have proposed a layered approach to analyse the vulnerabilities of data subjects. In *de lege ferenda* terms, this layered approach might be based either on an explicit mentioning of all possible layers of data subjects' vulnerability or on a general definition of dynamic and layered vulnerability that should then be contextualized by the data controller and the enforcement authorities.

It is possible to observe these two models in two existing examples of EU laws: the Clinical Trials Regulation (EU 536/2014) and the Unfair Commercial Practice Directive (2005/29/EC). The first model adopts a *category-based approach*, according to which many vulnerable categories are explicitly mentioned in the law with specific safeguards for each category. The second model adopts a *general approach*, according to which there is a clear distinction between the average data subjects and vulnerable ones, with one or more specific provisions defining vulnerability and requiring extra protection for vulnerable data subjects. This is the model inspired by the Unfair Commercial Practice Directive.

Before addressing these two perspectives, I note that the *de lege lata* interpretation of the GDPR is already an adequate solution to protect vulnerable subjects, and no further legislation or reforms are required to protect them. However, considering these two models, we might imagine a more foreseeable and harmonized protection of more vulnerable data subjects. It is possible to affirm that while the second model is preferable, the first one seems less appropriate. I will explain why below.

Policy option 1: the category-based approach to vulnerability

The *category-based approach* (1) would be based on an explicit recognition of all possible vulnerable categories. The Clinical Trials Regulation might be a good reference for this approach. In that Regulation, as observed in Chapter 3, every specific vulnerable group is the target of a specific provision with particular rules regarding the authorization to the trial and the informed consent to participate in clinical trials. Articles 10(2) and 31 address incapacitated subjects; Articles 10(1) and 32 address minors; Articles 10(3) and 33 address pregnant or breastfeeding women; and Article 34 (and indirectly also Article 10(4)) addresses individuals in

[149] See González Fuster, 'How Uninformed Is the Average Data Subject?' (n 50); Blume (n 45); see implicitly also N Helberger and others, 'The Perfect Match? A Closer Look at the Relationship between Eu Consumer Law and Data Protection Law' (2017) 54 Common Market Law Review 1427.

a hierarchical or institutional dependency, namely persons performing mandatory military service; persons deprived of liberty; persons who, due to a judicial decision, cannot take part in clinical trials; or persons in residential care institutions.[150] For all these categories, there are slightly different rules, based on the specificity of different vulnerability situations, except for the last category (hierarchical dependency), for which the Member States are free to set national rules and safeguards.

Some commentators propose to import such a category-based protection of vulnerable subjects in the data protection field. In particular, Blume seems to recommend different specific protections in the data protection law for different vulnerable groups, such as children, older people, and people affected by mental deficiency and illiteracy.[151] However, such sectorial protection of vulnerable individuals is already a reality in many current and former European national data protection laws. It is the case of the Spanish data protection law specifying the GDPR, where disabled people are mentioned explicitly as special addressees of security measures of the data controller.[152] Analogously, the UK Data Protection Act 2018 refers explicitly to disabled people or to 'individuals at risk', mentioning their care as a specific case of substantial public interest condition for processing special categories of data under Article 9(2)(g).[153] It was also the case of the former Danish Data Protection Act, which specifically protected data subjects affected by mental disabilities.[154] In addition, many data protection laws have whole chapters or titles dedicated to the protection of employees as special data subjects.[155]

The advantages of this approach are clarity, foreseeability, protections more tailored on single types of vulnerability, and better homogeneity and uniformity in the protection of these specific types of vulnerability. Indeed, having clear rules about well-defined and distinguished groups of data subjects would not only limit the arbitrary activity of data controllers in implementing data protection principles and accountability duties but would also help data controllers in their compliance tasks, guaranteeing a more homogenous application of vulnerability-based safeguards among different services and controllers. At the same time, these specific

[150] Gennet and others (n 28).

[151] Blume (n 45) 262–64.

[152] Ley Orgánica 3/2018, de 5 de diciembre, de Protección de Datos Personales y garantía de los derechos digitales, arts 3(3), 28(2)(e), and 96(1)(d).

[153] UK Data Protection Act, Sched 1, Part 2, ss 16 and 18. Individuals at risk are considered to be individuals about whom the controller has reasonable cause to suspect to be in need for care and support, to be experiencing, or at risk of, neglect or physical, mental or emotional harm, *and* that as a result of those needs is unable to protect himself or herself against the neglect or harm or the risk of it.

[154] Act No 429 of 31 May 2000 on Processing of Personal Data. This Act implements Directive 95/46/EC of 24 October 1995 on the protection of individuals with regard to the processing of personal data and on the free movement of such data, Section 30.

[155] See the Italian D.Lgs. 193/2003, as modified by Law 101/2018, Titolo VIII, arts 111–116. See also the Spanish Ley Orgánica 3/2018, arts 87–91; the German Bundesdatenschutzgesetz vom 30 Juni 2017, s 26.

vulnerable groups would have better protection from the outset, with less risk of being harmed and asking for after-harm redress.[156]

However, this proposal takes inspiration from a highly sector-specific framework (the clinical trials context), which cannot be easily compared to the wide scope of the GDPR. For example, the provision of a fixed list of vulnerable data subjects' categories might appear incomplete or problematic, in particular considering that many data subjects might belong to more than one vulnerable category, or might be in situations of temporary or transient vulnerability,[157] especially looking at the dynamics of the online environment.[158]

Policy option 2: the general approach to vulnerability

Now I move to the *general approach* (2). The alternative to the category-based approach is a broad legal definition of vulnerability in data protection law that could serve as an open clause to be contextualized in different situations. The Unfair Commercial Practice Directive is our reference here. There is a clear definition of the two different kinds of consumer in that model: the average and the vulnerable. The average consumer is assumed as a benchmark and defined in Recital 18,[159] while the vulnerable consumer is defined (though superficially) in Articles 5(3) and 18.[160]

The idea of reproducing such a general clause of vulnerable subjects as opposed to a broad definition of average subjects has also been proposed in the data protection field, in particular taking the consumer protection framework as an example.[161] The idea of a general clause defining data subjects' vulnerability has already been implemented by some national DPAs. In particular, as observed in Chapter 6, when developing the national lists of high-risk data processing deserving DPIA according to Article 35(4) GDPR, some DPAs only referred to some vulnerable groups of individuals. Even so, a group of DPAs proposed a general definition of data subjects' vulnerability to follow. This is the case of DPAs of Slovenia,

[156] I have already emphasized above the risk of an after-harm redress, in particular for vulnerable subjects. See Cavoukian and others (n 5) 11.

[157] S Commuri and A Ekici, 'An Enlargement of the Notion of Consumer Vulnerability' (2008) 28(2) Journal of Macromarketing 183.

[158] See eg R Calo, 'Digital Market Manipulation' (2013) 82 George Washington Law Review 995; Helberger and others (n 149) 1456.

[159] Recital 18 of the Unfair Commercial Practice Directive: the average consumer is 'reasonably well-informed and reasonably observant and circumspect, taking into account social, cultural and linguistic factors, as interpreted by the Court of Justice'.

[160] See T Wilhelmsson, 'The Informed Consumer v the Vulnerable Consumer in European Unfair Commercial Practices Law—A Comment' in G Howells and others (eds), *The Yearbook of Consumer Law 2007* (Routledge 2007).

[161] González Fuster, 'How Uninformed Is the Average Data Subject?' (n 50) 102. See indirectly also Helberger and others (n 149) 1458–60.

Poland, Ireland, the Czech Republic, and Greece. In particular, while Slovenian[162] and Polish[163] DPAs refer to the notion of power imbalance, the Irish DPA adopts a contextual definition of vulnerability in general,[164] and the Czech DPA defines the identifying factors for a layered notion vulnerability.[165]

This approach has several advantages: it explicitly recognizes the layered and flexible concept of data subject vulnerability.[166] A general definition can also encompass potential new forms of vulnerability—even temporary—that new technologies or new business models might induce, under all possible perspectives: processing-based vulnerability grounded on power asymmetry (with the risk of uninformed consent or incapability to exercise data protection rights) and effect-based vulnerability grounded on the adverse effects from the outcome of the data processing (discrimination, manipulation, etc). In addition, having a unique and flexible definition also helps in cases of individuals affected by more than one layer of vulnerability (ie belonging to more than one traditionally vulnerable group).

There are also several disadvantages in this approach: a general definition would be more open to diverging interpretations, creating more uncertainty and less foreseeability and homogeneity about the correct implementation of the GDPR. Indeed, contextualizing a general definition into practice could be problematic in many situations and might also generate the so-called pathogenic vulnerability: a too-extensive interpretation (or even abuse) of the concept that could even lead to stigmatization of individuals.[167]

To mitigate the risks mentioned above, a solution might be—rather than a fixed list of legislative definitions of vulnerable categories—some clear guidelines offered by the supervisory authorities (either the EDPB or the national DPAs), regularly updated, that explain how to interpret the concept of vulnerability, with a clear list of vulnerability examples of forbidden practices (as in the case of the Unfair

[162] Information Commissioner, The list of the kind of processing operations which are subject to the requirement for a Data Protection Impact Assessment under the Article 35(4) of the General Data Protection Regulation (EU) 2016/679 (GDPR) <https://www.ip-rs.si/fileadmin/user_upload/Pdf/Ocene_ucinkov/SI_DPIA_list_35-4_35-6_Slovenia_revised_21dec2018_OBJAVA_ZA_WEB.pdf> accessed 5 February 2022.

[163] Proponowany wykaz rodzajów przetwarzania, dla których wymagane jest przeprowadzenie oceny skutków dla ochrony danych <https://iapp.org/media/pdf/resource_center/poland_blacklist.pdf> accessed 5 February 2022.

[164] Data Protection Commission, List of types of data processing which require a DPIA <https://www.dataprotection.ie/sites/default/files/uploads/2018-11/Data-Protection-Impact-Assessment.pdf> accessed 5 February 2022: clarifying that processing the data of vulnerable data subjects is risky if the notion of vulnerability means 'audiences that may have particular or special considerations related to their inherent nature, context or environment'.

[165] Office for Personal Data Protection of the Czech Republic, List of processing operations subject to data protection impact assessment <https://iapp.org/media/pdf/resource_center/czech_blacklist.pdf> accessed 5 February 2022. For more details, see Chapter 5.

[166] Helberger and others (n 149) 1457–58.

[167] Rogers and others (n 68) 25.

Commercial Practice Directive).[168] The Spanish DPA[169] and the British one[170] have already published similar guidelines regarding children.

In sum, both the approaches (sectorial and general) have advantages and disadvantages. However, considering the conceptualization of vulnerability proposed in Chapter 3, I believe that the second approach (the general one) is more appropriate *de lege ferenda* to deal with a comprehensive notion of data subjects' vulnerability. Indeed, although the sectoral approach is more predictable in practice, it could increasingly reduce the potentialities of the concept of vulnerability. On the contrary, a general definition of the vulnerable data subject—in particular, if compared to a definition of an average subject—might be more durable, flexible, and adequate to deal with the impact of new technological challenges.

However, this general definition will be helpful and effective only if accompanied by clear guidelines. For example, the DPAs could indicate concrete criteria for identifying vulnerable individuals, with concrete measures to protect them and clear examples. The release of such guidelines could also follow the example of the Unfair Commercial Practice Directive: the European Commission periodically releases guidelines, though not legally binding ones, on the implementation and application of the Directive to facilitate enforcement activities and ensure legal certainty.[171]

Also, these Guidelines should be updated constantly and should meaningfully involve representatives of vulnerable subjects. Indeed, some authors have argued that involving individuals in the decision-making is fundamental to mitigate risks of vulnerabilities,[172] especially in the human–computer interaction field in the context of designing technologies.[173] If the participatory process is

[168] See Annex I of the Unfair Commercial Practice Directive.

[169] Agencia Española de Protección de Datos, 'Memoria 2016', 2107 <https://www.aepd.es/media/memorias/memoria-AEPD-2016.pdf> accessed 5 February 2022, 9–14

[170] Information Commissioner's Offices, 'Age Appropriate Design: A Code of Practice for Online Services', 2016 <https://ico.org.uk/about-the-ico/ico-and-stakeholder-consultations/age-appropriate-design-a-code-of-practice-for-online-services/> accessed 5 February 2022.

[171] See Commission Staff Working Document Guidance on the Implementation/Application of Directive 2005/29/EC on Unfair Commercial Practices Accompanying the document Communication from the Commission to the European Parliament, the Council, the European Economic and Social Committee and the Committee of the Regions. A comprehensive approach to stimulating cross-border e-Commerce for Europe's citizens and businesses, Brussels, 25 May 2016, SWD(2016) 163 final. See also the previous version: Commission Staff Working Document, Guidance on the Implementation/Application of Directive 2005/29/EC on Unfair Commercial Practices, Brussels, 3 December 2009, SEC(2009) 1666.

[172] See eg Convention on the Elimination of All Forms of Discrimination against Women, *General Recommendation 30*, para 57. See also: V Flegar and E Iedema, 'The Use of the "Vulnerability" Label by the Committee on the Elimination of Discrimination Against Women: Protecting or Stigmatizing Women and Girls in the Forced Migration Context?' (2019) Brill Open Law 27 <https://brill.com/view/journals/bol/aop/article-10.1163-23527072-20191021/article-10.1163-23527072-20191021.xml> accessed 20 February 2023.

[173] S Costanza-Chock, 'Design Justice: Towards an Intersectional Feminist Framework for Design Theory and Practice' (2018) in C Storni and others (eds), *Design as a catalyst for change - DRS International Conference 2018, 25–28 June, Limerick, Ireland* (Digital Ireland 2018) 529, 539; See also

meaningful, it can highlight and respond to experiences and situations of vulnerable communities.[174]

8. Conclusions

After investigating the notion of the data subject in the GDPR (Chapter 2) and the concept of vulnerable data subjects (Chapters 3 and 4), also considering the provisions of the GDPR (Chapters 5 and 6), I finally proposed a vulnerability assessment model with related mitigation measures (Chapter 7). However, such a vulnerability-aware interpretation model can have several limitations and problems. That is why this chapter has analysed possible criticisms of the data subjects' vulnerability model proposed in Chapter 7 (*de lege lata*) and possible alternative protection models *de lege ferenda*.

In other words, I addressed the research question about the limits of a vulnerability-aware interpretation of the GDPR and how these limits might be overcome by interpreting the existing law (*de lege lata*) or proposing legal reforms (*de lege ferenda*).

The possible limits of our interpretation model might be summarized as follows: (i) the risk of excessive limitation of data subjects' autonomy; (ii) the lack of legal certainty and foreseeability; (iii) the limits of analogical interpretation; and (iv) the limited convenience and effectiveness of an extensive interpretation of several GDPR provisions.

Section 2 observed that since the protection of vulnerable data subjects is grounded on the fundamental rights principle of dignity, the legal system needs to consider weaker individuals (especially in data protection law). Moreover, our model is not based only on limiting choice tools of individuals but to eventually considering such tools and only in cases of decision-making vulnerability (processing-based vulnerability), not in cases of effect-based vulnerability to the outcomes of the data processing.

Section 3 analysed the criticism of the lack of foreseeability in our vulnerability model: the controller might be unaware of possible vulnerable data subjects involved in the data processing. In addition, profiling them in order to discover their vulnerability seems a violation of data protection rules (especially of the rationale behind Article 11 GDPR). The solution proposed is a three-step test, in other words the data controller needs to implement specific vulnerability mitigation measures

L Jackson and others, 'Including Vulnerable Populations in the Assessment of Data from Vulnerable Populations' (2019) 2 Frontiers in Big Data 19, 7.

[174] H Zhu and others, 'Value-Sensitive Algorithm Design: Method, Case Study, and Lessons' (2018) 2 in K Karahalios and others (eds), *Proceedings of the ACM on Human–Computer Interaction* (ACM Press 2018) 1–23.

if they reasonably believe that: (i) the data controller specifically targets vulnerable individuals; (ii) the data processing uses knowledge about individual vulnerabilities; or (iii) the data controller has significant power in terms of intrusiveness of data processing techniques, extensive availability of other data, powerful data-mining capabilities, etc.

Section 4 analysed the risk of a too-individualistic approach to vulnerability: underestimating the structural and collective nature of many vulnerability sources might be a risk if we focus only on a case-by-case approach to vulnerability. In addition, the GDPR needs some form of group approximation in order to protect vulnerable data subjects better. However, a group-based vulnerability might be ineffective in describing the vulnerability situation and produce further stigmatization for vulnerable people. What is more necessary is to look at 'layers' as contextual sub-groups in which not only the characteristics of the data subjects are analysed (the traditionally vulnerable groups based on, for example, race, gender, sexual orientation, etc) but also the characteristics of the data controller and eventual vulnerability drivers/mechanisms: homogenous situations considering these three variables are still possible to find.

Section 5 then examined the risk of possible abuses of the analogical interpretation of vulnerable categories in the GDPR: exporting children-tailored rules to apply vulnerable adults by analogy might overestimate the importance of the category of 'vulnerable' data subjects as proposed by the GDPR (which is named only in the preamble, in Recital 75). I observed that all measures for children in the GDPR (apart from the age of consent in Article 8) are not meant *only* for children, but *in particular* for children: this means that the data controller has to apply those measures for similar situations as well as to children. In addition, the need to protect vulnerable subjects specifically is central in the data protection discourse, as revealed by the literature on fundamental rights, the risk-based approach (and the reference to power imbalance at Recital 43) in the GDPR, and the numerous references to vulnerability in the WP29 and EDPB opinions.

Section 6 analysed possible limits of a vulnerability-based implementation of the GDPR: from the vagueness of the fairness principle to the ineffectiveness of many rules implementing the lawfulness principle (the freedom of consent, the legitimate interest balancing test, the special categories of data), from the fallacy of many transparency measures to the delusive application of several data protection rights (eg the right to object, the right not to be subject to automated decision-making). However, to reach adequate protection for vulnerable people, those principles and rights should not be considered alone but jointly and should be interpreted extensively. However, some limitations cannot be easily overcome: further research is necessary.

Having analysed the relevant potentialities and the limits of a vulnerability-based interpretation of the GDPR, *de lege lata*, a final step has been to explore alternative models *de lege ferenda* in the view of a possible reform of the data protection framework.

I have thus taken into account two models: a sectoral approach (based on the example of the Clinical Trials Regulation) according to which specific vulnerable groups should be explicitly mentioned in law and protected with special rules; and a general approach (based on the example of the Unfair Commercial Practice Directive) where a broad definition of vulnerable subjects (in contrast to the notion of average subjects) should be formulated by law.

While the first model is more foreseeable but less flexible, the second is more dynamic and forward-looking. A combination of these two models might result in a core list of high-risk vulnerable data subjects, complemented with a generic provision for meaningful analogies. This would be an interesting opportunity for reform if accompanied by robust guidance activity by DPAs that would eventually involve representatives of vulnerable subjects in the decision-making process.

However, although I consider possible reforms of the GDPR, I do not believe that the current set of rules is inadequate to mitigate vulnerability layers of data subjects. Nevertheless, higher normative clarity in the definition of vulnerable data subjects and providing related safeguards will eventually help address several of the interpretational problems analysed above (eg predictability, limits of analogy, etc).

9
Conclusions
The layers of data subject's vulnerability and the way ahead

1. The need for a spectrum

The goal of this book has been to elucidate the notion of the data subject in the General Data Protection Regulation (GDPR), considering in particular different levels of data subjects' vulnerability and how the data protection framework can help protect vulnerable people. At this stage, we can reply that the notion of the data subject in the GDPR, though implicit, is twofold, based both on a general idea of the average data subject and on a layered concept of vulnerable subjects, who should be protected by exploiting all possible open clauses in the GDPR (from the general principles to the risk-based approach). The vulnerable and the average data subjects are the two poles of a spectrum composed of many shades of 'intermediate data subjects' (with an increasing level of vulnerability layers). This final chapter summarizes the main conclusions of this book, drawing the *fil rouge* between the findings of the different chapters.

2. Who is/are the data subject/s?

In Chapter 2, I observed that the definition of the data subject in the EU data protection framework is *broad* and *dynamic* for what concerns the identifiability and the relation to the information. At the same time, it is limited to natural living persons. In other words, it excludes legal persons and unborn or deceased persons, but the Member States may regulate post-mortem data protection. The definition is dynamic because the concepts of identifiability and 'relation'—according to the GDPR preamble[1] and the CJEU[2] and the WP29[3]—are relative and dynamic. I also observed that the definition of the data subject is apparently 'unique' (ie there is only one kind of data subject) and universal (nationality or citizenship cannot be a criterion to delimit the notion of the data subject).

[1] See Recital 36.
[2] Case C-582/14, *Patrick Breyer v Bundesrepublik Deutschland* [2016] ECLI:EU:C:2016:779.
[3] Article 29 Working Party (WP29), WP136.

Vulnerability and Data Protection Law. Gianclaudio Malgieri, Oxford University Press. © Gianclaudio Malgieri 2023.
DOI: 10.1093/oso/9780192870339.003.0009

However, even assuming that in the wording of the GDPR there is just *one* kind of data subject, we can still wonder whether personal variables of data subjects can have a legal relevance when applying the data protection rules (principles, rights, duties). Personal variables can include several different characteristics, for example legal status (legal capacity, familiar status, etc), mental conditions (including age, maturity, psychological health status), the level of awareness and understanding of data protection risks and rights, the likelihood of the fundamental rights being at risk, the resilience or reaction to such risks. Should the implementation of the existing data protection rules change according to these variables of the data subjects involved in the data processing?

A distinction between average and vulnerable data subjects is not explicit or clear in the data protection context, but a teleological interpretation of the Data Protection Directive and a comparison with the novelties of the GDPR seems to confirm this assumption: in the GDPR two different kinds of data subjects are assumed as a reference, an average data subject (coming from the historical tradition of data protection in Europe) and a vulnerable one, arising from several new inputs in the GDPR (including the risk-based approach).

3. The average data subject

Considering the well-established distinction in EU consumer law between average and vulnerable consumers, Chapter 2 analysed the notion of the average consumer in order to understand if it can be compared to an average data subject. The average consumer is 'reasonably well-informed and reasonably observant and circumspect, taking into account social, cultural and linguistic factors'.[4] It seems that this understanding of average consumers is not too distant from the GDPR notion of a data subject.[5]

In the first Proposal of the Commission for the Data Protection Directive, we can find that, for example, the right to information is seen as a tool to 'enable the data subject *to weigh the risks and advantages of the intended processing* of data relating to him and to exercise his rights under Article 14 of the Directive (rectification, erasure, blocking)'.[6] In other words, the legislator was relying on the reasonable and rational decision-making capabilities of the data subject, who alone can assess the risks and advantages involved in the data processing and take informed

[4] See Recital 18, UCPD.

[5] BW Schermer and others, 'The Crisis of Consent: How Stronger Legal Protection May Lead to Weaker Consent in Data Protection' (2014) 16 Ethics and Information Technology 171.

[6] Commission of the European Communities, Communication on the protection of Individuals In relation to the processing of personal data In the Community and Information security; Proposal for a Council Directive concerning the protection of individuals in relation to the processing of personal data Draft, COM(90) 314 final, SYN 287 and 288, Brussels, 13 September 1990, 26 <https://eur-lex.europa.eu/legal-content/EN/TXT/PDF/?uri=CELEX:51990DC0314&from=EN> accessed 4 February 2022.

decisions accordingly. Several commentators noted that the emphasis on information duties in the data protection discourse presupposes a rational, informed data subject who makes conscious decisions.[7]

Nevertheless, the new awareness about cognitive biases of even 'average' subjects,[8] and the empirical studies on data subjects' expectations and behaviour,[9] have revealed that such a positive view of an average data subject is not only unrealistic but also counterproductive.[10] This awareness is recently emerging in the Court of Justice of the European Union (CJEU) jurisprudence, which is adopting a more flexible understanding of the circumspect and informed average subject.[11] However, it is essential to analyse whether and how the data protection framework recognizes the notion of the non-average data subject. Accordingly, the main focus of Chapters 3 to 8 is about vulnerable data subjects.

However, the notion of the average subject is not the pure opposite of the vulnerable subject: there is an intermediate zone that I defined as the 'intermediate data subject'. This subject is neither reasonably informed and rational (average) nor at high risk of the fundamental rights and freedoms being harmed because of a power imbalance (not at risk of being vulnerable). Taking a layered approach, such a subject has a vulnerability layer that is not significant enough to trigger special protection. This non-vulnerable and non-average data subject seems to assume relevance under the GDPR: the CJEU is apparently open to recognizing a non-average, non-vulnerable data subject,[12] as is Article 12(1) requiring more intelligible and understandable transparency duties. On the other hand, the risk-based approach seems to lead data controllers to adopt safeguards proportional to the subjects' vulnerability layer. This book has focused on the average and the vulnerable person because they inspire the whole 'spectrum' of data subjectivity, though not denying the existence of many intermediate shades.

4. The compelling necessity to consider vulnerable data subjects

Chapter 4 argues that a notion of vulnerable data subjects, compared to average data subjects, exists in the GDPR. This term is explicitly mentioned only in Recital

[7] Schermer and others (n 5) 171.

[8] RH Thaler, 'The Psychology of Choice and the Assumptions of Economics' in AE Roth (ed), *Laboratory Experimentation in Economics: Six Points of View* (Cambridge University Press 2005).

[9] I Pollach, 'What's Wrong with Online Privacy Policies?' (2007) 50 Communications of the ACM 103; Schermer and others (n 5); A Acquisti, 'Nudging Privacy: The Behavioral Economics of Personal Information' (2009) 7 IEEE Security & Privacy Magazine 82.

[10] P Blume, 'The Data Subject' (2015) 1 European Data Protection Law Review 258; G González Fuster, 'How Uninformed Is the Average Data Subject? A Quest for Benchmarks in EU Personal Data Protection' (2014) 19 IDP Revista de Internet, Derecho y Política 92.

[11] CJEU, Case C-673/17, *Planet49* [2019], §55

[12] See ibid interpreting the 'rational' standards about transparency in a more lenient way.

75 among cases of data processing posing high risks of harm to fundamental rights and freedoms. Moreover, an implicit mention is in Recital 43 ('clear imbalance') but also in all references to children (especially Articles 6(1)(f) about legitimate interest, Article 12(1) on the legibility of communication from the data controller to the data subject, and also Recital 71 about the prohibition of automated decision-making).

The European Data Protection Board (EDPB) has developed the notion of vulnerable subjects in many different opinions.[13] Looking at the general picture of the GDPR, the new higher attention paid to 'risks' seems a relevant element toward the recognition of data subjects' vulnerability. The risk-based approach requires the data controllers to analyse different levels of risks to fundamental rights and freedoms and, accordingly, implement adequate safeguards. As affirmed in Chapter 3, a legal definition of vulnerability might be the situation of being at higher risk to fundamental rights and freedoms.[14] In other words, the notion of vulnerability would be a way to interpret and implement the risk-based approach on a subject-centred[15] (though not individualistic)[16] basis. How can the notion of vulnerability be useful to this goal? A layered analysis of data subjects' vulnerabilities might be a way to address risks beyond simplistic exercises of routine compliance, through a more mature, contextual, relational, and structural analysis of data subjects. In other words, the vulnerability-oriented interpretation of risks proposed in this book can be a model used to analyse how specific situations affect specific subgroups of data subjects considering their personal characteristics and the encounter between these characteristics, the data controller's power, and the existing socio-technical drivers of vulnerability. This approach might avoid standard and formalistic risk analyses and would impose a focus on structural and contextual asymmetries and concrete personal risks.

However, the reason to consider, identify, and protect vulnerable subjects goes beyond the mere textual analysis of the GDPR. The rationale for identifying and mitigating individual vulnerabilities is based on the protection of fundamental rights and, in particular, on the principle of dignity.[17] This is also confirmed by the

[13] See WP29, Guidelines on Transparency, WP260rev.01, 10; WP29, Opinion on legitimate interest, WP217, 40-41; WP29, Opinion on purpose limitation, WP203, 25 and 32; WP29 Guidelines on DPIA, WP248, 9; WP29, Guidelines on Profiling, WP251rev.01, 22. See indirectly also EDPB, Opinion 3/2019 concerning the Questions and Answers on the interplay between the Clinical Trials Regulation (CTR) and the General Data Protection Regulation (GDPR) (art 70.1.b)), 23 January 2019, 6 referring to the 'clear imbalance between the data subject and the controller'.

[14] See eg D Schroeder and E Gefenas, 'Vulnerability: Too Vague and Too Broad?' (2009) 18 Cambridge Quarterly of Healthcare Ethics 113; RE Goodin, *Protecting the Vulnerable: A Reanalysis of Our Social Responsibilities* (University of Chicago Press 1985).

[15] See WP29 Guidelines on DPIA, 21 M Macenaite, 'The "Riskification" of European Data Protection Law through a Two-Fold Shift' (2017) 8 European Journal of Risk Regulation 506, 536.

[16] See Chapter 8, Section 4.

[17] R Andorno, 'Is Vulnerability the Foundation of Human Rights?' in A Masferrer and E García-Sánchez (Eds.), *Human Dignity of the Vulnerable in the Age of Rights: Interdisciplinary Perspectives* (Springer International Publishing 2016).

ECtHR, which—as shown in Chapter 3—has developed a robust body of case law about vulnerable persons, accepting a broad, layered, and contextual concept of vulnerability.[18] In the privacy and data protection field, the protection of dignity[19] and, more specifically, the need to mitigate vulnerability seem to be the founding rationales for protecting natural persons. I know that the data protection framework itself was conceived to rebalance the power imbalance between subject and controller[20] but there are different levels of vulnerability that we should take into account. Children are a clear example, but many more cases need to be considered.

5. Human vulnerability: the layered approach

The definition of vulnerability is highly problematic and open to many diverse interpretations, as revealed by discussions in political philosophy, research bioethics, and law and economics. Despite the tension between universal vulnerability (everyone is vulnerable) and particular vulnerability (some people are more vulnerable than others), power imbalance and higher risk of harm seem two common elements in the different definitions.

A theory that overcomes the dualism universalism/particularism of human vulnerability is the theory of layered vulnerability of Luna.[21] The layers of vulnerability are not static attributes of certain groups of individuals but are features constructed by status, time, and location. This theory is in line with the studies on intersectionality: what qualifies the vulnerability level of the data subject is the 'intersection' of different layers.[22] Layers can be of different relevance and importance, temporary or permanent, physiological or pathological. The intersection of these layers (eg age, sexual orientation, sexual identity, cognitive issues, occupation, socio-economic condition, literacy, addictions) in a given structural and relational context qualifies a data subject's vulnerability level. The identification and assessment of vulnerability layers should be based on several criteria, including an analysis of the origins of vulnerability (ie an analysis of the stimulus conditions

[18] L Peroni and A Timmer, 'Vulnerable Groups: The Promise of an Emerging Concept in European Human Rights Convention Law' (2013) 11 International Journal of Constitutional Law 1056; F Ippolito and SI Sánchez, *Protecting Vulnerable Groups: The European Human Rights Framework* (Bloomsbury Publishing 2015).

[19] P De Hert and S Gutwirth, 'Privacy, Data Protection and Law Enforcement. Opacity of the Individual and Transparency of Power' in E Claes and others (Eds.), *Privacy and the Criminal Law* (Intersentia 2006) 81; L Floridi, 'On Human Dignity as a Foundation for the Right to Privacy' (2016) 29 Philosophy & Technology 307; JQ Whitman, 'The Two Western Cultures of Privacy: Dignity Versus Liberty' (2004) 113 The Yale Law Journal 72.

[20] O Lynskey, *The Foundations of EU Data Protection Law* (Oxford University Press 2015) 213–15.

[21] F Luna, 'Elucidating the Concept of Vulnerability: Layers Not Labels' (2009) 2 International Journal of Feminist Approaches to Bioethics 121; F Luna, 'Identifying and Evaluating Layers of Vulnerability—A Way Forward' (2019) 19 Developing World Bioethics 86.

[22] See Chapter 3, Section 4.

including if some layers are 'cascade vulnerability', in other words layers that have a cascade effect on other sources of vulnerability) and of its effects (ie probability and intensity of harms).

Potentially, any data subject can be vulnerable (eg to the lack of freedom of consent, manipulation, discrimination, physical damages, etc) in a particular context or circumstance. Therefore, the analysis must focus on the *layered* relationship between the data controller and the data subject. In other terms, vulnerability qualifies as the specific power imbalance between data subjects and controllers considering all particular characteristics and the higher risk of adverse effects for individuals.

Focusing on the vulnerability layers, law and economics scholars have analysed the three main components of consumer vulnerability: personal characteristics of consumers, external characteristics of suppliers, and vulnerability mechanisms (or drivers). As shown in Chapter 4, In the data protection framework, such components can also be relevant: personal characteristics of data subjects (eg cognitive issues, linguistic issues, etc., or being part of a social minority group, being physically or mentally weak); the data controller's power and potentials (eg hierarchical or institutional dominance of the data controller on the data subject or augmented information asymmetry, ie the enormous amount of information and predictive capabilities of the data controller); and vulnerability mechanisms (eg intrusive practices that actively exploit subjects' vulnerabilities, structural or technical factors that indirectly influence vulnerability, geographical or socio-economic contexts, political or institutional factors).

6. The two types of vulnerable data subject: a new taxonomy

In general, two types of vulnerability emerge from an analysis of the GDPR: *processing-based* vulnerability during the data processing (ie the risk of not being able to understand information, to give valid consent, or to exercise the data protection rights adequately) and *effect-based* vulnerability to the outcomes of data processing (ie the risk that the data processing can lead to discrimination, manipulation, damages, or any other interference with a fundamental right or freedom).

The first one (processing-based) appears evident when analysing the protection of children. The rationale for protecting children is their decisional vulnerability during the data processing, that is, the incapability of understanding information about the processing, the implications, risks, and related rights, and the incapability to give valid consent and exercise the data protection rights.[23] This form of decision-making vulnerability concerns not only children but also other data

[23] See Recital 38 of the GDPR. See also WP29, Guidelines on DPIA, 9.

subjects. We call it 'modal' because it refers to a modal power imbalance (ie not based on specific risks of effects on individuals but the structural imbalance inherent in a particular relationship between controllers and subjects).

The second category arises from Recital 75: vulnerability as the higher capability in incurring high risks to fundamental rights and freedoms. In particular, we need to consider rights and freedoms protected in the EU Charter of Fundamental Rights.

The identifying criteria of these two types of vulnerabilities are different: in one case, it is the structural or institutional power imbalance that makes data subjects vulnerable when providing consent or exercising their data protection rights; in the other, it is the higher risk of adverse effects for some data subjects that makes them vulnerable to the outcome of the data processing. The two kinds of vulnerability differ, thus, according to several other perspectives: (i) power imbalance structure (modal in the first case, causal in the second case);[24] (ii) manifestations in the GDPR (the first arises at the beginning or during the data processing, the second arises as an effect of the data processing); (iii) different effects on individuals (in the first case loss of control on personal data, in the second case interferences with other fundamental rights, including cases of discrimination and manipulation).

The distinction between these two categories is often blurred. There might be several overlaps between the two groups (eg an individual suffering from decision-making vulnerability during the data processing might also have higher adverse effects as an outcome of the data processing), and many conditions are often just temporary and difficult to detect.

7. Vulnerable to what? The choice of legal or similarly significant effects

Another difference between these two kinds of vulnerability is the fundamental rights and freedoms at issue: in the case of *processing-based* vulnerability, what might be at risk is the fundamental right to privacy and data protection (implying adverse effects on autonomy, dignity and informational self-determination); in case of *effect-based* vulnerability, the fundamental rights and freedoms at issue are many and diverse, such as non-discrimination, freedom of speech, freedom of thought, freedom of movement, etc. Although determining the concrete cases of manifestations of these interferences might be very difficult and result in a non-comprehensive massive list of cases, we could analyse the impact of such violations

[24] For these definitions see H Richter, 'The Power Paradigm in Private Law' in M Bakhoum and others (Eds.), *Personal Data in Competition, Consumer Protection and Intellectual Property Law: Towards a Holistic Approach?* (Springer Berlin Heidelberg 2018).

by looking at the minimum *severity threshold* that should trigger vulnerability-based protection.

As clarified in Chapter 8, our vulnerability definition has two components: (i) interference with a fundamental right or freedom; and (ii) severity of the effects produced by such an interference. As regards point (i), each significant effect needs to interfere with a fundamental right of the subject and, thus, must be relatable to one or more specific fundamental rights.

As regards point (ii), analysing the wording of the GDPR (and other relevant pieces of legislation), there are different degrees of severity of effects of data processing on the data subjects, from mere effects to damages. The borderline between them are not always clear, but they are gradual steps from the least to the most impactful contact between data controllers and subjects.

In terms of vulnerability assessment, each of these steps is relevant. Still, only from a certain severity level can we identify the legally relevant vulnerability of the data subject under the GDPR, as described in Chapter 7. According to the author, that minimum level of impact is '*legal or similarly significant effects*'. Indeed, these 'legal or similarly significant' effects have been described as a compromise between the subjective and objective perception of harms and can include the exploitation of not only effect-based but also processing-based vulnerability. Many forms of vulnerability may not reach the level of requiring quantifiable damages but are still very relevant (see eg the case of commercial manipulation as an outcome of intrusive profiling).

8. Vulnerability as a heuristic tool in the GDPR: a subject-centred perspective of the risk-based approach

One of the goals of this book is to promote the concept of the data subjects' layered vulnerability as a *heuristic tool* used to reinterpret the system of rights, duties, and safeguards in the GDPR and to reconceptualize the risk-based approach on a data subject-centred basis.

To develop such a heuristic tool, this book has proposed three steps: (i) a *descriptive step*, an analysis of the wording of the GDPR to understand which role individual vulnerability can have in the different provisions (Chapters 5 and 6); (ii) a *normative step*, a proposal of the mitigation measures that could be adopted to mitigate different layers of individual vulnerability (Chapter 7); and (iii) a *speculative step*, analysing limitations and counterarguments for such mitigation measures (Chapter 8).

Since analysing layers of data subjects' vulnerability means analysing risks to the fundamental rights and freedoms of data subjects, the Data Protection Impact Assessment (DPIA) model proposed by the GDPR seems useful for our purposes. To analyse risks, we might look at the groups of vulnerability factors and propose mitigation measures for each group. Chapter 4 has presented three factors: personal characteristics of the data subjects, data controller's power, or potentialities and vulnerability (social, technological, structural) drivers. Focusing on the data subjects' personal characteristics, the data controller might analyse the expectations, wishes, needs, and mental capabilities of the data subject concerned, and shape information duties and transparency rights accordingly. Looking at the data controller's potentialities, the data controller should perform a self-assessment of, for example, the intrusiveness of profiling and tracking operations and understand how to mitigate these. Looking at vulnerability drivers, the data controller should assess whether some of the business or societal practices or structures at issue can be considered unfair or problematic and how the eventual asymmetry between the controller and the subject could be rebalanced. At the same time, the Data Protection Authorities (DPAs) should release guidelines on how this self-assessment should be conducted and ensure correct implementation of these risk analysis acts, via relevant sanctions if needed. The enforcement should also rely on the cooperation with data subjects' representatives (eg non-governmental organizations (NGOs) and representatives of special categories of subjects).

It would be impossible to propose specific measures for each possible kind of vulnerability. However, Chapter 7 offered general guidelines of potential mitigation measures for vulnerable subjects. It is important to emphasize that the various GDPR safeguards for vulnerable people cannot be considered silos but must be seen in connection with each other and must be implemented beyond the mere letter of the law (eg enhancing the participation of impacted individuals or groups in the design of technologies and the impact assessment process, etc).

9. Is the GDPR enough?

Chapter 8 identified at least four possible criticisms to our vulnerability-based interpretation model: (i) the risk of paternalism; (ii) the lack of legal certainty and foreseeability (including a 'deflation' risk in defining vulnerable persons); (iii) the risk of a too-individualistic approach; (iv) the limits of analogical interpretation; and (v) the inconvenience and ineffectiveness of an extensive interpretation of several GDPR provisions, that could sometimes even amplify existing vulnerabilities.

I replied to all these possible criticisms of our model, but I acknowledge a remaining issue: the lack of clear recognition of vulnerable subjects makes their protection more difficult. The solution to this issue might be to reform the data protection law. Such a reform could follow two different models: a *category-based* approach (based on the example of Clinical Trials Regulation) according to which specific vulnerable groups should be explicitly mentioned in the law and protected with special rules; and a *general* approach (based on the example of the Unfair

Commercial Practice Directive) where the law formulates a general definition of vulnerable subjects (eventually in contrast to a notion of average subjects).

The first model is more predictable but cannot include layered and contextual situations of vulnerability. The second model is more appropriate for our definition of vulnerability and might be the best option. In addition, it would be essential to give examples of vulnerability layers and produce, for example, blacklists of unfair data processing operations that induce or exploit data subjects' vulnerability.

10. Call for further research

This research aimed to develop the definition of data subjects, particularly considering their dynamic vulnerability level. The author is aware that more points should be followed up in further discussion.

First, more research on subjects' vulnerability should be encouraged, considering, in particular, the notion of power imbalance both in competition law and in consumer law.[25] These two fields could help not only in the definitional efforts of vulnerability (eg how to define power in the algorithmic environment) but also in protection efforts (mitigating power imbalance at different levels).

Secondly, it will be necessary to check whether this analysis on data subjects' layered vulnerability is adequate to specific data protection sub-fields (processing data according to criminal procedure, international data transfers according to specific treaties, etc). It is possible that, in specific fields, a more circumscribed scope of vulnerability is desirable. Furthermore, the analysis of vulnerability drivers might be more nuanced in sectoral data protection law (eg which kinds of vulnerability drivers could exist in the data processing for criminal law purposes?).

Thirdly, it will be necessary to understand how data controllers (especially small and medium-size enterprises (SMEs)) could adequately assess and mitigate data subjects' vulnerability, particularly in terms of limited economic and human resources. I know that a vulnerability-aware interpretation of the GDPR requires building monitoring and evaluation capacities. Some help could come from DPA guidance or pan-European projects assisting SMEs in implementing the data protection rules.

Another element for further research might be the consideration of 'other' natural persons who are not data subjects but are still impacted by the data processing. The relevance of such categories is explicit in several parts of the GDPR. The risk-based approach refers to the risk to fundamental rights and freedoms of 'natural persons' (see Articles 24(1), 25(1), and 35(1)), not only of data subjects.

[25] See a similar call in N Helberger and others, 'The Perfect Match? A Closer Look at the Relationship between EU Consumer Law and Data Protection Law' (2017) 54 Common Market Law Review 1427, 1458.

In addition, Article 35(7)(d) states that data controllers should identify 'the measures envisaged to address the risks ... taking into account the rights and legitimate interests *of data subjects and other persons concerned*' (emphasis added). It is unclear who these 'other persons concerned' might be and whether and how data controllers could take those individuals into account. It could refer to, for example, the general group that may be impacted by some data processing operations or to other individuals whose data might be inferred from processing the data subjects' personal data. In both cases, these other impacted individuals might be vulnerable persons (according to our definition), and this is an issue that should be further investigated in the future. This issue becomes even more critical considering that predictive analytics and machine learning make the distinction between personal data of the data subject and 'of others' even more blurred.[26]

[26] J van Hoboken, 'The Privacy Disconnect' in RF Jørgensen (ed), *Human Rights in the Age of Platforms* (MIT Press 2019) 267.

Sources and bibliography

Secondary Sources

Guidance documents, opinions, recommendations, and statements

Article 29 Working Party

Article 29 Working Party, 'Opinion 4/2007 on the Concept of Personal Data' (Article 29 Working Party 2007) WP 136

Article 29 Working Party, 'Opinion 1/2010 on the Concepts of 'Controller' and 'Processor'' (Article 29 Working Party 2010) WP 169

Article 29 Working Party, 'Opinion 02/2010 on Online Behavioural Advertising' (Article 29 Working Party 2010) WP 171

Article 29 Working Party, 'Opinion 16/2011 on EASA/IAB Best Practice Recommendation on Online Behavioural Advertising' (Article 29 Working Party 2011) WP188

Article 29 Working Party, 'Opinion 02/2012 on Facial Recognition in Online and Mobile Services' WP 192

Article 29 Working Party, Opinion 03/2013 on purpose limitation Adopted on 2 April 2013, WP203

Article 29 Working Party, 'Opinion 06/2014 on the Notion of Legitimate Interests of the Data Controller under Article 7 of Directive 95/46/EC' (European Commission 2014) Opinion WP 217

Article 29 Working Party, 'Statement on the Role of a Risk-Based Approach in Data Protection Legal Frameworks' (2014) WP 218

Article 29 Working Party, 'ANNEX—Health Data in Apps and Devices, to the Letter to European Commission, DG CONNECT on MHealth, Brussels, 05 February 2015'

Article 29 Working Party, 'Guidelines on Data Protection Impact Assessment (DPIA) and determining whether processing is 'likely to result in a high risk' for the purposes of Regulation 2016/679', WP248

Article 29 Working Party, 'Guidelines on Automated Individual Decision-Making and Profiling for the Purposes of Regulation 2016/679' WP 251

Article 29 Working Party, 'Guidelines on Consent under Regulation 2016/679' (2017) WP259

Article 29 Working Party, 'Guidelines on transparency under Regulation 2016/679', WP260

European Data Protection Board

'European Data Protection Board, Guidelines 2/2019 on the Processing of Personal Data under Article 6(1)(b) GDPR in the Context of the Provision of Online Services to Data Subjects (Version for Public Consultation) Adopted on 9 April 2019'

European Data Protection Board, Opinion 3/2019 concerning the Questions and Answers on the interplay between the Clinical Trials Regulation (CTR) and the General Data Protection regulation (GDPR) (art 70.1.b), 6

European Data Protection Board, Guidelines 5/2019 on the criteria of the Right to be Forgotten in the search engines cases under the GDPR (part 1), 2 December 2019

European Data Protection Board, Letter in reply to Sophie In't Veld, Ref: OUT2020-0004, 29 January 2020

European Data Protection Supervisor

European Data Protection Supervisor, Opinion of the on the Communication from the Commission to the European Parliament, the Council, the Economic and Social Committee and the Committee of the Regions 'A comprehensive approach on personal data protection in the European Union', 14 January 2011, 22–23

European Commission and Parliament

European Commission, 'Communication from the Commission to the European Parliament, the Council, the Economic and Social Committee and the Committee of the Regions Consumer Policy Strategy 2002–2006 COM (2002) 208'

European Commission, 'First Report on the Application of Directive 2000/31/EC of the European Parliament and of the Council of 8 June 2000 on Certain Legal Aspects of Information Society Services, in Particular Electronic Commerce, in the Internal Market (Directive on Electronic Commerce)' <http://www.europarl.europa.eu/RegData/docs_autres_institutions/commission_europeenne/com/2003/0702/COM_COM(2003)0702_EN.pdf> accessed 6 August 2018

European Commission, 'Commission Staff Working Document Guidance on the Implementation/Application of Directive 2005/29/EC on Unfair Commercial Practices' SEC (2009) 1666, 20' <http://ec.europa.eu/justice/consumer-marketing/files/ucp_guidance_en.pdf> accessed 3 August 2017

European Commission, 'Communication from the Commission, Strategy for the Effective Implementation of the Charter of Fundamental Rights by the European Union, COM(2010) 573/4'

'European Parliament Resolution of 15 November 2011 on a New Strategy for Consumer Policy (2011/2149(INI))'

European Commission, 'DG Justice Guidance Document Concerning Directive 2011/83/EU of the European Parliament and of the Council of 25 October 2011 on Consumer Rights, Amending Council Directive 93/13/EEC and Directive 1999/44/EC of the European Parliament and of the Council and Repealing Council Directive 85/577/EEC and Directive 97/7/EC of the European Parliament and of the Council' (European Commission - DG Justice 2014) <https://www.cr-online.de/crd_guidance_en.pdf> accessed 16 February 2018

European Commission, 'Commission Staff Working Document Guidance on the Implementation/Application of Directive 2005/29/EC On Unfair Commercial Practices Accompanying the Document Communication from the Commission to the European Parliament, the Council, the European Economic and Social Committee and the Committee 345 of the Regions a Comprehensive Approach to Stimulating Cross-Border e-Commerce for Europe's Citizens and Businesses COM(2016) 320

National DPA documents

Belgian DPA, Autorité de Protection des Données, Liste des types d'opérations de traitement pour lesquelles une AIPD est requise, <https://www.autoriteprotectiondonnees.be/sites/privacycommission/files/documents/Liste_des_traitements_AIPD.pdf>

Bulgarian DPA, LIST of processing operations requiring data protection impact assessment (DPIA) pursuant to Art. 35, paragraph 4 of Regulation (EU) 2016/679, <https://iapp.org/media/pdf/resource_center/bulgaria_blacklist.pdf>

Croatian DPA, AZOP, ODLUKA o uspostavi i javnoj objavi popisa vrsta postupaka obrade koje podliježu zahtjevu za procjenu učinka na zaštitu podatak, <https://www.wpno.com/rss-news-feed/croatia-azop-issues-decision-on-processing-activities-requiring-dpias/>

Cypriot DPA, Office of the Commissioner for Personal Data Protection, Indicative list of processing operations subject to DPIA requirements under Article 35(4) of the GDPR, <https://iapp.org/media/pdf/resource_center/cyprus_blacklist.pdf>

Czechia DPA, Office for Personal Data Protection of the Czech Republic, List of processing operations subject to data protection impact assessment, <https://iapp.org/media/pdf/resource_center/czech_blacklist.pdf>

Dutch DPA, Autoriteit Persononsgegevens, Besluit inzake lijst van verwerkingen van persoonsgegevens waarvoor een gegevensbeschermingseffectbeoordeling (DPIA) verplicht is, Autoriteit Persoonsgegevens, <https://www.autoriteitpersoonsgegevens.nl/sites/default/files/atoms/files/stcrt-2019-64418.pdf>

Estonian DPA, Data Protection Inspectorate, List of cross-border processing operations which are subject to the requirement for a data protection impact assessment, <https://www.eurocloud.at/news/detail/news/the-estonian-data-protection-authority-issued-guidance-on-the-definition-of-large-scale-processing/

Finnish DPA, List compiled by the Office of the Data Protection Ombudsman of processing operations which require data protection impact assessment (DPIA), updated 21 December 2018, <https://tietosuoja.fi/en/list-of-processing-operations-which-require-dpia>

French DPA, CNIL, Délibération no 2018-327 du 11 octobre 2018 portant adoption de la liste des types d'opérations de traitement pour lesquelles une analyse d'impact relative à la protection des données est requise, <https://www.legifrance.gouv.fr/jo_pdf.do?id=JORFTEXT000037559521>

German DPA, Datenschutz Konferenz, Liste der Verarbeitungstätigkeiten, für die eine DSFA durchzuführen ist, 18.07.2018, <https://www.lda.bayern.de/media/dsfa_muss_liste_dsk_de.pdf>

Hungarian DPA, Nemzeti Adatvédelmi és Informacioszabadsag Hatosag, List of Processing Operations Subject to DPIA 35(4) GDPR, <https://www.naih.hu/list-of-processing-operations-subject-to-dpia-35-4--gdpr.html>

Irish DPA, Data Protection Commission, List of types of data processing which require a DPIA, <https://www.dataprotection.ie/sites/default/files/uploads/2018-11/Data-Protection-Impact-Assessment.pdf>

Italian DPA, Garante per la Protezione dei Dati Personali, Elenco delle tipologie di trattamenti, soggetti al meccanismo di coerenza, da sottoporre a valutazione d'impatto, <https://www.garanteprivacy.it/documents/10160/0/ALLEGATO+1+Elenco+delle+tipologie+di+trattamenti+soggetti+al+meccanismo+di+coerenza+da+sottoporre+a+valutazione+di+impatto>

Latvian DPA, Datu Valsts Inspekcija, List of processing operations requiring data protection impact assessment pursuant to Article 35 (4) of the GDPR, <https://edpb.europa.eu/sites/edpb/files/decisions/lv_sa_dpia_final_list_20181212.pdf>

Lithuanian DPA, Director of the State Data Protection Inspectorate, Order on the approval of the list of data processing operations subject to the requirement to perform data protection impact assessment 14, March 2019, <https://iapp.org/media/pdf/resource_center/lithuania_blacklist.pdf>

Luxembourgish DPA, CNDP, Délibération 34/2019 du 6 mars 2019 de la Commission nationale pour la protection des données portant adoption de la liste des types d'opérations de traitement pour lesquelles une analyse d'impact relative à la protection des données est requise

Maltese DPA, Office for the Information and Data Protection Commissioner, Data Protection Impact Assessment, <https://idpc.org.mt/en/Pages/dpia.aspx>

Norwegian DPA, Datatilsynet, The Norwegian Supervisory Authority's List of Processing Operations Subject to the Requirement of a Data Protection Impact Assessment, <https://edpb.europa.eu/sites/edpb/files/decisions/no_dpia_list_en_gb_20190316.pdf>

Polish DPA, Proponowany wykaz rodzajów przetwarzania, dla których wymagane jest przeprowadzenie oceny skutków dla ochrony danych, <https://iapp.org/media/pdf/resource_center/poland_blacklist.pdf>

Portuguese DPA, Aviso (extrato) no 17575/2018, <https://www.cnpd.pt/bin/decisoes/regulamentos/DR_Regulamento_1-2018_lista_de_AIPD.pdf>

Romanian DPA, DECIZIE nr. 174 din 18 octombrie 2018 privind lista operațiunilor pentru care este obligatorie realizarea evaluării impactului asupra protecției datelor cu caracter personal, <https://iapp.org/media/pdf/resource_center/romanian_dpa_blacklist.pdf>

Slovakian DPA, Urad Na Ochranu Osobnych Udajov, Slovak list of processing operations which are subject to the requirement for a data protection impact assessment, <https://iapp.org/media/pdf/resource_center/slovakia_blacklist.pdf>, 'Monitoring employee work on the ground of serious reasons based on the particular nature of the employer's activities (hereinafter "employee monitoring processing")'

Slovenian DPA, Information Commissioner, The list of the kind of processing operations which are subject to the requirement for a Data Protection Impact Assessment under the Article 35(4) of the General Data Protection Regulation (EU) 2016/679 (GDPR), <https://www.ip-rs.si/fileadmin/user_upload/Pdf/Ocene_ucinkov/SI_DPIA_list_35-4_35-6_Slovenia_revised_21dec2018_OBJAVA_ZA_WEB.pdf>

Spanish DPA, AEDP, List of the types of data processing that require a data protection impact assessment under Art 35.4, <https://www.aepd.es/media/criterios/listas-dpia-en-35-4.pdf>

UK DPA, ICO, Examples of processing 'likely to result in high risk', <https://iapp.org/media/pdf/resource_center/UK_ico_blacklist.pdf>

Academic literature

Acquisti A, 'Nudging Privacy: The Behavioral Economics of Personal Information' (2009) 7 IEEE Security & Privacy Magazine 82

Adjerid I and others, 'Sleights of Privacy: Framing, Disclosures, and the Limits of Transparency' in L Bauer and others (eds), *Proceedings of the Ninth Symposium on Usable Privacy and Security* (Association for Computing Machinery 2013) <https://doi.org/10.1145/2501604.2501613> accessed 20 January 2020, 1

Akehurst M, 'Equity and General Principles of Law' (1976) 25 International & Comparative Law Quarterly 801

Alexy R, *Theorie der Grundrechte* (Suhrkamp 2006)

Alvisi C, 'Il Consumatore Ragionevole e Le Pratiche Commerciali Sleali' (2008) 3 Contratto e impresa 700

Ananny M and Crawford K, 'Seeing without Knowing: Limitations of the Transparency Ideal and Its Application to Algorithmic Accountability' (2018) 20 New Media & Society 973

Andorno R, 'Is Vulnerability the Foundation of Human Rights?' in A Masferrer and E García-Sánchez (eds), *Human Dignity of the Vulnerable in the Age of Rights: Interdisciplinary Perspectives* (Springer International Publishing 2016)

Angwin J and Larson J, 'Bias in Criminal Risk Scores Is Mathematically Inevitable, Researchers Say' [2016] ProPublica <https://www.propublica.org/article/bias-in-criminal-risk-scores-is-mathematically-inevitable-researchers-say> accessed 2 February 2022

Angwin J and others, 'Machine Bias—There's Software Used across the Country to Predict Future Criminals. And It's Biased against Blacks' [2016] ProPublica <https://www.propublica.org/article/machine-bias-risk-assessments-in-criminal-sentencing> accessed 2 June 2019

Association for Psychological Science, 'Cognitive Bias' <https://www.psychologicalscience.org/tag/cognitive-bias> accessed 28 February 2022

Asquith NL and others (eds), *Policing Encounters with Vulnerability* (Palgrave Macmillan 2017)

Ausloos J, *The Right to Erasure in EU Data Protection Law* (Oxford University Press 2020)

Austin L, 'Enough About Me: Why Privacy Is About Power, Not Consent (or Harm)' in A Sarat (ed), *A World without Privacy: What Law Can and Should Do?* (Cambridge University Press 2014)

Bacciardi E, *Il recesso del consumatore nell'orizzonte delle scienze comportamentali* (Giappichelli 2019)

Baker SM and others, 'Building Understanding of the Domain of Consumer Vulnerability' (2005) 25(2) Journal of Macromarketing 128

Baker SM and others, 'Marketplace Experiences of Consumers with Visual Impairments: Beyond the Americans with Disabilities Act' (2001) 20 Journal of Public Policy & Marketing 215

Bar C von and others (eds), *Principles, Definitions and Model Rules of European Private Law: Draft Common Frame of Reference (DCFR)* (Oxford University Press 2010)

Barocas S, 'Data Mining and the Discourse on Discrimination' in K Jacobs and R Munro (eds), *Proceedings of the Data Ethics Workshop, Conference on Knowledge Discovery and Data Mining (KDD)* (Data Ethics 2014) <https://dataethics.github.io/proceedings/DataMiningandtheDiscourseOnDiscrimination.pdf> accessed 5 February 2023, 1–4

Barocas S and Selbst AD, 'Big Data's Disparate Impact' (2016) 104 California Law Review 671

Bartolini C and Siry L, 'The Right to Be Forgotten in the Light of the Consent of the Data Subject' (2016) 32 Computer Law & Security Review 218

Baumgärtel M, 'Facing the Challenge of Migratory Vulnerability in the European Court of Human Rights' (2020) 38(1) Netherlands Quarterly of Human Rights 12–29 <https://journals.sagepub.com/doi/10.1177/0924051919898127> accessed 26 May 2020

Beater A, *Verbraucherschutz und Schutzzweckdenken im Wettbewerbsrecht* (Mohr Siebeck 2000)

Beitz CR, *The Idea of Human Rights* (Oxford University Press 2011)

Berg M, 'Article 82 of the GDPR' in J Kühling and B Buchner (eds), *Datenschutz-Grundverordnung, Bundesdatenschutzgesetz Kommentar* (Beck 2018)

Bergemann B, 'The Consent Paradox: Accounting for the Prominent Role of Consent in Data Protection' in M Hansen and others (eds), *Privacy and Identity Management. The Smart Revolution: 12th IFIP WG 9.2, 9.5, 9.6/11.7, 11.6/SIG 9.2.2 International Summer School, Ispra, Italy, September 4–8, 2017, Revised Selected Papers* (Springer International Publishing 2018)

Bergkamp L, 'EU Data Protection Policy. The Privacy Fallacy: Adverse Effects of Europe's Data Protection Policy in an Information-Driven Economy' (2002) 18 Computer Law & Security Review 31

Bernhard Kresse, 'Article 82 of the GDPR' in G Sydow (ed), *Europaïsche Datenschutzgrundverordnung* (Nomos 2018)

Bloustein EJ, 'Privacy as an Aspect of Human Dignity: An Answer to Dean Prosser' (1964) 39 New York Law Review 962

Blume P, 'The Data Subject' (2015) 1 European Data Protection Law Review 258

Böhme R and Köpsell S, 'Trained to Accept? A Field Experiment on Consent Dialogs', *Proceedings of the SIGCHI Conference on Human Factors in Computing Systems* (Association for Computing Machinery 2010) <https://doi.org/10.1145/1753326.1753689> accessed 20 January 2020

Booth R, 'Facebook Reveals News Feed Experiment to Control Emotions' *Guardian* (29 June 2014) <https://www.theguardian.com/technology/2014/jun/29/facebook-users-emotions-news-feeds> accessed 2 June 2019

Böröcz I, 'Risk to the Right to the Protection of Personal Data: An Analysis Through the Lenses of Hermagoras' (2016) 2 European Data Protection Law Review 467

Brendan Van Alsenoy, *Data Protection Law in the EU: Roles, Responsibilities and Liability* (1st edn, Intersentia Uitgevers NV 2019)

Brenkert GG, 'Marketing and the Vulnerable' (1998) 8(S1) Business Ethics Quarterly 7

Bridges KM, *The Poverty of Privacy Rights* (Stanford University Press 2017)

Brkan M, 'Do Algorithms Rule the World? Algorithmic Decision-Making and Data Protection in the Framework of the GDPR and Beyond' (2019) 27(2) International Journal of Law and Information Technology 91–121 <https://academic.oup.com/ijlit/article/27/2/91/5288563> accessed 24 February 2022

Buitelaar JC, 'Post-Mortem Privacy and Informational Self-Determination' (2017) 19 Ethics and Information Technology 129

Burden R, *Vulnerable Consumer Groups: Quantification and Analysis* (Office of Fair Trading 1998)

Butler J, *Precarious Life: The Powers of Mourning and Violence* (Verso 2004)

Butterworth M, 'The ICO and Artificial Intelligence: The Role of Fairness in the GDPR Framework' (2018) 34 Computer Law & Security Review 257

Bygrave LA, 'Minding the Machine: Article 15 of the EC Data Protection Directive and Automated Profiling' (2001) 17 Computer Law & Security Review 17

Bygrave LA, *Data Protection Law, Approaching Its Rationale, Logic and Limits* (1st edn, Kluwer Law International 2002)

Bygrave LA, 'Article 22. Automated Individual Decision- Making, Including Profiling' in C Kuner and others (eds), *The EU General Data Protection Regulation (GDPR)—A Commentary* (Oxford University Press 2020)

Bygrave LA and Tosoni L, 'Article 4(1). Personal Data' in C Kuner and others (eds), *The EU General Data Protection Regulation (GDPR)—A Commentary* (Oxford University Press 2020)

Cadwalladr C and Graham-Harrison E, 'Revealed: 50 Million Facebook Profiles Harvested for Cambridge Analytica in Major Data Breach' *Guardian* (17 March 2018) <https://www.theguardian.com/news/2018/mar/17/cambridge-analytica-facebook-influence-us-election> accessed 17 December 2018

Calo MR, 'The Boundaries of Privacy Harm' (2011) 86 Indiana Law Journal 33

Calo MR, 'Digital Market Manipulation' (2013) 82 George Washington Law Review 995

Calo MR, 'Privacy, Vulnerability, and Affordance' (2017) 66 DePaul Law Review 591–604

Camardi C, 'La protezione dei consumatori tra diritto civile e regolazione del mercato. A proposito dei recenti interventi sul Codice del consumo' (2013) 5 Jus Civile 305–37

Cartwright P, 'Understanding and Protecting Vulnerable Financial Consumers' (2015) 38 Journal of Consumer Policy 119

Cavoukian A and others, 'The Unintended Consequences of Privacy Paternalism' (Information and Privacy Commissioner 2014) <https://collections.ola.org/mon/28003/326077.pdf> accessed 2 February 2023

Cees Van Dam, 'De Gemiddelde Euroconsument—Een Pluriform Fenomeen' (2009) 3 Tijdschrift voor Europees en economisch recht 11

Church P and others, 'Commentary on Article 15 of the Data Protection Directive' in A Bullesbach and others (eds), *Concise European IT Law* (Kluwer Law International 2010)

Citron D and Pasquale F, 'The Scored Society: Due Process for Automated Predictions' (2014) 89 Washington Law Review 1

Citron DK, 'Promoting Innovation While Preventing Discrimination: Policy Goals for the Scored Society' (2014) 89 Washington Law Review 1413

Clifford D and Ausloos J, 'Data Protection and the Role of Fairness' (2018) 37 Yearbook of European Law 130

Clifford D and others, 'Pre-Formulated Declarations of Data Subject Consent—Citizen-Consumer Empowerment and the Alignment of Data, Consumer and Competition Law Protections' (2019) 20 German Law Journal 679

Cohen J, 'What Privacy Is For' (2013) 126 Harvard Law Review 1904

Cohen JE, *Configuring the Networked Self* (Yale University Press 2012)

Cohen JE, 'Turning Privacy Inside Out' (2019) 20 Theoretical Inquiries in Law 1 <http://www7.tau.ac.il/ojs/index.php/til/article/view/1607> accessed 23 January 2019

Cole A, 'All of Us Are Vulnerable, But Some Are More Vulnerable than Others: The Political Ambiguity of Vulnerability Studies, an Ambivalent Critique' (2016) 17 Critical Horizons 260

Commuri S and Ekici A, 'An Enlargement of the Notion of Consumer Vulnerability' (2008) 28(2) Journal of Macromarketing 183 <https://journals.sagepub.com/doi/10.1177/0276146708316049> accessed 23 February 2022

Cooper FR, 'Always Already Suspect: Revising Vulnerability Theory' (2014) 93 North Carolina Law Review 43

Cordeiro ABM, 'Civil Liability for Processing of Personal Data in the GDPR' (2019) 5 European Data Protection Law Review 492

Costanza-Chock S, 'Design Justice: Towards an Intersectional Feminist Framework for Design Theory and Practice' in C Storni and others (eds), *Design as a catalyst for change—DRS International Conference 2018*, 25–28 (DRS Digital Library 2018) <https://doi.org/10.21606/drs.2018.679> accessed 9 February 2023

Custers B and others, 'Consent and Privacy' in P Schaber and A Müller (eds) *The Routledge Handbook of the Ethics of Consent* (Routledge 2018) 247

Davola A, 'The Death of Traditional Consumer Law at the Crossroads of Law, Economics and Cognitive Sciences: A Tentative Reaction' (Doctoral thesis, Sant'Anna School of Advanced Studies of Pisa 2019)

De Cristofaro G, 'Art. 20 Codice Del Consumo' in G De Cristofaro and A Zaccaria (eds), *Commentario breve al diritto dei consumatori (Codice del consumo e legislazione complementare)* (Cedam 2014)

De Hert P and Gutwirth S, 'Privacy, Data Protection and Law Enforcement. Opacity of the Individual and Transparency of Power' in E Claes and others (eds), *Privacy and the Criminal Law* (Intersentia 2006) de Montjoye Y-A and others, 'Cambridge Analytica Is Only the Beginning and You Might Have Your Friends to Blame for It', *Computational Privacy Group* (20 March 2018) <https://cpg.doc.ic.ac.uk/blog/cambridge-analytica-is-only-the-beginning> accessed 2 February 2023

Delacroix S and Lawrence ND, 'Bottom-up Data Trusts: Disturbing the 'One Size Fits All' Approach to Data Governance' (2019) 9(4) International Data Privacy Law 236

Demetzou K, 'GDPR and the Concept of Risk' in E Kosta and others (eds), *Privacy and Identity Management. Fairness, Accountability, and Transparency in the Age of Big Data: 13th IFIP WG 9.2, 9.6/11.7, 11.6/SIG 9.2.2 International Summer School, Vienna, Austria, August 20–24, 2018, Revised Selected Papers* (Springer International Publishing 2019)

Demetzou K, 'Data Protection Impact Assessment: A Tool for Accountability and the Unclarified Concept of 'High Risk' in the General Data Protection Regulation' (2019) 35 Computer Law & Security Review 105342

Douglas T, 'Biased Algorithms: Here's a More Radical Approach to Creating Fairness', *The Conversation* (21 January 2019) <http://theconversation.com/biased-algorithms-heres-a-more-radical-approach-to-creating-fairness-109748> accessed 22 January 2019

Ducato R and Marique E, 'Come to the Dark Side: We Have Patterns. Choice Architecture and Design for (Un)Informed Consent' (Social Science Research Network 2018) SSRN Scholarly Paper ID 3365952 <https://papers.ssrn.com/abstract=3365952> accessed 31 May 2020

Duivenvoorde BB, *The Consumer Benchmarks in the Unfair Commercial Practices Directive* (Springer International Publishing 2015)

Edwards L and Harbinja E, 'Protecting Post-Mortem Privacy: Reconsidering the Privacy Interests of the Deceased in a Digital World' (2013) 32 Cardozo Arts & Entertainment Law Journal 101

Edwards L and Veale M, 'Slave to the Algorithm? Why a "Right to an Explanation" Is Probably Not the Remedy You Are Looking For' (2017) 16 Duke Law & Technology Review 18

Eskytė I, 'Disabled People's Vulnerability in the European Single Market: The Case of Consumer Information' (2019) 42 Journal of Consumer Policy 521

Eubanks V, *Automating Inequality: How High-Tech Tools Profile, Police, and Punish the Poor* (St Martin's Press 2018)

European Commission, 'Consumer Vulnerability across Key Markets in the European Union' (2016) <https://ec.europa.eu/info/sites/info/files/consumers-approved-report_en.pdf>

European Network and Information Security Agency, *Guidelines for SMEs on the Security of Personal Data Processing* (ENISA 2016)

Faden RR and others, *A History and Theory of Informed Consent* (Oxford University Press 1986)

Falco G, *La buona fede e l'abuso del diritto: principi, fattispecie e casistica* (Giuffrè Editore 2010)

Fineman MA, 'The Vulnerable Subject: Anchoring Equality in the Human Condition' (2016) 20 Yale Journal of Law & Feminism 1 <https://digitalcommons.law.yale.edu/yjlf/vol20/iss1/2>

Fineman MA, 'The Vulnerable Subject: Anchoring Equality in the Human Condition' (2008) 20 Yale Journal of Law and Feminism 23

Fineman MA, 'Beyond Identities: The Limits of an Antidiscrimination Approach to Equality' (2012) 92 Boston University Law Review, 59

Fineman MA, 'Vulnerability and Social Justice' (2019) 53 Valparaiso University Law Review 341

Flegar V and Iedema E, 'The Use of the "Vulnerability" Label by the Committee on the Elimination of Discrimination Against Women: Protecting or Stigmatizing Women and Girls in the Forced Migration Context?' (2019) Brill Open Law <https://brill.com/view/journals/bol/aop/article-10.1163-23527072-20191021/article-10.1163-23527072-20191021.xml> accessed 20 February 2023

Floridi L, 'On Human Dignity as a Foundation for the Right to Privacy' (2016) 29 Philosophy & Technology 307

Fortuna-Zanfir G, 'Forgetting about Consent. Why the Focus Should Be on "Suitable Safeguards" in Data Protection Law' in S Gutwirth and others (ed), *Reloading Data Protection* (Springer 2014)

Foucault M and others, *Microfisica del potere. Interventi politici* (Einaudi 1977)

Frantziou E, 'Further Developments in the Right to Be Forgotten: The European Court of Justice's Judgment in Case C-131/12, Google Spain, SL, Google Inc v Agencia Espanola de Proteccion de Datos Recent Developments' (2014) 14 Human Rights Law Review 761

Fuster GG, *The Emergence of Personal Data Protection as a Fundamental Right of the EU* (Springer International Publishing 2014)

Future of Privacy Forum, 'Unfairness by Algorithm: Distilling the Harms of Automated Decision-Making' (2017) <https://fpf.org/2017/12/11/unfairness-by-algorithm-distilling-the-harms-of-automated-decision-making/> accessed 8 February 2020

Galhotra S and others, 'Fairness Testing: Testing Software for Discrimination', *Proceedings of the 2017 11th Joint Meeting on Foundations of Software Engineering—ESEC/FSE 2017* (ACM Press 2017)

Gandy OH, 'It's Discrimination, Stupid!' in J Brook (ed), *Resisting the Virtual Life: The Culture and Politics of Information* (City Lights Books 1995) 35

Garner BA (ed), *Black's Law Dictionary* (Thomson Reuters 2019)

Gellert R, 'Data Protection: A Risk Regulation? Between the Risk Management of Everything and the Precautionary Alternative' (2015) 5 International Data Privacy Law 3

Gellert R, 'We Have Always Managed Risks in Data Protection Law: Understanding the Similarities and Differences between the Rights-Based and the Risk-Based Approaches to Data Protection' (2016) 2 European Data Protection Law Review (EDPL) 481

Gellert R, 'On Risk, Balancing, and Data Protection: A Response to van Der Sloot' (2017) 2 EDPL 180

Gellert R, *The Risk-Based Approach to Data Protection* (Oxford University Press 2020)

Gellert R, 'Understanding the Notion of Risk in the General Data Protection Regulation' (2018) 34 Computer Law and Security Review 279

Gellert R, 'A Comparative Analysis of Anti-Discrimination and Data Protection Legislations' in Bart Custers and others (eds), *Discrimination and Privacy in the Information Society: Data Mining and Profiling in Large Databases* (Springer 2013)

Gennet É and others, 'Does the New EU Regulation on Clinical Trials Adequately Protect Vulnerable Research Participants?' (2015) 119 Health Policy (Amsterdam, Netherlands) 925

Gilliom J, *Overseers of the Poor: Surveillance, Resistance and the Limits of Privacy* (University of Chicago Press 2001)

Gilman ME, 'The Class Differential in Privacy Law' (2012) 77 Brooklyn Law Review 1389

Gilman ME and Green R, 'The Surveillance Gap: The Harms of Extreme Privacy and Data Marginalization' (2018) 42 Social Change 55

Gilson E, *The Ethics of Vulnerability: A Feminist Analysis of Social Life and Practice* (1 edition, Routledge 2014)

González Fuster G, 'How Uninformed Is the Average Data Subject? A Quest for Benchmarks in EU Personal Data Protection' (2014) 19 IDP Revista de Internet, Derecho y Política 92

González Fuster G, 'Inaccuracy as a privacy-enhancing tool' (2010) 12 Ethics and Information Technology 87

González Fuster G, *The Emergence of Personal Data Protection as a Fundamental Right of the EU* (Springer 2012)

González Fuster G and Paepe P, 'Reflexive Governance and the EU Third Pillar: Analysis of Data Protection and Criminal Law Aspects' in E Guild and F Geyer (eds), *Security versus Justice? Police and Judicial Cooperation in the European Union* (Ashgate 2008) 129

Goodin RE, *Protecting the Vulnerable: A Reanalysis of Our Social Responsibilities* (University of Chicago Press 1985)

Graef I and others, 'Fairness and Enforcement: Bridging Competition, Data Protection, and Consumer Law' (2018) 8 International Data Privacy Law 200

Gray CM and others, 'The Dark (Patterns) Side of UX Design' in R Mandryk and others (eds) *Proceedings of the 2018 CHI Conference on Human Factors in Computing Systems* (ACM 2018) Paper No 534, 1

Guerinoni E, *Pratiche commerciali scorrette. Fattispecie e rimedi* (Giuffrè 2010)

Gutiérrez Santiago P, 'La Llamada "Personalidad Pretérita": Datos Personales de Las Personas Fallecidas y Protección Post Mortem de Los Derechos al Honor, Intimidad y Propia Imagen' (2016) 5(1) 201–38

Harbinja E, 'Post-Mortem Privacy 2.0: Theory, Law, and Technology' (2017) 31 International Review of Law, Computers & Technology 26

Hart HLA, *Essays on Bentham: Jurisprudence and Political Philosophy* (Oxford University Press 1982)

Haselton MG and others, 'The Evolution of Cognitive Bias' in DM Buss (ed), *The Handbook of Evolutionary Psychology* (John Wiley & Sons, Inc 2015)

Helberger N and others, *EU Consumer Protection 2.0—Structural Asymmetries in Digital Consumer Markets, A joint report from research conducted under the EUCP2.0 project* (BEUC 2021) <https://www.beuc.eu/publications/beuc-x-2021-018_eu_consumer_protection.0_0.pdf> accessed 5 February 2022

Helberger N and others, 'The Perfect Match? A Closer Look at the Relationship between Eu Consumer Law and Data Protection Law' (2017) 54 Common Market Law Review 1427

Herring J, *Vulnerable Adults and the Law* (Oxford Univeristy Press 2016)

Herring J, *Law and the Relational Self* (Oxford University Press 2019)

Hewer RM, 'A Gossamer Consensus: Discourses of Vulnerability in the Westminster Prostitution Policy Subsystem' (2019) 28 Social & Legal Studies 227

Hildebrandt M, 'The Dawn of a Critical Transparency Right for the Profiling Era' in J Bus (ed), *Digital Enlightenment Yearbook* (IOS Press 2012)

Hildebrandt M, 'The Issue of Bias: The Framing Powers of ML' in M Pelillo (ed), *Machine Learning and Society: Impact, Trust, Transparency* (MIT Press 2020)

Hildebrandt M, *Law for Computer Scientists and Other Folk* (Oxford University Press 2020)

Howells G and others, *European Fair Trading Law: The Unfair Commercial Practices Directive* (1st edn, Routledge 2006)

Howells GG and others, *Rethinking EU Consumer Law* (Routledge 2018)

Huwiler B, 'Aequitas and Bona Fides Als Faktoren Der Rechtsverwirklichung. Zur Gesetzgebungsgeschichte Des Rechtsmissbrauchsverbotes (Art. 2 Abs. 2 ZGB)' in B

Schmidlin (ed), *Vers un droit privé européen commun? Skizzen zum gemeineuropäischen Privatrecht, Beiheft zur Zeitchrift für Schweizerisches Recht* (Heft 1994) 57

Incardona R and Poncibò C, 'The Average Consumer, the Unfair Commercial Practices Directive, and the Cognitive Revolution' (2007) 30 Journal of Consumer Policy 21

Information Commissioner Officer (ICO), *Children and the GDPR* (22 March 2018) <https://ico.org.uk/media/for-organisations/guide-to-data-protection/guide-to-the-general-data-protection-regulation-gdpr/children-and-the-uk-gdpr-1-0.pdf/> accessed 28 March 2022

Ippolito F, '(De)Constructing Children's Vulnerability under European Law' in F Ippolito and SI Sanchez (eds), *Protecting Vulnerable Groups* (Hart Publishing 2015) 23–48

Ippolito F and Sánchez SI, *Protecting Vulnerable Groups: The European Human Rights Framework* (Bloomsbury Publishing 2015)

Jackson L and others, 'Including Vulnerable Populations in the Assessment of Data From Vulnerable Populations' (2019) 2 Frontiers in Big Data 19

Janeček V and Malgieri G, 'Commerce in Data and the Dynamically Limited Alienability Rule' (2020) 21(5) German Law Journal 924

Janssen HL, 'An Approach for a Fundamental Rights Impact Assessment to Automated Decision-Making' (2020) 10(1) International Data Privacy Law 76

Jasmontaite L and others, 'Data Protection by Design and by Default' (2018) 4 European Data Protection Law Review 168

Jasmontaite L and De Hert P, 'The EU, Children under 13 Years, and Parental Consent: A Human Rights Analysis of a New, Age-Based Bright-Line for the Protection of Children on the Internet' (2014) 5 International Data Privacy Law 20

Johannes Stroux, *Summum Ius Summa Iniuria. Ein Kapitel Aus Der Geschichte Der Interpretation Iuris* (Teubner 1946)

Kahneman D, 'A Perspective on Judgment and Choice: Mapping Bounded Rationality' (2003) 58 The American Psychologist 697

Kamara I and De Hert P, 'Understanding the Balancing Act behind the Legitimate Interest of the Controller Ground: A Pragmatic Approach' in E Selinger and others (eds), *The Cambridge Handbook of Consumer Privacy* (1st edn, Cambridge University Press 2018)

Kaminski ME, 'Binary Governance: Lessons from the GDPR's Approach to Algorithmic Accountability' (2019) 92 Southern California Law Review 1529

Kaminski ME and Malgieri G, 'Algorithmic Impact Assessments under the GDPR: Producing Multi-Layered Explanations' (2021) 11(2) International Data Privacy Law 125

Kaminski ME and Malgieri G, 'Multi-Layered Explanations from Algorithmic Impact Assessments in the GDPR' in M Hildebrandt and others (eds), *Proceedings of the 2020 Conference on Fairness, Accountability, and Transparency* (Association for Computing Machinery 2020) 1 <https://doi.org/10.1145/3351095.3372875> accessed 29 January 2020

Kammourieh L and others, 'Group Privacy in the Age of Big Data' in L Taylor and others (eds), *Group Privacy: New Challenges of Data Technologies* (Springer International Publishing 2017)

Kerber W, 'Digital Markets, Data, and Privacy: Competition Law, Consumer Law and Data Protection' (2016) 11 Journal of Intellectual Property Law & Practice 856

Ladeur K.-H., 'Datenschutz—Vom Abwehrrecht Zur Planerischen Optimierung von Wissensnetzwerken. Zur "Objektiv-Rechtlichen Dimension" Des Datenschutzes' (2000) 24 Datenschutz Datensicherheit DuD 12

Kloza D and others, 'Data Protection Impact Assessments in the European Union: Complementing the New Legal Framework towards a More Robust Protection of

Individuals' (2017) d.pia.lab Policy Brief 1/2017 <https://cris.vub.be/files/32009890/dpialab_pb2017_1_final.pdf> accessed 5 February 2023

Kloza D and others, 'Towards a Method for Data Protection Impact Assessment: Making Sense of GDPR Requirements'(2019) d.pia.lab Policy Brief No. 1/2019 <https://cris.vub.be/ws/portalfiles/portal/48091346/dpialab_pb2019_1_final.pdf%20accessed.5> accessed 5 February 2023

Koops B-J, 'The Trouble with European Data Protection Law' (2014) 4 International Data Privacy Law 250

Kramer ADI and others, 'Experimental Evidence of Massive-Scale Emotional Contagion through Social Networks' (2014) 111 Proceedings of the National Academy of Sciences 8788

Laczniak GR and Murphy PE, *Ethical Marketing Decisions: The Higher Road* (Facsimile edition, Pearson 1992)

Lamond G, 'Precedent and Analogy in Legal Reasoning' in EN Zalta (ed), *The Stanford Encyclopedia of Philosophy* (Spring 2016, Metaphysics Research Lab, Stanford University 2016) <https://plato.stanford.edu/archives/spr2016/entries/legal-reas-prec/> accessed 8 April 2020

Langenbucher K, 'Argument by Analogy In European Law' (1998) 57 The Cambridge Law Journal 481

Lepri B and others, 'Fair, Transparent, and Accountable Algorithmic Decision-Making Processes' (2018) 31 Philosophy & Technology 611

Lievens E and Verdoodt V, 'Looking for Needles in a Haystack: Key Issues Affecting Children's Rights in the General Data Protection Regulation' (2018) 34 Computer Law & Security Review 269

Luhmann N, *Macht* (4th edn, UTB/UVK 2012)

Luna F, 'Elucidating the Concept of Vulnerability: Layers Not Labels' (2009) 2 International Journal of Feminist Approaches to Bioethics 121

Luna F, 'Identifying and Evaluating Layers of Vulnerability—A Way Forward' (2019) 19 Developing World Bioethics 86

Lunn P and Lyons S, 'Behavioural Economics and "Vulnerable Consumers": A Summary of Evidence' (2010) Communications Consumer Panel 1 <https://www.esri.ie/system/files?file=media/file-uploads/2015-07/BKMNEXT180.pdf> accessed 5 February 2023

Luño AEP, *Derechos humanos, Estado de Derecho y Constitución* (Tecnos 2010)

Lynskey O, *The Foundations of EU Data Protection Law* (Oxford University Press 2015)

Macenaite M, 'The "Riskification" of European Data Protection Law through a Two-Fold Shift' (2017) 8 European Journal of Risk Regulation 506

Mackenzie C and others, 'Introduction: What Is Vulnerability, and Why Does It Matter for Moral Theory?' *Vulnerability* (Oxford University Press 2013)

Mackenzie C and others (eds), *Vulnerability: New Essays in Ethics and Feminist Philosophy* (1st edn, Oxford University Press 2013)

Madden M and others, 'Privacy, Poverty and Big Data: A Matrix of Vulnerabilities for Poor Americans' (2017) 95 Washington University Law Review 53

Mahieu R and others, 'Responsibility for Data Protection in a Networked World: On the Question of the Controller, "Effective and Complete Protection" and Its Application to Data Access Rights in Europe' (2019) 10 Journal of Intellectual Property, Information Technology and Electronic Commerce Law 39

Mak V, 'Standards of Protection: In Search of the "Average Consumer" of EU Law in the Proposal for a Consumer Rights Directive' (2011) 19 European Review of Private Law 25

Malgieri G, 'Trade Secrets v Personal Data: A Possible Solution for Balancing Rights' (2016) 6 International Data Privacy Law 102

Malgieri G, '"User-Provided Personal Content" in the EU: Digital Currency between Data Protection and Intellectual Property' (2018) 32(1) International Review of Law, Computers & Technology 118

Malgieri G, 'R.I.P.: Rest in Privacy or Rest in (Quasi-)Property? Personal Data Protection of Deceased Data Subjects between Theoretical Scenarios and National Solutions' in R Leenes and others (eds), *Data Protection and Privacy: The Internet of Bodies* (Hart Publishing 2018) 300

Malgieri G, 'Automated Decision-Making in the EU Member States: The Right to Explanation and Other "Suitable Safeguards" in the National Legislations' (2019) 35(5) Computer Law & Security Review 105327

Malgieri G, 'The Concept of Fairness in the GDPR: A Linguistic and Contextual Interpretation' in M Hildebrandt and others (eds), *Proceedings of the 2020 Conference on Fairness, Accountability, and Transparency* (Association for Computing Machinery 2020) 1 <https://doi.org/10.1145/3351095.3372868> accessed 29 January 2020

Malgieri G, 'In/Acceptable Marketing and Consumers' Privacy Expectations: Four Tests from EU Data Protection Law' (2023) 40(2) Journal of Consumer Marketing 209 <https://doi.org/10.1108/JCM-03-2021-4571> accessed 2 January 2023

Malgieri G and Comandé G, 'Sensitive-by-Distance: Quasi-Health Data in the Algorithmic Era' (2017) 26 Information & Communications Technology Law 229

Malgieri G and Comandé G, 'Why a Right to Legibility of Automated Decision-Making Exists in the General Data Protection Regulation' (2017) 7 International Data Privacy Law 243

Malgieri G and González Fuster G, 'The Vulnerable Data Subject: A Gendered Data Subject?' (2022) 13(2) European Journal of Law and Technology 1 <https://www.ejlt.org/index.php/ejlt/article/view/843> accessed 29 September 2022

Malgieri G and Niklas J, 'Vulnerable Data Subjects' (2020) 37 Computer Law & Security Review 105415

Mantelero A, 'Children Online and the Future EU Data Protection Framework: Empirical Evidences and Legal Analysis' (2016) 2 International Journal of Technology Policy and Law 169

Rölli M, 'Vorüberlegungen Zu Einer Philosophie Der Privaten Macht—Im Ausgang von Einigen Allgemeinen Bemerkungen Zum Philosophischen Stand Der Machttheorie' in F Möslein (ed), *Private Macht* (Mohr Siebeck 2016) 83

Martini M, 'DS-GVO Art. 22 Automatisierte Entscheidungen Im Einzelfall Einschließlich Profiling' in BP Paal and D Pauly (eds), *Datenschutz-Grundverordnung* (Beck-online 2017)

Matz SC and others, 'Psychological Targeting as an Effective Approach to Digital Mass Persuasion' (2017) 114(48) Proceedings of the National Academy of Sciences of the United States of America 12714

Mayr CE, 'Il Parametro Del Consumatore' (2008) 17 AIDA 274

Mccullagh K, 'Data Sensitivity: Proposals for Resolving the Conundrum' (2007) 2(4) Journal of International Commercial Law and Technology 190

Meli VM, 'Pratiche Commerciali Scorrette' (2012) Diritto on line, Treccani <https://www.treccani.it/enciclopedia/pratiche-commerciali-scorrette_(Diritto-on-line)/> accessed 5 February 2023.

Metcalf J, '"The Study Has Been Approved by the IRB": Gayface AI, Research Hype and the Pervasive Data Ethics Gap', *Medium* (30 November 2017) <https://medium.com/perv

ade-team/the-study-has-been-approved-by-the-irb-gayface-ai-research-hype-and-the-pervasive-data-ethics-ed76171b882c> accessed 19 October 2022

Micklitz H-W, 'Unfair Commercial Practices and Misleading Advertising' in N Reich and others (eds), *European Consumer Law* (Intersentia 2014)

Minor J, 'Consumer Protection in the EU: Searching for the Real Consumer' (2012) 13 European Business Organization Law Review (EBOR) 163

Moerel EML and others, *Homo digitalis* (Wolters Kluwer 2016)

Montgomery KC and Chester J, 'Data Protection for Youth in the Digital Age: Developing a Rights-Based Global Framework' (2015) 1 European Data Protection Law Review 277

Moran M, *Are Objective Standards Worth Saving? Exploring the Feminist Debate* (Oxford University Press 2003)

Morgan FW, and others, 'A Framework for Examining the Legal Status of Vulnerable Consumers' (1995) 14 Journal of Public Policy & Marketing 267

Moritz R, 'Machtbegriffe Zwischen Privatrecht und Gesellschaftstheorie' in F Möslein (ed), *Private Macht* (Mohr Siebeck 2016) 505

Mortier R and others, 'Human-Data Interaction: The Human Face of the Data-Driven Society' (2014) arXiv:1412.6159 [cs] <http://arxiv.org/abs/1412.6159> accessed 21 October 2022

Mourali M and Nagpal A, 'The Powerful Select, the Powerless Reject: Power's Influence in Decision Strategies' (2013) 66 Journal of Business Research 874

Mulder J, 'Comparing Vulnerability? How Can EU Comparative Law Methods Shed Light on the Concept of the Vulnerable Consumer' (2019) 6 Journal of International and Comparative Law 209

Naffine N, *Law and the Sexes: Explorations in Feminist Jurisprudence* (Allen & Unwin 1990)

Nemitz P, 'EU-DSGVO Art. 82 Haftung und Recht auf Schadenersatz' in E Ehmann and M Selmayr (eds), *Datenschutz-Grundverordnung Kommentar* (Beck 2017)

Nissenbaum H, 'Privacy as Contextual Integrity' (2004) 79 Washington Law Review 39

Nótári T, 'Summum Ius Summa Iniuria—Comments on the Historical Background of a Legal Maxim of Interpretation' (2005) 45 Acta Juridica Hungarica 301

Noto La Diega G, 'Can the Law Fix the Problems of Fashion? An Empirical Study on Social Norms and Power Imbalance in the Fashion Industry' (2019) 14(1) Journal of Intellectual Property Law & Practice 18–24

Nussbaum MC, *Frontiers of Justice: Disability, Nationality, Species Membership* (Harvard University Press 2006)

Oddný Mjöll A, 'Vulnerability under Article 14 of the European Convention on Human Rights' (2017) 4 Oslo Law Review 150

Oostveen M and Irion K, 'The Golden Age of Personal Data: How to Regulate an Enabling Fundamental Right?' in M Bakhoum and others (eds), *Personal Data in Competition, Consumer Protection and Intellectual Property Law: Towards a Holistic Approach?* (Springer 2018)

Pasquale F, *The Black Box Society: The Secret Algorithms That Control Money and Information* (Harvard University Press 2015)

Pasquale F, *The Black Box Society: The Secret Algorithms That Control Money and Information* (Harvard University Press 2015)

Peroni L and Timmer A, 'Vulnerable Groups: The Promise of an Emerging Concept in European Human Rights Convention Law' (2013) 11 International Journal of Constitutional Law 1056

Picod Y, *Le devoir de loyauté dans l'exécution du contrat* (Librairie générale de droit et de jurisprudence 1989)

Pollach I, 'What's Wrong with Online Privacy Policies?' (2007) 50 Communications of the ACM 103

Poncibò C, 'Il Consumatore Medio' (2007) 2 Contratto e impresa Europa 734

Povel F, 'Perceived Vulnerability to Downside Risk' (2010) Discussion Papers, No 43, Georg-August-Universität Göttingen, Courant Research Centre—Poverty, Equity and Growth (CRC-PEG), Göttingen <https://econpapers.repec.org/paper/gotgotcrc/043.htm> accessed 23 February 2022

Powels J, 'The Seductive Diversion of "Solving" Bias in Artificial Intelligence' (2018) <https://medium.com/s/story/the-seductive-diversion-of-solving-bias-in-artificial-intelligence-890df5e5ef53> accessed 6 May 2022

Purtova N, 'Illusion of Personal Data as No One's Property' (2015) 7(1) Law, Innovation and Technology 83

Purtova N, 'Default Entitlements in Personal Data in the Proposed Regulation: Informational Self-Determination Off the Table ... and Back On Again?' (2014) 30 Computer Law & Security Review 6

Purtova N, 'The Law of Everything. Broad Concept of Personal Data and Future of EU Data Protection Law' (2018) 10 Law, Innovation and Technology 40

Quelle C, 'Not Just User Control in the General Data Protection Regulation. On the Problems with Choice and Paternalism, and on the Point of Data Protection' in A Lehmann and others (eds), *Privacy and Identity Management. Facing up to Next Steps, 11th IFIP International Summer School* (Springer International Publishing 2017)

Quelle C, 'The "Risk Revolution" in EU Data Protection Law: We Can't Have Our Cake and Eat It, Too' in R Leenes and others (eds), *Data Protection and Privacy: The Age of Intelligent Machines* (Hart Publishing 2017)

Quinn P, *Stigma, State Expressions and the Law: Implications of Freedom of Speech* (1st edn, Routledge 2019)

Quinn P and Malgieri G, 'The Difficulty of Defining Sensitive Data—The Concept of Sensitive Data in the EU Data Protection Framework' (2021) 22 German Law Journal 1583

Raiser L, 'Bürgerliches Recht' (1951) 6 Juristen Zeitung 716

Ramamurthy KN and others, 'Model Agnostic Multilevel Explanations' in H Larochelle and others (eds) *Proceedings of the 34th International Conference on Neural Information Processing Systems (NIPS'20)* (Curran Associates Inc. 2020) Article 501, 5968–79

Reisman D and others, *Algorithm Impact Assessment: A Practical Frameworks for Public Agency Accountability* (AI Now Institute 2018)

Reyna A, 'The Psychology of Privacy—What Can Behavioural Economics Contribute to Competition in Digital Markets?' (2018) 8 International Data Privacy Law 240

Richter H, 'The Power Paradigm in Private Law' in M Bakhoum and others (eds), *Personal Data in Competition, Consumer Protection and Intellectual Property Law: Towards a Holistic Approach?* (Springer Berlin Heidelberg 2018)

Rittenburg TL and Parthasarathy M, 'Ethical Implications of Target Market Selection' (1997) 17(2) Journal of Macromarketing 49

Robert R and Smit L, 'The Proposal for a Directive on Digital Content: A Complex Relationship with Data Protection Law' (2018) 19 ERA Forum 159

Rogers W and others, 'Why Bioethics Needs a Concept of Vulnerability' (2012) 5 International Journal of Feminist Approaches to Bioethics 11

Roig A, 'Safeguards for the Right Not to Be Subject to a Decision Based Solely on Automated Processing (Article 22 GDPR)' (2017) 8(3) European Journal of Law and Technology 1 <https://ejlt.org/index.php/ejlt/article/view/570> accessed 8 February 2023

Rösler H, 'Protection of the Weaker Party in European Contract Law—Standardised and Individual Inferiority in Multi-Level Private Law Schutz Des Schwächeren im Europäischen Vertragsrecht Typisierte and Individ' (2009) 73 Rabels Zeitschrift für ausländisches und internationales Privatrecht (RabelsZ) 889

Rossi A and Lenzini G, 'Transparency by Design in Data-Informed Research: A Collection of Information Design Patterns' (2020) 37 Computer Law & Security Review 105402

Rossi Carleo L, 'Consumatore, consumatore medio, investitore e cliente: frazionamento e sintesi nella disciplina delle pratiche commerciali scorrette' (2010) 3 Europa e Diritto privato 685

Rouvroy A, 'The End(s) of Critique: Data Behaviourism versus Due Process' in K de Vries and M Hildebrandt (eds), *Privacy, Due Process and the Computational Turn* (Routledge 2013)

Rouvroy A and Poullet Y, 'The Right to Informational Self-Determination and the Value of Self-Development: Reassessing the Importance of Privacy for Democracy' in S Gutwirth and others (eds), *Reinventing Data Protection?* (Springer 2009)

Sajfert J and Quintel T, 'Data Protection Directive (EU) 2016/680 for Police and Criminal Justice Authorities' in M Cole and F Boehm (eds), *Commentary on the General Data Protection Regulation* (Edward Elgar forthcoming) <https://ssrn.com/abstract=3285 873> accessed 5 February 2023

Sax M, *Between Empowerment and Manipulation: The Ethics and Regulation of For-profit Health Apps* (Kluwer Law International 2021)

Schermer BW and others, 'The Crisis of Consent: How Stronger Legal Protection May Lead to Weaker Consent in Data Protection' (2014) 16 Ethics and Information Technology 171

Schroeder D and Gefenas E, 'Vulnerability: Too Vague and Too Broad?' (2009) 18 Cambridge Quarterly of Healthcare Ethics 113

Schweitzer H, 'Wettbewerbsrecht und Das Problem Privater Macht' in F Möslein (ed), *Private Macht* (Mohr Siebeck 2016) 447

Selbst AD, 'Disparate Impact in Big Data Policing' (2018) 52 Georgia Law Review 109

Selbst AD and Powles J, 'Meaningful Information and the Right to Explanation' (2017) 7 International Data Privacy Law 233

Shultz C and Holbrook M, 'The Paradoxical Relationship between Marketing and Vulnerability' (2009) 28 Journal of Public Policy & Marketing 124

S Simitis, *Revisiting Sensitive Data, Review of the answers to the Questionnaire of the Consultative Committee of the Convention for the Protection of Individuals with regard to Automatic Processing of Personal Data* (ETS 108) (Strasbourg, 24–26 November 1999), Council of Europe study <https://rm.coe.int/16806845af> accessed 23 January 2023

Siry L, 'Forget Me, Forget Me Not: Reconciling Two Different Paradigms of the Right to Be Forgotten' (2014) 103 Kentucky Law Journal 311

Sloot B van der, 'Editorial' (2017) 3 European Data Protection Law Review 1

Smith NC and Cooper-Martin E, 'Ethics and Target Marketing: The Role of Product Harm and Consumer Vulnerability' (1997) 61(3) Journal of Marketing 1

Solove DJ, 'Privacy and Power: Computer Databases and Metaphors for Information Privacy' (2001) 53 Stanford Law Review 1393

Solove DJ, 'Privacy Self-Management and the Consent Dilemma' (2013) 126 Harvard Law Review 1880

Stearn J, 'Tackling Consumer Vulnerability an Action Plan for Empowerment' (2012) <https://www.bl.uk/collection-items/tackling-consumer-vulnerability-an-action-plan-for-empowerment> accessed 23 February 2020

Stein P, 'Equitable Principles in Roman Law' in RA Newman (ed), *Equity in the World's Legal Systems: A Comparative Study, Dedicated to René Cassin* (Établissements Émile Bruylant 1973)

Stoilova M and others, 'Children's Data and Privacy Online' (London School of Economics and Political Science 2019)

Stuyck J and others, 'Confidence through Fairness; The New Directive on Unfair Business-to-Consumer Commercial Practices in the Internal Market' (2006) 43 Common Market Law Review 107

Stuyck JHV, 'The Notion of the Empowered and Informed Consumer in Consumer Policy and How to Protect the Vulnerable under Such a Regime' in G Howells and others (eds), *The Yearbook of Consumer Law 2007* (Routledge 2007)167

Susser D and others, 'Online Manipulation: Hidden Influences in a Digital World' (2019) 4 (1) Georgetown Law Technology Review 1

Taylor L, 'Safety in Numbers? Group Privacy and Big Data Analytics in the Developing World' in L Taylor and others (eds), *Group Privacy: New Challenges of Data Technologies* (Springer International Publishing 2017)

Taylor L and others, 'Introduction: A New Perspective on Privacy' in L Taylor and others (eds), *Group Privacy: New Challenges of Data Technologies* (Springer International Publishing 2017)

Thaler RH, 'The Psychology of Choice and the Assumptions of Economics' in AE Roth (ed), *Laboratory Experimentation in Economics: Six Points of View* (Cambridge University Press 2005)

Thaler RH and Sunstein CR, 'Libertarian Paternalism' (2003) 93 American Economic Review 175

Thomas O, 'Two Decades of Cognitive Bias Research in Entrepreneurship: What Do We Know and Where Do We Go from Here?' (2018) 68 Management Review Quarterly 107

Thomas Wilhelmsson, 'The Informed Consumer v the Vulnerable Consumer in European Unfair Commercial Practices Law—A Comment' in G Howells and others (eds), *The Yearbook of Consumer Law 2007* (Routledge 2007)

Thouvenin F, 'Informational Self-Determination: A Convincing Rationale for Data Protection Law?' (2021) 12 Journal of Intellectual Property, Information Technology and Electronic Commerce Law 246

Tosoni L, 'Article 4(22). Supervisory Authority Concerned' in C Kuner and others (eds), *The EU General Data Protection Regulation (GDPR)—A Commentary* (Oxford University Press 2020)

Tosoni L, 'Article 4(23). Cross-Border Processing' in C Kuner and others (eds), *The EU General Data Protection Regulation (GDPR)—A Commentary* (Oxford University Press 2020)

Trites A, 'Black Box Ethics: Why the Rights to Explanation and to Be Forgotten Are Ethically Critical Components for Vulnerable Populations' (Master Thesis, Université Saint-Paul/ Saint Paul University 2019) <http://ruor.uottawa.ca/handle/10393/39126> accessed 10 May 2022

Trzaskowski J, 'Behavioural Economics, Neuroscience, and the Unfair Commercial Practises Directive' (2011) 34 Journal of Consumer Policy 377

Turner BS, *Vulnerability and Human Rights* (Pennsylvania State University Press 2006)

Tzoulia E, 'Imprints of Behavioural Research in EU Consumer Protection Legislation: The 'Average Consumer Test' in the Unfair Commercial Practices Directive' (2017) 6 Tijdschrift voor Consumentenrecht en handelspraktijken (TvC) 257 van der Hof S and Lievens E, 'The Importance of Privacy by Design and Data Protection Impact Assessments in Strengthening Protection of Children's Personal Data under the GDPR' (2018) 23 Communications Law 33

van der Hof S., 'I Agree… Or Do I? A Rights-Based Analysis of the Law on Children's Consent in the Digital World' (2017) 34 Wisconsin International Law Journal 409

van der Sloot B, 'Privacy as Human Flourishing: Could a Shift towards Virtue Ethics Strengthen Privacy Protection in the Age of Big Data?' (2014) 5 Journal of Intellectual Property, Information Technology and Electronic Commerce Law 230

van der Sloot B, 'Ten Questions about Balancing' (2017) 3 European Data Protection Law Review 187

van Dijk N, Gellert R and Rommetveit K, 'A Risk to a Right? Beyond Data Protection Risk Assessments' (2016) 32 Computer Law & Security Review 286

van Hoboken J, 'The Privacy Disconnect' in RF Jørgensen (ed), *Human Rights in the Age of Platforms* (MIT Press 2019)

Varney E, 'Redefining Contractual Capacity? The UN Convention on the Rights of Persons with Disabilities and the Incapacity Defence in English Contract Law' (2017) 37 Legal Studies 493

Veale M and Edwards L, 'Clarity, Surprises, and Further Questions in the Article 29 Working Party Draft Guidance on Automated Decision-Making and Profiling' (2018) 34 Computer Law & Security Review 398

Wachter S, 'Affinity Profiling and Discrimination by Association in Online Behavioural Advertising' (2020) 35(2) Berkeley Technology Law Journal 367

Wachter S and others, 'Why a Right to Explanation of Automated Decision-Making Does Not Exist in the General Data Protection Regulation' (2017) 7 International Data Privacy Law 76

Waddington L, 'Reflections on the Protection of 'Vulnerable' Consumers Under EU Law' Maastricht Faculty of Law Working Paper No 2013-2 (2014)

Warren ME, 'Max Weber's Nietzschean Conception of Power' (1992) 5 History of the Human Sciences 19

Weatherill S, 'Who is the Average Consumer' in S Weatherill and U Bernitz (eds), *The Regulation of Unfair Commercial Practices Under EC Directive 2005/29: New Rules and New Techniques* (1st edn, Hart Publishing Ltd 2007)

Weber M, *Economy and Society: An Outline of Interpretive Sociology* (University of California Press 1978)

Wenar L, 'Rights' in EN Zalta (ed), *The Stanford Encyclopedia of Philosophy* (Metaphysics Research Lab, Stanford University 2020)

Whitman JQ, 'The Two Western Cultures of Privacy: Dignity Versus Liberty' (2004) 113 The Yale Law Journal 72

Wilhelmsson T, 'Harmonizing Unfair Commercial Practices Law: The Cultural and Social Dimensions' (2007) 44 Osgoode Hall Law Journal 461

Wybitul T and others, 'Abwehr von Schadensersatzansprüchen nach der Datenschutz-Grundverordnung' (2018) 71 Neue Juristische Wochenschrift 113

Zarsky T, 'Understanding Discrimination in the Scored Society' (2014) 89 Washington Law Review 1375

Zarsky TZ, 'Privacy and Manipulation in the Digital Age' (2019) 20 Theoretical Inquiries in Law 157

Zeno-Zencovich V and Paglietti MC, 'Le droit processuel des consommateurs' (2014) 91 Revue de droit international et de droit comparé 321

Zhu H and others, 'Value-Sensitive Algorithm Design: Method, Case Study, and Lessons' (2018) 2 Proceedings of the ACM on Human-Computer Interaction 1

Zimmermann R and others, *Good Faith in European Contract Law* (Cambridge University Press 2000)

Zuiderveen Borgesius FJ, 'Behavioural Sciences and the Regulation of Privacy on the Internet' in A Alemanno and A-L Sibony (eds), *Nudge and the Law: A European Perspective* (Hart Publishing 2015)

Zuiderveen Borgesius FJ, *Improving Privacy Protection in the Area of Behavioural Targeting* (Kluwer Law International 2015)

Zuiderveen Borgesius FJ, 'Singling out People without Knowing Their Names—Behavioural Targeting, Pseudonymous Data, and the New Data Protection Regulation' (2016) 32 Computer Law & Security Review 256

Zuiderveen Borgesius FJ, 'Strengthening Legal Protection against Discrimination by Algorithms and Artificial Intelligence' (2020) 0 The International Journal of Human Rights 1

Index

For the benefit of digital users, indexed terms that span two pages (e.g., 52–53) may, on occasion, appear on only one of those pages.

Tables are indicated by *t* following the page number